THE
ENCYCLOPEDIA
OF THE
DOG

THE
ENCYCLOPEDIA
OF THE
DOG

DR. BRUCE FOGLE

Special photography by
TRACY MORGAN

DORLING KINDERSLEY
LONDON · NEW YORK · STUTTGART

A DORLING KINDERSLEY BOOK

Project Editor CANGY VENABLES
Senior Art Editor TIM SCOTT
Managing Editor KRYSTYNA MAYER
Managing Art Editor DEREK COOMBES
DTP Designer CRESSIDA JOYCE
Production Controller ADRIAN GATHERCOLE

Photography by TRACY MORGAN

First published in Great Britain in 1995
by Dorling Kindersley Limited,
9 Henrietta Street, London WC2E 8PS

Reprinted in 1996

*A CIP catalogue record for this book is available
from the British Library*

ISBN 0 7513 0204 X

Colour reproduced by GRB, Verona
Printed and bound in Italy
by A. Mondadori, Verona

CONTENTS

INTRODUCTION

FOR THOUSANDS OF YEARS the dog's closest relative, the wolf, followed primitive human groups and scavenged from the remains of their kills. However, when our distant ancestors settled into semi-permanent homesites, something unique in the history of evolution occurred. One intelligent social carnivore actively chose to live in close proximity to another. So began an extremely fruitful relationship that still exists today. It is so frequently written that it has become a cliché, but it is true – the dog is our best friend. Without its help in protecting campsites, assisting on the hunt, guarding our flocks, and pulling our loads, we would probably not have evolved as we have done. It is also unlikely that we would have survived in many parts of the world.

A long relationship

As the most dominant and powerful species in the world, we naturally assume that our ancestors actively chose to domesticate the wolf and create the obedient canine. It is more likely that, like the domestic cat, the dog is self domesticated, that 1,000 generations ago, its ancestors were adaptable enough to see the advantages of living in the territory that surrounded semi-permanent human campsites. The dog invaded this new ecological niche, and with time its fear and distrust of humans diminished. The relationship began well over 15,000 years ago, and by 12,000 years ago the modified wolf – what we now call the dog – had evolved. Smaller than

Bernese Hound
Pendulous-eared, long-nosed scent hounds first evolved in Asia, but were developed to a sophisticated degree in medieval Europe. The ancestors of this Bernese Hound probably arrived in the Balkans, Italy, or in Mediterranean France over 2,000 years ago. Through trade, travel, or migration, they accompanied people into the Bernese mountains of Switzerland.

the wolf, the primitive dog also had a head that was more domed or puppy-like than that of the wolf, and teeth that were smaller and more crowded. It was more playful, more obedient, and even had a shorter intestinal tract than the wolf.

Regional differences

The relationship we have with dogs varies dramatically and is deeply influenced by cultural perspectives. The ancient Chinese developed profound respect for the dog's abilities. Islam, on the other hand, labelled the dog "unclean", a sensible public health rule in a region where rabies was endemic, but one that has led to a strong distaste for canine companionship in traditional Islamic countries. However, the antiquity and utility of our relationship with the dog predates all modern religions. Although canine companionship is culturally discouraged in many Arab countries, the most ancient racing and hunting dogs, the breeds with the longest pedigrees – the Salukis and Sloughis – are of Arab origin. A similar ambivalent

Miniature Schnauzer
Selective breeding has both enhanced and diminished the size of the dog. Miniaturization began early, at least 5,000 years ago, in China. This white, rather than typically "salt-and-pepper" Miniature Schnauzer is the result of the more recent bantomization of the Standard Schnauzer, which has in turn been enlarged to create the Giant Schnauzer.

Sloughi
Throughout Australasia, mainland Asia, the Middle East, and North Africa, feral dogs are often long, lean, and light. The Sloughi was created by selectively breeding the fleetest and most obedient of these dogs.

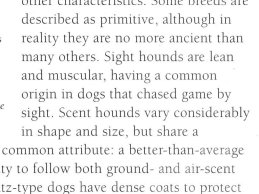

Canary Dog
Massive, muscular mastiff breeds may have been developed in Central Asia. They then spread eastwards into China and Japan, and westwards to Europe, and then the Americas. This Canary Dog was used as a cattle and fighting dog on the Canary Islands.

relationship towards the dog exists in the Far East. In Hong Kong, Taiwan, and Singapore, dog ownership is popular and unencumbered by excessive restrictions. In the People's Republic of China, and specifically in Beijing, government authorities use draconian financial penalties to discourage dog ownership. In spite of these obstacles, multitudes still keep canine companions.

The dog in society

Our evolving relationship with the dog can be followed by examining how it is portrayed in folklore and religion, literature, and art. The dog's role in past and present cultures and societies can be surveyed by exploring its involvement in our day-to-day activities – in agriculture, sport, defence, and security. Its roles and activities are many and diverse because its basic physical and psychological design is so superb. Physically, it is a robust carnivore with sophisticated senses, many of which are superior to ours. Its body systems are highly adaptable, permitting it to survive on a varied diet. Most important, when we consider its relationship with us, is its profoundly sociable behaviour. Like us, dogs are pack animals. They enjoy company, and because we communicate in ways that they understand, we make acceptable dog substitutes as companions.

Variety and function

The dog is a member of the canine family, or Canidae, and within this family there is a striking size variety, ranging from the tiny Fennec Fox to the massive Canadian Timber Wolf. The domestic dog has inherited the genetic potential to vary between these sizes, and through our intervention we have produced breeds varying

Austrian Pinscher
Aesthetics has only recently become a primary consideration in dog breeding. Most dogs evolved for practical reasons. This medium-sized, compact, muscular, and rugged Austrian Pinscher is a typical no-nonsense, multi-purpose farm dog, bred for ease of maintenance and to guard property, drive livestock, and hunt vermin.

Lucas Terrier
Virtually all of the small terriers have similar origins as vermin or small-game hunters. In this century, however, many terriers have been bred solely for companionship and have lost some of their original aptitudes. The Lucas Terrier has been developed to revive pack hunting.

dramatically in size, as well as in other characteristics. Some breeds are described as primitive, although in reality they are no more ancient than many others. Sight hounds are lean and muscular, having a common origin in dogs that chased game by sight. Scent hounds vary considerably in shape and size, but share a common attribute: a better-than-average ability to follow both ground- and air-scent trails. Spitz-type dogs have dense coats to protect them from the harsh, northern winter climate. Most terriers share common origins as game and vermin hunters, but vary considerably in size, from typical small, feisty terriers to the long-limbed, large, muscular Airedale Terrier. The gundogs are of recent European and American origin, bred to work to the gun. Livestock breeds, created initially to protect and latterly to drive livestock, are popular worldwide. From the original guarding breeds, war dogs, fighting dogs, and modern security dogs were developed.

There are over 400 breeds of dog. Some pure-bred dogs, and a large proportion of random-bred dogs, have particularly affable personalities and are primarily companions. It is our responsibility to care for them, and ensure that their lives are rewarding.

Chapter One

DEVELOPMENT OF THE DOG

The domestic dog descends from meat-eating mammals that evolved their distinguishing and unique shearing and cutting, carnassial teeth millions of years ago. By two million years ago, ten groups of carnivore had evolved within the canine family. The dog group consisted of the Coyote, jackals, and wolves. When humans settled in sites of permanent habitation, the wolf followed and altered its lifestyle. In doing so, it created the circumstances for selective breeding, through which the domestic dog was created.

EVOLUTION OF THE DOG

THERE IS ONLY FRAGMENTARY INFORMATION about the origins of mammals some 200 million years ago, but between 54 and 38 million years ago a unique branch of meat-eating mammals developed. These were the carnivores, a wide variety of predators distinguished from all other meat eaters by one shared characteristic, the possession of four carnassial teeth. Many other predators, both past and present, eat meat, but only the carnivorous mammals have teeth that originally evolved for crushing and chewing (the four upper premolars and first lower molars), and then adapted to cut through flesh. The evolution of the dog can be traced by examining the fossil remains of the teeth of its extinct ancestors.

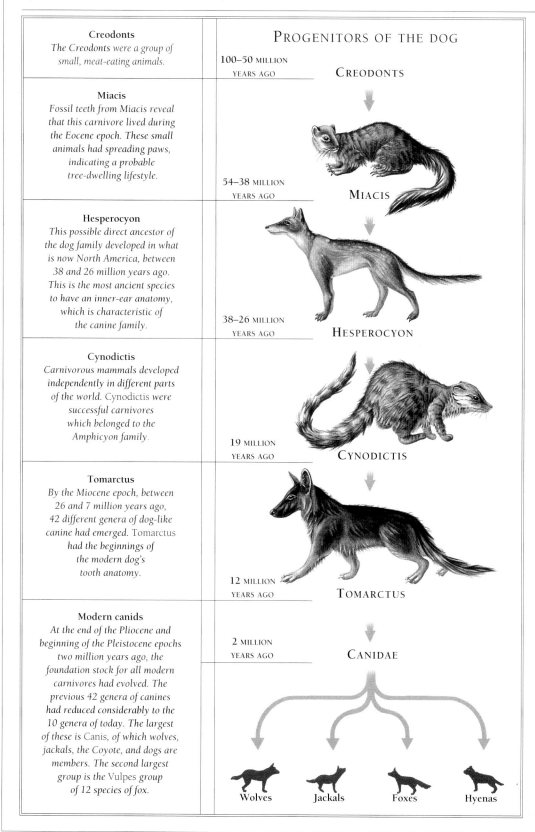

PROGENITORS OF THE DOG

Creodonts
The Creodonts were a group of small, meat-eating animals.

100–50 MILLION YEARS AGO
CREODONTS

Miacis
Fossil teeth from Miacis reveal that this carnivore lived during the Eocene epoch. These small animals had spreading paws, indicating a probable tree-dwelling lifestyle.

54–38 MILLION YEARS AGO
MIACIS

Hesperocyon
This possible direct ancestor of the dog family developed in what is now North America, between 38 and 26 million years ago. This is the most ancient species to have an inner-ear anatomy, which is characteristic of the canine family.

38–26 MILLION YEARS AGO
HESPEROCYON

Cynodictis
Carnivorous mammals developed independently in different parts of the world. Cynodictis were successful carnivores which belonged to the Amphicyon family.

19 MILLION YEARS AGO
CYNODICTIS

Tomarctus
By the Miocene epoch, between 26 and 7 million years ago, 42 different genera of dog-like canine had emerged. Tomarctus had the beginnings of the modern dog's tooth anatomy.

12 MILLION YEARS AGO
TOMARCTUS

Modern canids
At the end of the Pliocene and beginning of the Pleistocene epochs two million years ago, the foundation stock for all modern carnivores had evolved. The previous 42 genera of canines had reduced considerably to the 10 genera of today. The largest of these is Canis, of which wolves, jackals, the Coyote, and dogs are members. The second largest group is the Vulpes group of 12 species of fox.

2 MILLION YEARS AGO
CANIDAE

Wolves   Jackals   Foxes   Hyenas

THE EARLIEST CARNIVORES

The ancestors of modern mammals evolved to survive in the environment of their time. Most of these early mammals were herbivores, which fed solely on vegetation. Meat eaters then evolved to live off these vegetarians. Around 50 million years ago, when the now-extinct family of meat-eating mammals called Miacis evolved, the tooth shape and distribution of present-day carnivores developed. During the following 25 million years, the increasing diversity of vegetable food lead to a proliferation of herbivores. This increase was mirrored by an equally explosive expansion in the range of carnivores. Many authorities believe that the dog's most distant ancestors lived in North America and belonged to the extinct *Hesperocyon*, carnivores that evolved into an enormous range of families.

Scent marking
Social communication is important for species that hunt communally. All canines have a scent-marking gland on the dorsal surface of the tail. The gland leaves scent wherever the tail brushes.

Visual communication
All canines have a sophisticated repertoire of body language through which they communicate with each other. The tail's position and the state of its hair send explicit messages.

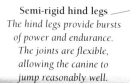

Semi-rigid hind legs
The hind legs provide bursts of power and endurance. The joints are flexible, allowing the canine to jump reasonably well.

MIGRATIONS OF THE DOG'S ANCESTORS

While the ancestors of today's carnivores were evolving in North America, similar carnivore evolution was occurring in Eurasia. A group of carnivores called Amphicyon dominated Eurasia for millions of years – the *Cynodictis* was once thought to be an ancestor of the dog, but the Amphicyon probably died out, leaving the *Hesperocyon,* a member of another family, to develop into today's carnivores. A canine (*Canis davisi*) evolved from this genus 10 million years ago, and migrated across the Bering land bridge, radiating throughout Asia, Europe, and Africa. During the next eight million years, it spread throughout Eurasia, diverging into the ancestors of today's canines. Having completed this evolution, several of the new species returned to North America.

MIGRATION OF EARLY CANINES

Early migration
The dog's earliest ancestors probably evolved in North America and spread to Eurasia.

Later migration
New canine species eventually returned to North America from Eurasia.

PHYSICAL TRAITS OF THE WOLF

Insulation and protection
The dense, double coat of harsh, protective hair and softer, finer inner hair provide protection from the elements.

Excellent hearing
Deep within the ears, the skull has evolved to house large cavities for enhanced hearing.

Large brain capacity
Skull capacity allows space for an advanced cerebral cortex necessary for coordinating group social activity.

Unique teeth
Large canine teeth developed to catch and hold prey. The lower molars and upper premolars are adapted for shearing and cutting.

Long skull
The typical carnivore skull is long, housing extensive and strong cheek muscles, necessary for holding onto prey, killing, and consuming.

Sturdy limbs
The radius and ulna bones are "locked" in position. This inability to rotate the forelimbs gives superb stability when running.

Compact feet
In order to capture prey, canines need stability. This is provided by soft pads, close toes, and non-retracting claws.

CANID FEATURES

Closely related to the wolf, the dog is distantly related to many other meat eaters. All seven families of today's carnivore – the cats (Felidae), raccoons (Procyonidae), weasels (Mustelidae), hyenas (Hyaenidae), civets and mongooses (Viverridae), bears (Ursidae), and dogs (Canidae) – share common ancestors. Until between 20 and 10 million years ago, bears and dogs were members of the same family; as they evolved along separate lines, the dog's modern family tree began. These ancient mammals all shared a wide range of characteristics still seen in modern canines such as the wolf, including long skulls, semi-rigid, sturdy hind legs, and lithe, loose front legs attached to the body only by muscle. Like the wolf, they had excellent insulating fur, compact feet, large teeth developed to catch, hold, and tear, an enormous brain capacity and, judging from the bony anatomy of the skull, excellent hearing and scenting abilities.

The ancestors of the dog evolved in response to climate changes and habitat opportunities. Distant ancestors of the dog may have been solitary hunters, but around two million years ago, when tropical forest and savannah gave way to open savannah and treeless steppes, herd behaviour of herbivores flourished. The dog's ancestors either already had a social structure, or were able to develop the social relationships needed for hunting in packs and bringing down and killing animals much larger than they. The dog's ability to form social relationships is the basis for its success as a species.

DISTANT RELATIVES

THE DOMESTIC DOG, and all other members of the canine family, or Canidae, evolved to successfully pursue and capture prey in open grasslands. The domestic dog is a member of the genus *Canis*, one of the 10 genera of Canidae. Other members of the *Canis* genus – wolves, jackals, and the Coyote – are the domestic dog's closest relatives. Members of the other nine genera are the domestic dog's distant but living relatives. They include 21 species of fox, the African Wild Dog, Dhole, Maned Wolf, Bush Dog, and Raccoon Dog. All of these share a common evolutionary past and a large variety of similar behaviours.

Bat-eared Fox
Two distinct populations of this fox exist, one from southern Zambia to the tip of Africa, the other from Tanzania north to Ethiopia. Puppies have a gestation period of 60 days, and reach full size at four months of age.

EARS ARE EXTREMELY LARGE IN RELATION TO HEAD AND BODY

Arctic Fox (below)
Coat colour changes from white in winter to dark brown in summer, and is determined by a single gene. Some Arctic Foxes have a steel-grey or "blue" winter coat. This is uncommon in Canada and mainland Alaska; isolated populations have higher percentages of blue.

EARS ARE SMALL AND DENSELY COVERED WITH HAIR

ADAPTABLE OPPORTUNISTS
The domestic dog's relatives vary in size from the 1.5 kg (3 lb) Fennec Fox of the North African, Arabian, and Sinai deserts, to the 80 kg (175 lb) Grey Wolf of the Canadian tundra. Curiously, this size variation among members of the Canidae family is mirrored in the size variation of domestic dogs within the genus *Canis*, which ranges from the 2 kg (4 lb) Chihuahua to the 86 kg (190 lb) English Mastiff. This is no coincidence – it is the Canidae's elastic ability to conform to environmental circumstances that has lead it to become the world's most successful living family of land predators, other than humans. Although they vary in size and appearance, all of the domestic dog's distant relatives share one characteristic – opportunistic and adaptive behaviour.

THE FOX FAMILY
The world's 21 species of fox make up the largest group within the Canidae family. The Red Fox (*Vulpes vulpes*) of Eurasia and North America evolved in Eurasia and crossed the Bering land bridge to the American continent. In recent history, it probably did not exist south of latitude 40 degrees in North America, but the introduction of European Red Foxes into New England in the 18th century by fox-hunting aficionados altered the natural picture. Even greater changes occurred in Australia, where the Red Fox, originally introduced for sport, proliferated and became a pest. The Red Fox's ability to adapt its behaviour ensures that its numbers will continue to multiply. The Arctic Fox (*Alopex lagopus*) is lighter in weight than the Red Fox, and has probably found it impossible to move out of its Arctic range

into territory already occupied by the more powerful Red Fox. The *Dusicyon* species of South American fox are also distributed according to size. The large Culpeo Fox (*D. culpaeus*) eats large rodents, while the smaller Argentine Grey Fox (*D. argenteus*) consumes smaller rodents, birds, and birds' eggs. Natives of South America domesticated these foxes and they filled the role of domestic dogs, until they were displaced by the dogs brought to South America by Europeans.

THIS DOG WAS ONCE FARMED FOR ITS FUR IN EUROPE

Raccoon Dog
Observations of this species indicate that it restricts itself to a small home territory, and has little contact with other social groups

WHEN IT WANTS TO BE CONSPICUOUS, THE MANED WOLF ERECTS ITS SHOULDER HAIR, AND SHOWS WHITE PATCH ON NECK

LONG AND LEAN LEGS ARE COVERED WITH DISTINCTIVE, DARK-BLACK HAIR

Maned Wolf
Adapted for hunting in tall grass, the Maned Wolf preys upon pacas, rabbits, small rodents, and occasionally fish and insects. Its long legs act like stilts, giving it added height to see the movement of its prey.

Red Fox
A malleable and versatile species, the Red Fox and its colour variants spread by natural migration to all continents. Through human intervention, it has also become endemic in eastern Australia.

THIS COAT IS NATURALLY COLOURED FLAME RED

NECK AND CHEEK MUSCLES ARE STURDY, FOR DRAGGING DOWN LARGE PREY

Bush Dog
Adults communicate with each other by whining, a practical method for maintaining group contact in forest and jungle overgrowth.

BEHAVIOURAL CHARACTERISTICS

Although foxes hunt on their own, they share with other members of the dog family a sophisticated variety of social behaviours. Radio-tracking studies have revealed that foxes often live in groups of three to six, consisting of a male and several related vixens. Like domestic dogs, both males and females may cock their legs to leave urine marks on vertical objects, especially near important places on their territory. They also use their anal glands to mark their faeces. Although the domestic dog has only a vestigial gland on the dorsal surface of its tail, the fox's gland is active, appearing as a black spot. Its scent is left on bushes that come in contact with the tail. Like domestic dogs, foxes yap, howl, bark, whimper, and scream.

The only fox to have largely abandoned mammalian prey is the termite- and dung-beetle-eating Bat-eared Fox (*Otocyon megalotis*) of the African plains. It, too, has a varied social repertoire – for example, communal nursing of the young has been observed.

OTHER DISTANT RELATIVES

All Canidae (except the Bush Dog) have four-toed feet. All have vestiges of a first toe on their front feet (except the African Wild Dog), but only domestic dogs (including the Dingo) have vestiges of first claws, called dewclaws, on their hind feet. All Canidae have a long, thin penis bone that helps the mating pair lock together. Although the African Wild Dog (*Lycaon pictus*) has these attributes, in many ways it is the most extreme of all Canidae, with a powerful and forbidding

MOBILE, ERECT EARS CAPTURE AND MAGNIFY SOUNDS

Dhole
Dholes hunt during the day, although evening moonlight hunts are not uncommon. Prey is located by scent. Individuals sometimes stand on their hind legs, scenting the air. Large mammals are attacked from behind and disembowelled.

array of shearing teeth and almost vestigial last molars. Like all the *Canis* species, the African Wild Dog regurgitates food for its young, hunts communally, uses urine and faeces to mark territory, and has one oestrus cycle per year, with gestation lasting about nine weeks. It rests, hunts, and eats as a pack. The pack hunts

LARGE EARS ARE USED FOR HEARING, SIGNALLING OTHER PACK MEMBERS, AND CONTROLLING BODY TEMPERATURE

African Wild Dog
This powerful hunter is now listed as being threatened with extinction. Its total population probably does not exceed 10,000 individuals.

at least once daily, kills by disembowelling prey, and feeds communally. Hunting techniques are passed on from one generation to the next. In India, the Dhole also hunts cooperatively, but competes for food by eating quickly. The Dhole is commonly seen running from a carcass with a piece of meat, and then eating it undisturbed by other pack members. These sandy-coloured hunters, averaging around 17 kg (37 lb) in weight, whistle in order to make contact with each other.

The Raccoon Dog (*Nyctereutes procyonides*) occupies the most easterly portion of the Dhole's Far East Asian territory and is the one member of the dog family that reputedly does not bark. Otherwise, its behaviour is typically canid – it uses its tail and scent glands for communication, mates with a "lock", and uses a toileting site, as other canids do.

The long-legged Maned Wolf (*Chrysocyon brachyurus*) of central and south Brazil, Paraguay, eastern Bolivia, Peru, and northern Argentina preys upon small mammals, but also eats fruit. Sharing its territory in Brazil, but extending north to Panama, lives the Bush Dog. Packs of these dogs hunt large animals.

With the possible exception of the South American Fox, the domestic dog's distant relatives are too remote on the evolutionary tree to successfully mate with any members of the genus *Canis*.

CLOSE RELATIVES

THE WOLF IS, AFTER THE HUMAN, the most widespread of all social predators, found throughout Europe, Asia, and North America. The Coyote, a smaller carnivore than the wolf, is widely distributed, but only in North America, while the four species of jackal are distributed throughout Africa, the Middle East, and India. These species are all closely related: they share the same number of chromosomes and are capable of breeding with each other. The Golden Jackal and Coyote share similarities in hunting methods, working either singly or in pairs. The wolf is far more sociable than either the Coyote or jackals, and this characteristic suggests that it provides the root stock for all of today's dog breeds.

THE COYOTE AND JACKALS

Simien Jackal
Small, slender, and dog-like in looks, the Simien Jackal is a lithe and muscular runner.

The Coyote (*Canis latrans*) is a typical opportunistic canine. As the wolf population of the continental United States was decimated by humans, the Coyote moved from the Great Plains, both northwards and eastwards. Its range now extends from deep in Mexico to high in Alaska, and from the Pacific Coast to central Canada and New England. The Silverbacked, Simien, and Sidestriped Jackals (*Canis mesomelas, C. simensis,* and *C. adustus*) live throughout Africa. The Golden Jackal (*Canis aureus*) exists from the Balkans to Burma. The Coyote and jackals can breed with wolves and domestic dogs, and it is possible that interbreeding has occurred.

Coyote
The image of the Coyote is as a lone hunter, but it forms packs with blood relatives to defend territory or carcasses. Extensive sheep farming in North America has been disrupted by this adaptable canine, and ranchers now employ European sheepdogs to defend their sheep.

North American Wolf
Like all other wolves, this largest member of the wolf family evolved in Eurasia and migrated to North America millions of years ago. It has a sophisticated social structure, involving ritualized dominance and submission.

Red Wolf (below)
Until recently, this light, small, lean wolf, weighing between 15 and 30 kg (33–66 lb) was thought to be a distinct species, given the name Canis rufus. Anatomists now believe that it is simply a colour and size variation of Canis lupus. When these variations occur in nature, the result is called a subspecies. If a variation occurs because of active human intervention, the result is classified as a breed. The Red Wolf subspecies is now probably extinct in the wild as a pure wolf. Wolf-like animals seen in the southeastern United States are most likely hybrids of the Red Wolf and eastwards-moving Coyote.

TYPICALLY GREY IN COLOUR, THIS WOLF IS WELL EQUIPPED TO ACT AS A PREDATOR

HEAD IS FLAT, WITH LONG MUZZLE

Mexican Wolf (right)
The small Mexican Wolf survives as a distinct subspecies in the mountains of central Mexico. Its presence indicates that ancient native peoples, such as the Aztecs and Incas, had the genetic material available to breed dogs.

THE MEXICAN WOLF IS SMALL BUT ROBUST

Kenai Wolf
This was among the largest of all subspecies of the Grey Wolf, seldom under, and often well in excess of, 45 kg (100 lb). It lived on the Kenai peninsula of Alaska, and became extinct in 1915.

Newfoundland White Wolf
In 1842, the Newfoundland government set a bounty on this hunter. In 1911, it became the first of many subspecies of North American Grey Wolf to be driven to extinction.

LARGE, WINTER COAT FOR CAMOUFLAGE

Japanese Wolf
Perhaps the smallest subspecies of wolf to survive into the 20th century, the Japanese Wolf lived on Honshu, Hokkaido, and in the now-disputed Kurile islands of the Japanese archipelago. The last of these small Grey Wolves was killed in 1905.

TAIL IS LONG, THICK, AND BUSHY

WORLD DISTRIBUTION OF THE WOLF

Arctic Wolf
This wolf inhabits Arctic Canada as far north as Ellesmere Island. Because food is scarce, each pack has an extensive home territory. Further south in Canada, where food is more plentiful, pack territories are smaller.

European Grey Wolf
Once a dominant subspecies, this canine has been driven to extinction in most parts of western Europe. It still survives in small numbers on the Iberian peninsula, in Scandinavia, and in central and eastern Europe.

THE WOLF FAMILY

The parentage of the domestic dog has been meticulously investigated by anatomists and behaviourists for over 100 years, and it is now a commonly held belief that the wolf is its direct ancestor. Of all the members of the Canidae family, wolves (*Canis lupus*) vary most in their social organization and size, and even in their coat colour. Until its numbers were decimated by human predation, the wolf was the most widespread of all land mammals. It is safe to assume that the opportunistic, scavenging wolf has been associated with human campsites for at least 40,000 years, since the emergence of *Homo sapiens*, eating human refuse or stealing food. Wherever groups of humans moved within the Northern Hemisphere, wolves are likely to have followed. Litters of wolf cubs may have been adopted by humans after the parents were killed. (The Coyote and jackals do not share the wolf's flexibility of social behaviour.) The process of taming began, and we know today that the evolution from wild to tame occurs far more rapidly than was once assumed. While the Coyote and jackals might have intermittently contributed their genes to the development of the domestic dog, most evidence indicates that today's dog is directly descended from the wolf.

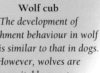

Wolf cub
The development of attachment behaviour in wolf cubs is similar to that in dogs. However, wolves are unsuitable as pets.

EARS ARE MUCH LARGER THAN THOSE OF OTHER WOLF SPECIES

Asiatic/Arab Wolf
This small subspecies is a likely progenitor of many European and Asian domestic dogs. Extensive throughout Asia, this adaptable and sociable wolf inhabited the areas from which domestic dogs first emerged. Its Chinese, European, and North American relatives added to the domestic dog's genetic pool.

Chapter Two

DOGS AND MAN

Although the first dogs were actually self-domesticated wolves, our ancestors found these "tame" wild carnivores to be extremely useful. Dog references in religion and folklore, and dog images in early art, illustrate the role they played in people's lives. The dog was involved in warfare, sport, and agriculture. More recently, it has become a theme for literature, art, and films. The role of the dog in human society continues to evolve and expand, reflecting changes in communities worldwide.

THE FIRST DOMESTIC DOGS

IT IS UNLIKELY THAT THE DOMESTIC DOG developed from the wolf as a result of intentional selective breeding. It is more probable that the dog is "self domesticated" – that changes in size, physiology, and behaviour occurred through natural selection. At least 12,000 years ago, wolves were attracted to the first sites of permanent human habitation. This new environment favoured the survival of small, sociable animals. No doubt humans took wolf cubs from their dens and cared for them. The dogs that evolved guarded campsites, assisted in hunting, and provided food when wild prey was scarce. At the same time, they retained the physical and behavioural stages of the wolf's development from puppy to adult.

MODERN DOGS AND THEIR ANCESTORS

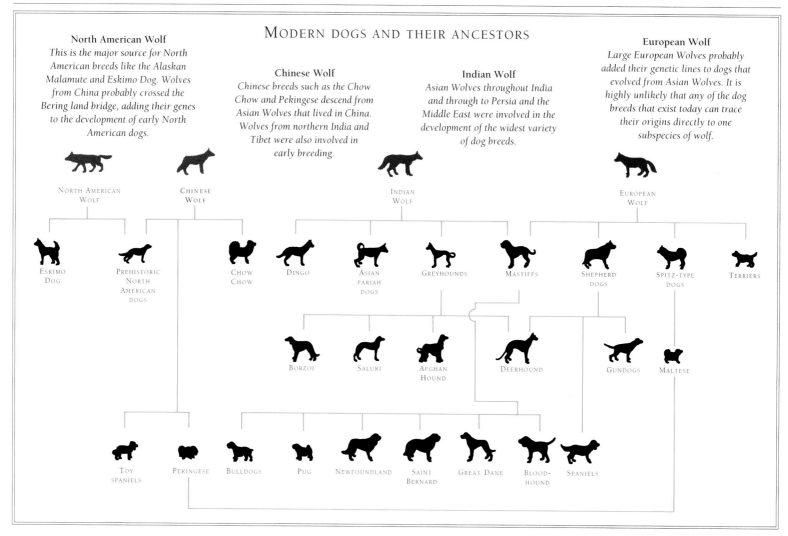

North American Wolf
This is the major source for North American breeds like the Alaskan Malamute and Eskimo Dog. Wolves from China probably crossed the Bering land bridge, adding their genes to the development of early North American dogs.

Chinese Wolf
Chinese breeds such as the Chow Chow and Pekingese descend from Asian Wolves that lived in China. Wolves from northern India and Tibet were also involved in early breeding.

Indian Wolf
Asian Wolves throughout India and through to Persia and the Middle East were involved in the development of the widest variety of dog breeds.

European Wolf
Large European Wolves probably added their genetic lines to dogs that evolved from Asian Wolves. It is highly unlikely that any of the dog breeds that exist today can trace their origins directly to one subspecies of wolf.

NORTH AMERICAN WOLF — CHINESE WOLF — INDIAN WOLF — EUROPEAN WOLF

ESKIMO DOG — PREHISTORIC NORTH AMERICAN DOGS — CHOW CHOW — DINGO — ASIAN PARIAH DOGS — GREYHOUNDS — MASTIFFS — SHEPHERD DOGS — SPITZ-TYPE DOGS — TERRIERS

BORZOI — SALUKI — AFGHAN HOUND — DEERHOUND — GUNDOGS — MALTESE

TOY SPANIELS — PEKINGESE — BULLDOGS — PUG — NEWFOUNDLAND — SAINT BERNARD — GREAT DANE — BLOODHOUND — SPANIELS

MODERN DOGS

Natural environmental pressures resulted in the wolf becoming small, relaxed with humans, and sociable, but it was only after many generations of selective breeding by humans that the great diversity of dog breeds developed. Intensive selection increased barking, valuable as a warning signal. Lopped ears and a different tail carriage were also selected to distinguish domesticated dogs from wild canids. The size of the frontal sinuses on the head increased for no apparent reason, other than to make the dog appear more intelligent. Initially, dogs were diminished in size, with the creation of miniatures and dwarfs. At a later stage size was enhanced, producing today's giant breeds.

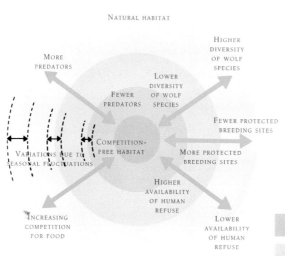

NATURAL HABITAT

MORE PREDATORS

HIGHER DIVERSITY OF WOLF SPECIES

FEWER PREDATORS

LOWER DIVERSITY OF WOLF SPECIES

FEWER PROTECTED BREEDING SITES

COMPETITION-FREE HABITAT

VARIATIONS DUE TO SEASONAL FLUCTUATIONS

MORE PROTECTED BREEDING SITES

HIGHER AVAILABILITY OF HUMAN REFUSE

INCREASING COMPETITION FOR FOOD

LOWER AVAILABILITY OF HUMAN REFUSE

ECOLOGICAL ZONES CREATED AROUND A SITE

Self domestication
Traits that developed at the beginning of the dog's domestication were determined by prolonged occupation of human sites by wolves. Human habitation created ecological zones, which graduated from areas of natural habitat to unnatural, but long-term, occupational sites. The development of the wolf varied according to the density of human occupation. For example, wolf species diversification increased in lightly exploited areas, where there was more competition from other predators.

LONG-TERM OCCUPATIONAL SITE

LIGHTLY EXPLOITED ZONE

HEAVILY EXPLOITED ZONE

CONTROLLED HUNTING

Central Asian Sheepdog
Self domestication reduced the dog's size, but eventually selective breeding intentionally enhanced size, producing large defence dogs like the powerful Asian sheepdogs.

ROBUST AND POWERFUL BODY IS LARGER THAN THAT OF LOCAL WOLVES

CAMPSITE SCAVENGERS
All canids scavenge when hungry, but dogs are especially efficient at finding nourishment. Just as reindeer in northern Europe became self domesticated by feeding on the salt in human urine around Sami campsites, throughout the world dogs found nourishment in the solid wastes of human campsites.

HARDY SURVIVORS
Human settlements were surrounded by heavily exploited ecological zones, where most wild animals existed in vastly reduced numbers. Vegetation often became sparse and, in times of drought, domesticated livestock died. Because it is at the end of the food chain, the dog managed to survive these conditions longer than other domesticated animal.

BLACK PIGMENTATION TO TONGUE ALSO OCCURS IN SHAR PEI

GUARDS AND SENTRIES
Because of its pack mentality, the dog warns other pack members of potential danger. Willing to become members of human packs, and with superior senses of hearing and smell, dogs originally warned people of intruders. When flock management developed about 10,000 years ago, the dog was already equipped to take on the responsibility of defending other animals from predators.

BODY IS THICKLY MUSCLED

Chow Chow
The modern Chow Chow was developed in Europe as a show dog, but its ancestors lived in China and were initially eaten as a necessity, and later as a delicacy.

SMALL BODY CAN SURVIVE ON TINY AMOUNT OF FOOD

PENDULOUS LIPS HELP TRAP ODOUR MOLECULES

DOG'S GREAT STRENGTH IS INTIMIDATING

Dingo
The Dingo arrived in Australia with seafarers about 3,000 years ago, having already been domesticated elsewhere. It seldom helped the Aboriginals on the hunt, but it did clean their campsites.

FURRY COMFORTERS
Anthropologists observe that it is a universal human condition to want to feed and comfort young, furry animals. The dog is unique in its positive response. Because it shares a number of social behaviours with us, it gives comfort and security in return. It is likely that the dog has provided warmth on cold nights, and affection to its owners, since it was first domesticated. It is only in this century, however, that the dog's role as companion has become its most important attribute.

Papillon
The behavioural range and shape of dogs reflects the wolf's development from puppy to adult. Companion dogs such as the Papillon retain the attractive shape, size, and behaviour of the young.

Brazilian Mastiff
Scent hounds such as the Bloodhound developed in Asia and the Middle East at least 5,000 years ago. The Brazilian Mastiff combines the scenting ability of the Bloodhound with the impressive size of a mastiff.

HUNTING COMPANIONS
The dog is a pack hunter, willing to work in tandem with other dogs or humans to locate, chase, capture, and kill prey. As our hunting methods developed, the dog's natural ability to track and retrieve game became overwhelmingly important. Dogs used both sight and scent for hunting. Later, as class systems emerged in human societies, social hunting with dogs became an important leisure activity.

COAT IS DENSE, SOFT, AND LUSH

DOGS IN FOLKLORE AND RELIGION

ALTHOUGH HUMANS HAVE utilized the dog for over 10,000 years, it has attracted very little folklore until relatively recently. In the great trilogy of world religions, Judaism, Christianity, and Islam, the dog is seldom mentioned and when it is, the reference is usually negative. Two outstanding exceptions exist – ancient Persia and China, where early folklore and superstition abound with dogs; indeed, they were regularly used to participate in religious rituals. Not without coincidence, these are the regions where some of the earliest and most important dog breeding took place.

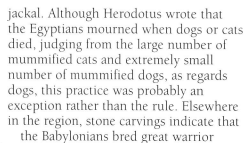

A good-luck talisman
There are many Chinese traditions concerning the dog. This 19th-century silken embroidery depicts the "Fu Dog", which was thought to bring good fortune and happiness.

A French werewolf
The "Wild Beast of Gevaudan", a ferocious werewolf, was reputed to have killed over 80 people in the Gavaudan region of France. Here, it appears in a medieval book of illustrations.

Dog deity
The Egyptian jackal-headed god Anubis personifies the popular tradition of worshipping a deity that is half man and half dog (or jackal).

BIBLICAL DOGS

Folklore, the tribal stories of our real or imagined ancestors, offers exciting clues as to how people thought and lived thousands of years ago. The Jewish Bible – the Old Testament – recounts, often in intimate detail, the tribal history of one ancient group of people. It contains about 30 references to dogs, of which all but two are negative. From the Old Testament we know that dogs guarded the flocks of the tribes of Israel, but nothing suggests that a bond of affection existed between them, and dogs were undoubtedly regarded as unclean scavengers.

Ancient Jewish tradition did not allow images of animals but in nearby Egypt, where animals were worshipped, artists portrayed a variety of different breeds. However, none of these played a significant role in religion or folklore. The Egyptian god Anubis, whose responsibility was to accompany the souls of the deceased to their final judgment, is depicted with a human body and what some consider to be a dog's head. It is more likely that the head is not that of a dog, but that of the jackal. Although Herodotus wrote that the Egyptians mourned when dogs or cats died, judging from the large number of mummified cats and extremely small number of mummified dogs, as regards dogs, this practice was probably an exception rather than the rule. Elsewhere in the region, stone carvings indicate that the Babylonians bred great warrior mastiffs. Nearby, the Assyrian nobility used dogs for hunting. A superb bas-relief in the British Museum in London shows the Assyrian King Assurbanipal hunting with great mastiff dogs. Dogs do not, however, seem to play any major role in local folklore.

GREEK MYTHOLOGY

Dogs do participate in a number of early Greek legends. Xanthippus, the father of Pericles, was said to have owned a dog that swam by the side of his master's galley to the city of Salamis when the Athenians were forced to abandon their city. The dog was buried beside his master at a site known ever since as Cynossema, the dog's grave. Alexander the Great is said to have founded and named a city, Peritas, in memory of his dog.

The line between folklore and early literature is difficult to define. The Greek writer Homer used figures from Greek mythology and historical events to create his incomparable epic stories. Homer's magificent description of the sagacious and faithful hound Argus, recognizing Ulysses on his return, when no one else could, and his sensitive account of the dogs belonging to the swine herder Eumaeus, demonstrate that Homer understood dog behaviour.

The dog's role in Greek religion was usually sacrificial. Kennels of dogs were kept at the sanctuary of Asclepius at Epidaurus, and Asclepius was occasionally represented accompanied by a dog that could heal the sick by licking them. More frequently, however, dogs were sacrificed because they were plentiful, inexpensive, and easy to control.

The dog in Christianity
This wooden bench finial of a dog, located in Swaffham, East Anglia, England was inspired by a local myth concerning a pedlar who gave money to rebuild the churches of Saints Peter and Paul.

An early Christian custom
In early Christian traditions, Saint Christopher is sometimes depicted with a dog's head, as is evident in this Byzantine icon.

ROMAN MYTHOLOGY

The early Romans also sacrificed dogs. For example, at the annual Roman festival of Robigalia, a dog was killed at the fifth milestone on the Via Claudia. Despite this, the Romans clearly view the dog with great affection, and their folklore abounds with stories of dogs' courage and fidelity.

REGIONAL INFLUENCES

Christian and Islamic cultures inherited attitudes to dogs from their ancestral religion. However, these attitudes were modified by the folklore and traditions of the regions in which these religions developed. In Europe, Christianity was influenced by regional and Roman folklore. Stories about the devotion of the

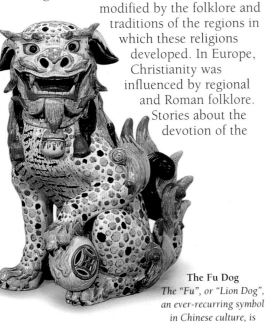

The Fu Dog
The "Fu", or "Lion Dog", an ever-recurring symbol in Chinese culture, is represented here in ceramic.

Allegorical representation
Throughout history, dogs have been used to portray human characters. In this 16th-century anti-Catholic allegory, the dog is used to play the part of the clergy.

dog developed throughout northern European folklore. The Norse Saga of Olaf Triggvason contains descriptions of the faithfulness of dogs, as does the story of Cavall, the favourite hound of the English King Arthur. The saga of Gelert, the Welsh Prince Llewellyn's great hound, is typical. Gelert was left at home with the king's son, Owain. Llewellyn returned to find blood on the dog's face and his son missing. He killed the dog with his sword, only to discover his son safe, beside the body of a slain wolf. In honour of the valour of Gelert, he had a statue cast in his memory.

In Islam, however, the dog was regarded as "unclean". Islam incorporates rules about sanitation and public health. In a region where rabies was, and still is, endemic, the Islamic responsibility to undergo a cleansing after being "contaminated" by dog saliva has obvious public health merit. Native American folklore is of more recent origin – legend says that dogs were sacrificed throughout the Americas.

POSITIVE ROLE

It is in the most sophisticated and earliest of civilizations, China, that the dog plays its greatest role in religion, folklore, and mythology. While black cats play a central role in European superstitions, in ancient China black dogs filled this role. Written records from over 4,000 years ago reveal that dog trainers were held in esteem and that kennel masters controlled large groups of dogs. The "Fu Dog", a recurring theme in Chinese culture, has the positive attribute of bringing happiness and good fortune.

A great deal of the dog's early domestication took place in ancient China. It is probably here that both dwarfing and miniaturization occurred, creating companion breeds. It is here, too, that the first pack-hunting dogs were bred.

The other ancient people with an extensive mythology about dogs are the Parsees of Persia. The religion Zoroastrianism was introduced into what is now Iran by a religious figure, Zarathustra, about 2,750 years ago. One of the volumes of the *Zend Avesta*, the seven sacred books of the religion, is devoted to the care and breeding of dogs, and one section describes the dog's many contrasting characteristics.

Dog-shaped vessel
This 100 BC terracotta vase, found in the Colima state of Mexico, may depict the Mexican Hairless Dog. This breed, originally bred for food, was particularly popular in Colima.

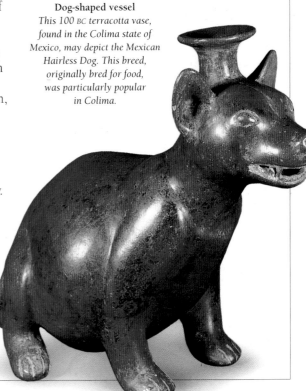

DOGS IN ART

THE EARLIEST EUROPEAN images of dogs and dog-like animals are found in cave paintings in Spain – these have existed for over 12,000 years. By the time Egyptian wall paintings and hieroglyphics were being produced 6,600 years ago, distinctive breeds had appeared, which were similar to today's greyhounds and mastiffs. Later, spitz- and terrier-type dogs were also depicted. In classical Greek art, stylized images of dogs appeared on both pottery and sculpture. Today, images of the dog appear in art forms throughout the world.

The hunt in 18th-century Europe (below)
In the 18th century, the English aristocracy led the fashion in Europe for large-scale hunts, as depicted here by George Stubbs.

The dog in Indian art
The Mughal emperors of India regarded hunting as an important pastime. Akbar (1542–1605) is shown here hunting Indian antelope with Saluki-type hounds.

EARLY EUROPEAN ART

The dog was frequently depicted in Greek art – images included Cerberus, the three-headed hound, guarding the entrance to the underworld, and the Virgin Goddess of the Chase, Diana, accompanied by hunting hounds. Portraits of dogs abounded, but by Roman times portraiture had nearly disappeared. With the decline of Rome's influence and the spread of Christianity across Europe, images of the dog were rarely seen in European art, although miniatures of dogs appeared in illuminated

The dog in medieval times
The Luttrell Psalter abounds in delightful details, such as this dog jumping through a hoop. These marginal illustrations give rare insight into the everyday medieval world.

manuscripts such as *Les Trés Riches Heures du Duc de Berry*. By 1066, the dog was again in favour, as tapestry illustrations of the period demonstrate. The Bayeux Tapestry, for example, shows King Harold of England setting out with a hawking party and five collared dogs.

The domestic dog
In this 17th-century Italian painting, the dog is included as the central figure of a domestic scene.

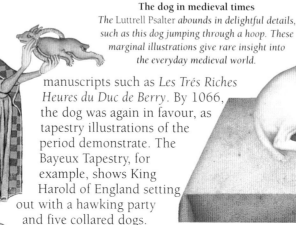

Dogs in satire
The Victorian artist Sir Edwin Landseer combined anecdote and anthropomorphism in popular depictions of the dog.

Dog portraiture
Many a proud dog owner in the 18th century would have aspired to have their pet lovingly delineated, as here by the French artist L.L. Boilly.

THE RENAISSANCE

During the Renaissance period, detailed portraits of the dog appeared in mythological, allegorical, and religious art throughout Europe, as an adjunct to the main subject. Titian (c. 1487–1576), in his portrait entitled *Giovanni dell'Acquaviva*, depicted a pensive, retriever-type dog with superb realism. Veronese (1528–88) accurately painted small, spaniel-type dogs, greyhounds, and Saluki-like gazehounds, but always as detail, never as main subject matter. Leonardo da Vinci produced detailed anatomical studies of the dog, but more as a scientist than as an artist. In Spain, both Antonio Moro (1517–75) and Diego Velasquez (1599–1660) depicted dogs in portraiture, particularly in the company of children.

In northern Europe, too, the dog appeared in many paintings. The great Flemish painter Jan Van Eyck (1390–1441) portrayed a sparky griffon terrier in *The Marriage of Giovanni Arnolfini and Giovanna Cenami*. Albrecht Dürer (1471–1528) painted anatomically superb greyhounds and hunting hounds in *The Vision of St. Hubert*.

In France, Alexandre-François Desportes (1661–1743), the official painter of King Louis XIV's hunt, and Jean-Baptiste Oudry (1686–1755), who followed him in the court of Louis XV, produced very colourful dog paintings.

The dog in Egyptian art
This Egyptian scene, in which a hyena is being chased by dogs, was sketched on limestone between 1555 and 1080 BC.

PORTRAITURE OF THE DOG

By the beginning of the 18th century, animal portraiture was becoming increasingly popular. British animal portraiture reached its apogee in the anatomically detailed works of George Stubbs (1724–1806), in the naturalism of Thomas Gainsborough (1727–88), and especially in the romantic drama of Sir Edwin Landseer (1802–73). In the United States, folk art recounts the history of that nation. Itinerant portrait painters travelled from town to town, gaining commissions from wealthy families. Dogs were portrayed in many of these paintings, often resting at the feet of the artists' subjects. Amni Phillips, one of the most successful of these painters, used the same resting dog in many of his portraits, including *Girl in Red Dress with Cat and Dog* (c. 1834). Folk painters also captured the relationship between African Americans and their dogs. In *Hauling the Whole Week's Picking* (c. 1842), William Henry Brown depicted a scene in which both the dog and its owners are weary.

THE MODERNIST MOVEMENT

Both in Europe and America, the romantic vision of the dog continued into this century. Impressionists such as Pierre-Auguste Renoir (1840–1919) produced works like *Tama, the Japanese Dog*, which portrayed the dog as cuddly fluff while others, such as Henri Toulouse-Lautrec (1864–1901), in *Bouboule: Mme. Palmyre's Bulldog*, sketched the dog as an extension of the owner's personality.

Modernism subjected the dog to all of its most outrageous experiments. Pablo Picasso (1881–1973) used them as cutouts; Otto Dix (1891–1969) made them as grotesque as the people he painted; Joan Miró (1893–1993) turned them into surreal and rather sinister images, while Alberto Giacometti (1901–66), in his sculptures, simply turned the dog inside out. Realism prevailed in North America, where two artists emerged – Andrew Wyeth (b. 1917) in the United States and Alex Colville (b. 1920) in Canada. Their dog paintings demonstrate the hardships of a natural world that is seldom benevolent.

Other 20th-century artists, including comic-strip caricaturist Roy Lichtenstein, emotionally detached Andy Warhol, boldly visual Alex Katz, and natural David Hockney, have all used the dog as a vehicle through which they can portray their feelings. The dog will undoubtedly continue to flourish in the future of art.

Hunting companion
In this medieval Flemish tapestry, the dog is portrayed as a companion in the hunt.

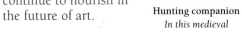

CANINE EPHEMERA

THE ROLES OF DOGS IN FOLKORE, religion, art, and literature indicate how dogs were perceived and treated in different cultures and at different stages of our relationship with them. Initially, dogs were bred for hunting, and the packs that developed symbolized power, wealth, and prestige. The dog became an important part of heraldry, and had its image imprinted on coats of arms, regal or otherwise. The dog has subsequently been depicted in an enormous variety of media – on gilt crests, china mugs, thimbles, greetings cards, and ceramic ash trays, to name a few. In addition, the dog's image has been used to assist sales of a range of products.

Cigarette cards
Here, the dog's image has been imprinted on a cigarette card from the 1920s, to assist sales of cigarettes.

CONSTANCY, FIDELITY, AND SECURITY
For thousands of years, in societies as diverse as ancient Egypt and Victorian Britain, the dog has symbolized constancy, fidelity, and security. Anubis, the dog-like guide to the underworld, was portrayed on drinking vessels and other ephemera of the Egyptians. Anubis prepared the body's spirit for its mysterious journey to the afterlife. In ancient Rome, the dog symbolized vigilance. In mosaic floors from Syria to Great Britain, with alert ears and an unblinking stare, the dog defends the home. *Cave canem*, reads the mosaic message – "Beware of the Dog".

Early depictions of medieval knights in armour often included small, faithful dogs at their feet; others featured lapdogs alongside the effigies of the ladies of the households. More recently, in 1986, Michael Leonard painted Great Britain's present monarch with her ubiquitous corgi, in celebration of her sixtieth birthday. This image was later disseminated to the populace in the form of royal souvenirs, such as posters, tea-towels, and place mats.

THE DOG AS ICON
Monuments to the fidelity of dogs exist in most societies. During the reign of the Roman emperor Hadrian, rabbinical Jewish tales tell of the shepherd dog that sees a serpent poison the shepherd's food. The dog barks a warning, but when the shepherd disregards this and moves to eat, the dog intercedes, swallows the poison, and dies. In gratitude, the shepherd builds a monument to his dog. Favoured pets of the nobility were sometimes honoured after their deaths by being immortalized in stone, either alongside their masters or mistresses, or in individual carvings. In Edinburgh, Scotland, between 1858 and 1872, Greyfriar's Bobby, a Skye Terrier, kept vigil in Old Greyfriar's graveyard for his master's return. After the dog's death, a memorial monument was built to honour his faithfulness. A similar monument to the loyalty of a Shiba Inu exists in Tokyo,

Dog-headed mummy
This Egyptian mummy of a dog represents Anubis, King of the Underworld.

Japan. In some countries, entire pet cemeteries testify to owners' affection for their pets. Although the dog cemetery in Hyde Park, London is justly famous, it is not unique. Dogs are memorialized worldwide. At the Atsugi Animal Memorial Park in Tokyo, Japan, life-size, painted, plaster-of-paris models of dogs greet you as you enter the facility.

THE POPULARIZED DOG
Dog-shaped household objects and ornaments have always been popular. The Romans made bronze lamps in the shapes of dogs' heads and delighted in purely decorative pieces such as bronze figurines. The diligent antiques hunter will not have to look far to unearth a pair of Dutch Delft spaniel money boxes, Swiss, enamelled gold snuff boxes shaped as hounds, and quantities of canine Meissen, Staffordshire, or Chelsea pieces. Clay "comforter" dogs, unwittingly mimicking the role of the guardian "Fu Dogs" in China, were produced in massive numbers in the potteries of Great Britain, France, Germany, and the Netherlands and transported around the world. From the 1800s, dogs also appeared on greetings cards, either humanized or turned into fantasy images. Noted dog portraitists

Dog engravings
In the 19th century, the illustrious gunmakers Purdy and Sons, of London, engraved a select number of their pieces with gundogs.

Roman mosaics
All around the world, Roman mosaics were often decorated with images of the dog – sometimes they were inscribed with the words Cave canem, or "Beware of the Dog".

The dog on magazine covers
In the 1920s, Harrison Fisher used the dog to adorn the covers of Cosmopolitan *magazine.*

Comforter dogs
Comforter dogs, modelled on a spaniel-type breed of lapdog, are among the most popular types of Staffordshire pottery animal. These pottery dogs have been produced since the 1860s, and are still made today.

Humanized dogs
On this 19th-century postcard, the dogs have been humanized by being represented as a romantic couple dancing.

were employed to give artistic cachet to this humble art form. One of the most popular of them was Arthur Wardle, whose studio contents, full of typically sensitive pastel canine studies, are often sold at auction. In this century, ornaments in dog form include sleek, bronze Art-Deco pieces, destined for chic coffee tables, nickel- and chromium-plated novelty-dog corkscrews inspired by cartoon characters, and wall plates with soft-focus, chocolate-box representations of fetching puppy groups. Contemporary American photographer William Wegmann has produced wonderful, imaginative photographs of his pet Weimaraner, dusted down with cooking flour, wearing women's clothing, and engaged in catching a ball, or entwined with Christmas tinsel. Many countries have portrayed a large number of dog breeds on stamps.

THE DOG IN ADVERTISING

The dog has also been used to assist sales, notably on cigarette cards produced by tobacco firms in the 1920s and 1930s, which were emulated later this century by tea cards made by several tea producers. Cigarette manufacturers produced numerous series of up to 50 cards, each showing a different dog breed, often charmingly depicted. These were extremely popular and are still avidly collected. Great Britain's famous HMV

(His Master's Voice) logo was based on a painting of Nipper, by Francis Barraud, painted in 1898. A Scottie and a West Highland White Terrier were used to advertise Black and White Whisky at the beginning of this century, and for a time were the world's most famous dog duo. Fashion magazines show the designer Versace using the sparky little Yorkshire Terrier as his symbol, while Christian Lacroix's slim, elegant, ice-queen models are accompanied by lean Afghan Hounds.

THE DOG INDUSTRY

Today, dogs often function as companions, rather than as workers. In contemporary Western societies, a major industry serves their needs and those of their owners. Functional necessities such as collars, leads, grooming brushes, identity discs, and food and water bowls are produced in an extraordinary variety of shapes and sizes. For centuries, a great deal of time and money has been expended in creating decorative dog collars, such as the lavishly ornamented examples produced in Paris in the 1900s. Today, a range of products is available for pampered pets, including monogrammed dog coats, four-poster beds, a wide range of toys, and gourmet treats. Canine accessories may be expendable, but their existence demonstrates that the dog is generally regarded by people with great affection, and is an important member of households all around the world.

The dog on postcards
In this humorous scene, a family of humanized canine characters is engaged in an energetic domestic brawl.

DOGS IN LITERATURE

HUMANS HAVE HAD a longer relationship with dogs than with any other domesticated animal, but only recently has literature developed that captures the essence of the close friendship we have with this species. The oldest literature concentrates on descriptions of the function and needs of the dog. Fables, in which the dog takes on human character, also exist in many cultures. Dog stories were originally written primarily for children, but in the last 200 years, dog literature has developed for adults, captivating readers with its portrayal of the dog's unique relationship with mankind.

The dog in poetry
Literature abounds with poetry about dogs. Rudyard Kipling's Almanac of Twelve Sports, *one of many publications to portray the dog as a hunting companion, is illustrated by Sir William Nicholson.*

Watercolour by Emily Brontë
Eminent woman of letters Emily Brontë is one of many Victorian novelists to revere the dog, which provided the inspiration for this watercolour that she painted in 1838, entitled Keeper – from life.

EARLY LITERATURE
The first recorded dog literature was written over 2,000 years ago by Marcus Terentius Varro, an officer in the Spanish Army, and a poet and philosopher. In *De Re Rustica*, Varro describes different types of dog, offering advice on how to examine them for soundness, where to buy them, what to feed them, how to breed them, and how to train them.

His book is less well known than that of the Roman Pliny the Elder's *Naturalis Historia*, but far more immediate and practical. Pliny quotes the Spaniard Columella when he describes rabies: "Madness in dogs is dangerous to human beings when Sirius, the dog star, is shining, and it is then that it causes hydrophobia (rabies). So it is a wise precaution in these days to mix dung, perhaps with that of fowls, in the dog's food, or if the disease has already taken hold, hellebore". Columella states that if, 40 days after being whelped, the dog's tail is docked and the end bitten off, the tail will not grow again and the dog is not susceptible to madness. This may be the origin of the senseless custom of amputating dogs' tails. The Roman Gratius wrote *Cynegetica* in the same period, likening dogs to their owners. He affirmed that dogs were similar to the people of their country of origin. Umbrian dogs from northern Italy, he said, ran away from their enemies, while Tartar dogs had ferocious tempers. Arcadian dogs were tractable, while Celtic dogs fought without training. He suggests cross breeding: "An Umbrian dam will give the slower-witted Gaul a lively intelligence; the Gelonians will inherit courage from a Hyrcanian sire; and the Calydonian from a Molossian sire will lose its greatest defect, a foolish tongue".

LITERATURE IN THE MIDDLE AGES
After the collapse of the Roman Empire, there is scant mention of dogs in literature for hundreds of years. We know of their roles in various countries through the wording of legislation passed to prevent poaching and protect game. In the 1300s, Guillaume Twici wrote *Le Art de Venerie* and Alfonso XI, King of Castile and Leon, wrote *Libro de la Monteria*, the first books on sport hunting in France and Spain respectively. The first book in the English language to discuss dogs was *The Master of Game*, authored by Edward, Duke of York and written in the early 1400s.

It was not until the late 1500s, when Dr. John Caius (or John Keys, founder of Gonville and Caius College, Cambridge and physician to successive English kings and queens) wrote *De Canibus Britannicis*, that an attempt was made to classify dogs. Elsewhere in Europe, dog literature remained devoted to writings about hunting. During this period, novelists made only passing references to dogs. Shakespeare anachronistically mentions spaniels (*Anthony and Cleopatra*), Beagles (*Twelfth Night*), greyhounds (*The Merry Wives of Windsor*), mongrels and curs (*Macbeth*), and hounds (*A Midsummer Night's Dream*).

Aesop's animal stories
For centuries, Aesop's Fables *have been enjoyed by readers all over the world. "The Dog and the Wolf", illustrated by Charles Bennett in 1857, is one of the many animal stories included in the book.*

The dog in pulp fiction
The American publication Weird Tales *is one of many examples of the popularization of the werewolf through pulp fiction. A.R. Tilburne provided the artwork.*

Shakespeare and the dog
The dog features in several of Shakespeare's plays. One of Shakespeare's most mischievous and memorable characters is Crab, the dog belonging to servant Launce in The Two Gentlemen of Verona.

with her in Kensington Gardens, where she spent most of her time peeping into perambulators." Capping his career as the most profound of social commentators, the novelist John Steinbeck, in *Travels with Charley*, circumnavigates the continental United States, accompanied by his canine friend and confidant. "Of course his horizons are limited," says Steinbeck, "but how wide are mine?"

The wittiest 20th-century dog literature is American, and comes from E.B. White and James Thurber. White tells of the stubbornness of his dachshund: "It stops in the doorway while returning to the house, pauses, lights a cigarette, inhales, then nonchalantly continues in". Thurber describes the attitude of his poodle: "She is not a hunter or a killer, but an interested observer of the life of lower animals of which she does not consider herself one". These humorists write with a deep understanding of canine behaviour; they also reveal great affection for the dog.

His most sensitive portrayal occurs in *The Two Gentlemen of Verona*, when the character Launce talks lovingly of the devotion of his dog, Crab. In *Memoirs from the House of the Dead*, Feodor Dostoevsky describes the anguish of prison life and talks of Sharik, a prison dog whom he befriends. Sharik responds by running to greet him when he returns from prison labour. " 'So this is the friend fate sends me!' thought I and after this, every time I returned from work during that first heavy and grievous period, before I went anywhere else I hurried first of all behind the barracks, with Sharik bounding along before me with yelps of joy, put my arms round his head and kissed him again and

A Fox Terrier's life story *(left)*
La Vie d'un Fox Terrier *was an early work by Czech writer Karel Capek.*

Nana the Newfoundland
Nana, the loveable Newfoundland who looks after the Darling children in J.M. Barrie's Peter Pan, *was inspired by the author's own dog, Luath.*

Popular wolfdog
Jack London's popular children's book, White Fang, *published in the United States in 1905, tells the story of a beast that is half wolf and half dog.*

again, and my heart ached with a feeling that was at once somehow sweet and agonisingly bitter."

20TH-CENTURY LITERATURE
Courage, fidelity, love, and devotion are the hallmarks of 20th-century dog literature. Jack London and Zane Grey wrote vivid accounts of the courageous endeavours of dogs. In *Peter Pan*, J.M. Barrie explains that the Darlings are too poor to have a nanny, so they acquire a Newfoundland, Nana, to look after the children. "She had always thought children important ... and the Darlings had become acquainted

DOGS ON FILM

FOR HUNDREDS OF YEARS, itinerant performers have used dogs to provide entertainment for people. By the 1700s, troupes of dogs were amusing the public in the circus ring, and the wealthy in private homes. Dogs demonstrated their physical prowess by jumping through fiery hoops, somersaulting backwards, doing handstands, and walking on their forepaws. To use the dog in films, and then advertising, was a logical step forwards. Producers and advertising managers realized that the emotive power of canines would appeal to the public. Indeed, some actors refused to work with them because they knew that the dogs might well steal the limelight.

EARLY HOLLYWOOD

Hollywood's first, some say greatest, canine superstar was Rin Tin Tin, a German Shepherd messenger dog found wounded in battle and subsequently adopted by an American soldier, Lee Duncan. Duncan lived close to Hollywood, California, and within a year, Rin Tin Tin was performing feats of canine intelligence and endurance in silent films. During a career lasting 14 years, Rin Tin Tin starred in 22 black-and-white films. His death in 1932 was front-page news. "The most celebrated dog in the world has left to go to the hunting grounds in the Elysian fields", said United Press in its obituary. Fifteen years later, when television appeared, Rin Tin Tin was resurrected in a series of weekly, half-hour episodes.

A calm German Shepherd is one of the most trainable of all breeds, but it is highly likely that the breed's current international stature as the world's most popular working dog is a direct result of the Rin Tin Tin films and television series. In 1940, the novel *Lassie Come Home* was bought by Hollywood. Three-hundred dogs were auditioned for

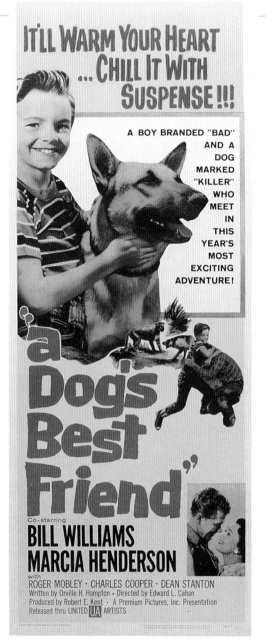

IT'LL WARM YOUR HEART ...CHILL IT WITH SUSPENSE!!!

A BOY BRANDED "BAD" AND A DOG MARKED "KILLER" WHO MEET IN THIS YEAR'S MOST EXCITING ADVENTURE!

a Dog's Best Friend

Co-starring
BILL WILLIAMS
MARCIA HENDERSON
with
ROGER MOBLEY · CHARLES COOPER · DEAN STANTON
Written by Orville H. Hampton · Directed by Edward L. Cahan
Produced by Robert E. Kent · A Premium Pictures, Inc. Presentation
Released thru UNITED UA ARTISTS

A unique friendship
In 1958, The Littlest Hobo *was produced in the United States. It has been broadcast on television internationally, most recently in Great Britain.*

The best of friends
During the 1940s and 1950s, numerous films like A Dog's Best Friend *were produced, celebrating the special friendship that exists between dogs and children.*

the role. One of them, a Rough Collie called Pal, had been sold for five dollars because he was too lively for his own family. Disregarding the fact that Pal was a male, the producers selected him to become Lassie, his luxuriously long coat successfully disguising his masculinity. In the following years, a series of Lassie films was produced. Pal, now Lassie in both his own mind and that of the public, had his own apartment, worked a maximum of seven hours a day, and had stunt doubles perform all the dangerous sequences. After he died, the film series continued, using other Rough Collies to play Lassie, but never with the panache of the original dog.

APPEALING SCREEN STARS

At the same time that Hollywood was using real dogs in life-like situations, Walt Disney was creating a new form of entertainment, the feature-length cartoon. He could see from the success of his short cartoons that dogs like Pluto caught the public's imagination, but in *The Lady and the Tramp* and *One Hundred and One Dalmatians*, dogs became human, with all the feelings and emotions of the audience. Tramp was masculine, cocky, and rather a "no hoper", until love and fatherhood changed him. Lady was all eyelashes and innocence – flirtatious and helpless. Disney pulled on the same emotional

The perfect team
The successful American film Turner & Hooch, *which was released in 1989, is centred on the relationship between a policeman and a large dog, who team up to solve a murder.*

A canine cop
The 1988 American film K9 *describes the extraordinary working relationship that developed between a narcotics cop and a German Shepherd Dog.*

A sentimental story
The Shop on the High Street, *a Czech film released in 1965, describes the friendship between a carpenter, an old Jewish lady, and a dog during the German invasion of Czechoslovakia.*

strings when he used real dogs in feature films like *The Incredible Journey*, the story of a sensible dog (a Labrador Retriever), a streetwise dog (a Bull Terrier), and a cat overcoming all obstacles to find their way home. Disney's rendition of the popular Canadian story jerked tears from the eyes of viewers all over the world. The worldwide, continuing popularity of Disney's feature films has had a significant effect on our

Hush Puppy dog
This is a prime example of the successful and powerful usage of dogs in order to promote a product.

perception of dogs. Loyalty, constancy, and reliability were already features of Victorian literature on dogs. "Near this spot are deposited the remains of one who possessed beauty without vanity, strength without insolence, courage without ferocity, and all the virtues of man without his vices", wrote Lord Byron, as an epitaph to his dog, Boatswain. Hollywood, and Disney, animated these feelings. In the 1940s through to the late 1950s, dogs were frequently seen in films as children's companions.

In the last 10 years the dog's role in Hollywood has changed. Until the 1980s, other than in cartoons, children's films, or tear jerkers, dogs were used as accessories to the characters. However, a new genre of Hollywood film – the canine buddy film – has recently emerged. In films such as *Turner & Hooch* and *K9*, the dog is the star's loyal friend.

DOGS IN ADVERTISING

The dog's devotion to the human race is the theme that advertising most frequently adopts. *His Master's Voice*, by the Victorian artist, Francis Barraud (1856–1924), is one of the most reproduced paintings in the world, recognizable nearly anywhere. In the words of 1950s advertising copy from The Gramophone Company, which owns the image, "The strong appeal of the picture lies probably in the fidelity of the dog. It is appropriate therefore that this quality of fidelity has been the keynote of His Master's Voice ever since". Dogs have been used elsewhere in advertising. Fragmenting the word "Optician" into its three syllables, O PTI CIEN, the French artist Jean-Leon Gerome produced a striking advertisement of a monocled little dog with a pun that simultaneously explains the nature of the business and says, "Oh, little dog" (*Au petit chien*).

Today, advertising companies use the dog to give an image of reliability, strength, comfort, and masculinity to their products. Dogs sit by men while they sip whisky; dogs accompany men while they smoke; dogs relax in cars; dogs sit by independent-looking men who are wearing Hush Puppies. As the dog's role of trustworthy companion grows, so too will its image in films and advertising.

A pensioner and his dog
The Italian film Umberto D, *which was released in 1952, explores the relationship between a retired, impecunious civil servant and his beloved dog.*

DOGS IN SPORT

THE DOG HAS PARTICIPATED in sport for as long as people have had free time to devote to leisure. Hunting simply for pleasure was enjoyed by the aristocracy of ancient China, India, Persia, and Egypt. It was taken up by Roman gentry and spread throughout Europe, reaching its apogee in France, where King Charles I of Lorraine created 800 royal parks in which hunting dogs were bred and trained. The Romans baited dogs with a variety of animals. Bull and bear baiting continued until the 1800s. In some countries, clandestine dog fighting persists even today. Dog and dog-sled racing continues worldwide, while agility sports and trials are increasing in popularity.

PACK HUNTING

Dogs have assisted in the hunt for thousands of years, and required little training to do so. By the 13th century, when the Italian explorer Marco Polo returned to Europe from Asia with stories of the Great Tartar Khan sport hunting with packs of up to 5,000 hounds, Europe's feudal nobles were fielding hundreds of hounds when they hunted. As guns replaced the bow and arrow, falcon, and net, new canine skills – setting and retrieving – were called into play. Dogs for these purposes evolved on the Iberian peninsula, and soon spread from there to the rest of Europe. As hunting became a popular sport with the common people of Europe and North America, new breeds were developed to assist men in their recreational activities. Recently, new sports that do not involve killing have developed. Hunters follow dogs, but rather than chasing foxes or raccoons, they follow a scent trail of aniseed.

FIGHTING AND BAITING

The cruelty of fighting and baiting sports has a universal appeal to human predatory instincts. Dogs have been selectively bred to participate in these dubious acitivities. The Romans used mastiff dogs in gladiatorial combat with a variety of other animals, including men. Bull baiting replaced bear baiting in popularity and soon enormous mastiffs, descendants of dogs of war, were selectively bred for this purpose. In old English these dogs were referred to as "Bandogges", a name recently revived in the United States to describe large fighting dogs. Fighting dogs such as the bulldog evolved from bull baiters in Europe and the Americas, while in other countries, such as Japan, Afghanistan, and Turkey, they were developed from mastiffs and herd guarders. Other dogs were created

Pheasant shoots
The single-purpose pointer is responsible for finding shot game both in water and on land.

to kill rats in enclosed pits. These dogs were originally large terriers, but by the 1800s short-legged breeds had been developed for sport-ratting contests. The Yorkshire Terrier comes from these origins. In 1689, the Netherlands became the first country to outlaw combat between animals. Great Britain and France did not pass similar laws for another 150 years. Dog fighting is illegal in most countries, but continues as a clandestine activity.

COURSING AND RACING

Hare coursing evolved into a sport at least 1,800 years ago. The Roman writer Flavius Arrianus (AD 95–175) wrote of the ethics of coursing in a manner that is appealing to modern thought. "The aim of the true sportsman", he wrote, "is not to take the hare, but to engage her in a racing contest or duel, and they are pleased if she happens to escape". Arrianus recommended using the Gallic Hound, an ancestor of today's Greyhound. Hare coursing continues today throughout Europe, using the Greyhound, Whippet, and Lurcher. The first National Coursing Club was founded in Great Britain in 1858, but its rules are almost identical to those written 300 years earlier in the time

Deer hunting
In medieval Europe, royalty kept packs of up to 800 scent-trailing and hunting dogs, which were used to pursue large game in the king's forests for the sporting pleasure of the king and his court.

Otter hunting
At one time, a king's responsibility included preventing otters from eating fish. By the 1800s, otter hunting had evolved into a sport. This sport is now illegal.

Sheepdog trials
In this century, sheepdog trials evolved as a sport, from the shepherd's need to train new dogs. Dogs must find and herd sheep, gaining points for working silently, while losing points for being too authoritative.

of Queen Elizabeth I. Racing Whippets on the straight also became popular during this period, the lure being a handkerchief waved by the owner. Racing greyhounds after an artificial hare was first attempted in 1876, but the course was straight and the dogs too consistent for worthwhile betting. The sport died out, but shortly after World War I, an Oklahoma farmer, O.P. Smith, was summoned for hare coursing his dogs in a paddock – an illegal activity in the United States. Smith then discovered an old patent for a mechanical hare and built a circular track in Oklahoma City.

Greyhound racing spread rapidly across the United States and in 1924 an American, Charles Munn, introduced track racing to Great Britain. In India, Spain, and Hungary, lean hounds had long been raced for pleasure, but these local breeds were no match for the American and British Greyhounds. Dogs of completely different stock are used for sled racing. In the first races over 100 years ago, muscular Eskimo Dogs and Alaskan Malamutes were used, but soon imported, lean Siberian Huskies were winning most races. Today, sled racing continues after the snow has melted, with dog teams pulling sleds mounted on roller blades.

FIELD TRIALS AND AGILITY
Sheepdog trials, field trials, and agility contests emerged at the beginning of this century. Frisbee and flyball contests were developed within the last 20 years. In Great Britain, Ireland, New Zealand, Australia, Canada, and the United States, competitions are organized exclusively for sheepdogs, in

which dogs find and herd sheep into an enclosure via a designated route. Points are attained for concentration, silence, speed, and efficiency. Field trials were originally developed to test the working abilities of shooting dogs, but in this century they have become sporting events in their own right. Trials are based on the working characteristics – retrieving, pointing, and flushing – of specific breeds, and retrievers, pointers, and spaniels participate in separate events. In North America, there are both daytime and night-time trial events – some trials involve water, others do not. Due to the popularity of this sport, dogs are now bred specifically for field-trial work. These dogs can be quite different from those that are bred for either hunting or companionship. The newest canine sports offer agility and obedience tests for all dogs, whether they are pure bred or random bred. Papillons, although not specifically bred for obedience, are particularly successful at obedience, while random-bred dogs are just as skilled as pure-bred dogs in agility. Catch and running contests with frisbees and balls will no doubt continue to increase in popularity.

Sled racing
The Inuit of Alaska, Canada, and Siberia relied upon sled dogs for transport. Competitive sled-dog racing began in Alaska in the late 1800s, and is now popular throughout North America and northern Europe.

Greyhound racing
Hounds were raced on the straight for hundreds of years. With the development of the "mechanical rabbit" early this century, greyhound racing became a popular sport worldwide.

Flyball competitions
New canine-agility sports have been developed in which all dogs can participate. In flyball contests, the dog activates the release of an object, which it then catches and carries back to the starting line.

DOGS IN THE SERVICE OF MAN

EVER SINCE THE DOG CHOSE to live near human habitation it has served people's needs. Originally used as a watchdog, it soon accompanied hunters in pursuit of game. Shepherds used dogs to guard and later herd their flocks. Throughout the Northern Hemisphere, dogs were used as draught animals to pull carts and sleds. For centuries, dogs have been used for a wide range of military purposes. Today, new roles have developed. Dogs are trained to see for blind people, hear for deaf people, assist the disabled, detect illicit drugs in airports, and for rescue work.

Truffle hunting
Dogs hunt truffles for the fun of the sport. They are not interested in eating these gourmet delicacies.

Search and rescue
In myth, the St. Bernard rescues victims lost in mountain snow.

or "retrieve" on command. Thousands of years ago, shepherds living in an area between China and Persia discovered that certain dogs could be trained to chase sheep, but not attack or kill them. Modern herding sheepdogs evolved from these animals.

DRAUGHT DOGS

At one time, draught dogs were used extensively in parts of Europe, and in the Antarctic and Arctic regions, to haul loads. While mastiffs pulled loads in continental Europe, huskies did so in North America, spitzen in Scandinavia, and laikas in Russia. In Europe, only a few dogs are still used to haul carts. In regions of central Asia, dogs are still occasionally used to turn spits or water wheels. The extinct Turnspit Tyke served this purpose in Great Britain until the mid-1800s, when laws forbad its continued use.

SERVING WITH THE NOSE

Dogs have accompanied people on the hunt for thousands of years, but also lend their noses in countless other ways. Pigs root around oak trees scenting for truffles because they want to eat them. Truffle dogs do so simply for a pat on the head. While military dogs are trained to sniff out ordnance, customs and excise dogs and drug-enforcement dogs scent out illicit chemicals. Springer and English Cocker Spaniels, Labrador Retrievers, and Belgian and Dutch shepherds all work efficiently, searching for specific substances, such as cocaine and marijuana. The American Department of Agriculture's "Beagle Brigade" works airports, searching for illicit fruit and meat. In Australia, sniffer dogs search hand baggage on incoming flights. In Scandinavia, Labrador Retrievers have been trained to detect mould in lumber yards, while in Great Britain dogs can scent traces of rising damp in homes. Throughout the

Draught dogs
Throughout continental Europe, but especially in Belgium, large dogs historically pulled milk carts from the farm to market. Few do so today, and only as a tourist attraction.

TO GUARD AND PROTECT

Dogs have guarded home sites since people first discovered that the wolf's natural ability to bark could be exaggerated through selective breeding. By the time the great ancient civilizations emerged in the Middle East, Assyria, Babylon, and Egypt, dogs were being used not only for defence, but also as dogs of war. Throughout the Middle Ages, Europe's rulers continued to use dogs in warfare. Even in this century, armies have employed dogs for a variety of military purposes – as messengers, guards, and mine and ordnance detectors. The police dog evolved from the war dog, and today it serves many roles. German and Belgian shepherds, Briards, Labrador Retrievers, and others are obedience trained to follow trails, and to either attack

world, but particularly in Europe and
North America, dogs are used in rescue
operations. Newfoundlands are
trained in France for sea rescue
but for mountain rescue, lighter
dogs are most efficient. German
Shepherds, Border Collies,
springer spaniels, and other
types of dog follow ground or
air scent in search of victims
in the aftermath of avalanches
and earthquakes, and during mountain
search and rescue operations.

ASSISTANCE DOGS

At the end of World War I, the German
government trained the first guide dogs
for war-blinded soldiers. This humane
endeavour was noted by an American
woman in Switzerland, Mrs. Harrison
Eustis, who created "L'Oeil Qui Voit", the
world's first guide dogs for blind people

Space dog
*For centuries, the dog's
service to science has
been uncomfortable,
usually lethal. Before
sending a man into space,
the Russians first sent
a dog resembling
a laika.*

organization. By 1930, a similar training
scheme had developed in Great Britain,
and shortly afterwards in the United States.
Today, dogs are trained worldwide to act as
eyes for blind people. More recently, dogs
have been trained to act as ears for deaf
people. Training was instituted in the
1970s in the United States, and developed
further in Great Britain in the 1980s. There
are organizations that train "hearing dogs"
throughout North America and Europe,
as well as in South Africa, Japan, Australia,
and New Zealand. Other centres train dogs
to assist people restricted to wheel chairs –
to open doors or pick up items that they
drop. All of these dogs
serve two functions. The
obvious role is to assist the
owner physically, to replace
a lost sense or ability. In
the 1970s, social workers
became aware that these
dogs serve another, equally

3rd Batln Grenadiers Pet Dog "Modder" Brought by the Regiment from the battlefield

War heros
*Recognizing the dog's positive role both as a
messenger and in finding injured soldiers on the
battlefield, after World War I the British created
a canine war medal for military valour.*

Tracker dogs
*Dogs naturally follow scent.
Militia worldwide use this
ability to detect ordnance in
the field, or intruders in
military installations.*

important role; they restore self esteem to
the disabled owners. The owners are
responsible for the continued training of
their service dogs and they feel needed. A
better understanding of this more
subliminal service role of the dog has led
to the development of dogs as residents in
retirement homes, hospitals, hospices, and
even prisons. Introducing a dog into a
regimented residential environment
reduces the feelings of helplessness that
many people experience when they are
confined. Carefully selected dogs are also
regularly taken to visit people housed in
institutions. In its mute but understanding
way, the dog is mysteriously therapeutic.

SPECIAL LIVERY
IDENTIFIES
QUALIFIED
HEARING DOG

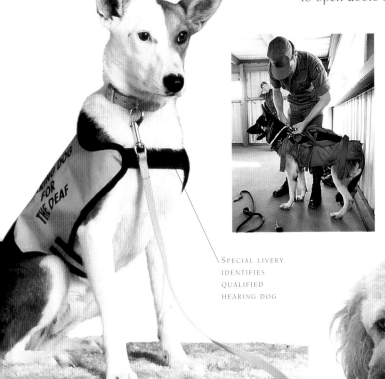

Social service dogs
*New service roles continue to develop. Ever-
alert, random-bred dogs act as ears for deaf
people, while calm, sensible dogs like Labrador
or Golden Retrievers, or retriever crosses,
make ideal guides for
blind people.*

DOGS AS COMPANIONS

THE DOG HAS PROVIDED people with companionship since it was first attracted to human habitation at least 12,000 years ago. Before the 20th century, this was a minor role for the dog – it was used primarily for work. However, today the dog is most valued for the companionship it offers. Although mass urbanization in Europe, North America, Australia, Japan, and the great cities of Asia and South America has cut many people off from the natural world, the dog has accompanied them to the cities. Its future is secure as an important member of both urban and rural households.

MUTUAL BENEFITS

It is only by happy accident that after the last Ice Age, the Northern Hemisphere's two most successful predators learned that they could not only survive better, but also actually thrive in each other's presence. Dogs are content to be our companions because they need to be guided by a pack leader, appreciate the simple availability of food, warmth, and comfort, and thrive on the knowlege that they have a defined territory to defend. We also offer them simple play (which provides them with a lifelong pleasure) and physical contact. We ourselves gain a great deal from canine companionship. Dogs make us feel loved, secure, and important, and they make us laugh. We enjoy stroking them because touch is pleasurable. We like talking to them, although most of us realize that their ability to understand what we are saying is very limited. We also like talking about them – describing something we love is probably good for our health. We feel content when we watch our dogs play, and we certainly feel loved when a dog comes over and gives an affectionate greeting. We feel immensely satisfied when we feed, groom, exercise, and care for our dogs in a variety of other ways.

AN EMOTIONAL BOND

Recently, science has investigated the role of dogs as companions. The companionship of dogs is not just a manifestation of a middle-class phenomenon. Scientists state, for example, that the Athabaskan Hare Native people in the Canadian Northwest Territories are "repressed, contained, and restrained", except in their relationships with children and puppies. Their puppies are spoiled, sheltered, given choice food, played with, and very rarely punished or scolded until they reach adulthood, when affection virtually ceases. Observers say that being in contact with a constant flow of puppies creates an outlet for natural, dormant feelings that are culturally repressed.

The great emotional satisfaction that dogs provide may well be mirrored in a number of more affluent societies. In Europe, the northern cultures of Scandinavia, Great Britain, northern France, and Germany are less comfortable with visible shows of human emotion than affluence. Dogs are the world's favourite companions, regardless of the culture or economic wealth of the region. In Zimbabwe and South Africa, over 40 per cent of all households keep dogs as companions. Anthropologists' reports from all the world's continents show that pet keeping is an international human

DOG ON BED EXPERIENCES SIMPLE PLEASURE

Fun to watch (above)
The dog's behaviour is genuine – its emotions are honest and uncomplicated. We enjoy observing the dog because we know we are seeing simple activity, which is uncomplicated by the veneers of human sophistication.

Something to care for
Most people have an irresistible, lifelong need to care for living things such as dogs.

DOG IS BATHED BY "PACK LEADER"

DOG TOYS COME IN ALL SHAPES AND SIZES; NEVER USE ANYTHING THAT MAY DAMAGE TEETH

JUMPING TO CATCH IS EXHILARATING AND SUPERB EXERCISE FOR LEAN, WELL-MUSCLED DOGS

Exercising together
Dogs need daily physical exercise but so, too, do people. International research shows that dog owners suffer fewer minor health problems and are less at risk from heart disease than people who do not have dogs. It is likely that the exercise gained from walking dogs plays a major role in these benefits.

Learning about life
Until only a few generations ago, most children routinely came into contact with a range of animals. Today, few urban children have the opportunity to touch any species of animal other than pets.

CHILDREN SHOULD BE INSTRUCTED HOW TO TALK TO, APPROACH, AND TOUCH A DOG THAT HAS NEVER MET THEM BEFORE

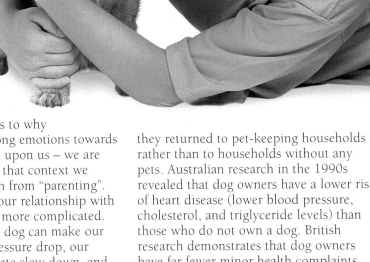

MOTHER RESTS ON HER SIDE, GIVING
PUPPIES AMPLE SPACE FOR BOTH
SUCKLING AND BODY CONTACT

SOFTNESS OF
COAT OFFERS
TACTILE PLEASURE

Learning about nature
*Adults and children can both learn
about the majesty of nature by watching
a dog give birth to and care for her
newborn puppies.*

Soft to touch
*Touching something soft
and warm gives sensual
pleasure. Dogs
also enjoy the
experience.*

the southern cultures of Spain, southern
France, Italy, Greece, and the Middle East.
Yet dog ownership is taken more seriously
in northern Europe than in southern
Europe. Dr. Aaron Katcher, an American
psychiatrist, has written that touching and
stroking dogs, and speaking to them
affectionately, are acceptable ways by
which people – men in particular – can
give and receive affection in public when
it is culturally unacceptable to show
emotion or affection to other people.

CULTURAL DIFFERENCES
Recent dog-population statistics
demonstrate that dog ownership in
central and eastern Europe is on
average considerably
higher than in
many affluent
western European
countries. Over
one-third of all the
households in the
United States, Australia,
Belgium, and France
have dogs. Elsewhere – in
Canada, New Zealand, Japan,
and the rest of western
Europe – between 10 to
25 per cent of homes keep
canine companions.

In Hungary, the Czech
and Slovak Republics, the
Baltic countries, and
especially Poland, dog
keeping is a common
pastime; virtually half of all
households in Poland keep dogs.
More people in central and eastern Europe
now live in cities, but many individuals
have retained cultural contact with their
rural roots and keep dogs, because dogs
have always been part of life.

DOGS AS THERAPISTS
Dogs do not judge us; they are loyal
and unquestioning, and do not criticize.
They comfort and protect – a striking
combination. Constance Perin, a cultural

THIS HEAVY
DOG MUST BE
LIFTED WITH CARE

**Understanding
responsibility**
*With the companionship
of a dog come
responsibilities for its
health and welfare.*

anthropologist, offers
an intriguing reason as to why
we can feel such strong emotions towards
dogs. They depend upon us – we are
care givers, and in that context we
derive satisfaction from "parenting".
However, our relationship with
them is far more complicated.
Stroking a dog can make our
blood pressure drop, our
heart rate slow down, and
our sense of anxiety
diminish. Dogs are
also intensely loyal –
they will defend and
protect us. Most
people feel secure when
a dog is around. Perin
says that the dog can be
perceived as the care giver,
while the person
receives. This
creates a
profound sense of
human attachment to
the dog, and explains
the sometimes
inexplicable
behaviour of some
dog owners. While
there is no evidence that if you
have a dog you will live longer,
there is substantial proof that
the quality of your life is
enhanced. American research in
the 1970s concluded that there
was a strong possibility that
heart-attack victims treated at
a hospital's cardiac intensive-
care unit were more likely
to be alive one year later if

they returned to pet-keeping households
rather than to households without any
pets. Australian research in the 1990s
revealed that dog owners have a lower risk
of heart disease (lower blood pressure,
cholesterol, and triglyceride levels) than
those who do not own a dog. British
research demonstrates that dog owners
have far fewer minor health complaints,
such as colds, sore throats, headaches,
stomach aches, and back pain, than those
without a dog.

There is nothing as yet to suggest
that dogs are directly responsible for
these health benefits. However, scientific
evidence firmly implies that if you have
something to care for, to play with, to
love, or to watch, the quality
of your life improves. Dogs
are superb companions –
they play significant roles
in cultures all over the
world, and the benefits to
be gained from having a dog
cannot be overestimated.

Playing games
*As a species, we retain a childlike,
lifelong enjoyment in playing games.
We have bred dogs to retain the
same characteristics.*

WHEN PLAYING TUG-OF-
WAR, HUMAN MUST
BE IN CONTROL

Chapter Three

CANINE DESIGN

The dog has a powerfully muscled body, a
resilient heart and lungs, teeth developed to
catch, hold, and tear, excellent insulating hair, and a
sense of smell so sophisticated that its power is far
beyond human comprehension. Although its attitude
to food still resembles that of the opportunist
hunter-scavenger, its reproductive cycles
have been enhanced through domestication.
Integrating all of its body functions, and
responsible for emotional control, is
a superbly adaptable nervous system,
augmented by an efficient group
of chemical hormones.

THE SKELETON

THE DOG'S SKELETON provides a superb framework for its body. A robust skull, with deep, protective pockets for the eyes and ears, surrounds the brain. Folds of nasal membrane are attached to delicate bone, housed inside the muzzle. The vertebrae in the neck and back have extensions to which powerful muscles are attached. The shoulder blades are unattached to the rest of the skeleton, allowing great flexibility for running. Long ribs form a cage to protect the heart, lungs, and liver. The shoulders and hips act as pivots, enabling the limbs to move gracefully and accurately. The system is held together by strong, elastic ligaments and tendons, and a complex of muscles adapted for endurance.

STRUCTURE OF THE SKELETON

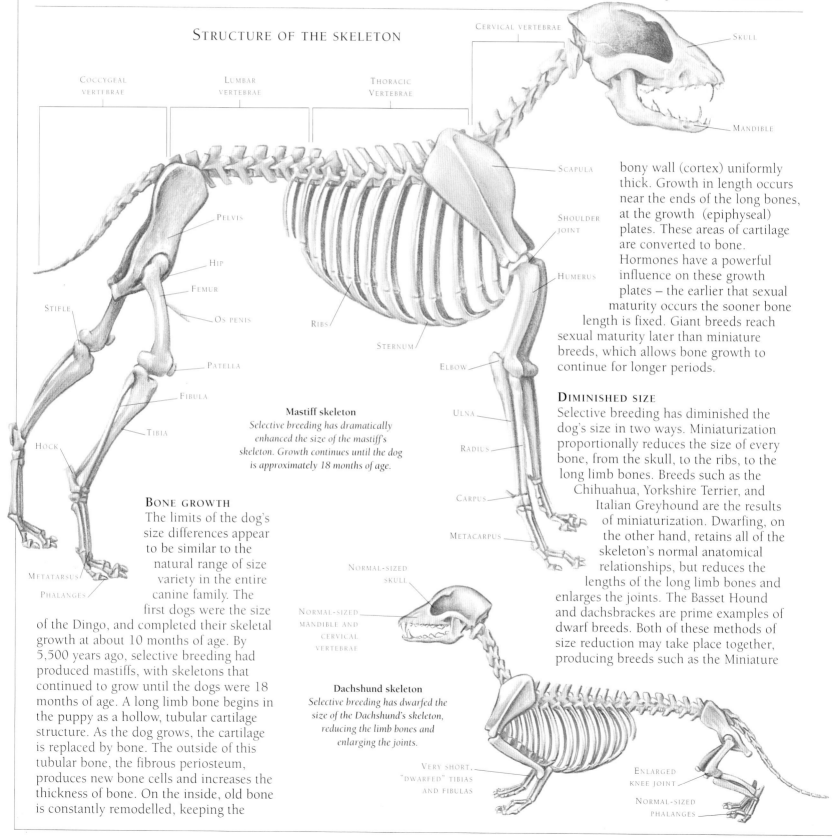

COCCYGEAL VERTEBRAE

LUMBAR VERTEBRAE

THORACIC VERTEBRAE

CERVICAL VERTEBRAE

SKULL

MANDIBLE

SCAPULA

SHOULDER JOINT

HUMERUS

ELBOW

ULNA

RADIUS

CARPUS

METACARPUS

PELVIS

HIP

FEMUR

OS PENIS

RIBS

STERNUM

STIFLE

PATELLA

FIBULA

TIBIA

HOCK

METATARSUS

PHALANGES

Mastiff skeleton
Selective breeding has dramatically enhanced the size of the mastiff's skeleton. Growth continues until the dog is approximately 18 months of age.

NORMAL-SIZED SKULL

NORMAL-SIZED MANDIBLE AND CERVICAL VERTEBRAE

Dachshund skeleton
Selective breeding has dwarfed the size of the Dachshund's skeleton, reducing the limb bones and enlarging the joints.

VERY SHORT, "DWARFED" TIBIAS AND FIBULAS

ENLARGED KNEE JOINT

NORMAL-SIZED PHALANGES

bony wall (cortex) uniformly thick. Growth in length occurs near the ends of the long bones, at the growth (epiphyseal) plates. These areas of cartilage are converted to bone. Hormones have a powerful influence on these growth plates – the earlier that sexual maturity occurs the sooner bone length is fixed. Giant breeds reach sexual maturity later than miniature breeds, which allows bone growth to continue for longer periods.

DIMINISHED SIZE

Selective breeding has diminished the dog's size in two ways. Miniaturization proportionally reduces the size of every bone, from the skull, to the ribs, to the long limb bones. Breeds such as the Chihuahua, Yorkshire Terrier, and Italian Greyhound are the results of miniaturization. Dwarfing, on the other hand, retains all of the skeleton's normal anatomical relationships, but reduces the lengths of the long limb bones and enlarges the joints. The Basset Hound and dachsbrackes are prime examples of dwarf breeds. Both of these methods of size reduction may take place together, producing breeds such as the Miniature

BONE GROWTH

The limits of the dog's size differences appear to be similar to the natural range of size variety in the entire canine family. The first dogs were the size of the Dingo, and completed their skeletal growth at about 10 months of age. By 5,500 years ago, selective breeding had produced mastiffs, with skeletons that continued to grow until the dogs were 18 months of age. A long limb bone begins in the puppy as a hollow, tubular cartilage structure. As the dog grows, the cartilage is replaced by bone. The outside of this tubular bone, the fibrous periosteum, produces new bone cells and increases the thickness of bone. On the inside, old bone is constantly remodelled, keeping the

DIFFERENT SKULL SHAPES

DOLICHOCEPHALIC, OR LONG NOSED (SALUKI)   MESOCEPHALIC (POINTER)   BRACHYCEPHALIC (BOXER)   EXTREME BRACHYCEPHALIC, OR SHORT NOSED (PUG)

There are three basic skull shapes. The wolf's skull has been elongated to create the Saluki's dolichocephalic skull, and diminished to produce the pointer's mesocephalic skull. It has been diminished again to create the brachycephalic Boxer. Taken to its brachycephalic extreme, the muzzle disappears, as in the Pug.

Dachshund. Both dwarfism and miniaturization are natural occurences, which have been accentuated through our intervention in dog breeding.

THE WORKING SKELETON

The skeleton consists of bony levers and lubricated joints, held together by fibrous ligaments, elastic tendons, and powerful muscles. Bone is a latticed structure of hard, calcified struts (trabecullae), filled in its hollow core with bone marrow. Bone needs nourishment, and this is supplied by blood vessels that enter the shaft of the bone through a hole (nutrient foramen). The growth plate itself is nourished by a profuse supply of tiny arteries. If a bone breaks, its fibrous surface (periosteum) produces new bone cells to bridge the gap of the fracture. Almost invariably, the periosteum produces too much new bone, but once the break has been filled, the fracture is remodelled from the inside out.

JOINTS

Bones are joined together at cartilaginous joints, which act like shock absorbers. Each joint is surrounded by a joint capsule, which is filled with lubricating joint fluid. The cartilaginous ends of bones have pearly, smooth surfaces, allowing easy movement and absorbing concussive force as the dog comes down on its legs while running. The articular cartilage of the joint obtains nourishment from the growth plate's blood supply and from joint (synovial) fluid. A joint may become inflamed (arthritis), or synovial fluid may be produced in excess (synovitis) through injury, disease, or even allergic reaction.

LIGAMENTS AND TENDONS

Ligaments anchor bones to each other and permit movements in specific directions, while preventing excessive movements that might injure delicate parts of the anatomy. Excess weight creates tension on some ligaments and can cause them to tear. Tendons are the elastic tips by which muscles attach themselves to the skeleton. The dog's tendons are superbly constructed and tendon injuries are rare.

SKELETON AND JOINT PROBLEMS

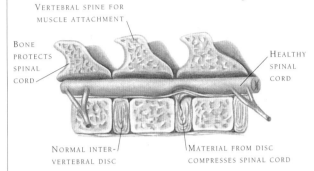

VERTEBRAL SPINE FOR MUSCLE ATTACHMENT
BONE PROTECTS SPINAL CORD
HEALTHY SPINAL CORD
NORMAL INTER-VERTEBRAL DISC
MATERIAL FROM DISC COMPRESSES SPINAL CORD

Disc prolapse

The spine is a hollow tube of back bones, held together by strong ligaments and cushioned from each other by shock-absorbing fibrous pads, called intervertebral discs. The spinal cord runs through this superbly protected structure. With age, especially in dwarfed breeds, the discs become gritty and dry, and tend to protrude up towards the spinal cord, causing disc prolapse.

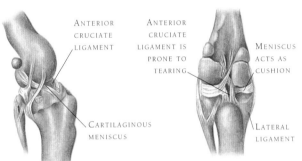

ANTERIOR CRUCIATE LIGAMENT
ANTERIOR CRUCIATE LIGAMENT IS PRONE TO TEARING
MENISCUS ACTS AS CUSHION
CARTILAGINOUS MENISCUS
LATERAL LIGAMENT

Side view   **Front view**

Torn knee ligaments

Anatomically, the weakest link in the hind legs occurs in the knees, where two crossed ligaments hold the structure together. Lateral ligaments hold the knee cap in place. If excessive pressure is consistently exerted on these crossed cruciate ligaments, with time the anterior ligament may fray or tear. This results in very little or no pain, but the leg can no longer bear weight and the dog limps. This occurs most frequently in overweight, middle-aged dogs.

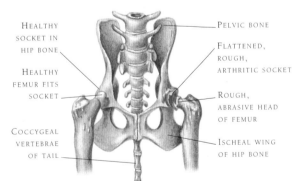

HEALTHY SOCKET IN HIP BONE
HEALTHY FEMUR FITS SOCKET
COCCYGEAL VERTEBRAE OF TAIL
PELVIC BONE
FLATTENED, ROUGH, ARTHRITIC SOCKET
ROUGH, ABRASIVE HEAD OF FEMUR
ISCHEAL WING OF HIP BONE

Hip dysplasia

This is a malformation of the ball-and-socket hip joint. It is a common problem in large and giant breeds, but can also occur in small breeds. The rough head of the femur does not fit securely into the hip. Eventually, the cartilage on the femoral head wears off on the uneven edges of the hip joint, producing a painful inflammation (arthritis). In certain breeds, there is a strong inherited component to hip dysplasia.

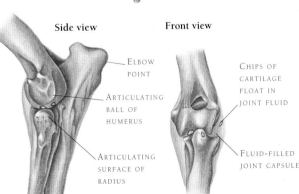

Side view   **Front view**

ELBOW POINT
ARTICULATING BALL OF HUMERUS
ARTICULATING SURFACE OF RADIUS
CHIPS OF CARTILAGE FLOAT IN JOINT FLUID
FLUID-FILLED JOINT CAPSULE

Elbow pain

In fast-growing breeds like the Bernese Mountain Dog, an area of surface cartilage in the elbow joint sometimes "dies" and breaks loose, floating into the joint capsule. This causes lameness and pain, sometimes accompanied by swelling and heat. It appears to be an inherited condition in some breeds, and surgery may be necessary to remove the loose lump of cartilage.

THE BRAIN AND SENSES

THE DOG'S BRAIN SYNTHESIZES, interprets, and acts on all the information it receives from the senses. Although the brain of an average dog accounts for less than half a per cent of its body weight, it needs a great deal of nourishment to function properly and receives over 20 per cent of the blood pumped out by the heart. Brain activity is, in part, predetermined by the "fixed wiring" of the dog's genes. Just as our brains are pre-wired to learn language, the dog's brain is pre-wired to learn to interpret scent, and a large part of the brain is devoted to this process. It is also able to interpret information from the other senses – touch, taste, hearing, and sight.

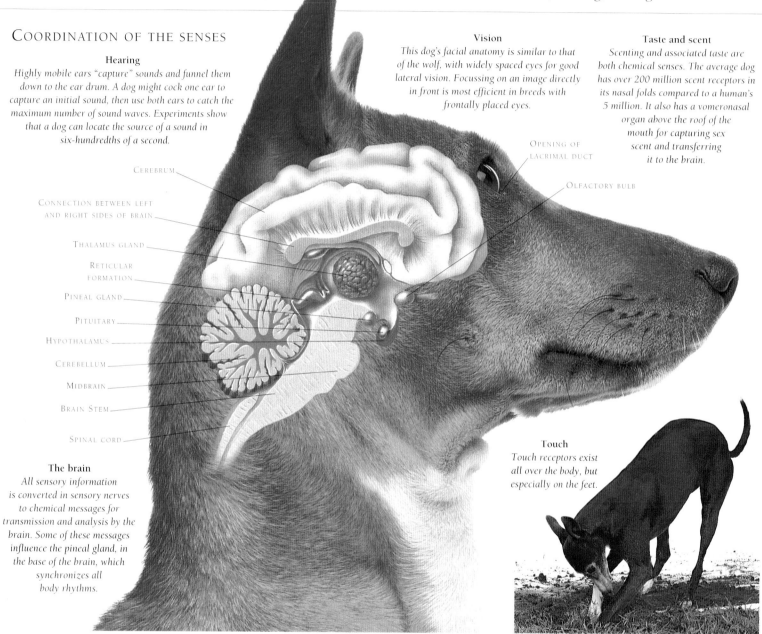

COORDINATION OF THE SENSES

Hearing
Highly mobile ears "capture" sounds and funnel them down to the ear drum. A dog might cock one ear to capture an initial sound, then use both ears to catch the maximum number of sound waves. Experiments show that a dog can locate the source of a sound in six-hundredths of a second.

CEREBRUM

CONNECTION BETWEEN LEFT AND RIGHT SIDES OF BRAIN

THALAMUS GLAND

RETICULAR FORMATION

PINEAL GLAND

PITUITARY

HYPOTHALAMUS

CEREBELLUM

MIDBRAIN

BRAIN STEM

SPINAL CORD

The brain
All sensory information is converted in sensory nerves to chemical messages for transmission and analysis by the brain. Some of these messages influence the pineal gland, in the base of the brain, which synchronizes all body rhythms.

Vision
This dog's facial anatomy is similar to that of the wolf, with widely spaced eyes for good lateral vision. Focussing on an image directly in front is most efficient in breeds with frontally placed eyes.

Taste and scent
Scenting and associated taste are both chemical senses. The average dog has over 200 million scent receptors in its nasal folds compared to a human's 5 million. It also has a vomeronasal organ above the roof of the mouth for capturing sex scent and transferring it to the brain.

OPENING OF LACRIMAL DUCT

OLFACTORY BULB

Touch
Touch receptors exist all over the body, but especially on the feet.

HOW THE BRAIN WORKS

The dog's brain stores information in two ways – it can either be conditioned or it can store what it learns. Both responses rely upon the individual dog's information-storage system and are, in part, determined by genetics. The brain consists of billions of cells (neurons), each of which may have up to 10,000 connections with other cells. The cells chemically communicate with each other through neurotransmitters. The speed of these transmissions depends partly upon a fatty substance called myelin. In the dog's prime, messages are transmitted at great speed, but as the brain ages, messages move more slowly. Anatomically, the dog's brain is similar to the brains of most other mammals. The cerebrum controls learning, emotions, and behaviour, the cerebellum controls the muscles, and the brain stem connects to the peripheral nervous system (see page 42). Each sense feeds into the brain through its own special nerves. A network of cells throughout the brain (the limbic system) almost certainly integrates instinct and learning. The conflict between what a dog instinctively wants to do and what we teach it to do probably takes place in the brain's limbic system. Humans can override this system by giving rewards to the dog for obeying its owners rather than its "instincts".

How the senses work

The dog's senses are similar in function to those of humans. Information from the senses feeds into the brain, where it triggers either a body response or hormonal activity. For example, if a dog steps on something and feels pain, it quickly steps back – a physical response. If it smells male or female dog scent, the pituitary gland in its brain activates and stimulates a hormonal response.

Sight

A dog's eyes are flatter than a human's; although the dog can change the shape of its lenses, thereby adjusting focal length, it cannot do so as effectively as a human. A dog's eyes are more sensitive to light and movement than those of a human, but their resolving power is correspondingly less efficient. The consequence is that a human finds it easier to see a lost tennis ball lying in the grass than a dog does, whereas a dog finds it easier to see slight movement out of the corners of its eyes than a human does.

Hearing

The dog's mobile ears allow it to scan the environment for sound. It may use one ear to scan, then both ears to capture and funnel sound waves. A dog can locate a source of sound in six-hundredths of a second, and it can hear sounds four times further away than a human can.

Touch

Touch is the first sense the dog develops, and remains a powerfully important sense throughout its life. Touch-sensitive hairs called vibrissae, which are capable of sensing air flow, develop above the eyes, on the muzzle, and below the jaws. The entire body, including the paws, is covered with touch-sensitive nerve endings.

Taste and smell

Dogs have far fewer taste buds than do humans, approximately one for every six. Although their limited number of taste buds register sweet, sour, bitter, and salty tastes, it is probably more realistic to think of the dog's response to taste as pleasant, indifferent, or unpleasant. Smell is the dog's most advanced sense – a large part of its brain is devoted to interpreting scent. In addition, it has a sex-scent-capturing vomeronasal organ in the roof of its mouth. This scenting apparatus transmits information directly to the limbic system, the part of the brain most intimately involved in emotional behaviour.

THE ANATOMY OF THE SENSES

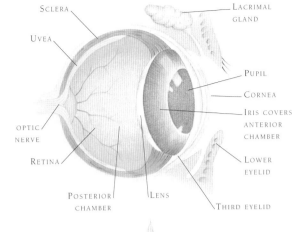

SCLERA
UVEA
OPTIC NERVE
RETINA
POSTERIOR CHAMBER
LENS
LACRIMAL GLAND
PUPIL
CORNEA
IRIS COVERS ANTERIOR CHAMBER
LOWER EYELID
THIRD EYELID

The eyes

The eye consists of the cornea, then an anterior fluid-filled chamber, followed by the three-part uvea – iris, ciliary body, and lens. Behind the lens is a large, fluid-filled posterior chamber, then the light sensitive retina which feeds information down the optic nerve to the brain. The third eyelid (nictitating membrane), which is hidden by the lower lid, sweeps the eye clean. The lacrimal gland produces tears to keep the cornea moist. Tears drain down the lacrimal duct into the nasal cavity. This can block, causing tears to overflow.

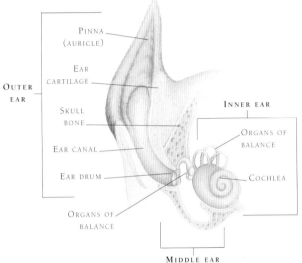

PINNA (AURICLE)
EAR CARTILAGE
OUTER EAR
SKULL BONE
EAR CANAL
EAR DRUM
ORGANS OF BALANCE
INNER EAR
ORGANS OF BALANCE
COCHLEA
MIDDLE EAR

The ears

The cartilaginous outer ear (pinna) captures sound, and funnels it down the external ear canal to the ear drum (tympanic membrane). Ear-drum vibrations stimulate the organs of balance in the middle ear – the hammer, anvil, and stirrup (malleus, incus, and stapes), which amplify and transmit sound, while at the same time protecting the inner ear from excessive vibration. The cochlea (part of the inner ear) captures these sounds and converts them to chemical signals to the brain. Adjacent to the cochlea are the semicircular canals – the saccule and utricle – the organs of balance in the inner ear, which feed the brain with information on the alignment of the head.

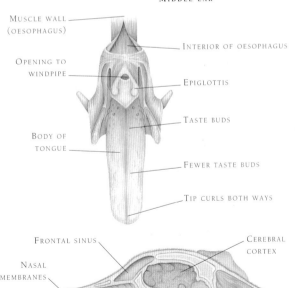

MUSCLE WALL (OESOPHAGUS)
OPENING TO WINDPIPE
BODY OF TONGUE
INTERIOR OF OESOPHAGUS
EPIGLOTTIS
TASTE BUDS
FEWER TASTE BUDS
TIP CURLS BOTH WAYS

The taste buds

Most taste receptors are on the anterior portion of the tongue and are sensitive to sweet, sour, bitter, and salty tastes. Other nerve endings act as touch or texture receptors. Although there are probably fewer than 2,000 taste receptors on the typical dog's tongue, as a "chemical" sense taste works in conjunction with the dog's infinitely more sensitive sense of smell. Odour initially attracts a dog to food, then taste and texture receptors take over.

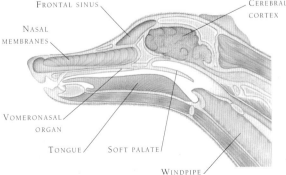

FRONTAL SINUS
NASAL MEMBRANES
VOMERONASAL ORGAN
TONGUE
SOFT PALATE
WINDPIPE
CEREBRAL CORTEX

The scent receptors

Moisture on the nose helps to capture scent, which is transmitted onto the nasal membranes, which cover the nose's wafer-thin turbinate bones. These bones have convoluted folds, ensuring that the tiniest amount of scent is captured within them. Sensory cells are closely packed along the nasal-membrane lining, and convert scent to chemical messages transmitted to the olfactory bulb region of the brain. Other scents are captured by the vomeronasal organ above the roof of the mouth, and transmitted to other parts of the brain.

NERVES, MUSCLES, AND MOVEMENT

THE DOG'S CENTRAL NERVOUS SYSTEM consists of the brain and spinal cord. Its peripheral nervous system includes 12 pairs of nerves that originate in the brain and supply the head and neck region. Further pairs of spinal nerves leave each opening between vertebrae and supply the entire body; the bodies of these nerves (neurons) are in the spinal cord. Nerve fibres (axons) are located outside the spinal cord. When a dog moves, its brain sends messages down the spinal cord and out through peripheral nerves to various muscles, telling some to contract and others to relax. Another part of the peripheral nervous system – the ANS (autonomic nervous system) – controls the dog's involuntary activities.

THE SPINAL CORD

The spinal cord, securely protected by the vertebral column, extends from the brain, down the dog's back, almost to the base of its tail. It is bathed in shock-absorbing cerebrospinal fluid. Whether the dog is asleep or awake, vast amounts of information from nerve receptors in the skin, muscles, and joints travel through peripheral nerves to the spinal cord and on to the brain. Most of this information is simply stored for future use, but some of it reaches the dog's consciousness and provokes movement. Using muscles efficiently involves training peripheral nerves that feed into body muscles to work so smoothly that they seem to respond almost involuntarily to stimulation. For example, a dog must learn, through trial and error, how fast to run and where it should be in order to catch a floating frisbee or ball in its mouth, but once it has done so its response seems almost instinctive.

THE AUTONOMIC NERVES

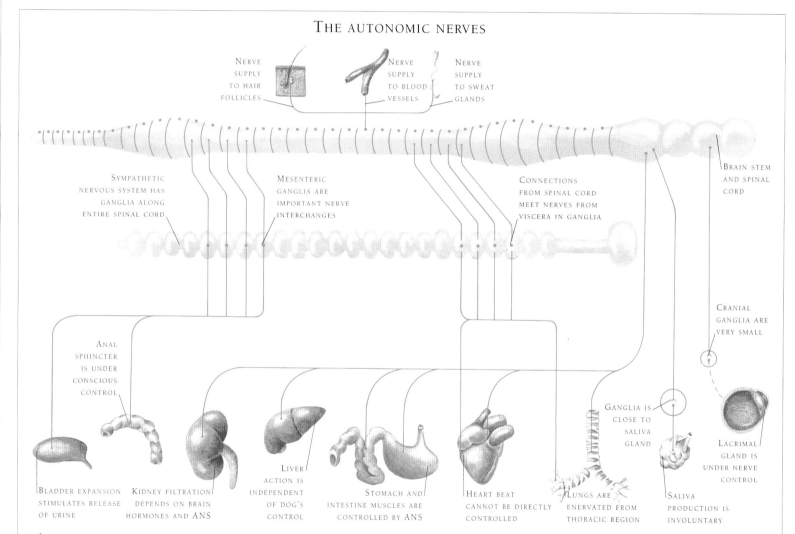

NERVE SUPPLY TO HAIR FOLLICLES

NERVE SUPPLY TO BLOOD VESSELS

NERVE SUPPLY TO SWEAT GLANDS

SYMPATHETIC NERVOUS SYSTEM HAS GANGLIA ALONG ENTIRE SPINAL CORD

MESENTERIC GANGLIA ARE IMPORTANT NERVE INTERCHANGES

CONNECTIONS FROM SPINAL CORD MEET NERVES FROM VISCERA IN GANGLIA

BRAIN STEM AND SPINAL CORD

ANAL SPHINCTER IS UNDER CONSCIOUS CONTROL

CRANIAL GANGLIA ARE VERY SMALL

GANGLIA IS CLOSE TO SALIVA GLAND

LACRIMAL GLAND IS UNDER NERVE CONTROL

BLADDER EXPANSION STIMULATES RELEASE OF URINE

KIDNEY FILTRATION DEPENDS ON BRAIN HORMONES AND ANS

LIVER ACTION IS INDEPENDENT OF DOG'S CONTROL

STOMACH AND INTESTINE MUSCLES ARE CONTROLLED BY ANS

HEART BEAT CANNOT BE DIRECTLY CONTROLLED

LUNGS ARE ENERVATED FROM THORACIC REGION

SALIVA PRODUCTION IS INVOLUNTARY

The autonomic nerves supply the smooth muscles of blood vessels, the heart, viscera (entrails), the glands of the digestive, respiratory, and urogenital systems, and the head and skin. Within the autonomic system is the sympathetic nervous system. This nervous system includes a chain of ganglia (junctions where nerves meet), which is located immediately outside the vertebral column. The sympathetic nerves leave the intervertebral spaces, enter the sympathetic chain of ganglia, and then proceed to various parts of the body. If these nerves become damaged, the organs that the nerves supply lose their control. For example, an injury that occurs in the middle lumbar region of the spine might cause damage to the autonomic nerve supply to the bladder, resulting in urinary incontinence.

Types of muscle

The dog has three types of muscle. Smooth muscle controls movements of the viscera, cardiac muscle makes up the bulk of the heart tissue, and skeletal muscle makes up the rest. The dog can control skeletal muscle, which can be contracted or relaxed at will. Under the microscope skeletal muscle appears striated, while smooth muscle does not. Most muscles consist of bundles of long cells and muscle fibres.

EARS ARE WELL MUSCLED FOR SOCIAL SIGNALLING

NECK MUSCLES PERMIT HEAD TO BE TURNED OVER 220 DEGREES

SHOULDER IS ATTACHED TO BODY ONLY BY MUSCLES

TAIL MUSCLES ALLOW RAISING AND CURLING, AS WELL AS WAGGING

POWERFUL FORELEG MUSCLES EXTEND LEG

HIP MUSCLES SUPPORT HIND LEGS

THIGH MUSCLES GIVE EXPLOSIVE ENERGY FOR CHASE

MUSCLES ATTACHED TO BONES BY TENDONS

DORSAL TENDONS EXTEND TOES

ACHILLES TENDON IS MOST PROMINENT TENDON ON DOG'S BODY

ABDOMEN HAS VERY THIN MUSCLE COVER

THE MUSCLES

POWERFUL JAW MUSCLES GIVE STRENGTH TO BITE OR HOLD

VENTRAL NECK MUSCLES PULL DOWN HEAD

MUSCLES PROTECT DELICATE OESOPHAGUS

MUSCLES ATTACHED TO BREASTPLATE

FORELEG MUSCLES RETRACT LIMB

THIN MUSCLE COVERS OUTER CHEST

MUSCLES PERMIT PAWS TO BE USED FOR DIGGING AND SCRATCHING

Voluntary activities

The peripheral nervous system consists of millions of individual nerve fibres, which conduct messages or signals from the brain to muscle fibres. Most of these nerve fibres are extremely long. In giant breeds such as the Great Dane, the nerve fibres to the toe muscles can be over 1 m (3 ft) long. These nerve fibres cannot repair themselves when damaged. A severed nerve results in permanent inactivity of its muscle.

MUSCLES AND MOVEMENT

A healthy dog has perfectly coordinated movement and a smooth gait. Inability to coordinate, and partial or even complete paralysis, are the most common reasons for neurological examinations. These conditions may be caused by muscle or nerve damage. Spinal or peripheral nerve damage deprives muscles of the ability to receive or send messages efficiently. Spastic movement often indicates damage in the spinal cord or the brain itself. Muscle rigidity may occur if a muscle loses its blood supply. Muscle shrinkage may occur if the muscles are not being used, or if their nerve supply has been damaged. A visit to the vet is essential if there are signs of disturbance in the dog's flexibility. By carrying out a number of tests to determine the efficiency of the dog's response mechanisms, the cause of the problem can generally be diagnosed.

Routine exercise is necessary for fluid muscle movement. Young dogs, in particular, need daily exercise – typically two periods – with combinations of walking, trotting, and galloping. Jumping is an excellent activity for lean dogs, but potentially dangerous for old, heavy dogs. Spinal-cord damage is possible if an overweight dog lands heavily. Certain dwarfed dogs are prone to compression of the spinal cord. A hereditary, ascending degeneration of the spinal cord causes a progressively drunken gait in other breeds, such as the German Shepherd Dog.

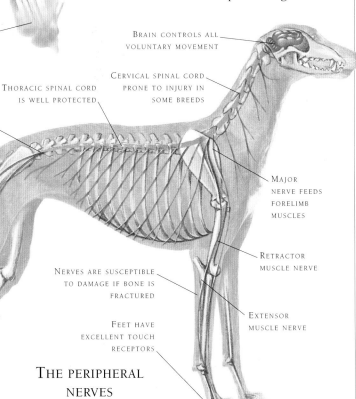

BRAIN CONTROLS ALL VOLUNTARY MOVEMENT

CERVICAL SPINAL CORD PRONE TO INJURY IN SOME BREEDS

THORACIC SPINAL CORD IS WELL PROTECTED

SPINAL CORD THINS AS IT EXTENDS TOWARDS TAIL

SACRAL REGION NERVES PRONE TO DAMAGE

MAJOR NERVES TO HIND-LIMB EXTENSOR AND RETRACTOR MUSCLES

MAJOR NERVE FEEDS FORELIMB MUSCLES

RETRACTOR MUSCLE NERVE

NERVES ARE SUSCEPTIBLE TO DAMAGE IF BONE IS FRACTURED

EXTENSOR MUSCLE NERVE

FEET HAVE EXCELLENT TOUCH RECEPTORS

THE PERIPHERAL NERVES

THE HEART AND LUNGS

THE DOG HAS A TYPICALLY efficient mammalian cardiovascular system. Blood carries nourishment in the form of oxygen around the body. The liver cleanses the blood of impurities, while the lungs exchange carbon dioxide for fresh oxygen. The spleen and bone marrow manufacture and store cells responsible for carrying oxygen. When a dog exercises vigorously, a great deal of oxygen is required, and waste products and carbon dioxide are produced in large amounts. The dog's respiratory and circulatory systems respond automatically, increasing blood flow through the heart and lungs. Blood is diverted away from regions like the intestines, to the body's muscles, providing the dog with extra stamina.

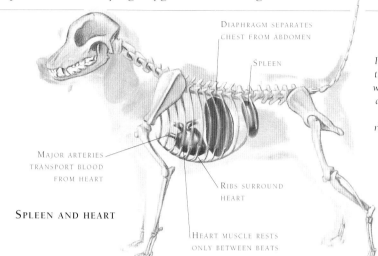

DIAPHRAGM SEPARATES CHEST FROM ABDOMEN

SPLEEN

MAJOR ARTERIES TRANSPORT BLOOD FROM HEART

SPLEEN AND HEART

RIBS SURROUND HEART

HEART MUSCLE RESTS ONLY BETWEEN BEATS

BLOOD PRODUCTION

Manufacturing blood

In the newborn puppy, blood cells are produced in the liver and spleen (where blood is manufactured while the puppy is still in the womb), but by young adulthood virtually all of the dog's blood cells are produced in the bone marrow, especially in the ribs, vertebrae, skull, and pelvis. All three types of blood cell – red cells that carry inhaled fresh oxygen or waste carbon dioxide (which is then exhaled), platelets needed to form clots and plug leaks when blood vessels are damaged, and white cells necessary to defend the body from microbes and parasites – are manufactured in the bone marrow. The spleen stores blood and pumps out extra cells when necessary.

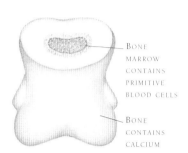

BONE MARROW CONTAINS PRIMITIVE BLOOD CELLS

BONE CONTAINS CALCIUM

CROSS SECTION OF BONE

THE HEART AND BLOOD SYSTEM

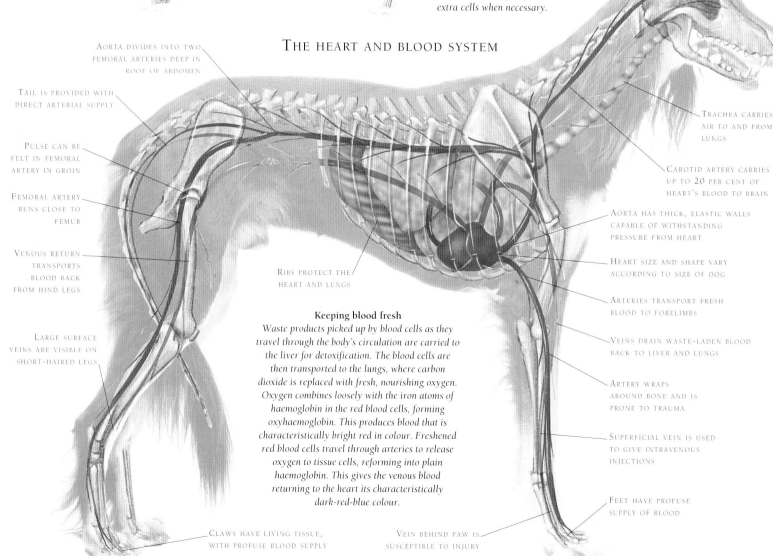

AORTA DIVIDES INTO TWO FEMORAL ARTERIES DEEP IN ROOF OF ABDOMEN

TAIL IS PROVIDED WITH DIRECT ARTERIAL SUPPLY

PULSE CAN BE FELT IN FEMORAL ARTERY IN GROIN

FEMORAL ARTERY RUNS CLOSE TO FEMUR

VENOUS RETURN TRANSPORTS BLOOD BACK FROM HIND LEGS

LARGE SURFACE VEINS ARE VISIBLE ON SHORT-HAIRED LEGS

RIBS PROTECT THE HEART AND LUNGS

TRACHEA CARRIES AIR TO AND FROM LUNGS

CAROTID ARTERY CARRIES UP TO 20 PER CENT OF HEART'S BLOOD TO BRAIN

AORTA HAS THICK, ELASTIC WALLS CAPABLE OF WITHSTANDING PRESSURE FROM HEART

HEART SIZE AND SHAPE VARY ACCORDING TO SIZE OF DOG

ARTERIES TRANSPORT FRESH BLOOD TO FORELIMBS

VEINS DRAIN WASTE-LADEN BLOOD BACK TO LIVER AND LUNGS

ARTERY WRAPS AROUND BONE AND IS PRONE TO TRAUMA

SUPERFICIAL VEIN IS USED TO GIVE INTRAVENOUS INJECTIONS

Keeping blood fresh

Waste products picked up by blood cells as they travel through the body's circulation are carried to the liver for detoxification. The blood cells are then transported to the lungs, where carbon dioxide is replaced with fresh, nourishing oxygen. Oxygen combines loosely with the iron atoms of haemoglobin in the red blood cells, forming oxyhaemoglobin. This produces blood that is characteristically bright red in colour. Freshened red blood cells travel through arteries to release oxygen to tissue cells, reforming into plain haemoglobin. This gives the venous blood returning to the heart its characteristically dark-red-blue colour.

FEET HAVE PROFUSE SUPPLY OF BLOOD

CLAWS HAVE LIVING TISSUE, WITH PROFUSE BLOOD SUPPLY

VEIN BEHIND PAW IS SUSCEPTIBLE TO INJURY

BLOOD CIRCULATION

Different parts of the dog's body need varying amounts of nourishment at various times. Although the dog's brain is relatively small compared to the rest of its body, it normally receives about 15 to 20 per cent of the blood pumped by the heart. At rest, the heart muscle receives half that amount and the rest of the body's muscles about twice that amount. When a dog is exercising strenuously, circulation changes dramatically. Although the supply of blood to the brain remains constant, flow to the heart muscle quadruples, and flow to body muscles increases twentyfold. About 90 per cent of the blood pumped out by the heart can be diverted to the muscles. At the same time, blood flow to other parts of the body diminishes.

BLOOD FLOW CONTROL

The ability to vary the quantities of pumped blood and to redirect it to the most needed areas is controlled by nerves and hormones that constrict or relax the muscles in the walls of the very smallest arteries – the arterioles. Any increase in local tissue activity, such as an increase in waste products produced when muscles are active, causes local arterioles to dilate. Blood flow to the region then increases; expansion of the elastic arteriole can increase the potential flow of blood through that vessel to 256 times the resting flow. During typical exercise, a dog's circulation normally increases muscle blood flow 20 to 30 times.

BLOOD PRESSURE

The blood circulation is a closed system, and pressure within the system varies at different sites. Pressure is highest in the blood vessels leaving the heart and lowest in the blood vessels returning to the heart. Blood vessels taking blood away from the heart (arteries and arterioles) have elastic walls which can expand and contract. Vessels returning blood to the heart (veins and venules) have thin walls, and pressure within this part of the system is lower.

CAPILLARY EXCHANGE

The dog's circulation sends fresh blood from the liver and lungs through arteries to tiny blood vessels (capillaries), where substances are exchanged by diffusion through cell walls. Highly concentrated substances, like oxygen, diffuse through capillary walls into tissue fluids. Carbon dioxide, found in tissue fluids, diffuses across the capillary wall into the blood vessel, to be carried by the veins back to the liver and lungs for detoxification.

THE HEART, DIAPHRAGM, AND LUNGS

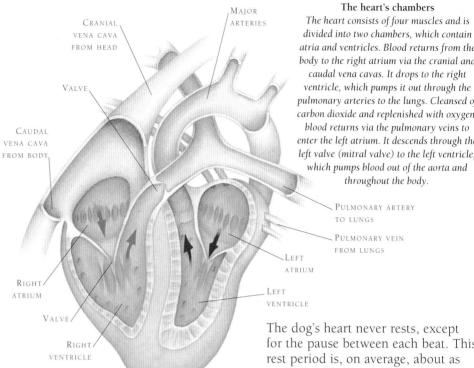

CRANIAL VENA CAVA FROM HEAD

VALVE

CAUDAL VENA CAVA FROM BODY

RIGHT ATRIUM

VALVE

RIGHT VENTRICLE

MAJOR ARTERIES

PULMONARY ARTERY TO LUNGS

PULMONARY VEIN FROM LUNGS

LEFT ATRIUM

LEFT VENTRICLE

THE HEART

The heart's chambers

The heart consists of four muscles and is divided into two chambers, which contain atria and ventricles. Blood returns from the body to the right atrium via the cranial and caudal vena cavas. It drops to the right ventricle, which pumps it out through the pulmonary arteries to the lungs. Cleansed of carbon dioxide and replenished with oxygen, blood returns via the pulmonary veins to enter the left atrium. It descends through the left valve (mitral valve) to the left ventricle, which pumps blood out of the aorta and throughout the body.

The dog's heart never rests, except for the pause between each beat. This rest period is, on average, about as long as the period of contraction but, unlike in the human heart, the length of the rest period normally varies considerably. Dogs rarely suffer from clots in the cardiac arteries but some breeds, the Dobermann in particular, have a high incidence of heart-muscle disease. Overwhelmingly, the most common canine cardiac problem involves the valves which separate the top chambers (atria) from the lower chambers (ventricles). For hereditary reasons, in breeds such as the Cavalier King Charles Spaniel, these valves do not shut properly. When the ventricles contract, rather than pumping all blood out of the heart, they pump some blood back into the atria from which it has come.

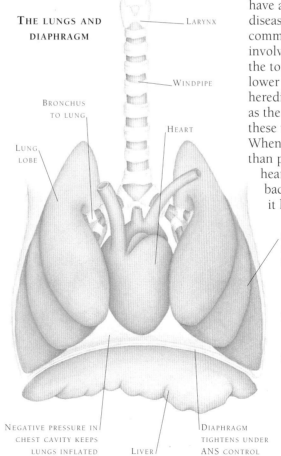

THE LUNGS AND DIAPHRAGM

LARYNX

WINDPIPE

BRONCHUS TO LUNG

HEART

LUNG LOBE

SMOOTH SURFACE LINING PREVENTS ADHESIONS TO CHEST WALL

NEGATIVE PRESSURE IN CHEST CAVITY KEEPS LUNGS INFLATED

LIVER

DIAPHRAGM TIGHTENS UNDER ANS CONTROL

The function of the lungs

The lungs are like inflated elastic balloons. The space that contains the lungs is called the thoracic cavity. As the diaphragm tightens, air is drawn into the lungs, which are forced to expand. Inside the lungs of a typical dog, in an area covering 50 sq m (164 sq ft) – the size of about half of a tennis court – fresh oxygen replaces existing carbon dioxide. The diaphragm relaxes and the lungs contract, expelling carbon dioxide from the dog's nose.

THE GASTROINTESTINAL SYSTEM

THE DOG'S GASTROINTESTINAL SYSTEM permits it to gorge on food infrequently but copiously. The teeth are adapted for killing prey, and for tearing meat. Little digestion occurs in the mouth – food passes through the oesophagus to the stomach, which allows portions of food to pass into the intestines at intervals. Enzymes produced by the pancreas and liver help break down food in the form of protein, carbohydrate, and fat into simple molecules that can be absorbed through the walls of the small intestine and transported by the blood stream to the body's cells. Further along, in the large intestine, water and salts are absorbed from the residue. Within 36 hours of eating, waste food is converted to faeces.

THE ALIMENTARY CANAL

Although the alimentary canal is structurally simple, its function is complex. Food enters one end and, while passing through the tube, is converted into nourishment that can be absorbed into the body. Waste is passed out of the other end of the tube. The teeth, jaws, and tongue break down food and move it to the back of the dog's mouth (pharynx), then lift it over the larynx and into the oesophagus for transport to the stomach. The oesophagus is very elastic, allowing large lumps of meat to pass through.

Unfortunately, this also permits undigestible objects such as bones and toys to be swallowed. At the stomach, a tight valve – the cardiac sphincter – opens for each bolus of food, then shuts tightly. Food leaves the stomach through another valve, the pyloric sphincter, and enters the small intestine, where contractions of intestinal muscles (peristalsis) both mix food and move it along. The large intestine has a large diameter and acts as the distal-holding tank in the alimentary system. Distension of the rectum stimulates the dog's urge to defecate.

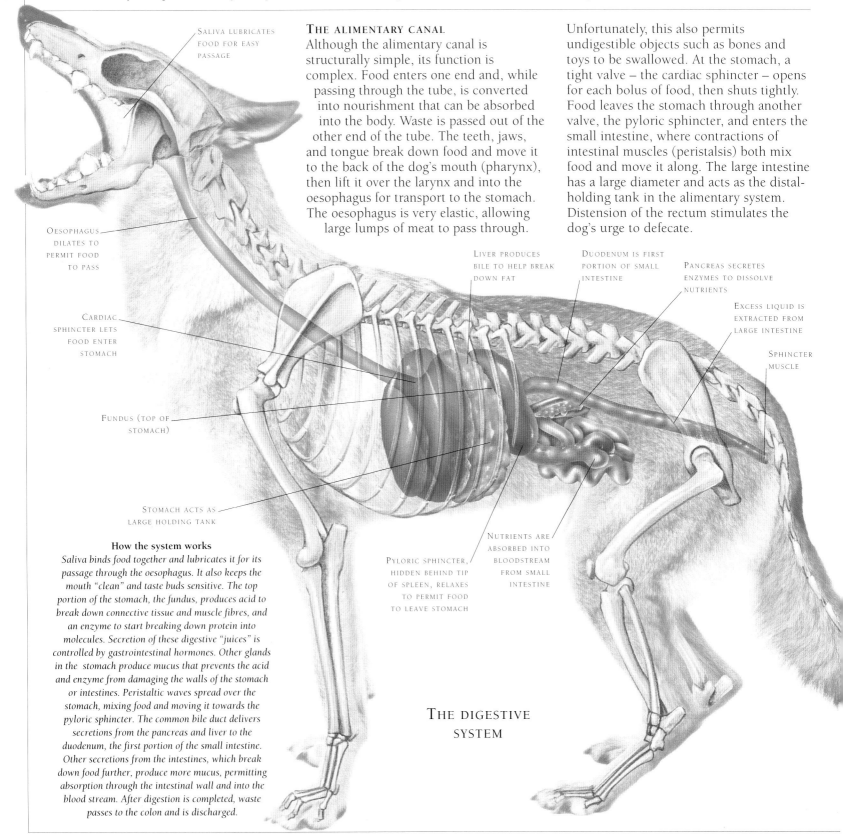

SALIVA LUBRICATES FOOD FOR EASY PASSAGE

OESOPHAGUS DILATES TO PERMIT FOOD TO PASS

CARDIAC SPHINCTER LETS FOOD ENTER STOMACH

FUNDUS (TOP OF STOMACH)

STOMACH ACTS AS LARGE HOLDING TANK

LIVER PRODUCES BILE TO HELP BREAK DOWN FAT

DUODENUM IS FIRST PORTION OF SMALL INTESTINE

PANCREAS SECRETES ENZYMES TO DISSOLVE NUTRIENTS

EXCESS LIQUID IS EXTRACTED FROM LARGE INTESTINE

SPHINCTER MUSCLE

PYLORIC SPHINCTER, HIDDEN BEHIND TIP OF SPLEEN, RELAXES TO PERMIT FOOD TO LEAVE STOMACH

NUTRIENTS ARE ABSORBED INTO BLOODSTREAM FROM SMALL INTESTINE

THE DIGESTIVE SYSTEM

How the system works

Saliva binds food together and lubricates it for its passage through the oesophagus. It also keeps the mouth "clean" and taste buds sensitive. The top portion of the stomach, the fundus, produces acid to break down connective tissue and muscle fibres, and an enzyme to start breaking down protein into molecules. Secretion of these digestive "juices" is controlled by gastrointestinal hormones. Other glands in the stomach produce mucus that prevents the acid and enzyme from damaging the walls of the stomach or intestines. Peristaltic waves spread over the stomach, mixing food and moving it towards the pyloric sphincter. The common bile duct delivers secretions from the pancreas and liver to the duodenum, the first portion of the small intestine. Other secretions from the intestines, which break down food further, produce more mucus, permitting absorption through the intestinal wall and into the blood stream. After digestion is completed, waste passes to the colon and is discharged.

How the gall bladder works

The dog's gall bladder is part of the liver, and stores bile acids. These emulsify fat and prevent the breakdown of pancreatic fat-digesting enzymes. Bile acids, which are manufactured in the liver, help to dissolve the fat-soluble vitamins. The gall bladder concentrates bile and, during digestion, delivers bile through the common bile duct to the duodenum.

GALL BLADDER STORES BILE MANUFACTURED IN LIVER

SECONDARY BILE DUCTS EXIST THROUGHOUT LIVER

BILE AND PANCREATIC ENZYMES ENTER DUODENUM THROUGH COMMON BILE DUCT

PANCREAS

DUCTS COLLECT PANCREATIC ENZYMES

DUODENUM

THE PANCREAS

The pancreas produces alkaline bicarbonate, which neutralizes stomach acid entering the duodenum. It also produces digestive enzymes that break down protein, carbohydrate, fat, elastic tissue, connective tissue, and even the nucleic acid of individual cells. These substances travel through the pancreatic duct to the common bile duct and enter the intestines with bile from the liver. Small regions of the pancreas produce insulin, which allows glucose to enter body cells. Without insulin, glucose fails to enter cells and builds up in the bloodstream, overflowing through the kidneys into the urine; this leads to sugar diabetes. Insulin is needed to build the dog's body – lack of it causes increased thirst, urinating, and body wasting.

THE INTESTINES

Enzymes from the liver and pancreas break food down into absorbable molecules, while waves of contractions mix food, and peristalsis of intestinal muscles moves food along. A great deal of water passes through the intestines. The rest is absorbed through the walls of the small and large intestines. The large intestine (colon) is inhabited by vast numbers of bacteria. These decrease the body's susceptibility to infection, synthesize vitamins, and break down waste material.

THE DOG'S DENTITION

UPPER JAW

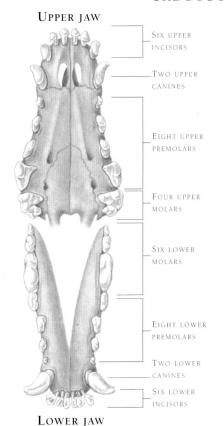

SIX UPPER INCISORS

TWO UPPER CANINES

EIGHT UPPER PREMOLARS

FOUR UPPER MOLARS

SIX LOWER MOLARS

EIGHT LOWER PREMOLARS

TWO LOWER CANINES

SIX LOWER INCISORS

LOWER JAW

The dog's mouth is ideally constructed for the carnivorous scavenger's diet. It is long and deep, with large canine teeth for stabbing, catching, and holding prey, small incisors for nibbling meat off bones and for grooming the dog's skin and coat, and premolars and molars adapted both for shearing and cutting meat, but also for grinding and chewing the roughage component of the omnivore's diet – foods such as roots and grass. Saliva lubricates food after it is chewed, to ease its entry into the digestive system. Canine teeth are sturdy and strong, although they may chip or fracture when bones are chewed. Far more common is a bacterial disease of the soft and hard tissues that surround and support the teeth, which is called periodontal disease. This is perhaps the most common preventable disease in companion dogs, affecting seventy per cent of dogs over four years of age. Periodontal disease can be prevented through routine dental hygiene.

Incisors

Twelve small incisors cut, nibble, groom, and bite. They usually meet in a scissors bite, where the top incisors fit neatly over the lower incisors.

Canines

The four canine teeth are the largest in the dog's mouth. Because their function is to hold and tear, they have extremely long roots.

Premolars

Sixteen premolars are used for shearing, cutting, and holding. The upper, fourth premolar and lower, first molar are called carnassial teeth.

Molars

The dog's ten molars have moderately flattened surfaces, useful for chewing and grinding the non-meat parts of the omnivorous dog's diet.

SIDE VIEW OF SKULL

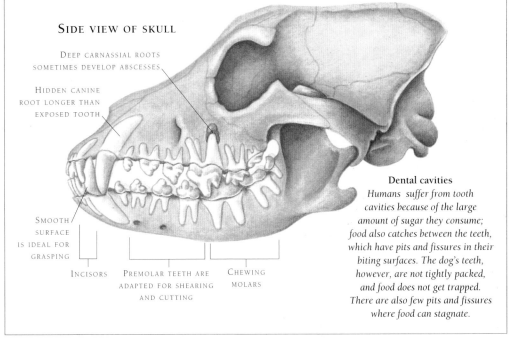

DEEP CARNASSIAL ROOTS SOMETIMES DEVELOP ABSCESSES

HIDDEN CANINE ROOT LONGER THAN EXPOSED TOOTH

SMOOTH SURFACE IS IDEAL FOR GRASPING

INCISORS

PREMOLAR TEETH ARE ADAPTED FOR SHEARING AND CUTTING

CHEWING MOLARS

Dental cavities

Humans suffer from tooth cavities because of the large amount of sugar they consume; food also catches between the teeth, which have pits and fissures in their biting surfaces. The dog's teeth, however, are not tightly packed, and food does not get trapped. There are also few pits and fissures where food can stagnate.

URINARY AND REPRODUCTIVE SYSTEMS

THE DOG'S URINARY AND REPRODUCTIVE systems are integrated in a typically mammalian fashion. Protected by the last ribs, the two kidneys hang from the roof of the abdomen. These filter the blood of unwanted or potentially toxic substances. Clear waste is then passed into the renal pelvis, from where it travels in peristaltic waves down two ureters to the bladder.

A single urethra discharges urine from the penis, or through the vulva. The reproductive system integrates itself into the latter part of the urinary system. Spermatic cords from the male dog's testes carry sperm through to the urethra. In the female dog, the vagina leads into a vestibule – the vulva – where the urethra empties.

HORMONAL INFLUENCES

The male dog mates opportunistically. He is always sexually active, and is attracted to the scent of the hormonally active female (*see page 52*). Scent stimulates the pituitary or "master gland" at the base of his brain to instruct his testes to produce more male hormone and sperm cells. The female usually has two hormonally active reproductive cycles each year. During pro-oestrus, which lasts on average

12 days, her vulva swells and she produces a discharge. During oestrus, which lasts about five days, her discharge stops and her ovaries release eggs into the fallopian tubes. Only then does she choose a mate.

WHEN TO MATE

A bitch willingly mates during her first oestrus, but emotional and physical immaturity often leads to small litters and poor mothering. During subsequent oestrus cycles, mating is usually more productive. Ovulation can vary, but most bitches ovulate some time between 10 and 12 days after the cycle begins. Breeders like to breed their bitches twice, on the tenth and twelfth, or eleventh and thirteenth days. Examining vaginal smears

under a microscope gives a reasonable indication of when a bitch has ovulated. More accurate assessment can be made by monitoring hormone levels in the blood.

MATING

Usually both dogs indulge in play activity before mating. When the bitch is ready, she holds her tail to the side, and stands still. The male mounts, enters, thrusts with his pelvis, and ejaculates. As he does so, his penis swells, becoming "locked" inside the female for twenty minutes. If mating does not occur, the female experiences a metoestrus stage of about eight weeks, when the uterus wall thickens, and a fifteen week anoestrus stage of reproductive rest until the next season.

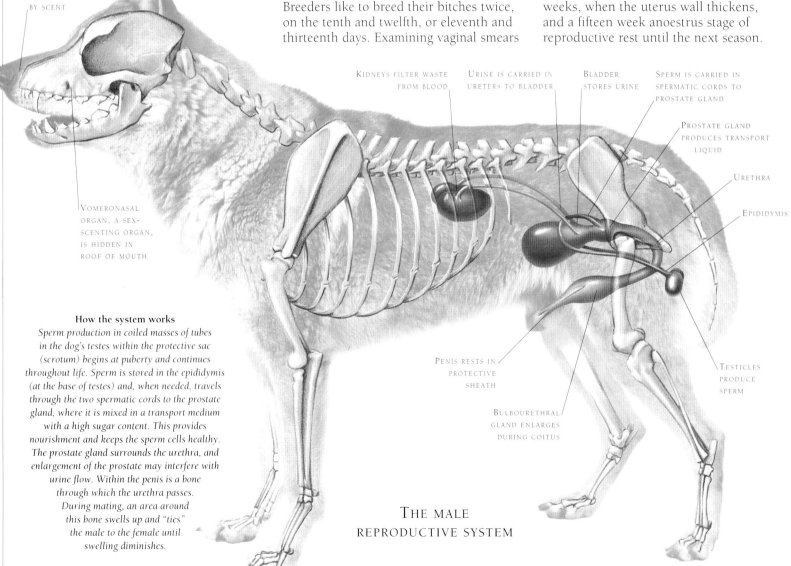

SEXUAL INTEREST IS STIMULATED BY SCENT

VOMERONASAL ORGAN, A SEX-SCENTING ORGAN, IS HIDDEN IN ROOF OF MOUTH

KIDNEYS FILTER WASTE FROM BLOOD

URINE IS CARRIED IN URETERS TO BLADDER

BLADDER STORES URINE

SPERM IS CARRIED IN SPERMATIC CORDS TO PROSTATE GLAND

PROSTATE GLAND PRODUCES TRANSPORT LIQUID

URETHRA

EPIDIDYMIS

PENIS RESTS IN PROTECTIVE SHEATH

BULBOURETHRAL GLAND ENLARGES DURING COITUS

TESTICLES PRODUCE SPERM

How the system works
Sperm production in coiled masses of tubes in the dog's testes within the protective sac (scrotum) begins at puberty and continues throughout life. Sperm is stored in the epididymis (at the base of testes) and, when needed, travels through the two spermatic cords to the prostate gland, where it is mixed in a transport medium with a high sugar content. This provides nourishment and keeps the sperm cells healthy. The prostate gland surrounds the urethra, and enlargement of the prostate may interfere with urine flow. Within the penis is a bone through which the urethra passes. During mating, an area around this bone swells up and "ties" the male to the female until swelling diminishes.

THE MALE
REPRODUCTIVE SYSTEM

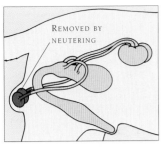

REMOVED BY NEUTERING

UNNEUTERED DOG

How neutering works

Neutering the male is relatively simple. A small incision is made just in front of the scrotum, and the testes are drawn through and removed, diminishing male hormone production. Neutering the female is more complex. Through an abdominal incision, the reproductive tract from the ovaries to the cervix is removed. This eliminates future reproductive problems and oestrus cycles, and diminishes oestrus-related behavioural changes.

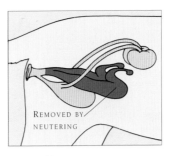

REMOVED BY NEUTERING

UNNEUTERED BITCH

BLADDER-STONE FORMATION

Minerals in the urine sometimes crystallize into granules, creating bladder stones. This can also occur in the renal pelvis, producing a painful kidney stone. Kidney stones are rare, but bladder stones are quite common. The mineral deposit irritates the lining of the bladder, causing straining and frequent passing of urine, sometimes with blood. Bladder-stone formation is ultimately diet controlled.

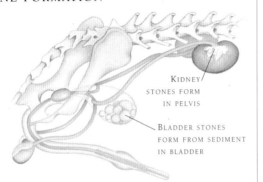

KIDNEY STONES FORM IN PELVIS

BLADDER STONES FORM FROM SEDIMENT IN BLADDER

THE FEMALE REPRODUCTIVE SYSTEM

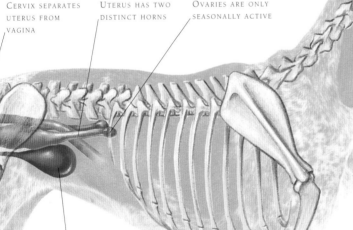

VAGINA OPENS AT VULVA

CERVIX SEPARATES UTERUS FROM VAGINA

UTERUS HAS TWO DISTINCT HORNS

OVARIES ARE ONLY SEASONALLY ACTIVE

INCREASING DAYLIGHT STIMULATES ONSET OF OESTRUS

SCENT PLAYS MODERATE ROLE IN REPRODUCTION

BLADDER TEMPORARILY STORES URINE FROM KIDNEYS

How the system works

Two ovaries hang from the roof of the abdomen, just behind the kidneys. They remain active for life, producing and releasing eggs, usually twice yearly. The eggs pass through the fallopian tubes to the uterus – this has two distinct horns which meet at the cervix. During pregnancy, the foetuses are positioned in rows in each horn. The cervix remains shut at all times except during oestrus, when it opens to allow the entry of semen, and at birth, to permit the passage of puppies. Occasionally, bacteria pass through the cervix into the womb, causing serious infection. This occurs particularly in old bitches, and demands urgent veterinary attention.

DEVELOPMENT OF THE FOETUS

Pregnancy lasts for about sixty-three days. All bitches have hormonal pregnancies, regardless of whether they are pregnant. The foetuses are initially encapsulated in amniotic sacs. By the time the foetus is seven weeks old, its bones are sufficiently calcified to show up on X-ray. Two weeks later, the cervix dilates and labour begins.

Twenty-eight days

Initially, the developing foetus receives its nourishment from a yolk sac, but after 28 days nourishment comes from the placenta. By this stage, the head, eyes, and limbs are developing. The most dangerous time, when drugs and other substances may cause overwhelming damage, has passed.

28 DAYS

Thirty-three days

The foetus is still tiny, but all the necessary components for life are established. The mother may only now give some indication that she is pregnant, although her abdomen has not changed shape.

33 DAYS

Forty days

The foetus is substantially larger, and the internal organs are functioning. The mother's nipples are pink, and her abdomen is changing shape.

40 DAYS

Fifty days

The foetus is now a perfect puppy in miniature, but cannot survive outside the womb. It will be another week before its lungs have developed sufficiently for it to breathe on its own. Its mother's abdomen is well distended and milk production has begun.

50 DAYS

Sixty days

The foetus will survive if its mother gives birth now, a few days earlier than average. A coat of hair covers its entire body, ensuring insulation when it is exposed to the outside world for the first time. Heat receptors in the nose will help it find its mother.

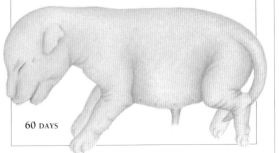

60 DAYS

THE SKIN AND COAT

THE DOG'S SKIN AND HAIR PROVIDE a physical barrier; this prevents harmful chemicals and microbes from entering the body. The skin is a sensory organ that controls the dog's body temperature. Raising or lowering of the hair also increases or decreases heat loss. Glands in the skin secrete or excrete substances that give the coat its shine and nourish the skin. Individual skin cells carry out surveillance for potential dangers to the dog's body, and influence the immune response when injuries occur. Regions of skin are modified for specific purposes – the paws for durability, the ears for social signalling, and the anal glands for scent marking.

HAIR FOLLICLES

Coats of hair vary more dramatically in dogs than in most other domestic species, because many hairs of varying texture can grow from an individual hair follicle. The central hair growing from the follicle is surrounded by up to five primary hairs, each with its own sweat gland, sebaceous gland, and erector (arrector pili) muscle. These solid and robust primary hairs may or may not be surrounded by small secondary hairs. Each secondary hair has a lubricating sebaceous gland, but neither a sweat gland nor an erector muscle. These hairs cannot be raised.

COAT TEXTURES

Primary hairs are often called guard hair or topcoat, while secondary hairs are called down or undercoat. The density of these hair types and their distribution are the most influential factors as regards coat types. Density varies substantially. A Yorkshire Terrier may have 100 hairs per square centimetre, while a Finnish Spitz may have 600 hairs to the same area. In wild canids such as wolves or the Coyote, and in breeds such as the German Shepherd Dog, the coarse primary hairs have many fine secondary hairs. Breeds like the Cairn Terrier have increased

Hairless
Hairlessness is a rare genetic accident that has occurred through human intervention. Virtually all of the hairless breeds give birth to some young with hair.

Wire coat
Wire-haired breeds have coats with increased numbers and density of harsh guard hairs. These create a superb physical barrier, offering insulation in cold weather, but also physical protection from the bites of other animals or damage from harsh vegetation.

HARSH, WIRY COAT OF THICK PRIMARY HAIR

density of primary hair and less secondary hair, while breeds with soft, short coats like the Boxer have decreased primary hair density and more secondary hair.

HAIR GROWTH

The dog's hair grows in cycles. There is an active growth period, followed by a transitional period, then a resting period. The hair is shed when another is ready to replace it. The growth cycle is controlled, or modified, by a range of side factors, including the surrounding temperature, increasing or decreasing daylight hours, body hormones,

nutrition, stress, and genetic influences. Typically, hair is shed most prolifically in spring, when the dense winter undercoat is no longer needed, and again in the autumn when the short summer topcoat is replaced by a long, dense coat, and new down grows. During the winter, the entire topcoat and 50 per cent of the undercoat may be in its resting phase. Because so many dogs live in centrally heated environments, or in regions where the ambient temperature is constant, this natural sequence of seasonal hair growth and loss is often altered. Many dogs shed their hair throughout the year. Changes in pituitary, thyroid, and adrenal hormone production have dramatic effects on coat texture and density. So, too, do sex hormones. Male hormones stimulate increased hair density, while female hormones have the opposite effect. In addition to normal body hair, there are two types of specialized hair. There are single hairs scattered all over the dog's skin (tyrotrich hairs), while the head and throat are covered by thick, stiff hairs (vibrissae). Both types act as specialized touch receptors.

Close coat
Dogs that evolved in warm climates often have close, short coats, in which fine secondary down is more prominent than primary or guard hair.

HIGH DENSITY OF SHORT, WATERPROOF HAIR PROVIDES GOOD INSULATION

Heavy coat
A prolonged growth phase for hair was probably actively selected not only to give thermal protection, but also because it was aesthetically pleasing. This aspect of the dog's coat has been dramatically emphasized since the formation of kennel clubs.

EXAGGERATED HAIR LENGTH

THE SKIN

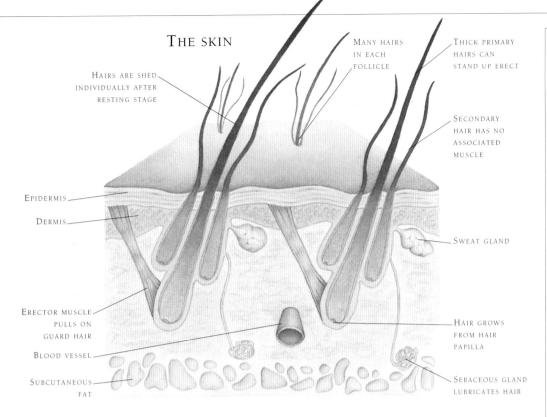

HAIRS ARE SHED INDIVIDUALLY AFTER RESTING STAGE

MANY HAIRS IN EACH FOLLICLE

THICK PRIMARY HAIRS CAN STAND UP ERECT

SECONDARY HAIR HAS NO ASSOCIATED MUSCLE

EPIDERMIS

DERMIS

SWEAT GLAND

ERECTOR MUSCLE PULLS ON GUARD HAIR

BLOOD VESSEL

HAIR GROWS FROM HAIR PAPILLA

SUBCUTANEOUS FAT

SEBACEOUS GLAND LUBRICATES HAIR

The structure of the skin
The skin consists of two main sections. The surface (epidermis) is not particularly strong, but preserves its protective function and integrity by continually laying down new cells and nourishing and lubricating itself through glandular secretions. Under the epidermis, the strong, elastic, and flexible dermis provides strength as well as the blood and nerve supply to the epidermis. Within the dermis are numerous skin glands, which vary on different parts of the body. The most common are the tubular sebaceous glands that secrete into hair follicles, providing nourishment and lubrication. Inside the ear canals, the sebaceous glands are modified to produce cerumin (wax). Some hair follicles also have sweat glands – these are most common on the footpads and in the ear canals. Elsewhere in the skin, for example around the anus and on the top of the tail, there are modified sebaceous glands that probably assist in social recognition.

THE ANAL SACS

The anal sacs are a part of the dog's skin. Sebaceous and sweat glands empty into each sac, secreting substances that play a role in both territory marking and social recognition. When a dog passes a stool, muscles around the anal sacs squeeze the sacs against the stool in the anal canal and empty a few drops of a sticky liquid. If stools are soft, anal sacs may become impacted and their contents thick and pasty.

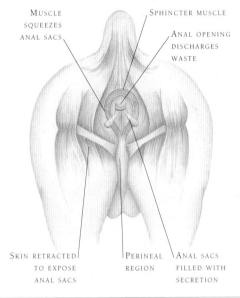

MUSCLE SQUEEZES ANAL SACS

SPHINCTER MUSCLE

ANAL OPENING DISCHARGES WASTE

SKIN RETRACTED TO EXPOSE ANAL SACS

PERINEAL REGION

ANAL SACS FILLED WITH SECRETION

VARIETY IN EAR SHAPES

NATURAL (WOLF) EARS

PRICKED OR ERECT GERMAN SHEPHERD-TYPE EARS

LOPPED EARS, SEMI AMPUTATED TO LOOK ERECT

ERECT, ROUNDED "BAT" EARS

SEMI-ERECT EARS ROLL OVER AT TIPS

"ROSE" EARS CAN BE FOLDED BACK

PENDANT EARS HANG CLOSE TO HEAD

"ROSE" EARS HANG PETAL-LIKE TO SIDES

"BUTTON" EARS ARE ERECT, BUT HANG IN V SHAPE

Selective breeding has modified the dog's ears to a greater extent than almost any other part of the body. Their natural shape, manifested in the wolf, is firmly erect and mobile. Many breeds have wolf-like ears, giving the impression of alertness. Selective breeding has, however, dramatically altered ear shape. The Dobermann has a naturally pendant ear, and to enhance a look of alertness, its ears are surgically amputated in some countries. Other breeds have "rose" ears, which can be raised or laid back flat when racing. The ground-scenting dog often has pendulous ears that touch the ground while it is trailing scent. Selective breeding has created ear-skin problems for some breeds. Hair does not naturally grow down the dog's ear canals, but skin change has produced this condition. Several breeds have hair growing in their ears that needs to be plucked out.

THE PAWS

The nails and pads of the foot are modified skin structures. Nail is produced from a specialized extension of the epidermis. The footpads have a thick, protective, insulating epidermal layer, and contain sweat-producing glands, which help to keep the pads supple. The footpads are much less sensitive to heat and cold than are other parts of the dog's skin.

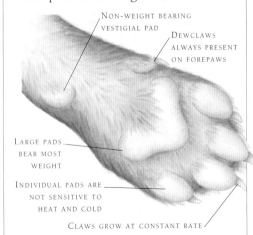

NON-WEIGHT BEARING VESTIGIAL PAD

DEWCLAWS ALWAYS PRESENT ON FOREPAWS

LARGE PADS BEAR MOST WEIGHT

INDIVIDUAL PADS ARE NOT SENSITIVE TO HEAT AND COLD

CLAWS GROW AT CONSTANT RATE

BIOFEEDBACK

BIOFEEDBACK IS A SYSTEM OF controlling actions with chemical messages carried in the blood stream. A sight, sound, smell, or even an emotional feeling stimulates hormones to be released. These travel through the blood stream to other glands, stimulating them to produce a number of different hormones. The new hormones also enter the blood stream, travel back to the gland that produced the first hormone, and then turn it off. The entire system is under the control of the master gland situated at the base of the brain, called the pituitary gland. The pituitary is in turn controlled by the hypothalamus gland, a chemical-producing part of the brain, which is located just above the pituitary.

INTEGRATING THE BODY

The hormones of the dog's endocrine system are responsible for carefully managing and maintaining body functions and responses to both internal and external changes. The dog's hormonal biofeedback system depends upon the nervous system. Nerve pathways in the brain feed into the hypothalamus, which controls the pituitary. In turn, the pituitary produces hormones that stimulate events elsewhere in the body.

PITUITARY HORMONES

TSH (thyroid-stimulating hormone) is produced at relatively constant levels by the pituitary. The thyroid hormone, produced by the thyroid gland, has a "negative" feedback effect on the pituitary, preventing excess production of TSH. The surface of the adrenal gland is stimulated by ACTH (adrenocorticotrophic hormone). Cortisol, produced by the adrenal cortex, feeds back to the pituitary and suppresses excess ACTH production. This system sometimes fails. The pituitary releases far more ACTH than the adrenal cortex can handle, creating a clinical condition called Cushingoid syndrome. Dogs drink and urinate copiously, develop pendulous abdomens, and lose hair on their bodies. The pituitary is also responsible for manufacturing and releasing a variety of sex-related, stimulating hormones such as leutenizing hormone, which induces ovulation in the female and sex-hormone production in the male.

HOW HORMONES WORK

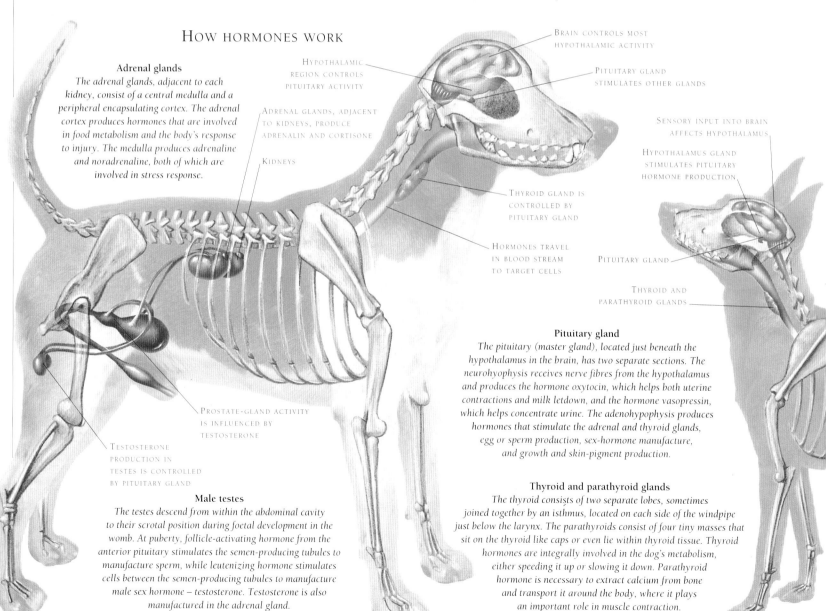

Adrenal glands
The adrenal glands, adjacent to each kidney, consist of a central medulla and a peripheral encapsulating cortex. The adrenal cortex produces hormones that are involved in food metabolism and the body's response to injury. The medulla produces adrenaline and noradrenaline, both of which are involved in stress response.

BRAIN CONTROLS MOST
HYPOTHALAMIC ACTIVITY

HYPOTHALAMIC
REGION CONTROLS
PITUITARY ACTIVITY

PITUITARY GLAND
STIMULATES OTHER GLANDS

ADRENAL GLANDS, ADJACENT
TO KIDNEYS, PRODUCE
ADRENALIN AND CORTISONE

KIDNEYS

SENSORY INPUT INTO BRAIN
AFFECTS HYPOTHALAMUS

HYPOTHALAMUS GLAND
STIMULATES PITUITARY
HORMONE PRODUCTION

THYROID GLAND IS
CONTROLLED BY
PITUITARY GLAND

HORMONES TRAVEL
IN BLOOD STREAM
TO TARGET CELLS

PITUITARY GLAND

THYROID AND
PARATHYROID GLANDS

PROSTATE-GLAND ACTIVITY
IS INFLUENCED BY
TESTOSTERONE

TESTOSTERONE
PRODUCTION IN
TESTES IS CONTROLLED
BY PITUITARY GLAND

Pituitary gland
The pituitary (master gland), located just beneath the hypothalamus in the brain, has two separate sections. The neurohyophysis receives nerve fibres from the hypothalamus and produces the hormone oxytocin, which helps both uterine contractions and milk letdown, and the hormone vasopressin, which helps concentrate urine. The adenohyophysis produces hormones that stimulate the adrenal and thyroid glands, egg or sperm production, sex-hormone manufacture, and growth and skin-pigment production.

Male testes
The testes descend from within the abdominal cavity to their scrotal position during foetal development in the womb. At puberty, follicle-activating hormone from the anterior pituitary stimulates the semen-producing tubules to manufacture sperm, while leutenizing hormone stimulates cells between the semen-producing tubules to manufacture male sex hormone – testosterone. Testosterone is also manufactured in the adrenal gland.

Thyroid and parathyroid glands
The thyroid consists of two separate lobes, sometimes joined together by an isthmus, located on each side of the windpipe just below the larynx. The parathyroids consist of four tiny masses that sit on the thyroid like caps or even lie within thyroid tissue. Thyroid hormones are integrally involved in the dog's metabolism, either speeding it up or slowing it down. Parathyroid hormone is necessary to extract calcium from bone and transport it around the body, where it plays an important role in muscle contraction.

NEGATIVE FEEDBACK

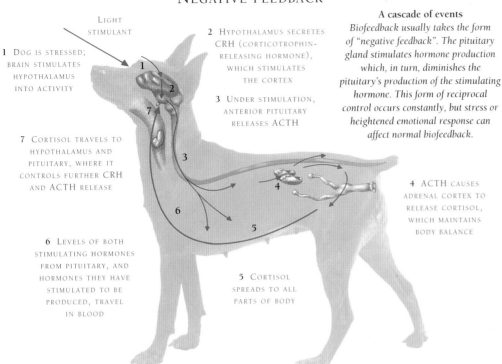

LIGHT STIMULANT

1 DOG IS STRESSED; BRAIN STIMULATES HYPOTHALAMUS INTO ACTIVITY

2 HYPOTHALAMUS SECRETES CRH (CORTICOTROPHIN-RELEASING HORMONE), WHICH STIMULATES THE CORTEX

3 UNDER STIMULATION, ANTERIOR PITUITARY RELEASES ACTH

7 CORTISOL TRAVELS TO HYPOTHALAMUS AND PITUITARY, WHERE IT CONTROLS FURTHER CRH AND ACTH RELEASE

4 ACTH CAUSES ADRENAL CORTEX TO RELEASE CORTISOL, WHICH MAINTAINS BODY BALANCE

6 LEVELS OF BOTH STIMULATING HORMONES FROM PITUITARY, AND HORMONES THEY HAVE STIMULATED TO BE PRODUCED, TRAVEL IN BLOOD

5 CORTISOL SPREADS TO ALL PARTS OF BODY

A cascade of events
Biofeedback usually takes the form of "negative feedback". The pituitary gland stimulates hormone production which, in turn, diminishes the pituitary's production of the stimulating hormone. This form of reciprocal control occurs constantly, but stress or heightened emotional response can affect normal biofeedback.

ADRENAL SECRETIONS
The adrenal medulla is primarily under the control of the nervous system. When the dog is stressed or sexually excited, the medulla produces adrenalin, a component of the fight or flight mechanism.

THYROID AND PARATHYROID PRODUCTS
The thyroid produces three hormones. T4 (Thyroxine) and T3 (Triiodothyronine) stimulate metabolism in body cells.

Calcitonin lowers blood-calcium levels and works in conjunction with the parathyroid's hormone (parathormone) to maintain a proper balance of calcium in body cells and fluids.

PANCREATIC INSULIN
Small islands of tissue within the pancreas produce insulin, which is necessary to lower blood-sugar levels. Increasing blood sugar triggers insulin release from the pancreas. The system involves negative feedback. As sugar goes up, insulin release increases. Then as blood-sugar levels drop, insulin production diminishes.

ADRENAL CORTEX SECRETES HORMONES THAT CONTROL CARBOHYDRATES AND SEX HORMONES

ADRENAL MEDULLA HORMONES AFFECT STRESS AND EMOTIONS

ANAL-GLAND SECRETIONS ARE INFLUENCED BY SEX HORMONES

OVARIES PRODUCE SEX HORMONE

EGG PRODUCTION DEPENDS ON PITUITARY HORMONES

PLACENTA PRODUCES HORMONE THAT TRAVELS BACK TO PITUITARY GLAND

Female ovaries
The ovaries are located in the abdomen, just behind the kidneys. At puberty, follicle-stimulating hormone and leutenizing hormone from the anterior pituitary stimulate egg-follicle development in the ovaries. One layer of the follicle manufactures the female sex-hormone oestrogen. Oestrogen production increases as the follicle increases in size, feeding back on the pituitary, and causing it to produce a surge of leutenizing hormone, which stimulates another layer of the follicle to manufacture the hormone progesterone. This hormone causes the follicle to rupture and release its egg into the fallopian tube.

HORMONAL INFLUENCES

Feeding calms mother
During lactation, the bitch's normal fight or flight mechanism is overridden. Her natural tendency to escape from potential danger might put her puppies at risk. Biofeedback, and the influence of hormones that stimulate milk letdown, increase her confidence and have a relaxing effect. This form of behaviour generally only lasts as long as hormonal changes influence maternal behaviour.

Play polishes biofeedback
Early experience is very important for puppies. The puppy's entire body is still actively developing. The puppy learns about itself and its environment. Play exercises muscles and improves senses such as balance, but it also encourages normal hormonal feedback. Early experience hones the sensitivity of biofeedback mechanisms. The puppy develops greater control of its emotional responses, which are integrated into hormonal biofeedback.

Training helps to control biofeedback
Training teaches dogs to control natural hormonal biofeedback mechanisms. Natural hormonal releases still occur but are rapidly dampened down by a highly developed biofeedback response. The trained guide dog, on seeing another dog, still gets excited. However, due to its training, that excitement is quickly overcome through "negative feedback", the dampening down of hormonal body response. Obedience training for dogs is really obedience training for their biofeedback mechanisms.

Chapter Four

THE LANGUAGE OF DOGS

The dog is a pack animal. Although it barks more than the wolf, most of its exquisite language is mute. The dog communicates both with us and with other dogs through its senses and a sophisticated understanding of body language. Very early in life, the dog learns to understand how body language communicates both affection and aggression. It uses scent to define its territory, to attract a mating partner, and to impart other precise information.

COURTSHIP, MATING, AND BIRTH

AS WITH ALL ANIMALS, the dog's survival is based upon the successful reproducing of new generations. While males are always sexually alert, females normally have just two short periods each year when they ovulate and willingly mate. While the male has no further role after mating, the female then finds a suitably secure birthing den, gives birth, cleans both the puppies and the site, and is responsible for her puppies' feeding and security. She may become aggressive if she feels her young are threatened.

Mating

Mating is perfunctory – the female stands motionless, remains passive, and allows the male to mount her. Using her back to support his weight, he clasps her body with his forepaws and thrusts his pelvis. Ejaculation occurs almost immediately, and lasts for only a few seconds.

THIS FEMALE SHOWS HIGH DEGREE OF RELAXATION

THE MALE THRUSTS HIS PELVIS; BONE IN HIS PENIS GIVES IT NATURAL RIGIDITY AND INCREASES LIKELIHOOD OF SUCCESSFUL ENTRY INTO VULVA

Locked together

During mating, a balloon-like apparatus at the base of the dog's penis swells and "locks" the dogs together.

WHEN "LOCKED" TOGETHER, NO OTHER MALE IS ABLE TO MATE WITH RECEPTIVE FEMALE

BECAUSE OF MALE'S GREATER HEIGHT, FEMALE FEELS MORE COMFORTABLE WITH HIND LEG RAISED SLIGHTLY ABOVE GROUND

MALE DOG'S TAIL IS CARRIED HIGH, A SIGN OF EXCITEMENT

FORELEGS ARE CLASPED FOR SUPPORT; IF FEMALE RESENTS THIS SHE SNAPS AT MALE

FEMALE REMAINS TOTALLY WILLING, BUT PASSIVE, DURING MATING

MATING

Mating is swift. While the female stands firmly, the male mounts her back, clasps her body with his forepaws, and thrusts with his pelvis. The combined rigidity of his already firm but now enlarged penis, and her enlarged vulva, ensures easy intromission. During pelvic thrusts, which often last for less than a minute, the female bears the male's weight. The male ejaculates, but during mating the base of his penis swells, preventing him from withdrawing his penis.

Although the transmission of sperm is quickly completed, the pair remain physically "tied" to each other for approximately half an hour. During this time the male dismounts from the female, often by drawing a hind leg over her back. They remain attached to each other, but tail to tail. At this stage their defences are reduced, but by standing tail to tail they are better able to defend themselves from possible danger. With time, the swelling in the male's penis deflates and they separate.

COURTSHIP

The male dog is sexually active the entire year and is attracted to the scent of any female in season. For most of the year the female is hormonally inactive, but under the influence of her twice-yearly production of the hormone oestrogen, she becomes interested in sex. Her vulva swells in order to accommodate the male's penis. Eggs are released from her ovaries and descend down her fallopian tubes to her uterus, where they await fertilization by sperm.

Often of short duration, courtship is filled with stereotyped behaviour. The female frequently demands "play" before accepting mating, and if she is not ready, she rolls over. Then she scents the male's prepuce and allows him to lick her vulva. After these rituals, mating proceeds.

PREGNANCY

Whether or not the female is actually pregnant, she enters a two-month pregnancy stage. After the eggs are released from the ovaries, the ovaries produce progesterone – the hormone of pregnancy – which initiates a variety of symptoms, including milk production. If she is not pregnant, this is called a false pregnancy. A true pregnancy lasts for about two months. Signs of pregnancy may include an increase in appetite and weight, but during the first half the female shows little evidence of physical changes.

TAIL IS ARCHED UP AND DRAWN TO SIDE

Brief courtship

Accepting the male as a mating partner, the female stands still, draws her tail to the side, and willingly prepares for mating. This hormonally induced behaviour occurs only after she has ovulated and pregnancy is likely.

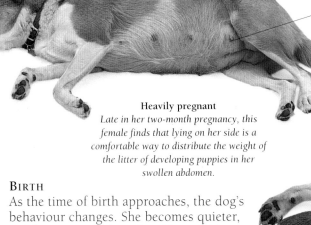

NIPPLES START TO
ENLARGE AND BECOME
PROMINENT

Heavily pregnant
*Late in her two-month pregnancy, this
female finds that lying on her side is a
comfortable way to distribute the weight of
the litter of developing puppies in her
swollen abdomen.*

BIRTH

As the time of birth approaches, the dog's
behaviour changes. She becomes quieter,
and less interested in play. About 24 hours
before labour begins she stops eating. She
spends more time than usual in her
chosen nest site, which is
often a covered or isolated
place. As labour approaches,
she becomes restless. Minor
contractions begin and the
first water bag is squeezed into
the birth canal and breaks,
leaving a puddle of fluid.
Contractions become firmer
and more rhythmic. The first puppy is
delivered within the next two hours.
Generally, the puppies are delivered head
first, although it is not unusual for some to
be delivered tail first. Most females lie on
their sides and deliver the puppies on to
the ground, although some prefer to stand.

The firmest contractions are necessary
to push each puppy's head and shoulders
through the birth canal. Once these
are visible, the rest of the puppy
follows easily. Each puppy is enveloped
in a membrane, which the mother licks
from its face and body. The massaging of
her tongue stimulates the puppy to take its
first breath and also dries it, reducing the
risk of hypothermia. After each delivery,
the mother expels a placenta. In the
womb, this was the puppy's
nutritional lifeline, feeding into its
umbilicus. The mother usually eats the
afterbirth, chewing off the umbilical cord
from the puppy's body. Within 30 minutes
she is in labour again, expelling the next
puppy and its afterbirth.

Healthy puppies, attracted by the heat
from her body, stay close. Only after the
last puppy has been delivered does the
mother relax and provide milk for her
newborn. She does so by
exposing her nipples, which
she has cleaned throughout
the latter stages of her
pregnancy. For the next 24
hours, most mothers do not
leave their young. Their
crying concerns the mother:

Giving birth
*The mother contracts
her abdominal muscles
and expels a puppy in
its birth sac.*

THIS PUPPY EMERGES
TAIL FIRST, WRAPPED IN
PROTECTIVE SAC, WHICH
WILL BE LICKED FROM
FACE AND BODY

Cleaning the birth site
*The mother licks the birth membranes
from the puppy, permitting it to
inflate its lungs for the first time
and to breathe on its own.
She eats all
remnants of the
afterbirth and
keeps her den as clean as possible,
perhaps to reduce signs to predators
of defenceless newborns.*

crying usually means hunger and she
quickly positions herself to feed them. She
licks their anogenital regions to stimulate
them to urinate and defecate, consuming
their body-waste products to hide evidence
of their vulnerable presence. Typically, in
a litter of seven, one puppy is born
handicapped, and dies soon after birth.

POTENTIAL PROBLEMS

Birth is a dangerous time for the mother
and her offspring. If she is not in excellent
condition, she may not have the strength
to expel her litter. Highly strung females
may abandon their young after birth.
Others may have difficulty letting down
milk. Prompt veterinary advice is usually
sufficient to overcome most problems.

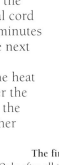

The first feed
*Only after all the puppies have
been born, cleaned, and dried, does
the mother relax on her side and offer
them a first feed. Heat sensors in the
puppies' noses draw them to their
mother's teats for this first
and most important meal.*

PUPPY'S SENSE
OF SMELL ALREADY
EXISTS; IT CLASPS ITS
MOUTH ONTO A NIPPLE
AND SUCKLES MILK

GROWING UP

ALTHOUGH A DOG is born with a superb array of natural instincts and abilities, it is the early experiences that refine the use of these attributes. From the day it is born, the puppy's relationship with its mother and littermates has a significant influence on its personality. Learning refines the uses of its senses and biofeedback system. The puppy learns to solve problems; it learns the limits of acceptable behaviour with other animals, including dogs and humans. The wider the range of early experiences, the more adaptable and responsive the dog will be as an adult.

MOTHER STANDS WHILE PUPPIES FEED, OCCASIONALLY LICKING PUPPIES

Experiments with objects
As soon as the puppy can walk it begins to learn about its environment. Using all its senses it watches, listens to, feels and, most important, smells and tastes the world outside its nest. By playing with toys, it begins to understand its physical abilities.

Natural dominance
The male puppy's brain is "masculinized" just before birth when, for a short period, it produces a male sex hormone. However, dominance does not depend upon hormone alone. This female puppy mounts another simply to show her dominance.

Dependence
Earliest learning is provided by the mother. She offers nourishment, comfort, and security. Gradually, during the puppy's first three months, the mother's comforting lick is replaced by our stroking hands, and her provision of milk by our provision of bowls of food.

PRESSING FULL WEIGHT ON MALE PUPPY'S BACK, THE FEMALE THRUSTS WITH PELVIS IN SEX-RELATED MANNER

DOMINANT PUPPY CLASPS OTHER PUPPY'S BODY

MOTHER'S INFLUENCE
Puppies inherit a wide range of instincts, but many of these are subtly influenced by the behaviour of the mother, who is responsible for feeding and protecting her litter. For the first three weeks she provides milk; during the next three weeks she continues to provide milk but may regurgitate food for her litter or allow them to eat some of her solid food. Then, during the following weeks she still allows the puppies to suckle for comfort and security – this natural action can soothe a puppy. If a youngster acts too gregariously, the mother disciplines it with a controlled bite. Puppies learn from their mothers and perpetuate their mother's specific skills.

CRITICAL PERIODS
A dog's early life is divided into what are sometimes called "critical periods". The first period begins when the puppy is still in the womb. It is quite possible that if a mother is stressed during pregnancy, her young might develop into more nervous than typical progeny. For two weeks after birth the puppy is wholly dependent on its mother. During this neonatal period its senses develop rapidly. Balance, sight, hearing, touch, taste, and smell all evolve towards maturity. Recent research suggests that even during the neonatal period, regular handling of puppies by humans has a positive effect on their later emotional development. In the next two weeks the puppy enters a transitional period, during which time it begins to move away from complete maternal dependence. The puppy growls, barks, and wags its tail for the first time. Its temperature-control mechanism improves sufficiently to allow it to leave the warmth of its mother for the first time.

SOCIALIZATION
The dog's social life commences at about four weeks of age, when it starts to communicate with other dogs and with humans. It begins to play, and through play learns about pack behaviour, dominance, and submission. The puppy uses play to test adversaries in a ritualized manner, free from danger. Play encourages cooperative behaviour and improves the

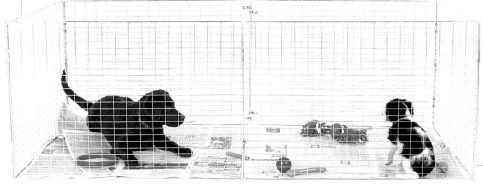

Training
If a puppy is introduced to a crate at less than three months of age, for the rest of its life it regards a crate as a safe refuge.

Paternal role
The father has a limited role in the puppy's early life. Some males will occasionally lick and groom puppies, but they rarely regurgitate food for them, as mothers sometimes do. Fathers are more likely to teach discipline by nipping puppies when they become too exuberant.

FATHER TAKES ACTIVE INTEREST IN PUPPY'S SCENT, SNIFFING ITS FACE AND EARS

RAISED TAIL INDICATES THAT PUPPY'S FATHER IS ALERT AND INTERESTED IN SCENT HE HAS FOUND ON PUPPY

Maternal control
Because of her size and maturity, the mother is firmly in control. Puppies' baby teeth are sharp, and when they playfully nip her, she responds by nipping back and chiding them. By doing so, she demonstrates that there are limits to their behaviour which they should not exceed.

MOTHER'S EARS ARE HELD IN RELAXED FASHION

THIS PUPPY IS NOT LEARNING AS MUCH AS THE OTHERS

Living with other dogs
The subtleties of relationships are discovered through play. Playful activity allows puppies to experiment. They inherit body language that dramatically portrays feelings and emotions, and through play actively learn how to use these gestures for the most beneficial response.

HIGH-WAGGING TAIL INDICATES THAT MOTHER IS ACTIVE AND ALERT

PUPPY ADOPTS SUBMISSIVE POSE WITH ITS MOTHER

FACE CHEWING ALLOWS PUPPY TO LEARN HOW TO INHIBIT ITS BITE

DOMINANT PUPPY BRACES ITSELF WITH ITS HIND LEGS, PERMITTING IT TO GAIN THE HIGHER AND MORE DOMINANT POSITION

puppy's use of its body.
Puppies that are denied play activity during the socializing period, which is from four to twelve weeks of age, often develop bizarre behaviour habits in adult life. These puppies have a greater fear of people, animals, and noises, and are more shy and antisocial than puppies that play freely both with each other and with people during this crucial period.

INSTINCTIVE AND ACQUIRED BEHAVIOUR
A puppy is born with the instincts of a pack animal. It has an exclusive range of sensory building blocks, but must learn how to use these faculties to adapt to existing circumstances. This ability is at the core of the dog's success in integrating itself into the ecological patterns of a different species. Puppies derive greater

benefit from watching their mothers than from watching other dogs. Early learning ensures that puppies have the ability as adults to hunt collectively and also to communally protect territory. Early, daily exposure to humans when a puppy is under six weeks old ensures that it will not be afraid of people, and that it will have a lifelong capacity to learn from humans. For the next six weeks, the puppy's mind remains fully open

Playing with people
The dog learns best when it is very young. Through early human contact it develops a lifelong attitude towards us. Positive and pleasurable early experience ensures a lasting relationship.

to a vast range of experience. The more it smells, sees, tastes, hears, and touches, meets other species, and experiences different situations, the more adaptable it will be later in life. If basic training is initiated at this early stage, the sophisticated training that follows will be less complicated.

INTELLIGENCE
We often talk of the dog's intelligence, but usually we do so without a complete understanding of what we mean by the the word. Compared to primates, the dog has limited problem-solving abilities. If a dog learns to open a door by the handle, it first does so by accident rather than premeditation. Dogs vary in their inherited abilities – for example in their ability to herd sheep, retrieve game, or listen and learn. When talking about dogs we often confuse instinctive abilities, trainability, or obedience with intelligence.

THE PACK

THE DOG'S WILLINGNESS, even eagerness, to share a social life with other dogs is based upon the pack mentality that it has inherited from the wolf. The pack works together to find a source of food, and to protect both food and the pack's territory from other wolves and scavengers. Pack behaviour is well defined, with a leader – nearly always a male – and his almost equally dominant consort, controlling most pack activity. The rest of the pack follows its leader, although dominant members occasionally challenge him. The domestic dog's pack behaviour is still present. We become pack leaders and our dogs willingly obey us, at the same time defending the pack's territory.

THE NATURAL PACK

The dog's natural pack behaviour is perhaps the most important reason why it has so successfully integrated itself into human communities worldwide. The sophistication of pack behaviour varies considerably within the canine family. Foxes, for example, having left their mothers, have little inclination to behave socially with other foxes. Wolves, on the other hand, remain gregariously sociable throughout their lives. This results in the pack – a group of genetically related individuals who work together with common cause. They hunt together, share food, and keep each other warm, all of which involve communicating in a variety of ways. The domestic dog experiences a few months of natural pack activity from birth until it leaves its litter and joins a human pack, of which it will become a member. In the litter, each puppy learns how to behave with its littermates and with its mother. The mother is the leader because she controls food,

WOMEN AND MEN MAKE EQUALLY GOOD PACK LEADERS

Part of the family
When raised with people from puppyhood, dogs regard them as full members of their pack. The dogs happily engage in the activities of their human packs. These Golden Retrievers willingly join their owners on the sofa when given the opportunity.

warmth, and security. Beginning at about three weeks of age, puppies start to play with each other. Play offers the satisfaction of physical contact with other puppies, while at the same time providing learning experience for muscle control. Equally important, it teaches the puppies how to behave with other dogs. Play remains a lifelong activity among pack members.

THE HUMAN PACK

People discovered over 10,000 years ago that the dog's mind is most malleable and impressionable in the first three to four months of its life. When a puppy is taken from the litter at between eight and twelve

PACK LEADER STANDS UNCHALLENGED BY THE OTHERS

The human pack leader
Sled dogs form a pack hierarchy among themselves. The dominant dog receives the first food reward from its handler, but even this canine pack leader accepts the superiority of the human pack leader.

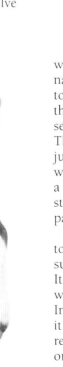

weeks of age, and homed with people, it naturally transfers its innate pack mentality to this distinctly different species. Because they control food, warmth, comfort, and security, people are seen as pack leaders. The puppy naturally begs for food. It jumps up to lick a human face just as it would jump up to lick its mother's face, a behaviour that in wolves and some dogs stimulates the mother to regurgitate a partly digested meal for her puppies.

As the puppy matures, it continues to treat its human pack as an acceptable substitute for the canine pack it has left. It plays with people, nipping them as it would nip its littermates or its mother. In a natural pack, if a puppy nips too hard it is reprimanded, either by a squeal and reluctance to play further by a littermate, or by a controlled bite from its mother – a bite not meant to damage the puppy but

MOTHER GROOMS PUPPIES AND DISCIPLINES THEM IF THEY BITE TOO HARD

Learning pack behaviour
Learning about pack activity begins almost at birth. The mother dictates and controls virtually all of her puppies' activities. Within the litter, puppies subtly challenge each other for the most productive teats.

Barking warns rest of pack of danger

Defending territory
Pack mentality drives most dogs to warn the rest of the pack about potential danger to the pack's territory. The markers we build to define our own territories, such as fences, are adopted by dogs as the limits of their territories to guard and defend.

sufficiently intense to teach it not to play quite so vigorously. By these means, the puppy learns how to behave with other members of the pack.

STATUS WITHIN THE PACK

As the puppy matures into adulthood, its pack behaviour evolves, eventually to be influenced both by cumulative experience and by the onset, at puberty, of sex-hormone production. It is also influenced by selective breeding. Certain breeds have been intentionally bred to work together as packs, with as little internal conflict as possible. Pack hounds follow scent trails together, eat communally from large feeding troughs, and look upon the human pack master as their leader.

Within typical human households, the adult dog's pack instinct drives it to find a suitable niche in the family. Although sexual maturity arrives early in life, usually at between six and twelve months of age, emotional maturity is not complete until a year later, the time of emotional maturity in wolves. A dominant dog, particularly if it is male, can challenge its designated position in the human pack at any time between sexual and emotional maturity. It does so by refusing to follow instructions given by another pack member or by

intentionally challenging someone. The dog usually chooses what it considers to be the weakest member of the pack. It might, for example, bite a child over possession of a toy, or refuse to obey a command given by the child's mother, but still obey the same command given by the deeper voiced, more assertive sounding father. The dog's position in the pack is not always static. Especially while young and robust, it may challenge in an attempt to move closer to pack leadership.

THE TERRITORIAL INSTINCT

All members of a pack are equally responsible for the security of their territory. This is, of course, one of the earliest reasons why our ancestors permitted wolves to live near and then in their campsites. When canine and human family groups share territory, they warn each other of potential dangers. After companionship, security is the most common reason for dog ownership.

The dog's territorial instincts have their origins in pack activity. Almost every dog becomes alert and inquisitive when it hears, sees, or smells something different. Most dogs will alert other members of the pack by barking, sometimes aggressively, but just as often simply to alert the rest of the pack that someone or something is approaching their communal space. Some members of the pack actively defend that communal space, while most prefer to leave this to the initiative of the pack leader. As well as communal space, each pack member has its own personal space within the territory. This is often a bed provided for the dog, but some individuals choose their own space – a chair, sofa, or "den" beneath a table – and defend that space from incursions by other pack members, including ourselves.

Natural pack activity
Wolf-pack activity is clearly defined, with a dominant leader. Control of the pack gives the leader the right to mate. Dog-pack activity follows similar principles.

GOING SOLO

In parts of Central and South America, Eastern Europe, Asia, and Africa, pariah dogs breed, feed, and travel together as independent packs. However, in North America, northern Europe, Japan, Australia, and New Zealand, few dogs form packs with other dogs. Free-ranging dogs (owned by people but allowed to roam freely) never form social packs, and only congregrate together when they are following an oestrus female. No scientific observation of groups of free-ranging dogs has shown any indication of territorial pack behaviour, probably because there is no need for these dogs to defend either a source of food or themselves. Free-ranging dogs in groups are not cohesive units, as are wolf packs, or even a single human hunter and his canine companion. They are simply individuals with irresponsible human pack leaders.

Dog feels secure in its wicker basket

Having a personal space
In addition to pack territory, each member of the pack naturally wants its own personal space. Each of these Golden Retrievers has its own personal basket.

Dog can sleep comfortably in large basket

AGGRESSION AND AFFECTION

MOST ANIMALS HAVE SOPHISTICATED body language that dramatically implies either defensive behaviour or forthright aggression, but only sociable species like dogs also have the body language of intimacy, which we sometimes regard as "affection". We tend to equate our own forms of human body language with that of the dog. As a result, dogs communicate with us surprisingly well, considering we are such physically different species. They seem to understand our feelings and emotions. Their apparent understanding is based upon their own sophisticated social behaviour. Dogs behave with each other in a variety of ways, ranging from passive submission, through indifference, to outright dominance.

EARLY LEARNING

The degree of dominance or submission that a dog develops depends on both its genetic potential and its experiences in youth. At an early stage, the puppy learns how to threaten other puppies by showing its teeth, raising its hackles, and barking. It may feign attacks. Although it looks comical, this behaviour is significant – the puppy is learning the body language of dominance and submission.

Puppies learn the signals of threat and friendship by the time they are 12 weeks old. Power and confidence may be shown by stalking other members of the litter. With its head and tail down but its hindquarters raised and its ears erect, the stalker chases, ambushes, or pounces on a littermate. Or it circles the other puppy while walking imperiously and stiffly wagging its tail. It may stand over the puppy, forming a T-shape with its adversary. Other ways in which puppies threaten each other during play include boxing, shoulder slams, erecting their hackles, baring their teeth, mounting, and pelvic thrusting. A direct stare is a direct threat. Just as important are the submissive or surrendering behaviours:

Submission to mother
While still fully dependent on their mother for nourishment, puppies learn to pester her for food. These puppies are jumping up to lick their mother's mouth, a physical inducement for her to regurgitate a meal for them.

the tail between the legs, avoidance of eye contact, depressed ears, retracted lips forming a "smile", the head hung low, lying on the side or back, exposing the belly and genitals, and even urinating. Between these extremes are the cooperative behaviours, activities that we see as socially affectionate – grooming each other, sniffing, nosing, licking and pawing each other, investigating, barking together, feeding, sleeping, lying down, walking or running together, and perhaps most important, playing with each other.

BEHAVIOUR WITH PEOPLE

Dogs transfer this range of behaviours from other dogs to humans. They understand that we are a different species from themselves, but are only able to behave with us in the way they behave with other dogs. This difficulty applies to us, too. We realize that dogs are a distinctly different species, but we too have an inherited range of behaviours that makes us behave with dogs, and treat them, in the way we behave with and treat other people. This is

Submission to humans
Even though this Leonberger is as tall and as heavy as its owner, it jumps up to lick his face submissively, re-enacting its behaviour as a puppy with its own mother. Juvenile submissive behaviour is perpetuated in the dog's relationship with us.

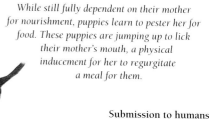

TO REACH OWNER'S FACE, DOG JUMPS UP AND ALMOST KNOCKS HIM OVER

ALTHOUGH THIS APPEARS TO BE THE "UNDERDOG", IT MAY BE PLAYING AT MOCK SUBMISSION

Youthful experiments
Dogs learn the most important lessons about how to behave with each other during puppyhood. These puppies seem to be playing mindlessly, but in fact are learning about each other's abilities and weaknesses. At this stage during play, the dog on top is dominant, but roles may change quickly.

why we willingly adopt them as members of the family and are able to love them, but it is also why we can be so abusive to them. Potentially, the dog can display its complete range of behaviours with people. However, by training it to look upon the humans in its pack as the inherent pack leaders, the dog is trained to control its aggression and to use its social affection and submission.

Selective breeding plays an important role. Some breeds, such as the guarding Causasian Shepherd Dog, are selectively bred for enhanced dominance, while other breeds, like working Labrador Retrievers, are bred for enhanced "togetherness" or social affection. Social affection, which specialists call allelomimetic activities,

Reluctance to compete
Body language can express a wide range of behaviours, from assertive dominance to extreme submission. This Whippet has tucked back its ears, pulled its tail down between its legs, laid down, averted its eyes from a dog it considers dominant, and is about to raise its leg in a very distinct display of submission.

BELLY IS EXPOSED IN ABJECT SUBMISSION

is the basis for obedience training, and this is why dogs that seem to have the greatest potential to show "affection" are often the individuals or breeds that are easiest to train. The dog manifests the same range of aggressive and affectionate behaviours as that of the wolf. However, through selective breeding we have enhanced some behaviours and diminished others. Then, through training, we further influence these behaviours.

FORMS OF AGGRESSION
Dogs have developed a sophisticated array of theatrical threats of aggression, all of which are intended to intimidate the opposition but avoid any bloodshed. Dogs threaten aggression by staring, body posturing, or growling and barking. Different expressions of aggression are influenced by the sex, age, sometimes the size, hormonal status, territory, personal distance, position in the order of rank, and previous experience of the individual.

Generally, aggression is a form of competition over food, territory, shelter or, curiously, our affection. Some dogs fight with each other for the right to be stroked and talked to first by the human pack leader. Dominance is an inherited form of aggression, usually shown in males between two and two-and-a-half

years old, who disobey or threaten people. Training can be useful (*see pages 306–307*). Some dogs aggressively protect objects such as food bowls or toys. Fearful aggression is defensive and is manifested by submissive dogs, while protective aggression might apply to defence of territory. Aggression between male dogs is related to sex status, and is the only form of aggression that is likely to respond to castration.

SUBMISSION AND AFFECTION
Just as selective breeding has enhanced different types of aggression in some breeds of dog, so too it has accentuated social togetherness in others. All breeds of dog play willingly, but submissive dogs play more frequently than dominant ones. Overt dominance and overt submission are simply the extremes of dog behaviour. Most dogs fall between these two extremes, into a category some specialists call "subdominance". These dogs are at ease with their positions in a hierarchy with other dogs or with people. They willingly play with both. Play serves many purposes. It maintains physical and mental dexterity, and stimulates inventiveness and problem solving.

When dogs play with us, they sometimes carry out dominant activities, such as tug-of-war, or hide-and-seek, but they do so either in intentionally exaggerated or inhibited ways. The activity is distinctly "playing". In play activity we should dominate, which means "win", if the dog in question is overly confident. However, with insecure dogs, we should sometimes let them win. Ultimately, dogs must always behave submissively with their human pack leaders.

The typical canine companion is a "subdominant", or submissive animal. It obeys people. It also seeks out human companionship; for example, it brings a toy and asks for play. We interpret these activities as signs of "affection", and they probably are. They are certainly signs of attachment. The dog feels content in the presence of its own humans. It wants to eat with them, sleep with them, and play with them. Some animal behaviourists say that these are simply signs of dependence. Others, and many dog owners, believe that dogs are capable of a range of emotions, and that affection is one of them.

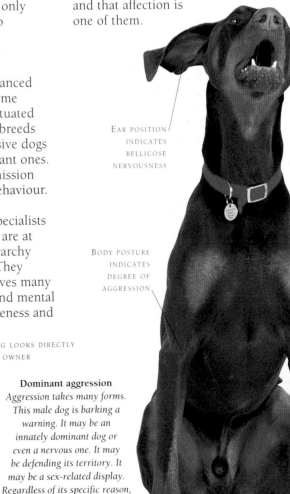

EAR POSITION INDICATES BELLICOSE NERVOUSNESS

BODY POSTURE INDICATES DEGREE OF AGGRESSION

DOG LOOKS DIRECTLY AT OWNER

Dominant aggression
Aggression takes many forms. This male dog is barking a warning. It may be an innately dominant dog or even a nervous one. It may be defending its territory. It may be a sex-related display. Regardless of its specific reason, the display of aggression is easily understood by both other dogs and other species of animal.

TAIL IS RELAXED, NOT TUCKED BETWEEN LEGS

Waiting for a tickle
This Billy's body posture is almost identical to that of the submissive Whippet above, but it is simply asking for its belly to be tickled. We call this "affection", but it may be a sign of submission.

COMMUNICATION

THE SOCIABLE DOG HAS A VARIETY of often subtle ways of communicating with other dogs. It uses its voice to express sounds, ranging from warnings to expressions of pleasure. It leaves scent markings in its urine and faeces, primarily to tell other dogs whether it is male or female, and probably to display an extensive selection of further facts beyond human comprehension. Dogs sometimes scratch the earth in the vicinity of these body-waste scent markers as an added visual sign, pointing to the communication site. Finally, the dog communicates elegantly through body language. By subtly altering the positions of its ears and tail, it expresses its feelings and emotions in vivid detail.

VOCAL EXPRESSION

Vocal canine communication is surprisingly effective. A mother quickly learns the vocal differences of each of her puppies, and understands their sounds of hunger, pain, and pleasure. Dogs express themselves vocally with five varieties of sound – infant cries, whimpers, and whines; warning growls and sharp barks; attention-seeking, plaintive barks and howls; painful yips; yelps and screams; and pleasurable moans.

Sophisticated sound analysis of wolf howls indicates that each wolf has a specific howl, as unique as a fingerprint. Some dogs sing by howling; certain music appears to stimulate this pleasure response. Dogs howl less than wolves but bark more, a trait intentionally enhanced through domestication. The dog's alarm bark was perhaps one of the first canine traits our ancestors selected for.

TERRITORY MARKING

The dog leaves visual and scent markers on its territory that act as business cards, giving information about the status of the depositor. Dogs produce chemicals called pheromones, which are present in saliva, faeces, and urine, and in vaginal and preputial secretions. By mixing

Scent marking
Urine scent markers contain information on sex and status. Dogs cock their legs to leave their urine marks as close as possible to the nose level of other dogs.

URINE IS DEPOSITED IN SMALL AMOUNTS ON VERTICAL OBJECTS

or coating body-waste products with these chemicals, dogs use their waste to distribute information. After a dog empties its bowels, a muscular anal contraction squeezes out two drops of pheromone-laden substance from the glands of its two anal sacs (small, grape-shaped reservoirs on either side of the anus), and deposits this offensive-smelling cornucopia of scents on the faeces. Anal-sac-gland

Body-gland information
The Basenji gathers information about the sex and perhaps even the family of the Italian Spinone by scenting odours from the anal-sac gland and the perineal glands.

THE SPINONE ADOPTS A SUBMISSIVE STANCE

secretion contains at least 12 distinct substances. With the dog's acute sense of smell, it is highly likely that anal-sac-gland substance transmits a wealth of information. Surrounding the anus are perineal glands. Although the specific function of these glands in the dog is unknown, in other species they produce sex-related pheromones. Pheromones that are found in urine transmit information about the reproductive condition of the female and the power and authority of the male. Vaginal and preputial discharge also transmit information on sexual status. Males

TAIL HELD HIGH INDICATES CONFIDENCE

ERECT EARS HELD FORWARDS INDICATE DOMINANT ASSURANCE

Using body language
By raising its head high, carrying its ears erect, and drawing its tail up, this young puppy tells the intruding puppy that it is dominant. The intruder lowers its head to say that it understands this body language.

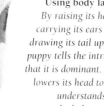

TAIL, USEFUL IN COMMUNICATION, DROPS SLACK AND TUCKS BETWEEN HIND LEGS

Communicating subordination
With ears flattened against her lowered head, and tail dropped between her legs, this Whippet vividly communicates through her body language that she is not a threat.

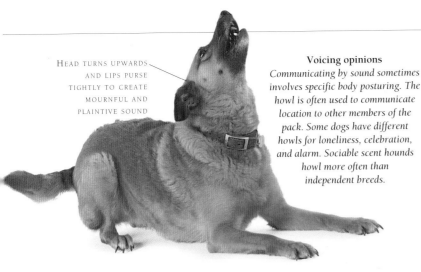

Voicing opinions
Communicating by sound sometimes involves specific body posturing. The howl is often used to communicate location to other members of the pack. Some dogs have different howls for loneliness, celebration, and alarm. Sociable scent hounds howl more often than independent breeds.

Requesting play
Body language is instinctive in dogs, just as the basis of verbal language is instinctive in humans. This puppy has dropped into a "play bow", a distinctive and vivid gesture that simply, eloquently, and silently asks another dog to join in play.

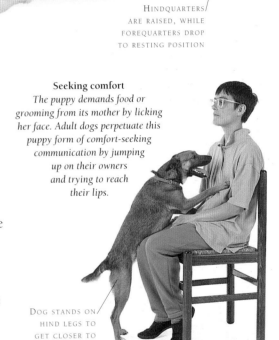

DIRECT EYE
CONTACT AND
PERKED,
ALERT EARS

HINDQUARTERS
ARE RAISED, WHILE
FOREQUARTERS DROP
TO RESTING POSITION

attempt to leave as much information about themselves as possible on marking posts at nose level. It is not unusual for a male dog to mark eighty distinct sites with his urine in a four-hour period. The cleaner the environment, the less need a dog has to mark it with his own urine. Urban dogs that share territories such as parks with many other dogs, urine mark more frequently than do rural dogs. Females do not scent mark as much as males, but some females will try to leave elevated urine markers by lifting one leg slightly when they urinate. Both males and females occasionally scratch at the earth around their urine or faeces. These marks act like arrows, pointing towards the scent mark, but they are also scent marks themselves, impregnated with sweat-gland secretions from the dog's feet.

USING BODY SCENTS
Body odours are produced in saliva, ear secretions, anal sacs, vaginal and preputial discharges, and from glands around the anus and on the top of the tail. All these

odours transmit information. Dogs sniff each other's lips and ears to pick up data. Ear odours, in particular, may contain substances that indicate sexual status. The dorsal tail gland is a remnant scent gland. Other canines – wolves and the Coyote for example – have more active dorsal tail glands, used to deposit scent on bushes as their tails brush against them.

BODY LANGUAGE
The dog displays its emotions, thoughts, and demands through detailed body language. Subtle changes in the positions of the ears, tail, mouth, face, hair, or posture convey a wealth of facts. Eye contact is particularly potent. The dominant dog stares, while the submissive dog avoids direct eye contact by averting its gaze. Body posture is equally explicit. The dominant dog stands erect; the submissive dog grovels. We understand these methods of communication because we communicate with each other and with dogs in similar ways.

Body postures are not static; they respond to the dog's changing emotions. The calm dog has relaxed tail and ears, but as it becomes alert both are raised. If the dog then feels aggressive, it raises its hackles, lifts its tail higher, and pulls back its lips to display its teeth. It

Seeking comfort
The puppy demands food or grooming from its mother by licking her face. Adult dogs perpetuate this puppy form of comfort-seeking communication by jumping up on their owners and trying to reach their lips.

DOG STANDS ON
HIND LEGS TO
GET CLOSER TO
OWNER'S FACE

THREATENING BARK IS
MEANT TO PREVENT FURTHER
INCURSION ON DOG'S
TERRITORY

Barking determination
Growls and barks are the dog's warning sounds. Cries, whimpers, whines, yelps, and moans all communicate other forms of information. Some dogs bark demands. This dog is protecting its territory.

displays further aggression by leaning forwards and snarling. If the dog becomes frightened, its ears flatten back and it drops both its tail and its body profile. If it feels completely overwhelmed, it drops abjectly to the ground, averts its eyes, lifts a hind leg, and urinates. The eyes, ears, hair, and tail are used to communicate mood or emotion.

Through either selective breeding or surgery we sometimes interfere with these features. Non-verbal communication is affected if hair covers the eyes, or is so long that the hackles cannot be raised. Amputating the ears and tail also inhibits communication. Unless there are sound medical reasons for operating, these amputations should be avoided.

Chapter Five

DOMESTIC DOG BREEDS

There are over 400 recognized breeds and breed varieties throughout the world, but this selection is not static. Breeds – groups of dog that when bred together produce descendants which both look and behave like their parents – come and go. Many breeds have become extinct this century, while new ones have been created. These changes will continue. Although breeds are categorized according to their utility, conformation, or place of origin, these classifications are purely arbitrary. Every dog ultimately has an equally long pedigree.

SELECTIVE BREEDING

THE VARIETY OF SHAPE, SIZE, colour, coat, and temperament of dog breeds is a testament to the dog's inherent genetic elasticity, but also to the lucid judgments made thousands of years ago by highly skilled dog breeders. All of the major aspects of selective breeding – dwarfing and miniaturization, enhanced size, speed, scent following, herd guarding, sociability, friendliness, and dependence – were selected for at least 5,000 years ago. At a later stage, "arrested" behaviours, such as pointing, setting, and retrieving, produced new uses for the dog. Today, most dogs are bred to kennel club rather than working standards. One consequence is that today's breeds may look unlike even recent ancestors.

Modern English Bulldog
This English Bulldog has a delightful personality, but with so many inherited defects its life expectancy is at least 20 per cent less than that of most other dogs of its size. Selective breeding gives it an elongated soft palate, which produces breathing and heart problems, crowded teeth creating gum and tooth disease, and skin folds causing chronic infection.

LEGS ARE SET SO WIDE APART THAT WALKING BECOMES DIFFICULT; BREATHING DIFFICULTIES EXACERBATE SITUATION

SHAPE OF ANATOMY ALLOWS DOG TO MOVE FREELY

Early working English Bulldog
This engraving from the early 1800s illustrates what the Bulldog looked like before it was bred to conform to a written breed-club standard. Its legs are under, rather than beside, the rib cage. The head is proportional to the rest of the body, with a distinctly visible neck. There are fewer infection-prone skin folds than in today's Bulldog, and a lean, extended, rather than a corkscrew, tail.

SHAPE AND BEHAVIOUR

The exceptionally successful dog breeders of ancient China, Central Asia, Persia, and the Middle East bred their dogs for utilitarian purposes. Some were bred for watchdog barking; others were bred to defend either territory or herds of livestock from predators. For the majority of the 12,000 years during which we have intervened in dog breeding, we selected for the dog's function, rather than for aesthetic appeal. With no understanding of the science of genetics, dog breeders successfully accentuated certain shapes and behaviours by breeding dogs that shared these conditions. Breeding a large male to a large female enhanced size; breeding together two dogs that alarm barked enhanced watchdog barking. By selectively breeding for a specific purpose, certain forms began to emerge.

Nordic and high-mountain dogs have dense, insulating coats. Middle Eastern, North African, Indian, and Southeast Asian breeds have short coats that retain very little heat. Variations according to climate and terrain, as well as those imposed by selective breeding, produced groups of dog that were similar in both appearance and abilities. However, it was only with the development of "leisure time" that selective breeding for looks as well as for form intensified.

ROYAL INFLUENCES

For thousands of years, the emperors of China, moguls of India, kings of European countries, and other rulers hunted for pleasure and took pride in their hunting dogs. While still being selectively bred for hunting ability, dogs were also bred for looks. Rulers and their courts set fashions for the wealthier of their subjects. As royalty started to breed for looks as well as for temperament, so too did land owners and other aristocrats. Many of the women of the imperial courts of Asia and Europe, especially those of China, Japan, France, Spain, and Italy, kept small dogs as companions. These were bred for their coat texture, colour, size, and affectionate personalities.

THE ROLE OF KENNEL CLUBS

By the mid-1800s, ownership of selectively bred dogs was common among the affluent throughout Europe. The first dog show was a social affair held by English aristocrats to raise funds for charity. In 1860, the first dog-show society came into existence in Birmingham, England. Within three years, the "Acclimitation Société" held the first dog show on the European continent in Paris, France, exhibiting a range of breeds, although the definition of

The natural poodle
Probably a descendant of guarding breeds, the poodle once had a dense and insulating corded coat. The breed evolved to become a water dog, retrieving game or fallen arrows for hunters. Until recently, it retained an almost rustic, curly, and very functional coat, as pictured in this illustration from 1867.

PRACTICAL COAT OFFERS SUPERB, WEATHERPROOF INSULATION AND IS LEFT UNCUT

The elegant dog-show poodle (right)
Selective breeding has both softened the poodle's coat and made it more luxurious. Its density is emphasized by cutting it according to precepts laid down by breed clubs. These cuts have their origins in the breed's previous function as a water dog. Hair insulated the chest, but was cut from the hips and hind legs to reduce drag.

Early Afghan Hounds
Afghans started to appear in dog shows this century, and received recognition in the late 1920s. These Afghans, pictured with their breeder in 1933, are typical of those first show quality dogs.

COAT IS SHORT AND
"SELF CLEANING", A
NECESSITY IN DOGS
USED FOR HUNTING
IN AFGHANISTAN

DEEP CHEST OF THIS RACING
HOUND IS COVERED BY
DENSE, INSULATING HAIR

Sleek, refined supermodel
Seventy years of selective breeding for coat texture and richness have produced a remarkable change. The Afghan Hound now has a robust beard and long fringes on its ears, legs, and tail. The hair is so dense on its legs that they are no longer visible.

THICK, LONG HAIR COVERING
PAWS READILY PICKS UP DIRT
AND BITS OF VEGETATION

HAIR IS DENSE
ENOUGH TO STAND
ON ITS OWN,
RATHER THAN
FALLING TO
SIDES

POODLES DO NOT
MOULT; HAIR IS
TRIMMED BEFORE
A SHOW

HAIR IS LEFT
LONG AND
TRIMMED INTO
A BALL

a "breed" remained open to interpretation. In 1873, a kennel club was formed in Great Britain – this produced a stud book, containing the pedigrees of over 4,000 dogs divided into 40 breeds. In 1880, this kennel club decided that no dog could be exhibited at a show held under kennel club rules unless it had been registered with the Kennel Club. This rule had more influence on the future selective breeding of dogs worldwide than any other factor, because it defined a breed as a group of dogs recognized by a kennel club.

In 1882, the French Société Centrale Canine was founded, followed a year later by the American Kennel Club. These, too, ruled that dogs and their pedigrees must be registered with the respective club. When the International Cynological Federation was formed in 1911, under the auspices of the Austrian, Belgian, Dutch, French, and German canine societies, it also passed a similar regulation.

Kennel clubs have had more influence on the development of dog breeds than any other factor since the original diversification of dogs according to function. For example, the English Bulldog was once bred to attack and hold on to the neck of a bull. Later, Bulldogs were used to bait bulls for amusement. By the mid-1800s, this "sport" was banned, but Bulldogs retained some of their looks from their working antecedents. However, breed-club standards emphasized the size of the head. To win at shows, Bulldogs

were bred for increasingly large heads, until they were so large that many Bulldogs had to be born by Caesarean section because their heads did not fit through the birth canal. Other breeds were bred to conform to breed standards for coat length or texture. The Afghan Hound, once an independent mountain dog, now has a luxurious coat, but no longer has the instinct to course gazelles or hunt wolves.

SENSIBLE BREEDING

Breeding away from a dog's origins sometimes accentuates features such as short noses, excessive facial folds, and short, crooked legs. If left to nature, traits that interfere with the dog's vigour and ability to survive on its own are eliminated simply because the dog with these traits cannot compete with dogs with more robust physical characteristics. However, what nature determines to be a fault, selective breeding sometimes labels "desirable". Selectively breeding dogs to breed standards that lead to disease or discomfort is inhumane – and any breed standard that predisposes to disease or discomfort should be modified.

Today, many breeders are aware of the genetics of breeding and breed clubs are reviewing standards to remove the most worrying aspects. Some undesirable genetic characteristics, affecting health, may be carried by certain members of a breed. Medical ailments can occur in descendants when two carriers of these genetically caused diseases are mated. The best breeders try to ensure that selective breeding eliminates these disorders.

THE BREED SECTION EXPLAINED

CLASSIFICATIONS OF BREEDS and breed types are arbitrary. The Romans classified dogs as house dogs, shepherd dogs, and sporting dogs. The latter category was subdivided into war dogs, sight hunters, and scent hunters. More recently, as for example in the former Soviet Union, breeds have sometimes been divided into only two groups, professionals and amateurs. Professionals served functional roles such as herding, guarding, or hunting, while amateurs were strictly companions. Breeds come and go according to our whims. The history of the dog consists of gains and losses. Many breeds have been lost this century, but today organizations exist in several countries to save endangered individuals.

HOW THE BREED ENTRIES WORK

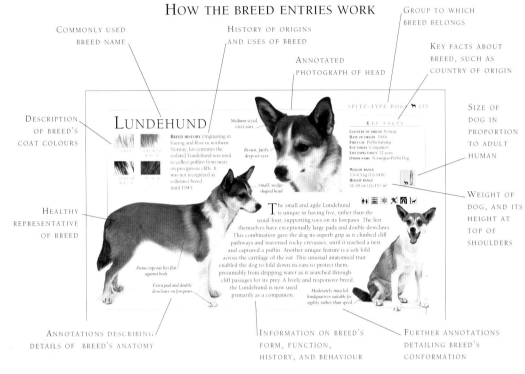

COMMONLY USED BREED NAME

HISTORY OF ORIGINS AND USES OF BREED

ANNOTATED PHOTOGRAPH OF HEAD

GROUP TO WHICH BREED BELONGS

KEY FACTS ABOUT BREED, SUCH AS COUNTRY OF ORIGIN

DESCRIPTION OF BREED'S COAT COLOURS

SIZE OF DOG IN PROPORTION TO ADULT HUMAN

HEALTHY REPRESENTATIVE OF BREED

WEIGHT OF DOG, AND ITS HEIGHT AT TOP OF SHOULDERS

ANNOTATIONS DESCRIBING DETAILS OF BREED'S ANATOMY

INFORMATION ON BREED'S FORM, FUNCTION, HISTORY, AND BEHAVIOUR

FURTHER ANNOTATIONS DETAILING BREED'S CONFORMATION

CLASSIFICATION SYSTEMS

In this encyclopedia, a simple and logical classification system is used, but like many others, it is an arbitrary one. No attempt to improve upon the Roman classification of dogs was made until the late Middle Ages, when the Englishman Dr. John Caius divided dogs into three groups – hunters, homely dogs, and curs. He subdivided hunters into terriers, harriers, bloodhounds, gazehounds, greyhounds, spaniels, setters, and water spaniels. Homely dogs were subdivided into gentle spaniels and comforters, while the curs were divided into shepherds, mastiffs, and bandogges. Two centuries later, in the 1700s, the Swedish scientist Carl Linneaus published his *System of Nature*, in which he listed and named 35 breeds of dog. The French naturalist Buffon classified them into five groups, according to both shape and behaviour. In the late 1800s, German experts applied modern scientific

THE PARTS OF A DOG

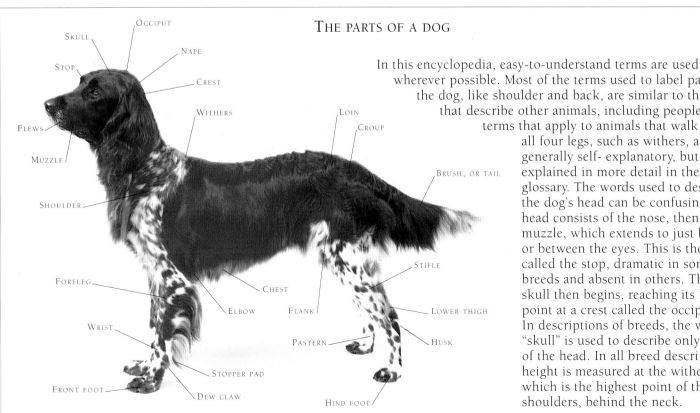

OCCIPUT

SKULL

NAPE

STOP

CREST

WITHERS

LOIN

CROUP

FLEWS

MUZZLE

BRUSH, OR TAIL

SHOULDER

STIFLE

FORELEG

CHEST

ELBOW

FLANK

LOWER THIGH

WRIST

PASTERN

HUSK

FRONT FOOT

STOPPER PAD

DEW CLAW

HIND FOOT

In this encyclopedia, easy-to-understand terms are used wherever possible. Most of the terms used to label parts of the dog, like shoulder and back, are similar to those that describe other animals, including people. Other terms that apply to animals that walk on all four legs, such as withers, are generally self-explanatory, but are explained in more detail in the glossary. The words used to describe the dog's head can be confusing. The head consists of the nose, then the muzzle, which extends to just before or between the eyes. This is the point called the stop, dramatic in some breeds and absent in others. The skull then begins, reaching its highest point at a crest called the occiput. In descriptions of breeds, the word "skull" is used to describe only the top of the head. In all breed descriptions, height is measured at the withers, which is the highest point of the shoulders, behind the neck.

knowledge to the classification of dogs. In 1878, Professor Fitzinger recognized 180 breeds and varieties of dog according to their external features. In 1901, Herr Studer, applying evolutionary principles, reclassified all dogs according to evidence from ancient bones and skulls. His was a valiant attempt, but unfortunately many of his arguments proved incorrect.

OFFICIAL CLASSIFICATIONS

By the late 1800s, kennel clubs and canine societies had come into existence in many countries, each with its individual method of classifying and grouping dog breeds. To rationalize these differences, the canine societies of several European countries formed the FCI (International Cynological Federation). It has its own unique canine nomenclature, dividing all breeds into 10 groups and numerous subgroups. This is as much a political document as a method of breed classification.

ALTERNATIVE CLASSIFICATIONS

Original breed clubs retain the right to define the standards for their own breeds, but all clubs affiliated with the FCI (and that is most of the world's canine societies) submit their standards to that tribunal for international recognition. In different countries these standards may be interpreted in varying ways, and this has led to breeds developing distinctly different looks in different countries.

In this book, FCI standards are used as the norm, but variations according to the standards of different countries are also included. Because the FCI classification of breeds is rather complicated, a streamlined method is used, based in part on the origins and physical characteristics of breeds, and in part on their behaviour. The eight categories – primitive dogs, sight hounds, scent hounds, spitz-type dogs, terriers, gundogs, livestock dogs, and companion dogs – are arbitrary. Some breeds, especially obvious crosses between one type and another, could just as accurately be listed in different groups.

EXTINCTIONS AND PRESERVATION

Curiously, in the 1800s, before canine societies existed, there were many more breeds of dog than there are today. Breeders worldwide could see that the danger of extinction loomed over regional breeds, and successfully categorized differences before they were lost. However, within the last generation we have lost a number of breeds, such as the Belgian Braque Belge, the French Braque Dupuy, Levesque, and Chambray, the German Harlequin Pinscher and Sheep Poodle, and the Canadian Tahl Tan Bear Dog. In Denmark, the Broholmer has become extinct but is being "recreated" through judicious breeding of dogs with similar looks and temperament. Any loss of a regionally successful breed is needless.

PRIMITIVE DOGS

THE LABEL "PRIMITIVE" is an arbitrary one applied to a small group of dogs that are descended from the Indian Plains Wolf, *Canis lupus pallipes*. Some members of this group, such as the Dingo and New Guinea Singing Dog, are genuinely primitive, in that they are at an early or at least an arrested stage of domestication. Others, such as the Mexican Hairless and Basenji, although they are descended from the same root stock, have been dramatically affected by human intervention in their breeding.

Ibizan Hound
Five-thousand-year-old images of hounds that are almost identical to the Ibizan Hound have been discovered in Egypt.

BODY IS LONG, WITH SLIGHTLY ARCHED NECK; SMOOTH, FIRM SKIN IS SUSCEPTIBLE TO SUNBURN

Miniature Mexican Hairless
One of three recognized sizes, the Mexican Hairless also exists in smaller toy (see opposite) and larger standard versions.

LONG, STRAIGHT LEGS GIVE THIS BREED DAZZLING SPEED, MAKING IT ONE OF THE FASTEST PACED HUNTING DOGS

FIRST MIGRATIONS
Experts are quite certain that wandering groups of humans spread out of south-west Asia between 10,000 and 15,000 years ago, accompanied by pariah dogs. The dog had reached the Middle East and North Africa at least 5,000 years ago, through migration and trade. Images of the oldest recorded breed, the Pharaoh Hound, grace the tombs of ancient Egyptian pharaohs. This dog was probably a descendant of

the breed known as the Phoenician Hound – the Phoenicians traded dogs throughout the Mediterranean, introducing the breeds which are today known as the Canaan Dog, Cirneco dell'Etna, and Ibizan Hound.

EARLY EVOLUTION
Dogs eventually spread into the heart of Africa, and although the Basenji is the only primitive African breed commonly recognized today, there were until recently many other similar breeds. In West Africa, the Liberian Dog, a terrier-like, neat, small, reddish brown dog evolved; in Kenya, the East African Dog, a larger, more powerfully muzzled dog, found a niche as a scavenger and hunter's companion. The Bagirmi Dog was of similar size and shape, but pied in colour, while the Bantu Dog, which was used for hunting and as a watchdog, was much more slender, with a pointed muzzle. In South Africa, the small, powerful, fawn-coloured, square-muzzled Zulu Dog also acted as a guard and hunter. In Zaire, the pygmies kept the long-headed, prick-eared Bush Dog, while the Hottentots owned a bushy tailed, spitz-like breed. The fox-like Kabyle, or Douar Dog, acted as a herder and guard, while the ring-tailed, longer limbed Baganda Dog functioned as a pack dog. All of these related breeds existed in pure form until this century. While some pariah dogs migrated westwards, others accompanied people as they journeyed eastwards. Many accompanied humans as they traversed the land bridge to the Americas, across what are now the Bering Straits. A number of these Asian pariah dogs interbred with North American Wolves, but fossil records indicate that unsullied, distinctly Dingo-like dogs spread first to the south-west of North America, to what is now Arizona, and then on to the south-east, to what are now the states of Georgia and South Carolina. The Canadian Tahl-tan Bear Dog, which became extinct only recently, might be part of that chain.

Peruvian Inca Orchid
This breed may descend from Asian dogs brought to the Americas 12,000 years ago, although it may be of more recent African origin.

EARS ARE RATHER LOW SET ON SMALL HEAD; HAIR USUALLY GROWS ON TOP OF HEAD BETWEEN EARS

LEGS ARE THIN BONED, AND COVERED BY DELICATE SKIN; NATURAL HEAT LOSS MAKES BREED A GOOD HOT-WATER BOTTLE

Cirneco dell'Etna
Smaller than the Pharaoh and Ibizan Hounds, the Cirneco also descends from primitive Asian hounds traded in the Mediterranean.

VERY MOBILE EARS ARE BROAD AT BASE AND TRIANGULAR IN SHAPE, WELL ADAPTED FOR ACUTE HEARING

SLIGHTLY ARCHED, LONG, MUSCULAR NECK IS COVERED BY SMOOTH, SHORT COAT OF RED HAIR

So, too, are the extinct Kentucky Shell Heap Dog and Basketmaker Dog. The origins of Central and South American dog breeds will always be uncertain. The indigenous dogs of Mexico and Peru may well be hairless

COAT OVER CHEST IS DENSER THAN THAT OF MANY PRIMITIVE DOGS

Canaan Dog
This medium-sized, robust dog descends from the pariah dogs of the Middle East.

Wire-haired Podengo Medio
One of three different-sized Portuguese Podengos, the Medio is much smaller than the Standard, which was the original size. Its small size helped it survive in harsh conditions.

TOUGH, INSULATING, ROUGH HAIR PROVED TO BE VERY USEFUL FOR SURVIVAL

WRINKLED FOREHEAD AND POINTED EARS GIVE DOG QUERULOUS EXPRESSION

Basenji
The Basenji is the only primitive African dog to have achieved widespread popularity outside its native territory. Like the wolf and the Dingo, it comes into season only once each year.

to live off Australian marsupials infests some wild dogs in Asia, strongly suggesting that there was a two-way trade of the Dingo between Australia and Asia. The breed may have travelled back and forth with the seafarers, who took it with them to Australia in order to hunt marsupials in the Australian bush. The oldest dog fossils found in New Guinea are a mere 2,000 years old, implying that the dog only arrived on that island relatively recently. The dog was highly prized by some tribes, but looked upon with disgust, or simply as food, by others. The Orokaiva and Elema peoples, both of whom respected

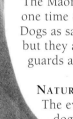

LARGE, ERECT, BROAD, AND VERY MOBILE EARS GIVE BREED DISTINCTIVE APPEARANCE

Pharaoh Hound
Bearing a striking resemblance to the Egyptian jackal god, Anubis, the Pharaoh Hound continued to be bred in the isolation of Malta, until its discovery by European dog breeders in the 1960s.

descendants of the Asian pariah dogs, transported further south through migration and trade. It is equally likely that they are more recent descendants of African pariah dogs brought to Central and South America by European traders. If this is the case, the Mexican Hairless and the Peruvian Inca Orchid are more closely related to the African Basenji than to the Carolina Dog.

AUSTRALASIAN BREEDS
Spreading down through Southeast Asia, the Dingo arrived in Australia only 4,000 years ago, at least 1,000 years after the Pharaoh Hound was already being venerated in Egypt. A parasite that evolved

Toy Mexican Hairless
Smallest of the three sizes of Mexican Hairless, the Toy is also the most fragile, and is susceptible to body heat loss, especially in cold, northern climates.

ELEGANT NECK IS LONG AND SLIGHTLY ARCHED

LEGS ARE LONG IN COMPARISON WITH BODY

LEGS ARE STRAIGHT AND PARALLEL

the dog's hunting and guarding abilities, reserved eating dog for only the most important ceremonies. This was the hapless fate of many other primitive dogs that were traded throughout the Pacific. The Maori of New Zealand at one time offered their Kuri Dogs as sacrificial offerings, but they also valued them as guards and companions.

NATURAL SELECTION
The evolution of primitive dogs involved, to a certain extent, self domestication. Ecological pressures naturally selected for small size, and they are not as large as their Indian Wolf progenitors. When the numbers of dogs increased around human habitation, small dogs needing less food were most likely to survive. Evolutionary changes occur much faster than previously thought; so does the speed with which a species can colonize new land. The Red Fox took only 130 years to spread from Victoria in South Australia to the Kimberley mountains in the north. It probably took less than 500 years for the Dingo to colonize that entire continent.

With the exception of the Dingo and New Guinea Singing Dog, pariah breeds are reasonably easy to train in obedience. They are always alert, and can be rather aloof. Some remain at an early stage of human intervention, and lack selected traits such as enhanced sight-scenting ability, power, or friendly, outgoing natures.

New Guinea Singing Dog
This dog is native to New Guinea, although anthropological evidence shows that it only arrived on that island 2,000 years ago.

TEETH ARE CLOSER TOGETHER THAN THOSE OF THE ASIAN WOLF – ITS ANCESTOR

THE PEQUEÑO'S LUCID, BRIGHT EYES MAKE IT A COMPELLING COMPANION

Smooth-haired Podengo Portugueso Pequeño
A miniaturized version of the original primitive Podengo, this breed is a very competent ratter.

DINGO

Intense eyes vary from yellow to orange in colour

Typical coat colour is yellow-ginger, but can occur in black or white

Tail is relaxed and has good length

Very mobile ears are naturally erect

KEY FACTS

COUNTRY OF ORIGIN Australia
DATE OF ORIGIN Antiquity
FIRST USE Camp follower, sentry
USE TODAY Rarely kept
LIFE EXPECTANCY 10 years
OTHER NAMES Maliki, Warrigal, Noggum, Mirigung, Boolomo

WEIGHT RANGE
10–20 kg (22–44 lb)
HEIGHT RANGE
up to 53 cm (21 in)

BREED HISTORY
The Dingo arrived in Australia about 4,000 years ago, and its arrival coincided with the decline of the indigenous carnivorous marsupial, the thylacine, on mainland Australia.

Hindquarters are lean and muscular

VARIETY
OF
COLOURS

All pure-bred Dingos have white hair on feet

The Dingo is a breed that has never been fully domesticated. This is partly due to its remote isolation, but also through lack of human intervention. It does not have the same degree of tooth crowding and shortening of the jaw that distinguish other dog breeds from their ancestor, the Asian Plains Wolf. Also like the wolf, the female Dingo has only one breeding cycle each year. Originally kept by some Australian Aboriginal groups as a pet, the breed also served as a sentry, camp cleaner, and even as an emergency source of food. Today, the Dingo is almost never kept as a companion.

NEW GUINEA SINGING DOG

Bases of small, mobile ears are on line with eyes

Ears are erect

KEY FACTS

COUNTRY OF ORIGIN New Guinea
DATE OF ORIGIN Antiquity
FIRST USE Pariah – scavenger
USE TODAY Pariah – scavenger, companion
LIFE EXPECTANCY 10–12 years

WEIGHT RANGE
8–10 kg (18–22 lb)
HEIGHT RANGE
35–38 cm (14–15 in)

VARIOUS
SHADES
OF RED

Eyes are small

Coat occurs in various shades of red

BREED HISTORY This breed is a close relative of ancient dogs that were domesticated from Asian Wolves between 10,000 and 15,000 years ago.

Jaw structure is more advanced than a Dingo's

Hindquarters are lean

Hair on feet is always white

Explorers in the 1800s described the varying popularity of dogs in the lowland villages of New Guinea – in some they were treated as pets, while in others they were abused. By this century, hybridization with imported dogs had made the indigenous, lowland New Guinea Dog almost extinct. In the 1950s, however, two pure dogs were captured in the isolated

Lavanni valley in the southern highlands, and eventually sent to Taronga Park Zoo in Sydney, Australia. In the 1970s, another pair was captured in Irian Jaya's Eipomak valley, part of Indonesia. Virtually all Singing Dogs in Europe and North America descend from these pairs. This boisterous breed has a unique sing-song howl, which is curiously plaintive.

CANAAN DOG

WHITE SANDY

BROWN BLACK

Eyes are dark and slant very slightly

Pricked ears have broad base and rounded tip, and are set low

Bushy tail curls over back when dog is alert

The Canaan Dog was originally employed by the Bedouins as both a herder and guard dog in the Negev desert. Today's breed, which was developed in the 1930s, has proved to be exceptionally versatile. During World War II, a number of Canaans were trained for mine detection; after the war, members of the breed were even used as guide dogs for the blind. The Canaan Dog is now used for herding, guarding, tracking, and search and rescue. Although rather aloof, it does make a good companion. Increasingly popular in its country of origin, the breed has now spread to the United States.

Forehead appears wide

Strong body, with moderately deep chest

BREED HISTORY Originally a pariah, the Canaan Dog has existed in the Middle East for centuries. In the 1930s, Dr. Rudolphina Menzel, an Israeli authority on dogs, conducted a selective breeding programme in Jerusalem, producing today's resourceful, versatile breed.

Coat is straight and harsh

KEY FACTS

COUNTRY OF ORIGIN Israel
DATE OF ORIGIN Antiquity
FIRST USE Pariah – scavenger
USE TODAY Livestock guarding, herding, tracking, search and rescue, companion
LIFE EXPECTANCY 12–13 years
OTHER NAME Kelef K'naani

WEIGHT RANGE
16–25 kg (35–55 lb)
HEIGHT RANGE
48–61 cm (19–24 in)

PODENCO CANARIO

GOLDEN
WHITE

RUST-
ORANGE

Small, slanted eyes have alert expression

BREED HISTORY Closely related to the Ibizan Hound, and the largest of the three Portuguese podengos, this isolated breed is probably as ancient as its mainland Iberian relatives.

Rigid ears are usually directed forwards

Long, narrow head, with pink nose

In repose, low-set tail is carried low

Chest is deep and narrow

Slightly arched, muscular neck

The Podenco Canario arrived in the Canary Islands from the Iberian mainland only in the last 400 years. It is probably a direct descendant of the ancient dogs brought to Spain by Mediterranean traders thousands of years ago. Unusual for a sight hound, this breed uses hearing and scenting as much as it uses sight to find prey. Equally unusual, it participates with hunters in pack hunting for rabbits – it can point and retrieve. This adaptation to work as a pack gundog on the volcanic soil of the Canary Islands is representative of the amazingly elastic nature of dog behaviour, with the ability to change function to suit the conditions in which the species finds itself.

Coat is smooth, short, and hard

KEY FACTS

COUNTRY OF ORIGIN Canary Islands
DATE OF ORIGIN Antiquity
FIRST USE Rabbit hunting with nets
USE TODAY Hunting, companion
LIFE EXPECTANCY 12–13 years
OTHER NAME Canary Islands Hound

WEIGHT RANGE
16–22 kg (35–48½ lb)
HEIGHT RANGE
53–64 cm (21–25 in)

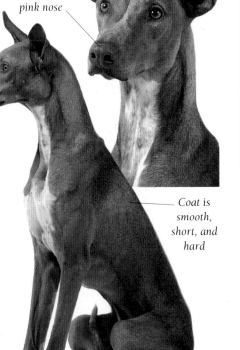

Hare-like feet, with well-spaced toes

Long, straight bones

BASENJI

Pointed ears are erect; short fur allows for heat loss, which is important in hot climates

Dark-hazel eyes have penetrating expression

BREED HISTORY Although its exact origins are a mystery, dogs similar to the Basenji are depicted in Egyptian tombs from the Fourth Dynasty. Today's Basenji descends from dogs that came from Zaire in the 1930s.

Tail curls in a ring, and is held close to body

Loose skin is covered by short coat, with silky texture

Muzzle tapers from eyes to tip of nose, which is usually black

BLACK/WHITE TAN/WHITE BLACK

Long, lean legs allow for free movement, much like horse trotting

This quiet and graceful dog is typical of the breeds that evolved in temperate and warm climates. Tan colour provides camouflage, and white patches on the fur and a short coat on the ears and body all help with heat tolerance. These factors, as well as the Basenji's silence while tracking game, make it an efficient hunter. Most breeds of dog have two sex cycles each year but the Basenji, in common with wild canids such as the wolf, has only one. Also like the wolf, it rarely barks. Instead, it howls in a curious voice not unlike the sound of an Alpine yodeller. Docile with humans, it has a tendency to wander.

Wrinkles give dog surprised expression

Chest is only moderately deep and wide

Long jaws are typical of most ancient breeds

Ears are highly visible and mobile

Neck is quite long and muscular; nape is prominent

KEY FACTS

COUNTRY OF ORIGIN Central Africa
DATE OF ORIGIN Antiquity
FIRST USE Hunting
USE TODAY Companion
LIFE EXPECTANCY 12 years
OTHER NAME Congo Dog

WEIGHT RANGE
9.5–11 kg (21–24 lb)
HEIGHT RANGE
41–43 cm (16–17 in)

PERUVIAN INCA ORCHID

Thin, light boned, and graceful, this breed typifies the human fascination with the unusual or bizarre. Hairlessness in dogs is a genetic accident; without the physical protection and insulation of hair, dogs are more prone to illness. The ancient Incas perpetuated this calm and intelligent breed and, although it became quite rare, breeding continued in Peru until this century, when it was introduced to North America and Europe. The Peruvian Inca Orchid has a high incidence of teeth, eye, and skin problems, all of which need veterinary attention.

Hair grows on top of head

Dark, round eyes

Thin, leathery ears sometimes have wisps of hair

Lips are wrinkled

White or pink skin is prone to sunburn

VARIETY OF COLOURS

BREED HISTORY Spanish explorers came upon this breed in the homes of the Inca nobility, when they first entered the Peruvian empire in the early 1500s.

INCA HAIRLESS DOG

VARIETY OF COLOURS

Ears are quite small

Expressive, gentle eyes

The shape of the Inca Hairless is similar to that of sight hounds, and the breed was developed in three sizes. Small dogs weighing 4–8 kg (9–18 lb) would originally have made ideal bed warmers, while medium varieties of 8–12 kg (18–26 lb), and large dogs of 12–25 kg (26–55 lb), especially coated varieties, may have been used for sight hunting. The existence of these breeds before the arrival of the Spanish suggests that they either evolved from North American Timber Wolves, or that Asians, Polynesians, or North Africans introduced them to South America before it was discovered by Europeans.

Nose is deep black, but can be mottled with pink

Hairless skin needs oiling to prevent sunburn

Lean, long, sinewy legs are built for speed

BREED HISTORY For the breed to survive, the Incas recognized that intermittent breeding with coated members of the breed was necessary.

Thin skin susceptible to abrasions

Nails are easy to trim

CAROLINA DOG

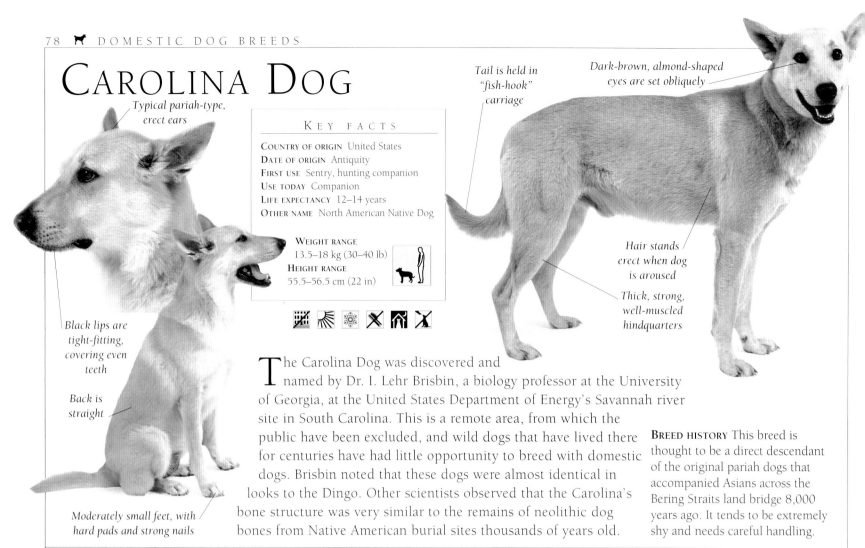

Typical pariah-type, erect ears

Tail is held in "fish-hook" carriage

Dark-brown, almond-shaped eyes are set obliquely

Hair stands erect when dog is aroused

Thick, strong, well-muscled hindquarters

Black lips are tight-fitting, covering even teeth

Back is straight

Moderately small feet, with hard pads and strong nails

KEY FACTS

COUNTRY OF ORIGIN United States
DATE OF ORIGIN Antiquity
FIRST USE Sentry, hunting companion
USE TODAY Companion
LIFE EXPECTANCY 12–14 years
OTHER NAME North American Native Dog

WEIGHT RANGE
13.5–18 kg (30–40 lb)
HEIGHT RANGE
55.5–56.5 cm (22 in)

The Carolina Dog was discovered and named by Dr. I. Lehr Brisbin, a biology professor at the University of Georgia, at the United States Department of Energy's Savannah river site in South Carolina. This is a remote area, from which the public have been excluded, and wild dogs that have lived there for centuries have had little opportunity to breed with domestic dogs. Brisbin noted that these dogs were almost identical in looks to the Dingo. Other scientists observed that the Carolina's bone structure was very similar to the remains of neolithic dog bones from Native American burial sites thousands of years old.

BREED HISTORY This breed is thought to be a direct descendant of the original pariah dogs that accompanied Asians across the Bering Straits land bridge 8,000 years ago. It tends to be extremely shy and needs careful handling.

STANDARD MEXICAN HAIRLESS

Head is rather broad, with tapering muzzle

ORANGE

SLATE

BLACK

Deep chest is fairly narrow, descending as far as elbows

Forelegs are long and straight

Supple back ends in a rounded rump

Eyes are slightly almond shaped

How this breed arrived in Mexico will probably remain a mystery. Images of what appear to be hairless dogs appear in ancient Aztec ruins; it is more likely, however, that these are some other indigenous mammals – it seems that the Aztecs at one time "created" naked animals by using a resin to remove the hair from guinea pigs, which then served as food and bed warmers. This alert, lively, and affectionate breed is often compared to both ancient African pariah dogs and European terriers. Its physical structure is reminiscent of classic sight hounds, while its personality can be very similar to the Fox Terrier's.

KEY FACTS

COUNTRY OF ORIGIN Mexico
DATE OF ORIGIN Unknown
FIRST USE Companion, comforter
USE TODAY Companion
LIFE EXPECTANCY 12–15 years
OTHER NAMES Xoloitzcuintli, Tepeizeuintli

WEIGHT RANGE
9–14 kg (20–31 lb)
HEIGHT RANGE
41–57 cm (16–22½ in)

BREED HISTORY
Most references indicate that this hairless breed existed in Mexico at the time of the Spanish Conquest, in the early 1500s. It was probably introduced to Central and South America by Spanish traders.

MINIATURE MEXICAN HAIRLESS

Ears are usually set at an angle of between 50 and 80 degrees

BREED HISTORY Although its origins are lost, the Miniature either arrived in Mexico at the same time as the Standard, or was bred down in size after the latter arrived in Mexico. Hairlessness is a genetic rarity in dogs, but can occur in other animal breeds.

Slender head has narrow skull

KEY FACTS	
COUNTRY OF ORIGIN Mexico	
DATE OF ORIGIN Unknown	
FIRST USE Companion, comforter	
USE TODAY Companion	
LIFE EXPECTANCY 12–15 years	
OTHER NAMES Xoloitzcuintli, Tepeizeuintli	
WEIGHT RANGE 6–10 kg (13–22 lb)	
HEIGHT RANGE 30–38 cm (12–15 in)	

Muzzle is pointed and tipped

Long, low-set tail tucks in and tapers to a tip

Skin feels hot to the touch because of dog's high body temperature

Small, hare-like feet have retracted toes

Much more common than the Standard, and enjoying a resurgence of popularity in North America as well as in Mexico, about one out of every three puppies in this breed is covered in fine, downy fur. This "powder-puff" version of the breed is not recognized by breed clubs and cannot be exhibited at dog shows, but it still makes an excellent pet, and its use in breeding programmes ensures the health and vigour of the breed. The Miniature's skin, like that of other Mexican Hairless, needs careful attention in order to keep it it supple and healthy.

SLATE

LIVER, BRONZE

CHARCOAL

TOY MEXICAN HAIRLESS

KEY FACTS	
COUNTRY OF ORIGIN Mexico	
DATE OF ORIGIN 1950s	
FIRST USE Companion, comforter	
USE TODAY Companion	
LIFE EXPECTANCY 12–15 years	
OTHER NAMES Xoloitzcuintli, Tepeizeuintli	
WEIGHT RANGE 4–8 kg (9–18 lb)	
HEIGHT RANGE 28–31 cm (11–12 in)	

BREED HISTORY This miniaturization of the Mexican Hairless is the result of a breeding programme that was initiated by the Mexican Kennel Club in the 1950s.

Thin ears, like those of a bat

There are no wrinkles to lips, and no flews

Back is firm and muscular

SLATE

LIVER, BRONZE

CHARCOAL

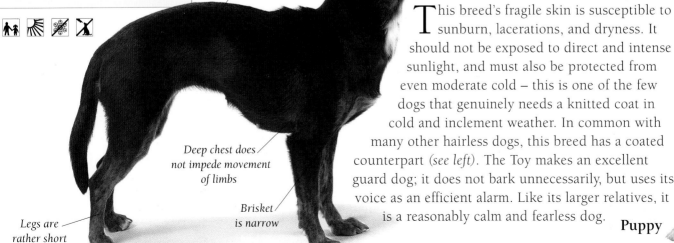

Deep chest does not impede movement of limbs

Brisket is narrow

Legs are rather short

This breed's fragile skin is susceptible to sunburn, lacerations, and dryness. It should not be exposed to direct and intense sunlight, and must also be protected from even moderate cold – this is one of the few dogs that genuinely needs a knitted coat in cold and inclement weather. In common with many other hairless dogs, this breed has a coated counterpart (*see left*). The Toy makes an excellent guard dog; it does not bark unnecessarily, but uses its voice as an efficient alarm. Like its larger relatives, it is a reasonably calm and fearless dog.

Puppy

PHARAOH HOUND

Mobile, medium-sized
ears are carried erect
when alert

Elegant neck is long,
lean, muscular, and
slightly curved

Oval, rather closely set eyes
give excellent binocular vision
necessary for sight hunting

Tail, which is
fairly thick at base
and tapers off, is
relaxed

Shoulders are laid
well back

Skeleton remains indicate that hunting
dogs similar to the Pharaoh Hound have
existed in the Middle East for at least 5,000
years. After the Roman invasion of Egypt 2,000
years ago, similar dogs spread around the rest of
the Mediterranean, possibly traded by Phoenicians
and Carthaginians. They survived particularly well
as distinct breeds in relatively isolated places such as
the Maltese and Balearic islands, and Sicily, but also
in France and mainland Italy. Perhaps due to its rich,
red colour and its rediscovery by dog breeders in the
1960s, the Pharaoh Hound, always clean in appearance,
has become the most popular of these descendants of
the "Egyptian Hound". Unlike the greyhound, which
 hunts by sight alone, the Pharaoh Hound hunts by
 sight, sound, and smell.

Strong and
muscular thighs

BREED HISTORY The elegant, dignified
Pharaoh Hound is probably descended from
the small, lithe wolf that inhabited the Arabian
peninsula. Phoenician traders brought the
breed to the islands of Malta and Gozo
approximately 2,000 years ago, where it
has remained isolated in a pure state.

Eyes are amber,
moderately deep set,
keen, and alert

Long, lean face has
chiselled look

Short, glossy, but slightly harsh,
coat needs little grooming

Flesh-coloured nose
blends with colour of
coat and flushes when
dog is excited

White-tipped feet
are strong and firm;
pads and claws are
light in colour

CIRNECO DELL'ETNA

BREED HISTORY Another classic descendant of the Egyptian prick-eared running dogs, the Cirneco dell'Etna has been bred true to type in the relative isolation of Sicily since its arrival there 2,000 years ago.

Alert, inquisitive-looking dog, with broad, upright ears

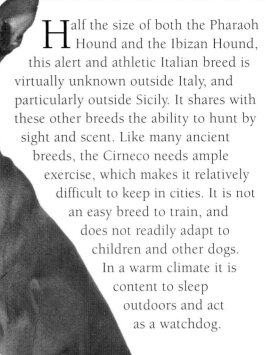

Half the size of both the Pharaoh Hound and the Ibizan Hound, this alert and athletic Italian breed is virtually unknown outside Italy, and particularly outside Sicily. It shares with these other breeds the ability to hunt by sight and scent. Like many ancient breeds, the Cirneco needs ample exercise, which makes it relatively difficult to keep in cities. It is not an easy breed to train, and does not readily adapt to children and other dogs. In a warm climate it is content to sleep outdoors and act as a watchdog.

Tail is thick at base, then tapers to just below hock

Short, glossy, rustic-looking coat has no feathering

Hard thigh muscles, visible through fine skin, give rapid bursts of power

Long, sinewy forelegs are ideal for racing

Compact feet, with tan-coloured pads

IBIZAN HOUND

Strong, lean thighs are well suited to bursts of speed

Steep, rather short shoulders above long, straight legs

Large ears on long, flat head funnel sounds to assist in hunting

BREED HISTORY Traders brought the Ibizan Hound to Mediterranean islands thousands of years ago. The breed spread to Mediterranean France, where it was known as the Charnique.

The coat of the Ibizan Hound can be wiry, smooth, or long, and variously coloured. Although named after Ibiza, one of the Balearic islands, the breed spread a long time ago to mainland Spain, where it was used both as a gundog, and to course rabbits and hares. Affectionate and even tempered with its owner, it is sometimes sensitive with strangers.

WHITE

FAWN

FAWN/WHITE

RED

RED/WHITE

Amber eyes are clear and alert

Well-arched toes, with light-coloured claws

Flesh-coloured nose lightens in colour when dog is unwell

Tail is long and low set

PODENGO PORTUGUESO MEDIO

Although its closest relative, the Podengo Grande, is now quite rare, this lively and alert, medium-sized hound remains a popular dog, particularly in rural parts of northern Portugal, where it is sometimes still used as a small-game hunter. Human intervention in breeding has reduced the Medio's size, while leaving other characteristics intact. Colour and coat variety are relatively unimportant – some individuals are solid coloured, others are marked with white; some have short, shiny coats, others have long, coarse hair. One benefit of our relatively limited intervention in the Podengo's breeding is that it has a very low incidence of known inherited defects or diseases.

BREED HISTORY There are two possible origins of all Podengo Portugueso. The Grande, from which the Medio and Pequeño evolved, is similar to the tan-coloured sight hounds, such as the Pharaoh Hound, which spread out of North Africa to the Iberian peninsula. The Podengo could, however, be a descendant of small Iberian wolves.

Triangular ears are highly mobile

Nose is usually brown, but may be black

Smooth-haired variety

Thick, pointed tail is set high, and curves slightly

Ears turn forwards to catch sound

Muscular chest is not prominent

YELLOW TAN BLACK

Round feet have well-arched toes

Back line only has a slight arch

Nose, oblique at tip, is darker than coat colour

Ears are naturally upright

Wire-haired variety

Eyes are honey to brown in colour

Long legs are moderately feathered with hair

Hard, strong pads

KEY FACTS

COUNTRY OF ORIGIN Portugal
DATE OF ORIGIN Antiquity
FIRST USE Rabbit/hare hunting
USE TODAY Companion, rabbit/hare hunting
LIFE EXPECTANCY 12–14 years
OTHER NAME Medium Portuguese Hound

WEIGHT RANGE
16–20 kg (35–44 lb)
HEIGHT RANGE
39–56 cm (15–22 in)

PODENGO PORTUGUESO PEQUEÑO

Highly mobile, triangular ears are erect

YELLOW   TAN   BLACK

Shoulders are well muscled

KEY FACTS

COUNTRY OF ORIGIN Portugal
DATE OF ORIGIN Antiquity/1600s?
FIRST USE Ratting, game flushing
USE TODAY Companion, ratting
LIFE EXPECTANCY 12–14 years
OTHER NAME Small
Portuguese Hound

WEIGHT RANGE
4–6 kg (9–13 lb)
HEIGHT RANGE
20–31 cm (8–12 in)

Slightly slanted, honey-brown-coloured eyes

Skin is rather fine and close, without slackness

Smooth-haired variety

Forearm is powerful for size of dog

Round paws have hard, strong pads

Long, strong neck has no dewlap

Like the Podengo Portugueso Medio, the Pequeño has been bred for size alone, rather than for colour or coat, which occur in all the varieties of the larger breed. The short-haired variety looks somewhat like a Chihuahua, but there is no ancestral link between the two. The wire-haired variety looks distinctly like a small terrier. The lively, alert Pequeño sometimes goes rabbit hunting with the Medio. The Pequeño enters the warren and, like a terrier, flushes out the rabbits, while the faster Medio chases those that are above ground. The Pequeño gets on well with children and with other animals, and is easy to train, so it is popular as a house pet, particularly in cities. Small as it is, this vibrant dog thrives on plenty of exercise.

Back is long and fairly straight

Feathered face and muzzle are a distinctive feature

Erect ears are well covered with hair

Wire-haired variety

BREED HISTORY The Pequeño is simply a miniaturized version of the original greyhound-sized Grande. Although it was, and still is, used for flushing out small game, the Pequeño has been a city dog for at least three centuries. In his paintings of the poor of Seville, Bartolomé Esteban Murillo (born in that city in 1617) featured dogs that bear a striking similarity to the Pequeño of today.

Feathering on legs

Tail hangs down when dog is relaxed

SIGHT HOUNDS

ROUND EYES
ARE SOFT AND
QUESTIONING

BRED FOR SPEED, with an aerodynamic build for flying like arrows after their prey, sight hounds are almost invariably tall, long, lean, lithe, running hounds. They are products of selective breeding thousands of years ago that was as sophisticated as any selective breeding today. Some of them are obviously close relatives of the primitive dogs, such as the Ibizan and Pharaoh Hounds, and the distinction between the two groups is strictly arbitrary. All sight hounds emanated from south-west Asia.

ANCIENT ORIGINS

Arabia is the heartland of the oldest recorded sight hounds. The Saluki and Sloughi have both been selectively bred there for at least 5,000 years, to outrun desert gazelles. In ancient Persia, the streamlined Saluki once existed in 16 different varieties, including the Taji. Today, in Kazakstan, Uzbekistan, and Turkmenistan, the Tasy, another variety, still exists in a large assortment of colours. Unfortunately, with no breed organizations to assure its future, and with unrest throughout the central Asian Republics, its numbers are decreasing and it is in danger of becoming extinct.

In its Afghanistan homeland, the Afghan Hound originally hunted the desert fox and gazelle by day and guarded the tent at night. There, it still exists in two varieties, the thick-coated northern variety from which the elegant, frosted blond show dog derives, and a light-coated southern variety, seldom seen in the West, but still used as a working dog in parts of Pakistan. A closely related sight hound, the Taigan, never seen in western Europe or the Americas, still exists in the Tien Shan mountains of Kirgizia, where it is used to hunt foxes and hares. The Russian Kennel Club recognizes both the Tasy and the Taigan, and is trying to find breeding stock in order to maintain these sight hounds.

HISTORICAL INFLUENCES

In Russia, the Chortai, or Russian Greyhound, was developed from two now-extinct breeds, the Krymskaja and Gorskaja sight hounds. After the October Revolution of 1917, Chortai from the deserted kennels of the Russian nobility were bred with local dogs, producing what is now recognized as the South Russian Steppe Hound. With the breakup of the Soviet Union, Russian breeders are now more interested in pre-revolution breeds and, sadly, this industrious, trusty hare hunter is in danger of extinction. Russia's most popular and distinctive sight hound, the elegant Borzoi, existed in numerous forms in Czarist times. Russian breeders are currently looking to recreate many of the lost varieties of Borzoi.

Sight hounds thrived further south, in India, and still exist there today, although only the Rampur Hound of northern India, and the Mahratta and Banjara Hounds of the nomadic Banjara tribe, are recognized by the Indian Kennel Club.

Rampur Greyhound
The Rampur is rarely seen outside its area of origin, although some individuals now exist in Canada.

LEGS ARE WELL
BONED AND
FIRMLY MUSCLED

PAWS ARE ROUND, FIRM,
AND WELL PADDED

Smooth-haired Lurcher
The favourite sight hound of Irish and English gypsies, the Lurcher was originally a cross between a collie and a greyhound.

Greyhound
The dog world's most accomplished professional athlete reached Great Britain at least 2,900 years ago.

MUSCULAR NECK AND
FOREQUARTERS ARE
NECESSARY FOR SUDDEN
BURSTS OF SPEED

BREED HAS
DISTINCTIVE
BEARD

Irish Wolfhound
The world's tallest breed, this inveterate wolf slayer almost became extinct, until Scottish Deerhound bloodlines were used to revive it.

Spanish Greyhound
Partly descended from the primitive dogs brought by traders to Spain, today this breed has a considerable amount of English Greyhound blood.

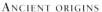

HEAD IS LONG
AND NARROW,
WITH EARS
FALLING BACK

Afghan Hound
First brought to Europe in the late 1800s by soldiers returning from war, the Afghan has been popular in the West since the turn of the century.

SELECTIVE BREEDING
HAS ARTIFICIALLY
THICKENED COAT

Ears tend to be small and semi-erect, although size varies considerably

Wire-haired Lurcher
The Wire-haired Lurcher is well adapted to course hares in tempestuous weather conditions. This breed has always been bred for utility, never for form – as a consequence there are no breed standards.

Azawakh
Deep in Mali, in the southern Sahara, the Tuareg people have for centuries bred the Azawakh to chase gazelles.

Chest is deep and powerful, with well-sprung, long ribs

Powerful legs are very long, allowing dog to sprint with great speed

Saluki
At one time, there were over a dozen varieties of Saluki in Iran. This high-stepping gazelle hound has been bred by the Bedouin for over 2,000 years.

Long, mobile ears are covered in long hair

then crossed with mastiff breeds, producing the muscular, enduring, and powerful Irish Wolfhound, which became the sight hound of the nobility. Likewise, the sleek Scottish Deerhound evolved to become the esteemed sight hound of Scottish Highland chieftains. The English Greyhound, today's thoroughbred racing king, may have been introduced into Great Britain by the Celts, to course hares and foxes. More recently, the Whippet was bred as the working man's sight hound, as was, and still is, the Lurcher. There are few sight hound breeds outside Asia and Europe. The Brazilian Greyhound is almost certainly a cross between the English Greyhound and

In southern India, the lean, hare-hunting Chippiparai Hound still exists, as does the Poligar Hound, native to the districts around Madras, and the Mudhol Hound – the Greyhound of Maharashtra. These powerful, leggy hounds evolved to chase jackals and hares.

Sight hounds were probably introduced into Mediterranean Europe and Africa by Phoenician traders. The now-rare Greek and Albanian Greyhounds resemble the Saluki, and the tall, athletic-looking Spanish Greyhound is closely related to the Podenco. The Hungarian Greyhound is significantly smaller, while the greyhound was transformed, probably by Spanish breeders, into a miniature sight hound, the Italian Greyhound, to act as a companion.

ROYAL CONNECTIONS
It is possible that the Phoenicians, while trading in tin, also introduced sight hounds into Great Britain over 2,500 years ago. Here, they were selectively bred and

Head is broadest at ears; eyes have black rims

Deerhound
This breed was developed in Scotland to hunt deer. Its dense, shaggy coat protects it against the elements.

Foxhound, while the powerful Australian Greyhound is descended from exceptionally muscular English Greyhounds.

HUNTING BY SIGHT
Many sight hounds are now kept solely for companionship, but at one time they were all bred to hunt primarily by sight – to detect movement, then to chase, capture, and kill prey. Although in fundamentalist Islamic societies dogs are despised, sight hounds are excluded from

these cultural taboos. This is probably because the relationship between the hunter and his sight hound predates Islam.

Sight hounds thrive on physical activity, and need regular access to open space. They generally have benign temperaments, but are not overly demonstrative. They are quiet, usually reliable with children and, although some breeds are good watchdogs in their natural forms, in their pure-bred forms, they are not very territorial. All sight hounds have a strong instinct to chase small animals.

Black pigmentation to lips gives striking outline to face

Whippet's head is typical of all the sight hounds – streamlined and narrow

Whippet
The Whippet began life in Great Britain as the poor man's racing dog, but today it is more likely to be seen on a carpet by a warm fire.

Sloughi
This Moroccan breed is still used in its native land as a flock guard and hunter. It is likely that it originated in Saudi Arabia, or the Yemen, and is a smooth-coated, close relative of the Saluki.

GREYHOUND

Capable of reaching 60 km/h (37 mph), the elegant Greyhound is the dog world's most important speed merchant. This surprisingly gentle breed uses speed and sight to overtake prey, be it a living animal in the field or desert, or a mechanical rabbit on a dog track. The pet Greyhound is a delightful and relaxed companion, although dogs that have retired from racing have a tendency to chase anything that moves.

KEY FACTS

COUNTRY OF ORIGIN Egypt/Great Britain
DATE OF ORIGIN Antiquity
FIRST USE Large-game coursing
USE TODAY Racing, coursing, companion
LIFE EXPECTANCY 10–12 years

WEIGHT RANGE
27–32 kg (60–70 lb)
HEIGHT RANGE
69–76 cm (27–30 in)

WHITE FAWN RED

RED-BRINDLE BLACK-BRINDLE BLACK

Small, fine-textured, rose-shaped ears

Face is long and moderately wide, with flat skull

BREED HISTORY
A 4,900-year-old carving on an Egyptian tomb confirms the antiquity of this breed. Exported to Spain, China, Persia, and elsewhere, the Greyhound was developed to its present form in Great Britain. Its name derives from the old Saxon word *grei*, meaning fine, or beautiful.

Capacious chest provides ample room for heart and lungs

Long, straight forelegs are well boned

Fine, close hair on long, arched, muscular neck

BORZOI

In Russia, *borzoi* is a general term for sight hounds, with the Tasy, Taigan, South Russian Steppe Hound, and Chortaj all being classified as borzois. The size, speed, strength, and symmetry of this breed made it a superb hunter. Wolf coursing was at one time popular among the Russian aristocracy. The Borzoi could outrun most wolves – working in pairs, the dogs would grab their prey behind the ears, and hold it to the ground. For almost a century, the breed has been bred outside Russia strictly for companionship. In losing its interest and aptitude for hunting, it has become a gentle and amenable companion for people of all ages.

KEY FACTS

COUNTRY OF ORIGIN Russia
DATE OF ORIGIN Middle Ages
FIRST USE Wolf hunting
USE TODAY Companion
LIFE EXPECTANCY 11–13 years
OTHER NAME Russian Wolfhound

WEIGHT RANGE
35–48 kg (75–105 lb)
HEIGHT RANGE
69–79 cm (27–31 in)

BREED HISTORY Originally developed to protect its Russian masters from local wolves, the Borzoi is probably descended from the Saluki, Greyhound, and a lean variety of Russian sheepdog.

Oblong eyes are set quite close together

Long and hare-like feet are covered in short, flat hair

Shoulders are close to body

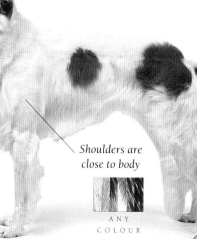

ANY COLOUR

AFGHAN HOUND

Foreface is very long and elegant

Dark-golden eyes have almost triangular openings

Head is long, but not too narrow

BREED HISTORY It is not clear how this breed made its way from the Middle East to Afghanistan. There, it exists in three varieties; short haired like the Kirghiz Taigan (of the former Soviet Union country that now exists above Afghanistan), fringe haired like the Saluki, and long and thick haired, like the true mountain dog first seen in the West in 1907.

Thick hair covers large, strong feet

Long hair on chest has very fine texture

ANY
COLOUR

KEY FACTS

COUNTRY OF ORIGIN Afghanistan
DATE OF ORIGIN Antiquity/1600s
FIRST USE Large-game hunting
USE TODAY Companion, guarding, hunting
LIFE EXPECTANCY 12–14 years
OTHER NAMES Tazi, Baluchi Hound

WEIGHT RANGE
23–27 kg (50–60 lb)
HEIGHT RANGE
64–74 cm (25–29 in)

At speed, there is no other breed with the beauty, grace, elegance, and dignity of the Afghan Hound. Developed in the West wholly for looks rather than function, it is a superb fashion accessory and show dog, lending a feeling of sophistication to any environment. In Afghanistan, however, this beautiful and sensitive animal is still used to guard sheep and goats, and to hunt wolves and foxes. The thick, long coat serves as protection against the cold in the mountainous regions of the north. On the companion Afghan, this dramatic coat must be groomed daily, otherwise it rapidly forms thick mats. Like most other sight hounds, the breed has a strong independent streak, and therefore requires extensive obedience training and careful handling from an early age.

Low-set, sparsely feathered tail

Hair on neck becomes short and close on back

Ears are low, set well back, and carried close to head

Forelegs are straight, and very well boned

SALUKI

KEY FACTS

COUNTRY OF ORIGIN Middle East
DATE OF ORIGIN Antiquity
FIRST USE Gazelle hunting
USE TODAY Companion, hare coursing
LIFE EXPECTANCY 12 years
OTHER NAMES Arabian Hound, Gazelle
  Hound, Persian Greyhound

WEIGHT RANGE
14–25 kg (31–55 lb)
HEIGHT RANGE
58–71 cm (22–28 in)

Ears have very long hair

BREED HISTORY The Saluki, which closely resembles dogs depicted on the tombs of Egyptian pharaohs, was the hunting companion of nomadic Bedouin tribesmen. It is possible that the Saluki has been selectively bred for longer than any other breed of dog.

According to fundamentalist Islam, dogs are unclean. Special dispensation was given to Salukis, permitting them to live in the home of a true believer. When the Bedouins hunted, they used trained hawks to swoop on prey to slow it down until the Saluki caught up and trapped it for the hunter. Originally the Saluki was carried to the hunt on camels to protect its feet from the burning sand. Today, it is more likely to be taken to hunts in vehicles.

Deep chest built for stamina

Leg muscles less developed than a greyhound's

Small, deep-set hazel to brown eyes

Long, lean, straight bones covered by thin skin

WHITE, CREAM   RED, GOLDEN

BLACK/ TAN   FAWN   TRICOLOUR

SPANISH GREYHOUND

Dark, oval-shaped eyes have lively, but soulful, expression

KEY FACTS

COUNTRY OF ORIGIN Spain
DATE OF ORIGIN Antiquity
FIRST USE Sight hunting
USE TODAY Companion, racing, hunting
LIFE EXPECTANCY 12 years
OTHER NAME Galgo Español

WEIGHT RANGE
20–30 kg (44–66 lb)
HEIGHT RANGE
60–70 cm (23–28 in)

CREAM   TIGER   CHESTNUT/ WHITE   BLACK

GOLD

Protective wire-haired coat is now very rare

Rose-shaped ears fall to back

Muscles more like a Sloughi's than a greyhound's

Very long, thin tail almost always carried low

Long, powerful limbs allow speeds in excess of 48 km/h (30 mph)

BREED HISTORY The breed's antecedents almost certainly include the North African Sloughi, which accompanied the Moors when they occupied Spain over 1,000 years ago.

Somewhat timid and almost always independent, the Spanish Greyhound suffers little from the inherited disorders that afflict more modern breeds. The Spanish Greyhound is smaller in size than the English Greyhound, and not as fast. In Spain this breed is preserved by breeders as a show dog and companion, but for field and racing purposes it is commonly bred with the English Greyhound. Although a friendly companion, this is a rather aloof dog. It needs plenty of space for ample exercise, has a mild tendency to be snappy, and can be difficult to obedience train.

SLOUGHI

KEY FACTS

COUNTRY OF ORIGIN North Africa
DATE OF ORIGIN Antiquity
FIRST USE Guarding, hunting
USE TODAY Companion
LIFE EXPECTANCY 12 years
OTHER NAMES Arabian Greyhound, Slughi

WEIGHT RANGE
20–27 kg (45–60 lb)
HEIGHT RANGE
61–72 cm (24–28 in)

Like the Saluki, the Sloughi was treated as a member of the family in its native lands, and was mourned for when it died. This breed is very similar in shape and behaviour to the Saluki but has a smooth, close coat. Its range of sand and fawn colours provided an ideal camouflage for hunting desert animals such as gazelles, hares, and Fennec Foxes. Being naturally vigilant, the Sloughi may behave aggressively with strangers. It is not ideal in a home with children – its nervous temperament makes it most content in a quiet atmosphere.

Fine, smooth, close hair does not retain heat

Large, dark eyes, with gentle, sad expression

Large rib cage gives excellent lung capacity

Hocks are close to ground, but not abruptly bent

Nose is black, with large, open nostrils

Long, lean paws are lighter than a greyhound's

BREED HISTORY The Sloughi probably accompanied the nomadic Arab tribes that invaded northwest Africa over 1,000 years ago. It may come from the Yemeni town of Saloug.

AZAWAKH

KEY FACTS

COUNTRY OF ORIGIN Mali
DATE OF ORIGIN Antiquity
FIRST USE Guarding, hunting
USE TODAY Companion, guarding, hunting
LIFE EXPECTANCY 12 years
OTHER NAME Tuareg Sloughi

WEIGHT RANGE
17–25 kg (37–55 lb)
HEIGHT RANGE
58–74 cm (23–29 in)

The Azawakh has a natural tendency to guard. These dogs often can be seen sleeping on the low, straw roofs of the village homes of their Mali owners. As a hyena or other night predator approaches, the first Azawakh to see it jumps down and is quickly joined by others; they form a pack and chase away or kill the intruder. The breed is alert, independent, and exceptionally fast, reaching speeds of up to 65 km/h (40 mph).

Flat head is slightly heavier than that of a greyhound

Well-developed nose allows dog to scent and sight hunt

Chest is not wide, but deep, reaching to elbow

Soft, short coat, typical of dogs that evolve in hot climates

Thighs are well dropped and flat

Forelegs are long, lean, elegant, straight, and well muscled

Elbows are carried compact to brisket; bones are flat and each tendon is distinct

BREED HISTORY Originally bred by the Tuareg tribes of the southern Sahara as a hunter and guardian, this African sight hound can now be found outside its native land. Used to course game such as hares and gazelles, the Azawakh slows the quarry until its owner arrives.

IRISH WOLFHOUND

BREED HISTORY Present in Ireland almost 2,000 years ago, this noble breed had almost completely vanished by the mid-1800s, when it was revitalized by Captain G.A. Graham, a British army officer.

Originally used by the Celts to hunt wolves, this majestic dog was probably transported to Ireland by the Romans. In the latter half of the 19th century, the breed was successfully recreated, using stock related to the ancient Wolfhound. Affectionate and loyal, today's Wolfhound makes an excellent companion and an effective guard dog. However, due to its enormous size, it needs a great deal of space and is therefore not ideally suited for city life.

KEY FACTS

COUNTRY OF ORIGIN Ireland
DATE OF ORIGIN Antiquity/1800s
FIRST USE Wolf hunting
USE TODAY Companion
LIFE EXPECTANCY 11 years

WEIGHT RANGE
40–55 kg (90–120 lb)
HEIGHT RANGE
71–90 cm (28–35 in)

Deep chest, with long body

Thighs are long and straight, like a greyhound's

Long head has little indentation between eyes

Muscular legs and forearms, with sturdy, straight bones

Rough, hardy topcoat is particularly wiry and long over eyes and under jaw

VARIETY
OF
COLOURS

DEERHOUND

Long head tapers slightly to eyes, then decidedly to nose

KEY FACTS

COUNTRY OF ORIGIN Great Britain
DATE OF ORIGIN Middle Ages
FIRST USE Deer hunting
USE TODAY Companion
LIFE EXPECTANCY 11–12 years
OTHER NAME Scottish Deerhound

WEIGHT RANGE
36–45 kg (80–100 lb)
HEIGHT RANGE
71–76 cm (28–30 in)

FAWN   RED   RED-BRINDLE

BLUE-GREY   GREY   BLACK-BRINDLE

Hair on body is harsher and more wiry than hair on belly

Long tail, thick at root, tapers at tip and almost reaches ground

Feet are compact, with very little feathering on legs, and only short hair between toes

BREED HISTORY The recorded history of the wistful-looking Deerhound begins in the Middle Ages, when Scottish chieftains used it for hunting. The collapse of the clan system in 1746 threatened its existence, until it was revived by a local breeder, Duncan McNeil.

Black-rimmed, dark-brown eyes, with gentle expression

Strong neck is well developed

Ownership of the graceful and gentle Deerhound was once restricted to the Scottish nobility; this is when the breed was developed to course deer through the dense forests of the Scottish Highlands. With the felling of the forests in the early 1700s and the introduction of the gun for hunting, the breed lost its popularity. Today, this dignified hound is most common in South Africa, while in Scotland its numbers are quite small. It is very much like a greyhound in appearance, but with a weather-resistant coat. A good-natured breed, it gets on well with other dogs.

WHIPPET

KEY FACTS

COUNTRY OF ORIGIN Great Britain
DATE OF ORIGIN 1800s
FIRST USE Coursing, racing
USE TODAY Companion, coursing, racing
LIFE EXPECTANCY 13–14 years

WEIGHT RANGE
12.5–13.5 kg (27–30 lb)
HEIGHT RANGE
43–51 cm (17–20 in)

Rose-shaped, small, finely textured ears are very mobile

Long, tapering tail is carried between legs when not in action

ANY COLOUR

BREED HISTORY In the 1800s, rabbit coursing was a popular sport in the north of England. To improve the acceleration of the terriers used in this sport, good coursing terriers were bred with small greyhounds, producing today's graceful Whippet.

Long, lean head tapers to nose

Bright, alert, brown eyes, with quiet, retiring look

The Whippet's aerodynamic body design is ideal for racing – over short distances it is capable of achieving speeds of up to 65 km/h (40 mph). At one time the breed was referred to as the "snap-dog", a possible reference to the snap of a whip. It may look and behave like a delicate breed, and it certainly enjoys the pleasures of curling up on sofas and beds, but in the field its personality changes to that of a robust, fearless, and successful hunter. The breed is gentle and affectionate, and has a good life expectancy. Its coat requires very little grooming, although its thin skin is prone to laceration.

Legs are well muscled and strongly boned, and covered by very thin skin

HUNGARIAN GREYHOUND

ANY COLOUR

Rarely seen outside Hungary and the Transylvania region of Rumania, this breed is still used in Hungary for coursing hares, and for racing over long distances. Its temperament is similar to that of its close relative, the English Greyhound: it is quiet, retiring, and does not make a very good watchdog, but it is by instinct a lively chaser. When worked as a coursing dog, it acts like a classic sight hound – it almost always follows by sight, and rarely relies on scent to track hares and larger game. An affectionate and docile companion, the breed is unlikely to snap or bite, and usually gets on well with other dogs. Its short coat offers little weather protection, even when it has grown to full length.

Short, smooth coat is noticeably longer during winter

Oval eyes are clear and bright, with gentle expression

Button-shaped ears are half raised when dog is alert

KEY FACTS

COUNTRY OF ORIGIN
Hungary
DATE OF ORIGIN Antiquity
FIRST USE Small-game hunting
USE TODAY Companion, coursing
LIFE EXPECTANCY 12–14 years
OTHER NAME Magyar Agar

WEIGHT RANGE
22–31 kg (49–68 lb)
HEIGHT RANGE
64–70 cm (25–27½ in)

Neck is long, muscular, and gently arched

Muzzle narrows to prominent nose, with large nostrils

BREED HISTORY This breed's predecessors accompanied the Magyars to present-day Hungary and Rumania in the 900s. In the centuries that followed, its development involved Asiatic sight hounds and the English Greyhound.

AMERICAN STAGHOUND

Rough, hard topcoat covers dense, fine undercoat

VARIETY OF COLOURS

Muzzle is long and slightly pointed, with only a slight indication of a stop

Jaws are long and powerful

Long tail reaches well below hocks

BREED HISTORY This rugged sight hound, which resembles a rough-coated greyhound, descends from the Scottish Deerhound, English Greyhound, and Irish Wolfhound, which were all exported to the United States in the late 1800s.

When the American West was being opened to settlers in the 1800s, wolves and Coyotes presented a threat to both people and livestock. The American Staghound evolved from the British coursing hounds that were large enough to take on and defeat a full-sized wolf. These dogs accompanied hunters as they cleared the land of predators. After settlements were established, hunting continued as a sport. Robust, muscular Staghounds were bred for fitness, but also to tolerate and work with other dogs. Hunters say that the Staghound is swift enough to catch and bring down the largest deer. Today, this breed is used exclusively for deer hunting; it is also becoming increasingly popular as a companion.

KEY FACTS

COUNTRY OF ORIGIN United States
DATE OF ORIGIN 1800s
FIRST USE Large-game hunting
USE TODAY Large-game hunting
LIFE EXPECTANCY 10–12 years

WEIGHT RANGE
29.5–45 kg (65–100 lb)
HEIGHT RANGE
63.5–84 cm (25–33 in)

LURCHER

BREED HISTORY Bred in Ireland and Great Britain by Irish gypsies and tinkers, the Lurcher's name is derived from the Romany word *lur*, meaning thief. Most prized was the short-haired Lurcher, descended mainly from greyhounds, and used for poaching rabbits and hares.

Rarely, if ever, seen outside Ireland and Great Britain, and never bred to a specific standard, the Lurcher is still an extremely common dog in its native islands. Historically, it was a cross breed, the result of matings between greyhounds and either collies or terriers. Today, breeding is carried out in a more systematic manner, with Lurcher bred to Lurcher to perpetuate the breed's prowess at rabbit and hare coursing. Gentle with people, it makes an amenable companion, but it has high-energy demands and is not well suited to city life. It is a natural racer, and will chase and kill any small game.

Long-haired variety

Small, dark, round eyes are alert

Small, wire-haired ears are high set

Short-haired variety

VARIETY OF COLOURS

Coat is short and smooth; undercoat thickens in winter

Legs are long and straight

Deep chest provides lung capacity for endurance

KEY FACTS

COUNTRY OF ORIGIN Great Britain/Ireland
DATE OF ORIGIN 1600s
FIRST USE Hare/rabbit coursing
USE TODAY Coursing, companion
LIFE EXPECTANCY 13 years

WEIGHT RANGE
27–32 kg (60–70 lb)
HEIGHT RANGE
69–76 cm (27–30 in)

RAMPUR GREYHOUND

BREED HISTORY An indigenous sight hound of the Indian subcontinent, the Rampur Greyhound may be related to the Afghan, but its smooth coat suggests that it is probably a close relative of the Sloughi. The breed's form was considerably altered with the introduction of English Greyhound blood in the 1800s.

Flat forehead has pronounced stop

Small eyes are set forwards and give excellent vision

KEY FACTS

COUNTRY OF ORIGIN India
DATE OF ORIGIN Antiquity
FIRST USE Game coursing
USE TODAY Game coursing
LIFE EXPECTANCY 10–12 years
OTHER NAME Rampur Dog

WEIGHT RANGE
23–32 kg (51–70½ lb)
HEIGHT RANGE
56–76 cm (22–30 in)

Tail is long and lean

Deep chest gives excellent space for large lungs and heart

Thick hindquarters provide power for rapid acceleration

Sure-footed feet are moderately small

Oone of the three remaining, distinct sight hound breeds of India (the others are the Banjara and Mahratta Greyhounds), this breed is named after the Indian State of Rampur, where it probably originated. It is rarely seen outside its native land, although it has reached Canada. A classic sight hound, the Rampur has been bred for eyesight, speed, and power. It is an instinctive courser, and is seldom kept as a companion. Its striking head has a pronounced stop and light-coloured eyes, giving it a distinctive and rather charming appearance. This is a powerful breed that is unsuitable for urban living.

Coat is short and smooth

Puppy

ITALIAN GREYHOUND

Small, high-set ears have dropped tips

Aperfect miniature, the high-stepping Italian Greyhound has been the companion of pharaohs of Egypt, rulers of the Roman Empire, and kings and queens of Europe. Discerning, a little bashful and retiring in temperament, but still a typically determined and resourceful dog, this sleek breed is an ideal companion for fastidious people. Its smooth, close coat sheds very little hair and produces almost no odour. Relaxed in temperament, it is not demanding; however, it does enjoy the comforts of life. Although its refined, thin-boned body is rather delicate, the breed's good nature is an asset in any dog-loving home.

 CREAM   FAWN   BLUE   BLACK

Skull and muzzle, separated by large eyes, are of equal length

Short, fine, smooth coat covers thin, close-fitting skin

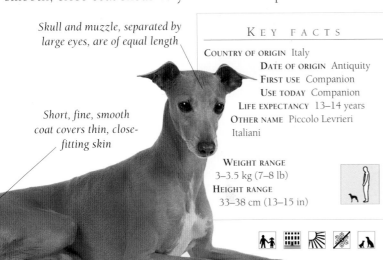

KEY FACTS

COUNTRY OF ORIGIN Italy
DATE OF ORIGIN Antiquity
FIRST USE Companion
USE TODAY Companion
LIFE EXPECTANCY 13–14 years
OTHER NAME Piccolo Levrieri Italiani

WEIGHT RANGE
3–3.5 kg (7–8 lb)
HEIGHT RANGE
33–38 cm (13–15 in)

Slender tail is low set

BREED HISTORY This graceful breed dates back to the classical Greek and Egyptian eras. It is a perfect sight hound in miniature, undoubtedly created thousands of years ago as a companion, by breeding down from standard-sized greyhounds.

Deep chest is suitable for endurance, but is rarely used to full capacity

SCENT HOUNDS

WHILE SIGHT HOUNDS rely upon vision and great speed to capture or corner prey, scent hounds use their noses and profound stamina to wear down game and bring it to bay. The Bloodhound, whose membrane lining to its nasal cavity is of a greater surface area than its entire body,

is the supreme scent follower. Although dogs use all their senses when hunting, hearing is relatively unimportant to the scent hound. The sight hound chases silently; the scent hound hunts methodically, but will bark or howl when it encounters the scent trail of its prey.

PENDULOUS EARS HELP DOG TO PICK UP SCENT

ROBUST LEGS ALLOW DOG TO CARRY OUT ENDURING, HARD WORK

Basset Hound
The Basset is a dwarf, with normal-length body but short bones and large joints.

Bloodhound
The world's largest scent hound originated in Belgium over 1,000 years ago, the result of careful breeding by the monks of St. Hubert's monastery.

Kerry Beagle
Bred as a pack-hunting scent hound in southern Ireland for hundreds of years, this breed has never been formally recognized.

CROOKED LEGS ARE COVERED WITH DENSELY FURRED SKIN

HUNTING COMPANIONS

No country was more efficient in developing varieties of scent hounds than medieval France. Hundreds of packs of scent hounds, some consisting of up to 1,000 dogs, worked the parks and forests of France for the pleasure of the king and his friends. Some scent hounds were smooth haired; others were wire haired – these were griffons. Yet others, called bassets, were bred with short legs so that hunters could

HEAD IS ROUND AND ELEGANT

accompany them on foot. For 1,000 years, until the French Revolution in 1789, the abbots of the Benedictine monastery of St. Hubert delivered annually to the king of France six St. Hubert Hounds. Today's Bloodhound is a descendant of this breed.

France produced other large hounds, including the Grand Bleu de Gascogne, Grand Gascon Saintongeois, Grand Griffon Vendéen, Grand Griffon Nivernais, Billy, and Poitevin. Some breeds, including the Chambray and Levesque, are now extremely rare, or even extinct. Smaller hunting dogs, called harriers (from the Norman *harier*, meaning to hunt), developed at the same time – the Ariégois, Porcelaine, Briquet Griffon Vendéen, Petit Bleu and Petit Griffon Bleu de Gascogne, and Griffon Fauve de Bretagne. Basset breeds developed in France included the Basset Bleu de Gascogne, Basset Fauve de Brétagne, Grand and Petit Basset Griffon Vendéens, and the Basset Artésien Normand, from which Great Britain's popular Basset Hound evolved. British aristocrats routinely acquired French scent hounds; likewise French breeders developed a great variety of Anglo-French scent hounds, many of which still exist today.

All scent hounds were bred for efficiency at work, not for looks or conformation. It was in Great Britain that the work which began in France reached its highest degree of sophistication, with the development of the Basset Hound, Beagle Foxhound, Otterhound, Staghound, and Harrier. Descendants of these dogs made their way to the United States, forming the genetic pool from which the American Foxhound and virtually all the American coonhounds derive.

SPECIALIZED SKILLS

Germany presented an exceptional contribution to the pool of scent hounds. The dachshund is a dwarfed scent hound, but because it has been intensively bred for aggressive temperament and going to earth, it is more appropriate to classify it with terriers. Crossing dachshunds with long-legged German scent hounds has, however, produced a unique

SOLID DOG, WITH WELL-MUSCLED BODY AND DEEP CHEST

Porcelaine
This is thought to be the oldest breed of French scent hound, descending from the now-extinct Montaimboeuf. It has a typically sensitive sense of smell and a delightfully musical voice.

Styrian Rough-haired Mountain Hound
One of Austria's finest scent hounds, this kindly breed is kept primarily by hunters and is rarely seen outside the regions in which it works.

FACIAL HAIR OFTEN PROTECTS EYES

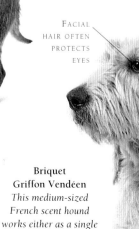

Briquet Griffon Vendéen
This medium-sized French scent hound works either as a single hunter or in packs.

Basset Bleu de Gascogne
A typical working basset, unlike the show-ring Basset Hound, the Basset Bleu de Gascogne has straight legs and strong, oval-shaped feet.

EARS ARE LONG AND PENDULOUS

Dobermann
Herr Louis Dobermann used a variety of dogs – the Rottweiler, Pinscher, and others – to produce this elegant breed.

Istrian Smooth-coated Hound
The most ancient of all the Balkan scent hounds, this dog probably traces its origins back to the primitive dogs brought to the area that is now Slovenia by Phoenicians.

EARS ARE SOMETIMES CROPPED TO GIVE DOG FIERCE EXPRESSION

Catahoula Leopard Dog
Originating in Catahoula, in the state of Louisiana, this breed is still used to round up pigs and cattle.

Poitevin
This pack dog, favoured by the nobility, was nearly wiped out during the French Revolution.

THIS TYPICAL SCENT HOUND'S COAT IS SMOOTH AND DENSE

THIS BREED HAS SERENE EXPRESSION

group of dogs, the dachsbrackes. The Swedish Drever evolved from dachsbrackes which were imported from Germany. In other parts of Germany, especially in Bavaria, cold-trailing hounds capable of following a blood trail that was days old were developed to fill that specific niche in the hunter's requirements. The Dobermann, bred for modern guard work, is a direct descendant of German black-and-tan hounds. In Switzerland, hunters generally accompanied their dogs on foot, so they produced robust but short-legged breeds such as the

Small Bernese Hound
One of eight different varieties of Swiss scent hound, the Small Bernese is a dwarfed, or "basseted", version of the Bernese Hound.

LEGS HAVE BEEN SHORTENED IN A TYPICAL DWARF STYLE

laufhunds. In the Austro-Hungarian Empire, however, the aristocracy hunted on horseback. In order to fulfil the hunters' demands, long-legged mountain hounds evolved in Transylvania, the Styrian mountains, and throughout the mountainous regions of the Balkans.

NEWEST BREEDS
In northern and Central Europe, Norwegian, Swedish, Finnish, and Polish breeders assiduously developed an efficient range of scent hounds in the 1800s, using stock from both central Europe and Russia. The Norwegian Dunker is the

living descendant of the now-extinct Russian Harlequin Hound. Russian scent hounds, such as the Tartary Hound, red-coloured Russian Hound, and black-and-fawn Russian Hound, used to work in tandem with the Borzoi, but most of these breeds became extinct after the Russian Revolution. New breeds such as the Estonian and Latvian Hounds also came into existence in the 19th century, and with the independence of the Baltic States, it is likely

Segugio Italiano
A delightfully distinctive breed, the Segugio was an extremely popular hunter in Renaissance Italy. It fell into decline, but today is enjoying a welcome revival both in Italy and abroad.

THICK SKIN HANGS IN FOLDS FROM NECK; THERE IS ALSO A MUCH RARER, ROUGH-COATED VARIETY

that a large proportion of these breeds will eventually increase in numbers. Scent hounds were the property of the nobility and existed primarily in Europe. A Chinese hound, however, which was similar in appearance to the European hounds, could be found in Jun-Han Province, China, until the beginning of this century. Elsewhere in the world, in countries such as Japan, indigenous dogs were frequently used to trail scent.

GENERAL CHARACTERISTICS
Scent hounds are generally amenable, and more willing to live together than other types of dog. Their formidable scenting ability is beyond human comprehension. They possess certain physical characteristics that help them to pick up the faintest scent; for example, their lopped and generally long ears create air currents that help them to detect scents, and their pendulous, moist lips can also trap scents. The intensity with which these dogs work is staggering. Some breeds do not have the killer's instinct, leaving the dirty work of the hunt to other dogs, such as terriers, or to humans.

Scent hounds are usually reliable with children and often with other dogs. As a group, they are not as demonstrative as terriers, as affectionate as companion dogs, or as trainable as gundogs. Scent hounds are most content when working, be it following the trail of a fox, or the paw prints of the last dog to cross its path.

BLOODHOUND

BREED HISTORY For centuries, the monks of the St. Hubert monastery in Belgium bred superb, scent-tracking hounds. At the same time, virtually identical hounds were bred in Great Britain. Both breeds had a common source – they may have accompanied crusaders who were returning to Europe from the Middle East.

Lower lids of eyes fall away to reveal part of inner surface

Eyes are set deeply in their sockets

Invariably black nose sits on tip of long muzzle

Short and fairly hard coat of hair covers body; hair feels softer on skull and ears

Skull is very high and prominent

Extremely long and graceful ears are low set

Forelegs are straight, solid, and muscular

Hocks are well developed on robust, straight back legs

Paws are compact and trim in relation to size of dog

RED   LIVER/TAN   BLACK/TAN

KEY FACTS

COUNTRY OF ORIGIN Belgium
DATE OF ORIGIN Middle Ages
FIRST USE Tracking ground scent
USE TODAY Companion, tracking
LIFE EXPECTANCY 10–12 years
OTHER NAMES St. Hubert Hound, Chien St. Hubert

WEIGHT RANGE
36–50 kg (80–110 lb)
HEIGHT RANGE
58–69 cm (23–27 in)

Powerful shoulders allow dog to work for long hours without a break

Tail is carried in elegant curve above topline of back

Lower lips hang 5 cm (2 in) below jaw bone

Neck is very well muscled and has pendulous dewlap

Back is extraordinarily strong for size of dog

Throughout the world, breeds such as the American coonhounds, Swiss Jura hounds, Brazilian Fila Brasileiro, Bavarian Mountain Hound, and many others trace their lineage back to this ancient scent tracker. Today, all Bloodhounds are black and tan, liver and tan, or red, but in the Middle Ages they occurred in other solid colours. The white variety, which existed in medieval Europe, was called the Talbot Hound. By the 1600s, this strain had died out as a breed, although its genes continue in dogs as diverse as white Boxers and tricoloured Basset Hounds. The Bloodhound thrives on the hunt rather than the kill – it revels in tracking and has been used to hunt animals, criminals, runaway slaves, and lost children. Today, this plodding, sonorously voiced breed is both tracker and companion. Although affable in temperament, it is not easy to obedience train.

HARRIER

Expressive head is not quite as broad as that of a Beagle

Rather small, somewhat oval-shaped, brown eyes give good binocular vision

Long neck is well rooted in shoulders and slightly rounded at upper part

Feet are compact, but less so than a cat's

Upper lips overhang lower jaw

Puppy

Muzzle is pointed rather than wedge shaped

Historical records reveal that a pack of British Harriers, the Penistone pack, existed as early as 1260 in the west of England. Later records demonstrate that the Harrier was also a popular pack hound in Wales. By this century, however, the breed was near extinction in its country of origin. It was revived through the introduction of foxhound bloodlines – today's Harrier, be it a leopard hunter in Sri Lanka, a fox hunter in the Eastern United States, or a scent trailer in the Columbian mountains, is a successful mix of foxhound and Beagle temperaments. It is a breed that is at ease with its own kind and bonds well with other dog breeds. The Harrier also makes an excellent companion – slightly smaller than a foxhound, its future in Europe and North America is likely to be in the home rather than in the pack.

Lightly tufted, medium-length tail is carried high

Straight, well-muscled back is free of inherited defects

Skull is quite flat, with slight prominence to occipital bones

Smooth coat is short and flat

Chest is deeper than it is broad

BREED HISTORY The Harrier was developed in the west country of England at least 800 years ago, and probably descends from the Bloodhound crossed with ancestors of today's Beagle. Its name derives from the Norman French word *harier*, which means hunting dog. Today, this breed is secure in both Great Britain and the United States.

VARIETY OF COLOURS

Forelegs are straight, muscular, and robust

KEY FACTS

COUNTRY OF ORIGIN Great Britain
DATE OF ORIGIN Middle Ages
FIRST USE Hare hunting
USE TODAY Hare/fox hunting, companion
LIFE EXPECTANCY 11–12 years

WEIGHT RANGE 22–27 kg (48–60 lb)
HEIGHT RANGE 46–56 cm (18–22 in)

GRAND ANGLO-FRANÇAIS BLANC ET NOIR

BREED HISTORY The Grand Anglo-Françaises occur in three colour variations – tricolour, black and white, and orange and white. Recognized as three separate breeds, they were produced by crossing the English Foxhound with French hounds.

Head is relatively flat

Long ears are set level with eyes

Moderately thick tail hangs with curl

Upper lips are moderately tight and do not overhang lower lips

Black-and-white coat colour distinguishes this breed from the tricolour

Straight hind legs like a foxhound's

Eyes always have gentle expression

KEY FACTS

COUNTRY OF ORIGIN France
DATE OF ORIGIN Late 1800s
FIRST USE Large-game hunting
USE TODAY Deer/wild boar/fox hunting
LIFE EXPECTANCY 10 years
OTHER NAME Large Anglo-French Black-and-white Hound

WEIGHT RANGE
34.5–35.5 kg (76–78 lb)
HEIGHT RANGE
62–72 cm (24–28 in)

The Grand Anglo-Français Blanc et Noir is virtually indentical to its cousin, the Tricolore. As its name indicates, it is black and white in colour, and it is probably related to the Bleu de Gascogne and Gascon Saintongeois. A powerful dog, with a strong bone structure, it has immense stamina and is used to hunt large game such as red and roe deer, and wild boars. It is less popular than the Tricolore and is rarely, if ever, kept as a companion.

GRAND ANGLO-FRANÇAIS TRICOLORE

Tapering tail distends to hocks when limp and rises above back when dog is excited

Tricolour, double coat of short, thick topcoat and fine, softer undercoat

Eyes are moderate in size, with gentle expression

Large ears hang with soft fold; base rises to eye level when dog is alert

Head is long and moderately broad, with distinct stop

The Grand Anglo-Français Tricolore is the most popular of the large French hound breeds and is, in part, descended from the Poitevin and English Foxhound. Although this breed looks predominantly like a French hound, its foxhound origins are apparent in its solid stature and unsculptured head. Its striking appearance and gentle disposition have attracted non-hunters, and it is sometimes kept as a companion. However, it is primarily a working dog, and is happiest when hunting with the pack.

Eyes may vary considerably in colour

KEY FACTS

COUNTRY OF ORIGIN France
DATE OF ORIGIN 1800s
FIRST USE Large-game hunting
USE TODAY Hunting, companion
LIFE EXPECTANCY 10 years
OTHER NAME Large Anglo-French Tricoloured Hound
WEIGHT RANGE
34.5–35.5 kg (76–78 lb)
HEIGHT RANGE
62–72 cm (24–28 in)

BREED HISTORY Like the Grand Anglo-Français Blanc et Noir, this breed is descended from old-type French hounds, which were crossed with the English Foxhound. The third colour, white and orange, is now extremely rare. There are separate standards for each colour variation.

Français Blanc et Noir

Tail is thick at root and carried high when dog is alert

Neck is long and moderately strong

Nose is large and black, with big, open nostrils

Dense, rugged, short coat has extended, black-saddle marking

KEY FACTS

COUNTRY OF ORIGIN France
DATE OF ORIGIN 1900s
FIRST USE Small-game hunting
USE TODAY Small-game hunting
LIFE EXPECTANCY 10 years
OTHER NAME French Black-and-white Hound

WEIGHT RANGE
34.5–35.5 kg (76–78 lb)
HEIGHT RANGE
65–72 cm (25½–28 in)

Long legs, with muscular thighs

BREED HISTORY Henri de Falandre, a French breeder, produced this classic, black-and-white scent hound by crossing the English Foxhound with the Bleu de Gascogne and other large French hounds.

The Français Blanc et Noir has a majestic presence, an arresting coat pattern, and a superb voice. Its powerful build and robust bone structure are reminiscent of its close relative, the Gascon Saintongeois. Generally used to hunt small game, it is an excellent working dog and has boundless energy. Like the Grand Anglo-Françaises, it has a kindly, gentle disposition – good with children and easy to obedience train, this breed very rarely snaps at people. However, it is not bred for city life and may not be suitable for urban environments.

Head is moderately domed

Low-set ears can reach tip of nose

Français Tricolore

Large, alert-looking eyes

Ears are set at eye level and fold inwards at tips

BREED HISTORY A re-creation of an historic pack hound, this breed was developed by Henri de Falandre by crossing the Poitevin, Billy, Saintongeois, and perhaps the Bleu de Gascogne with the English Foxhound. The Français Tricolore was officially recognized in 1965.

Head is elongated and slightly domed

Short, fine coat has black-and-tan saddle

Thighs are long and muscular, with well-angulated hocks

The second most common of the French hounds, the Français Tricolore is sturdy but elegant. Used to hunt all types of small game, this breed can move very quickly, over a variety of terrain. It has immense stamina, and is able to work for long hours at a time. The breed is content to live outdoors, needs little coat maintenance, and is unlikely to snap at people, although it may snap at other dogs. If taken from a working pack, it makes a poor watchdog, and an equally poor companion. If raised from puppyhood in a family home, it can make a reasonably good house dog. However, it needs a great deal of exercise and is happiest when on the trail of game.

Nose is large and black, with wide-open nostrils

KEY FACTS

COUNTRY OF ORIGIN France
DATE OF ORIGIN 1900s
FIRST USE Small-game hunting
USE TODAY Small-game hunting, companion
LIFE EXPECTANCY 10 years
OTHER NAME French Tricoloured Hound

WEIGHT RANGE
34.5–35.5 kg (76–78 lb)
HEIGHT RANGE
62–72 cm (24–28 in)

GRAND BLEU DE GASCOGNE

BREED HISTORY The origins of this ancient dog may lie in racing breeds brought to France by Phoenician traders. It is certainly one of the oldest of hounds whose ancestry cannot be traced.

Deep-chestnut eyes look mournful but gentle

Nose is black and well developed, with long, strong bridge

Very low-set and distinctive ears are slightly curled

Coat is fairly thick, quite long, and profuse

Oval, wolf-like feet, with lean toes

Well-muscled forelegs support massive shoulders

Originating in the hot, dry Midi region of south-west France, this breed is now more numerous in the United States, where it has been bred since the 1700s, than in its country of origin. On both sides of the Atlantic, the elegant and majestic Grand Bleu is used almost solely as a scent-trailing working dog. It is not particularly fast, but has formidable staying power. It declined in numbers when wolves in France became extinct. The Grand Bleus exhibited at French dog shows 100 years ago were predominantly black in colour.

KEY FACTS

COUNTRY OF ORIGIN France
DATE OF ORIGIN Middle Ages
FIRST USE Deer/wild boar/wolf hunting
USE TODAY Gundog work, sometimes in packs
LIFE EXPECTANCY 12–14 years
OTHER NAME Large Blue Gascony Hound

WEIGHT RANGE
32–35 kg (71–77 lb)
HEIGHT RANGE
62–72 cm (24–28 in)

PETIT BLEU DE GASCOGNE

KEY FACTS

COUNTRY OF ORIGIN France
DATE OF ORIGIN Middle Ages
FIRST USE Rabbit hunting
USE TODAY Gundog for rabbits and hares
LIFE EXPECTANCY 12 years
OTHER NAME Small Blue Gascony Hound

WEIGHT RANGE
18–22 kg (40–48 lb)
HEIGHT RANGE
50–60 cm (20–23 in)

Rarer than the Grand Bleu, the Petit Bleu, which is still most prevalent in south-west France, is small only in name. Its superior nose makes it an excellent hound to follow the faint scent of the hare. It is a resourceful and determined breed, which is relatively easy to obedience train and gets on extremely well with other dogs. Its thick, dense coat provides effective protection against the elements, and it is primarily a working hound, well suited to the countryside.

BREED HISTORY This breed was created through selective breeding of the Grand Bleu de Gascogne for reduction in size, in order to hunt small quarry.

Refined looking head is long, light, and delicate

Low-set ears are thicker and less curled than a Grand Bleu's

Thighs are quite flat, with powerful muscles

Oval, fairly long feet have black pads and usually tan hair

Deep chest houses ample space for large lungs

Forelegs are surprisingly strong in relation to rest of body

PETIT GRIFFON DE GASCOGNE

Large, prominent nose is always jet black

Ears, set at eye level, hang quite flat

BREED HISTORY This rare breed's rough appearance is probably the result of breeding the slightly larger Petit Bleu de Gascogne with the Wire-haired Pointing Griffon. This produced a dog with size and markings similar to the Petit Bleu.

Slightly wavy coat is never woolly or frizzy

Bright, golden eyes are less prominent than a Petit Bleu's

This breed retains the colour distribution of the Petit Bleu – slate-blue body with black spots and tan restricted to the head and feet – but with the addition of the coarse, bushy coat of the Griffon. Its temperament is similar to that of the Petit Bleu – good natured, hard working, uncomplaining, and diligent. When kept in a hunting pack, however, it can be aggressive. Despite the breed's working ability, and favourable looks and temperament, it is surprisingly uncommon.

Slanting shoulders are well muscled

Round, compact feet have hard, black nails

BASSET BLEU DE GASCOGNE

BREED HISTORY The breed's origins are lost, and today's Basset Bleu de Gascogne is a re-creation of the original breed by the French breeder Alain Bourbon.

Deep-brown eyes have gentle, melancholy appearance

Long, thin, folded ears are as long as muzzle

Lips are quite accentuated; roof of mouth is black

Forehead is long, with slight curve; markings are always symmetrical

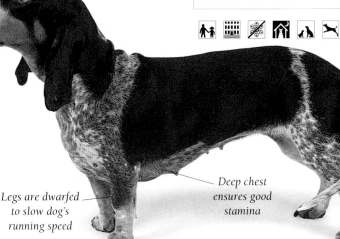

The Basset Bleu is an excellent companion and hunter, suitable for either town or countryside. It is not difficult to obedience train, and with a little encouragement can make a moderately good watchdog. Its relatively short coat makes it rather sensitive to the cold. Breeders in France are of the opinion that this breed is susceptible to gastric torsion, a life-threatening condition that occurs when the stomach twists on itself, usually after a large meal. The Basset Bleu has a good voice and a fine nose.

Legs are dwarfed to slow dog's running speed

Deep chest ensures good stamina

Oval feet have hard, black nails and strong, black pads

CHIEN D'ARTOIS

BREED HISTORY One of the oldest French scent hounds, its other French name, Briquet, may be a modification of *braquet*, meaning small braque or small hound. The breed nearly disappeared in the 1800s, but was retained in almost pure form by the Prince de Conde.

Short, thick, tricolour coat over thick skin

Long, arched tail has "sickle" shape

Moderately wide chest is covered in short hair

Muscular thighs are wide

Strong, lean feet, with fairly long toes

Dogs similar to this medium-sized scent hound appear in descriptions of French kings' hunting scenes from the 1400s. Because of their small size, they survived the ravages of the French Revolution more successfully than the long-legged scent hounds. By the mid-1800s, these pack hounds were used on small game, and were at their best working through thick undergrowth. With popularity, however, came indiscriminate cross breeding with imported British gundogs. Only a few packs retained their original type, but through the efforts of breeders earlier this century, type was re-established. This breed requires firm training, and males can be dominant.

KEY FACTS

COUNTRY OF ORIGIN France
DATE OF ORIGIN 1400s
FIRST USE Hare hunting
USE TODAY Companion, gundog
LIFE EXPECTANCY 12–14 years
OTHER NAME Briquet

WEIGHT RANGE 18–24 kg (40–53 lb)
HEIGHT RANGE 52–58 cm (20½–23 in)

Drooping lips give melancholy look

ARIÉGEOIS

BREED HISTORY This breed is probably the result of a crossing of the Chien d'Artois with either, or both, the Bleu de Gascogne and Gascon Saintongeois. First recognized in 1912, it is seldom seen outside France.

Head is long and lean

KEY FACTS

COUNTRY OF ORIGIN France
DATE OF ORIGIN 1900s
FIRST USE Small-game hunting
USE TODAY Small-game hunting, companion
LIFE EXPECTANCY 12 years

WEIGHT RANGE 25–30 kg (55–66 lb)
HEIGHT RANGE 53–61 cm (21–24 in)

Thin ears are low set

Dark eyes have gentle expression

Base of wide-set ears is at eye level

Forelegs are straight

Lean feet have thick pads

Fine hair covers supple skin

Easygoing, affectionate, relaxed with children, and amenable with other dogs, this scent hound has successfully made the transition from pack hound to household companion. The Ariégeois is, however, primarily a hunter and, given the opportunity, uses it fine nose and its sonorous and beautiful voice while following hares and other small game. Its origins in Ariége, south-west France, have prepared it for living in warm climates. Although a relative newcomer, this breed is similar in form and function to the ancient Petit Bleu de Gascogne.

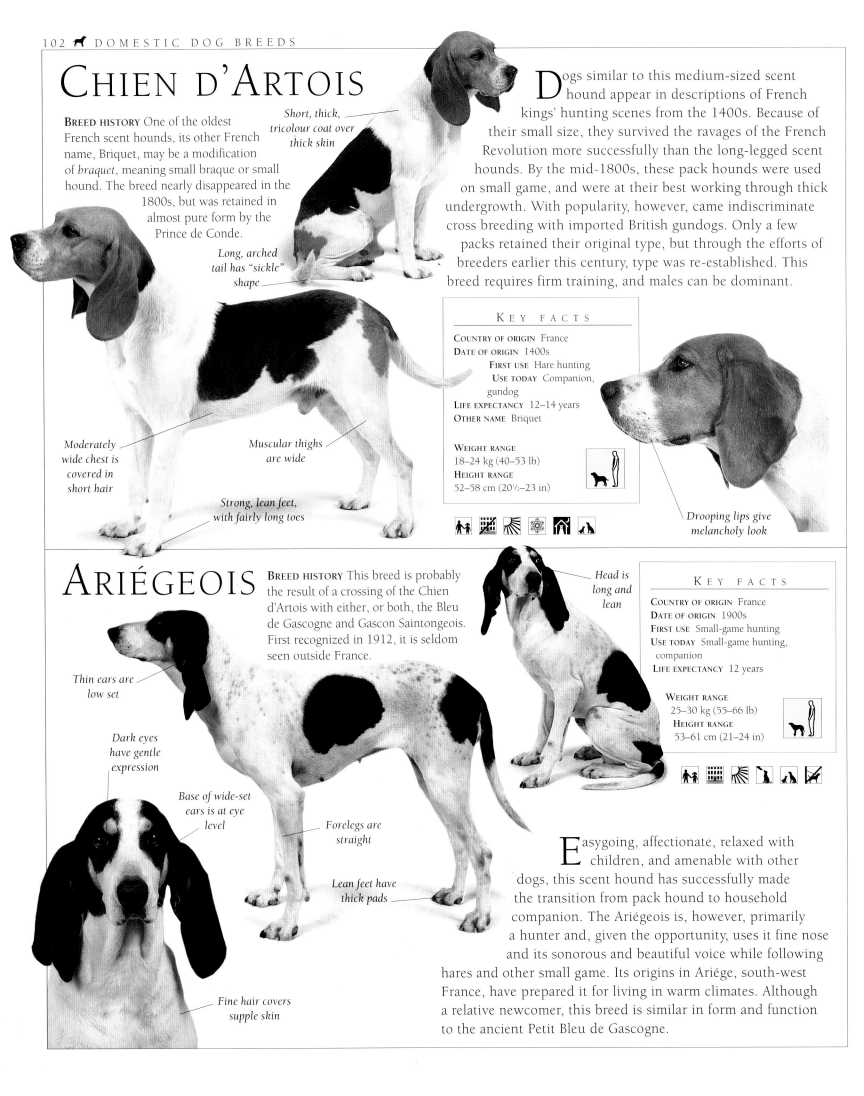

GRIFFON NIVERNAIS

BREED HISTORY Rough-coated, long-legged hounds have existed in France for at least 800 years. This breed may descend from the now-extinct Gris de St. Louis (the greyhound described by King Charles IX in *La Chasse Royale*) and the Chien de Bresse, a local breed.

There is slight beard on chin

The Griffon Nivernais may trace its ancestry back to rough-coated hounds brought to central Europe by Mediterranean traders. The descendants of these dogs thrived especially well in the central Nivernais and Vendéen regions of France. The French Revolution decimated and scattered this rustic breed, but it was revived by breeders at the turn of the century. The Griffon Nivernais needs firm training and is sometimes slow to respond to obedience work. It is built for endurance, rather than just for speed, and it tends to run after anything that moves.

Longish head, with bristly eyebrows

Topcoat is long and shaggy

Fairly short tail

Ears have slight twist at tips

FAWN GREY BLACK

Shoulders are set close to body

Brisket is not very wide

Feet are slightly elongated

KEY FACTS	
COUNTRY OF ORIGIN France	
DATE OF ORIGIN 1200s	
FIRST USE Large-game hunting	
USE TODAY Game hunting, companion	
LIFE EXPECTANCY 12 years	
OTHER NAME Chien de Pays	

WEIGHT RANGE
23–25 kg (50–55 lb)
HEIGHT RANGE
53–64 cm (21–24 in)

BASSET ARTÉSIEN NORMAND

BREED HISTORY Originating in Artois and Normandy, this short but straight-legged hound is the forebear of the more crooked-legged, and popular, British Basset Hound. This century's European wars decimated its numbers, but the breed was saved from extinction by a French breeder, Leparoux de Combrée.

Robust tail tapers at tip

Long back is prone to disc disease

Large, black nose protrudes slightly beyond lips

Supple, fine ears hang in folds

Large, serious-looking eyes

Upper lips cover lower lips

TAN/WHITE TRI-COLOUR

Bassets are dwarfed, full-sized hounds, retaining the body lengths of their forebears, but with enlarged heads, shortened long bones, and bigger joints. Their short stature allows hunters to follow them easily on foot. By the turn of this century, this breed was developing into two distinct lines, straight-legged hunters and crooked-legged, droopy-eared companion and show dogs. Around 1900, Léon Verrier, a French breeder, developed today's standard, which blends attributes of both varieties. The breed makes a charming companion – it is happy living in town or country, is fairly easy to obedience train, and gets on well with people.

KEY FACTS	
COUNTRY OF ORIGIN France	
DATE OF ORIGIN 1600s	
FIRST USE Rabbit/hare/roe deer tracking	
USE TODAY Companion, hunting	
LIFE EXPECTANCY 13–15 years	
OTHER NAME Basset Artois	

WEIGHT RANGE
14.5–15.5 kg (32–34 lb)
HEIGHT RANGE
25–36 cm (10–14 in)

GRAND GASCON-SAINTONGEOIS

BREED HISTORY In the 1840s, Baron Joseph de Caryon Latour de Virelade, using careful and selective breeding, crossed the Grand Bleu de Gascogne with the Santongeois and the Ariégeois to produce this breed.

Dark-brown eyes

KEY FACTS

COUNTRY OF ORIGIN France
DATE OF ORIGIN 1800s
FIRST USE Roe-deer hunting
USE TODAY Gundog, companion
LIFE EXPECTANCY 11–12 years
OTHER NAME Virelade

WEIGHT RANGE
30–32 kg (66–71 lb)
HEIGHT RANGE
63–71 cm (25–28 in)

Skull is long and pointed

Well-set, round tail

Thin ears hang in folds

Hocks are set well down

Legs are long, straight, and well boned

Rather large, oval feet

This muscular, leggy hound is an inveterate hunter, and is still used to hunt roe deer and other large game. Although virtually never seen outside France, it remains a popular pack hound, especially in the south-west, near the Pyrenees. The Grand Gascon-Saintongeois is gentle and safe with children, gets on well with other dogs, and will rarely snap or bite. It has never been bred solely for companionship, but if raised in a home from puppyhood, it makes a reasonable house dog. Easy to obedience train, the breed requires frequent exercise.

ANGLO-FRANÇAIS DE PETITE VÉNERIE

ORANGE/ WHITE   BLACK/ WHITE   TRI- COLOUR

Eyes are small

Once known simply as the Petit Anglo-Français, this breed, unlike the Anglo-Français and Français hounds, is the result of planned breeding. Produced in the first half of this century from crosses between the French Poitevin, Porcelaine, and Beagle or Beagle Harrier, breeders are continuing to develop it as a pack hound for scent trailing small game such as pheasants, quails, and rabbits. It has proved to be an amenable house dog – a little reserved – but otherwise obedient and willing. In the early stages of the breed's development some rough-coated puppies emerged, but this coat variety is no longer seen. Dignified and calm, it is very possible that its popularity as a companion will soon increase.

Head is well rounded

Pointed muzzle, with black nose

Eyes are quite deeply set

KEY FACTS

COUNTRY OF ORIGIN France
DATE OF ORIGIN 1970s
FIRST USE Small-game hunting
USE TODAY Hunting, companion
LIFE EXPECTANCY 12 years
OTHER NAME Small Anglo-French Hound

WEIGHT RANGE
16–20 kg (35–44 lb)
HEIGHT RANGE
48–56 cm (19–22 in)

BREED HISTORY A smaller version of the Grand Anglo-Français hounds, this is the most recent development in French hounds, produced by crossing the Beagle or Beagle Harrier with medium-sized, French, short-haired hounds. Its first standard was prepared in 1978.

GRIFFON FAUVE DE BRETAGNE

BREED HISTORY The wolf-hunting Fauve de Bretagne is mentioned in 1570 by King Charles IX in *La Chasse Royale* as one of four different French hounds. The Griffon Fauve and Basset Fauve are direct descendants of this breed. It may also be related to the Welsh Foxhound.

Hard coat, with pronounced eyebrows

WHEATEN, GOLD, FAWN   RED

Muzzle is long, straight, and slightly hooked

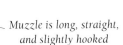

Shoulders slope to sturdy forelegs

Strong, muscular thighs

Neat feet, with firm, hard pads

An ancient breed, the Griffon Fauve de Bretagne remains an excellent scent hound – Brittany farmers once used its prowess in tracking wolves. In 1885 the breed nearly became extinct, and breeders introduced Briquet Griffon Vendéen blood in order to revive it. Visually, it bears a close resemblance to the Griffon Vendéen. In France today, working ability remains integral to the breed's show standard, although it now acts more frequently as a gundog than as a pack hound. With its elongated muzzle and strong build, the dog makes a tenacious hunter. It is also an affable companion and an excellent house dog, although, like most scent hounds, it makes a poor watchdog.

Ears are covered with soft hair

BASSET FAUVE DE BRETAGNE

FAWN   RED

Longish skull has pronounced occiput

Long muzzle leads to large, black nose

Golden hair is thick and harsh

Thick tail is not too long

Thick ears are set below eye level

A typical basset, with a long body and short legs, the Basset Fauve has neither the smooth coat of the Artésien Normand nor the rough, wiry coat of the Griffon Vendéen, but rather a coarse, hard coat. Tenacious and durable, it both scents and flushes game, and is most at home working difficult terrain. Traditionally, this basset hunted in packs of four, but when it works today it is more likely to hunt singly or with a partner. It is a lively, opinionated breed, more difficult to obedience train than the Griffon Fauve. Although it makes a fine companion, like most dogs, it is unhappy when confined and thrives on physical activity.

Straight forelegs

Long bones are dwarfed

BREED HISTORY Produced by crossing the Griffon Fauve de Bretagne with short-legged hounds from the Vendée region, the Basset Fauve de Bretagne is still rarely seen outside France, except in Great Britain, where it has endeared itself to many breeders.

GRAND GRIFFON VENDÉEN

Relaxed look to eyes, although breed can be excitable

WHITE, CREAM | WHEATEN -ORANGE | TRICOLOUR

Dense coat protects skin from damage, and body from cold

BREED HISTORY This breed, which was developed hundreds of years ago in the Vendée region of France, is descended from the Italian St. Hubert Hound and the Griffon Nivernais.

Muscular, robust, and well-proportioned thighs

KEY FACTS

COUNTRY OF ORIGIN France
DATE OF ORIGIN Middle Ages
FIRST USE Boar hunting
USE TODAY Large-game (roe-deer and wild-boar) hunting
LIFE EXPECTANCY 12 years
OTHER NAME Large Vendéen Griffon

WEIGHT RANGE
30–35 kg (66–77 lb)
HEIGHT RANGE
60–66 cm (23–26 in)

Walks softly – can be a sign of nervousness

Strong thigh muscles for hunting

Grass seeds catch easily in dense fur between toes

T his ancient breed had almost completely disappeared from France by the end of World War II. Breeders revived it by introducing bloodlines from the Anglo-Français and the Billy. The result is a dog with a rough and wiry topcoat and a thick, downy undercoat. This combination makes it extremely suitable for working in water, but also means that the coat needs routine grooming if you want to avoid a strong, natural dog odour. The breed is structurally very sound, but this is the rarest of the hunting Vendéens and its future is uncertain.

BRIQUET GRIFFON VENDÉEN

Large, black nose is surrounded by facial whiskers

BREED HISTORY The Briquet was developed from the Grand Griffon Vendéen to hunt small game. Griffon is a variation of the old French word *greffier* (clerk). One of the original breeders was the French king's clerk.

T his ancient breed, never prevalent, was severely reduced in numbers during World War II. Still relatively unknown, even in France, the Briquet has a tendency to be stubborn and needs experienced handling if it is to be used as a gundog. Its dense, waterproof coat makes it an ideal gundog for all types of weather and terrain, including water. The Briquet makes a reasonably good watchdog, and adapts to city life if raised in an urban environment from an early age. Some individuals have a tendency to be snappy, although the breed is usually good with children.

Thick-boned, muscular legs are ideal for active work

CREAM

TRICOLOUR | WHITE/ ORANGE

Pendulous upper lips can produce copious saliva

Dense, wiry coat is never woolly

KEY FACTS

COUNTRY OF ORIGIN France
DATE OF ORIGIN 1600s
FIRST USE Gundog
USE TODAY Gundog, companion
LIFE EXPECTANCY 12 years
OTHER NAME Medium Vendéen Griffon

WEIGHT RANGE
22–24 kg (48–53 lb)
HEIGHT RANGE
50–55 cm (20–22 in)

GRAND BASSET GRIFFON VENDÉEN

WHITE GREY BLACK/WHITE TAN/WHITE TRICOLOUR

Fur on eyebrows does not completely cover friendly eyes

BREED HISTORY The breed was selectively created by a French breeder, Paul Desamy. Its bloodline was established by the middle of the 1940s.

Ears hang to tip of nose when scenting

Long, robust neck is thickest at shoulders

KEY FACTS

COUNTRY OF ORIGIN France
DATE OF ORIGIN 1800s
FIRST USE Gundog, hare coursing
USE TODAY Companion, gundog
LIFE EXPECTANCY 12 years
OTHER NAME Large Vendéen Griffon Basset

WEIGHT RANGE
18–20 kg (40–44 lb)
HEIGHT RANGE
38–42 cm (15–16 in)

Taller than most bassets, the Grand Basset is a handsome and independent breed, with a strong will of its own. Although obstinate, it is not a dangerous dog. It is an affectionate breed, with a lower-than-average tendency to snap or bite. The Grand Basset enjoys working on its own or in a pack, and with proper training makes a good rabbit and hare hunter. Adaptable and content to live in a city environment, its dense coat needs regular grooming.

Skull is domed, elongated, and not too wide

Straight, lean shoulders, well muscled over heavy bone

Trim feet permit effortless walking

PETIT BASSET GRIFFON VENDÉEN

The most popular of all the griffon vendéens, the Petit Basset has gained the affection of breeders and owners in many parts of the world, including Great Britain and the United States. Truly basset in shape, this alert, enthusiastic dog has a tendency to suffer from back pain. Males are known to fight among themselves for "top dog" recognition from their human caretakers. The breed prefers brisk, cool weather to sultry, humid heat.

Petit

Large, dark eyes have engaging and relaxed expression

Short legs are, nevertheless, firm and straight

Grand

BREED HISTORY The Petit Basset has its ancient origins in the Vendée region of France. In 1947, its characteristics were fixed by Abel Desamy, a French breeder.

KEY FACTS

COUNTRY OF ORIGIN France
DATE OF ORIGIN 1700s
FIRST USE Hare coursing
USE TODAY Companion, gundog
LIFE EXPECTANCY 12 years
OTHER NAME Little Griffon Vendéen Basset

WEIGHT RANGE
14–18 kg (31–40 lb)
HEIGHT RANGE
34–38 cm (13–15 in)

Chest is as deep as a Grand Basset's

WHITE ORANGE/WHITE TRICOLOUR

ENGLISH FOXHOUND

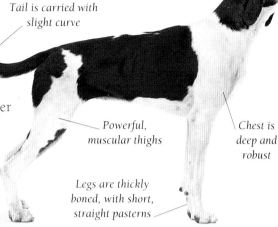

Tail is carried with slight curve

Powerful, muscular thighs

Chest is deep and robust

Legs are thickly boned, with short, straight pasterns

A good voice, a keen nose, a rugged constitution, and an ability to get on with other dogs are all hallmarks of the English Foxhound. At one time the shape and size of individuals varied across Great Britain. Hounds from Yorkshire were the fastest, while those from Staffordshire were larger and slower, with deeper voices. Today, most English Foxhounds share a similar shape and personality. Although rarely kept as a domestic pet, the breed does make an excellent companion, and its solid voice and attentive nature make it a good guard dog. It is gentle, affectionate, and even tempered, although it can be rather difficult to obedience train. It also has a strong instinct to chase and kill fox-sized animals.

BREED HISTORY In 14th-century Great Britain, fox hunting became popular, creating a demand for speedy dogs. From imported French hounds and native stock, fast, lean hounds eventually evolved.

Eyes are large and set well apart

Muzzle is quite square and straight

BICOLOUR

TRICOLOUR

KEY FACTS

COUNTRY OF ORIGIN Great Britain
DATE OF ORIGIN 1400s
FIRST USE Fox hunting
USE TODAY Fox hunting
LIFE EXPECTANCY 11 years

WEIGHT RANGE
25–34 kg (55–75 lb)
HEIGHT RANGE
58–69 cm (23–27 in)

OTTERHOUND

KEY FACTS

COUNTRY OF ORIGIN Great Britain
DATE OF ORIGIN Antiquity
FIRST USE Otter hunting
USE TODAY Companion
LIFE EXPECTANCY 12 years

WEIGHT RANGE
30–55 kg (65–120 lb)
HEIGHT RANGE
58–69 cm (23–27 in)

ANY HOUND COLOUR

Harsh, bristly topcoat covers woolly undercoat

Hindquarters are well muscled

BREED HISTORY The Otterhound could be descended from the Bloodhound. Alternatively, it could be a cross between large, rough-coated terriers, ancient foxhounds, and the French Nivernais Griffon.

Deep-set eyes have serious expression

Lips are fairly heavy

G reat Britain produced different hounds for different game, such as the Foxhound for foxes, the Harrier for hares, and the Bloodhound for boars. The Otterhound was created to enter the coldest river and follow an otter to its den. Now that otters are no longer regarded as pests, the Otterhound's original function no longer applies. Fortunately, it has a cheerful disposition, enjoys human companionship, and is reasonably good with children and with other animals. The breed can, however, be stubbornly independent, especially when it sees or smells water.

Back is long, strong, slightly arched, and covered by dense, insulating double coat

Toes are suitably webbed for efficient swimming

BASSET HOUND

Often stubborn, but usually gentle and benign, the Basset was once a superb hunting dog. Its pendulous ears may have been useful for picking up scent, particularly on damp mornings. Even now, lighter boned Bassets with slightly longer legs and shallower bodies participate in field trials, but the typical pet Basset is heavy, long, and low. Today, the breed is the cartoonist's and advertiser's delight. In the United States, the cartoon character, Fred Basset, personifies droll good humour, while worldwide the Basset has been used to symbolize the comfort of well-fitting shoes.

BREED HISTORY The Basset Hound may descend from "dwarfed" bloodhounds. Although it originated in France, it is now popular in Great Britain and the United States.

Slightly sunken eyes look soft

TRICOLOUR LEMON/ WHITE

Weight is born evenly on centre of paws without splaying toes

Thick tail is carried with slight curve

Head is large and long

Ears hang in loose folds

KEY FACTS

COUNTRY OF ORIGIN France
DATE OF ORIGIN 1500s
FIRST USE Rabbit/hare hunting
USE TODAY Companion, hunting
LIFE EXPECTANCY 12 years

WEIGHT RANGE
18–27 kg (40–60 lb)
HEIGHT RANGE
33–38 cm (13–15 in)

Ears are long and low set

Hocks are straight; legs point ahead

Elbows are set against deep chest

BEAGLE

KEY FACTS

COUNTRY OF ORIGIN Great Britain
DATE OF ORIGIN 1300s
FIRST USE Rabbit/hare hunting
USE TODAY Companion, gundog, field trials
LIFE EXPECTANCY 13 years
OTHER NAME English Beagle

WEIGHT RANGE
8–14 kg (18–30 lb)
HEIGHT RANGE
33–41 cm (13–16 in)

Although the Beagle is independent, with a strong tendency to wander off when distracted, it is a popular companion because of its affectionate nature and low degree of aggression. An endearing trait of this tranquil breed is its rather elegant and harmonious voice. Its actual size and look vary quite significantly from country to country. Some kennel clubs solve this problem by recognizing different varieties of Beagle with different sizes. At one time in Great Britain, mounted hunters carried small Beagles in their saddlebags.

Long, fine-textured ears hang in graceful fold

Head has slightly domed skull

Dark at birth, the nose often turns brown-pink

ANY HOUND COLOUR

Lips are well defined, with distinct flews

Moderately deep chest, with well-sprung ribs

Thighs have excellent propulsive power

Erect tail is white tipped

Smooth coat; can also be wiry

BREED HISTORY The Beagle may be descended from the Harrier and ancient English hounds. Small hounds, which were capable of accompanying rabbit hunters on foot, have existed since the 1300s.

Compact but sturdy feet are very well padded

DUNKER

Round-tipped, silky ears are low set

Moderately long muzzle; cheeks are not prominent

Dark eyes, with relaxed expression

Sloping shoulders are well muscled

Black nose, with large nostrils

BREED HISTORY Wilhelm Dunker, a Norwegian breeder, developed the placid, good-natured Dunker by crossing the merle-gened Russian Harlequin Hound with other reliable scent hounds.

Straight coat covers durable, resistant skin

KEY FACTS

COUNTRY OF ORIGIN Norway
DATE OF ORIGIN 1850s
FIRST USE Hare hunting
USE TODAY Companion, hare hunting
LIFE EXPECTANCY 12 years
OTHER NAME Norwegian Hound

WEIGHT RANGE
16–22 kg (35–49 lb)
HEIGHT RANGE
47–57 cm (18½–22½ in)

Although Norway has a relatively small population, its hunting tradition remains strong, and several breeds have evolved to fit the specific niche required of a northern hunting dog. The Dunker is a classic example, "designed" to hunt and retrieve hares by scent, rather than by sight. It is a mild-mannered and friendly breed, sleek and poised in appearance, but with tremendous stamina and staying power. Although hip dysplasia can occasionally be a problem, the Dunker is otherwise a sound dog, adapted to hunting over a wide variety of terrain. With its attractive looks and engaging personality, it is also a valuable companion.

Compact, well-arched toes

HALDENSTÖVARE

Smooth and shiny coat is very fine

Like all other Norwegian hounds, the Haldenstövare is not a pack hound – it hunts hares individually with its owner. Also in common with other Norwegian hounds, this breed has a placid and amenable disposition. It can be particularly affectionate with people and is rarely snappy, although – like most breeds – it should be supervised when meeting children it does not know. The striking tricolour coat with predominant black-and-tan markings contributes to its attraction. Although the coat needs little attention, it is not as thick as that of northern spitz breeds, and the Haldenstövare should be protected from extreme cold.

KEY FACTS

COUNTRY OF ORIGIN Norway
DATE OF ORIGIN 1900s
FIRST USE Hare hunting
USE TODAY Companion, hare hunting
LIFE EXPECTANCY 12 years
OTHER NAMES Halden Hound, Haldenstover

WEIGHT RANGE
23–29 kg (51–64 lb)
HEIGHT RANGE
51–64 cm (20–25 in)

If extended, velvety, wide-set ears reach middle of muzzle

Black nose is prominent, with wide-open nostrils

Brown eyes have serene expression

BREED HISTORY Relatively unknown even in other parts of Scandinavia, the Haldenstövare evolved in the south of Norway, near Halden, from a cross between the English Foxhound and local hounds. The breed was fixed in its present form in the 1950s.

Legs are well boned and muscular

Oval feet, with well-arched toes

HYGENHUND

Medium-sized, dark-brown eyes have earnest expression

BREED HISTORY The Hygenhund, another retrieving hound named after its first breeder, was created by crossing hounds from Hölstein, in northern Germany, with various Scandinavian hounds, including the now-extinct Ringerike Hound.

Tail is in line with back

Moderately thick, velvety ears

Black nose, with wide nostrils

Forelegs are straight and lean

Hair in between toes

Compact in size, the short-backed but strong Hygenhund is used primarily for hunting; it has gained little popularity as a companion. Livelier than the other indigenous Norwegian hounds, the Hygenhund is excellent at hunting small game. It makes a reliable watchdog, gets on moderately well with other dogs, needs vigorous exercise, and has a tendency to snap or bite. It is not a city dog and, when the weather permits, is content to live outdoors, although it must be protected from very cold temperatures. The breed is not well known outside Norway.

Smooth, very dense, shiny coat

 CHESTNUT YELLOW-RED BLACK/CHESTNUT

KEY FACTS

COUNTRY OF ORIGIN Norway
DATE OF ORIGIN 1830s
FIRST USE Hare hunting
USE TODAY Hare hunting, companion
LIFE EXPECTANCY 12 years
OTHER NAME Hygenhound

WEIGHT RANGE
20–24 kg (44–53 lb)
HEIGHT RANGE
47–58 cm (18½–23 in)

FINNISH HOUND

Sturdy tail is carried below line of back

Fairly harsh, dense coat is only moderately long

High-set, long ears

KEY FACTS

COUNTRY OF ORIGIN Finland
DATE OF ORIGIN 1700s
FIRST USE Deer/hare hunting
USE TODAY Companion, hunting
LIFE EXPECTANCY 12 years
OTHER NAMES Suomenajokoira, Finsk Stövare

WEIGHT RANGE
20–25 kg (45–55 lb)
HEIGHT RANGE
56–63 cm (22–25 in)

Powerful shoulders are oblique

Pasterns are sturdy

Straight neck, with no dewlap

Head is lean and noble looking

BREED HISTORY Although summer hunting hounds have existed in Finland since the 1700s, today's breed results from a breeding programme in the 1800s, which involved French, German, and Swedish hounds. The Finnish Hound has become Finland's most popular native working breed.

Unlike the Norwegian hounds, the Finnish Hound follows scent but does not retrieve, although it leads hunters to shot woodcocks and other gamebirds in dense forest cover. This large and gentle breed thrives on physical activity, is good with children, and is content to sleep outdoors alone during the Scandinavian summer months. Although the close coat does not offer much protection from the elements, it needs little attention. The breed makes only a moderately good watchdog, due to its placid nature. Males can be temperamental with other male dogs.

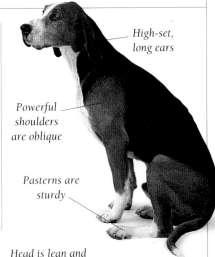

HAMILTONSTÖVARE

Long muzzle is tipped
with large, black nose

Except in Great Britain, where it is rapidly becoming a successful show dog and working hound, the handsome Hamiltonstövare is virtually unknown outside Scandinavia. One of Sweden's 10 most populous breeds, this is a single rather than a pack hunter, capable of tracking, trailing, and flushing game. It bays in a typical hound-like fashion when it finds wounded quarry. With a coat that thickens considerably in the winter, the industrious Hamiltonstövare is content working in snow-covered Swedish forests.

Long, powerful neck merges with shoulders

BREED HISTORY Created by Adolf Patrick Hamilton, the founder of the Swedish Kennel Club, by crossing varieties of German Beagle with the English Foxhound and local Swedish hounds, the Hamiltonstövare was first shown in 1886.

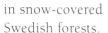

Brown eyes have
almost serene
expression

Tail is thick at
root, and tapers
to tip

KEY FACTS

COUNTRY OF ORIGIN Sweden
DATE OF ORIGIN 1800s
FIRST USE Game tracking
USE TODAY Companion, gundog
LIFE EXPECTANCY 12–13 years
OTHER NAME Hamilton Hound

WEIGHT RANGE
23–27 kg (50–60 lb)
HEIGHT RANGE
51–61 cm (20–24 in)

Strong, dense topcoat
covers short, thick,
soft undercoat

SMÅLANDSSTÖVARE

Dark eyes, with
calm expression

Artwork and manuscripts suggest that the compact and stocky Smålandsstövare has been a successful Swedish working hound since the Middle Ages, but it was not until 1921 that it was formally recognized by the Swedish Kennel Club. Virtually unknown outside its home country, this steady hound uses stamina rather than speed to hunt rabbits and foxes in the dense forests of Småland. Amputating dogs' tails is an illegal procedure in Sweden, and the Smålandsstövare's short tail is a result of the original selective breeding carried out by Baron von Essen in the 1800s, by crossing local hounds with the Schillerstövare.

Muzzle is well
developed, but not too
heavy or pointed

Topcoat is thick, heavy,
smooth, and glossy

Rather high-set
ears hang flat, and
are rounded at tips

Tail is
unusually
short

BREED HISTORY Perhaps the oldest of the Scandinavian hounds, this breed originated in Småland, south Sweden, where it was bred to work in the forests. Its standard was established in 1921.

KEY FACTS

COUNTRY OF ORIGIN Sweden
DATE OF ORIGIN Middle Ages/1800s
FIRST USE Hare/fox hunting
USE TODAY Companion, gundog
LIFE EXPECTANCY 12–14 years
OTHER NAME Smålands Hound

WEIGHT RANGE
15–18 kg (33–40 lb)
HEIGHT RANGE
46–50 cm (18–20 in)

Legs are muscular
and thickly boned

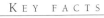

SCHILLERSTÖVARE

BREED HISTORY Local working hounds have existed throughout Sweden since the Middle Ages. In the 1800s, Per Schiller, a farmer wanting a light, fleet-footed hound, imported hounds from Germany, bred them with local hounds, and produced the breed that now bears his name. It was officially recognized in 1952.

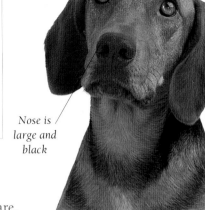

Nose is large and black

KEY FACTS

COUNTRY OF ORIGIN Sweden
DATE OF ORIGIN Middle Ages/1800s
FIRST USE Hare/fox hunting
USE TODAY Companion, gundog
LIFE EXPECTANCY 12–14 years
OTHER NAME Schiller Hound

WEIGHT RANGE
18–24 kg (40–53 lb)
HEIGHT RANGE
53–57 cm (21–22 in)

Thick-rooted tail is carried high, and has a slight curve

High-set, soft-textured ears hang flat, without folding

Muscular thighs are covered by smooth topcoat

Compact feet have robust, large pads and elastic toes

Unlike the Hamiltonstövare, this breed remains primarily a hunter's dog. Seen only in Scandinavia, and rarely even outside Sweden, it is an excellent tracker of snow hares and foxes. Its harsh winter coat offers good protection from cold and snow, and its speed and stamina make it a durable hunting companion. It is a typical Scandinavian gundog – it does not touch live quarry, but rather bays until the hunter arrives. In Sweden, where hunting is a popular recreational activity, the hunt is often more important than the kill. The hunter frequently calls off the dog, and allows the hare or other game to survive. The Schillerstövare is increasingly seen in the show ring, and its obedient nature makes it an ideal companion.

DREVER

BREED HISTORY A re-creation of the type of short-legged dog used to drive game towards the gun, the Drever was developed from the now-rare Westphalian Dachsbracke and local hounds.

Head is large, long, and well proportioned

Clear, alert eyes have thin, close-fitting eyelids

Although quite short, forelegs are vertical and parallel

Coat is thick, close fitting, and flat over body

Tail is carried with downwards curve

KEY FACTS

COUNTRY OF ORIGIN Sweden
DATE OF ORIGIN 1900s
FIRST USE Game tracking
USE TODAY Companion, gundog
LIFE EXPECTANCY 12–14 years
OTHER NAME Swedish Dachsbracke

WEIGHT RANGE
14.5–15.5 kg (32–34 lb)
HEIGHT RANGE
29–41 cm (11½–16 in)

The Drever is rare outside Sweden, but it is almost as popular as the Labrador Retriever in its home country. In a short period of time, this industrious and resilient breed has become the Swedish hunter's most popular companion. Its personality is typical of other dachsbrackes and dachshunds, and if it were criticized, it would be for overzealousness. Headstrong and tenacious, the breed often wants to continue working long after its human companion has satisfied his own hunting instinct. The Drever has a first-class nose and is a powerful tracker. Due to its short legs, it is slower than other hounds – this makes it ideal for manoeuvering game towards the hunter's gun.

BLACK/ WHITE   TRICOLOUR   FAWN/ WHITE

Upper lip is quite tight, and fits firmly over lower jaw

AMERICAN FOXHOUND

Eyes are set well apart

ANY COLOUR

Head is fairly long, with moderately domed skull

Flews hang below jaw

BREED HISTORY The first pack of working English Foxhounds arrived in America from Great Britain in 1650. Kerry Beagle-type Irish hounds and French hounds helped create today's lean and fast breed.

Medium-dense coat is hard and close

Long ears are set at eye level

The American Foxhound is taller and lighter boned than its European counterpart, although until this century new blood was routinely introduced from Europe. When working, it tends to act individually, rather than in a group, with each dog being willing to take the lead. Fox hunting varies in form across the Eastern Seaboard of the United States. In northern states it follows traditional European patterns – hunting takes place during the day and the fox is killed. In southern states a hunt may take place day or night, and the chase is most important – the fox is not necessarily killed. Each of these strong-willed dogs has a distinct voice, which can be recognized by its owner.

KEY FACTS

COUNTRY OF ORIGIN United States
DATE OF ORIGIN 1800s
FIRST USE Fox hunting
USE TODAY Fox hunting, companion
LIFE EXPECTANCY 11–13 years

WEIGHT RANGE
30–34 kg (65–75 lb)
HEIGHT RANGE
53–64 cm (21–25 in)

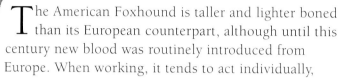

CATAHOULA LEOPARD DOG

Skull is broad and flat

Named after a Parish in north-east Louisiana, at one time the "Cat" was used to round up feral pigs and cattle – livestock that had escaped, and was living in woods and swamps. (More accurately, it would pick fights with, and then be chased by the pigs.) Hunters sometimes used the Catahoula to trail and tree raccoons, but this dominant breed is more at home acting the thug with recalcitrant boars. Breeding is based on the survival of the fittest.

Breed is named after mottled spots on coat

Legs are solid and strong boned

BREED HISTORY The Catahoula evolved in the deep south of the United States, and probably descends from war dogs brought there by the Spaniards, and from dogs belonging to Native Americans. In 1979, the breed was designated the state dog of Louisiana.

Deep chest provides for good heart and lung capacity

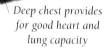

MERLE   BLACK/TAN

KEY FACTS

COUNTRY OF ORIGIN United States
DATE OF ORIGIN 1700s
FIRST USE Deer hunting, herding
USE TODAY Herding, companion
LIFE EXPECTANCY 12–13 years
OTHER NAMES Catahoula Hog Dog, Catahoula Cur

WEIGHT RANGE
18–23 kg (40–50 lb)
HEIGHT RANGE
51–66 cm (20–26 in)

PLOTT HOUND

BLUE

BRINDLE

Considered the hardiest of the coonhounds, this large and gregarious dog has been bred by members of the Plott family for almost 250 years, to hunt bears and raccoons in the Appalachian, Blue Ridge, and Great Smoky mountains of the Eastern United States. The Plott has a curiously sharp and high-pitched voice, unlike the sonorous bawl common to other coonhounds. Well muscled and rather lean boned, it has the endurance and stamina to work all day and well into the night. It has the typical deep chest of the American coonhounds. It eats large quantities of food quickly, which makes it susceptible to gastric torsion, a life-threatening twisting of the stomach. It is extremely rare outside the southern states, and is seldom kept solely as a companion.

KEY FACTS

COUNTRY OF ORIGIN United States
DATE OF ORIGIN 1700s
FIRST USE Bear hunting
USE TODAY Gundog, companion
LIFE EXPECTANCY 12–13 years

WEIGHT RANGE
20–25 kg (45–55 lb)
HEIGHT RANGE
51–61 cm (20–24 in)

BREED HISTORY The only American hound without a British ancestry, its progenitors were German hounds brought to North Carolina in the 1750s by the Plott family.

Long tail is held high when dog is alert

Ears hang with slight fold

Short coat is thick, dense, and glossy

Strong feet have webbed toes

Lean, powerful thigh muscles provide energy

TREEING WALKER COONHOUND

An efficient and reliable hunter of raccoons, squirrels, and possums, this coonhound has retained the looks of its ancestor, the English Foxhound. The Treeing Walker "trees" its prey, and can then sometimes virtually climb the tree to get at it. With a little training, however, it will merely bay its distinctive howl, telling the hunter that the prey has been cornered. The breed has been bred for arduous physical exercise, and although it is a gentle companion, it is not suitable for urban life.

Ears are large for size of head

Powerful shoulders are very mobile

Upper lips hang well below lower jaw

KEY FACTS

COUNTRY OF ORIGIN United States
DATE OF ORIGIN 1800s
FIRST USE Raccoon hunting
USE TODAY Gundog, companion
LIFE EXPECTANCY 12–13 years

WEIGHT RANGE
23–32 kg (50–70 lb)
HEIGHT RANGE
51–69 cm (20–27 in)

BREED HISTORY A descendant of the English Foxhound, which Thomas Walker imported to Virginia in 1742, the Treeing Walker was not recognized as a separate breed until 1945.

Smooth coat is fine and glossy

Forelegs are long, straight, and lean

TRI-COLOUR

BICOLOUR

BLACK-AND-TAN COONHOUND

Rich tan colour above eyes

Typical large, black, hound nose, with well-opened nostrils

Hazel-brown eyes are alert and friendly

Ears are set well back and hang gracefully

Sloping, muscular neck is of medium length

Deep chest for physical endurance

Americain Coonhounds are among the world's most specialized breeds, with a highly developed instinct to follow the scent trail of a raccoon or opossum, and tree the animal. Once the quarry has been cornered, the coonhound changes the tone of its voice. It remains at the tree, baying its "I've got it cornered" call until the hunter arrives. The Black-and-tan is the most common coonhound and is assertive, watchful, and obedient. Grooming, with special attention to the ears, and exercise, are vitally important.

Prone to hip dysplasia

Long, strong limbs built for prolonged running and swimming

BREED HISTORY Ancestry includes the Bloodhound, Irish Kerry Beagle, and foxhound, in particular the Virginia Foxhound of the 1700s. The breed may also be related to the 12th-century Talbot Hound.

BLUETICK COONHOUND

BREED HISTORY Selective breeding in Louisiana of foxhounds, curs, English Coonhounds, and French hounds produced the Bluetick Coonhound.

Tail is set just below level of back line

Nose adept at picking up scent

Each dog has unique "voice" recognizable by owner

The Bluetick Coonhound is an exceptionally elegant animal. Its name is not entirely accurate – it is, in fact, a tricoloured dog. Like all coonhounds, the Bluetick has a strong instinct to tree animals. Raccoons inhabit all states and provinces in the United States mainland and Canada, and have for centuries been pursued by hunters. Each year, hundreds of licensed night trials take place. Each trial lasts about three hours and involves three to four dogs. Points are given according to the dog's ability to find a trail and tree a raccoon; however, points are lost for treeing game other than raccoons.

Tan colour on neck gives way to elegant blue ticking

Long hind legs are sinewy and muscular

Eyesight is extremely good and enables Bluetick to work well at night

Compact feet, with well-arched toes, are of similar tan colour to muzzle

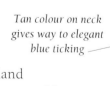

ENGLISH COONHOUND

ALL HOUND
COLOURS

*Clear eyes give
good lateral and
binocular vision*

*Hearing is
acute, but
drooping ears
are prone to
injury*

*Shoulders are powerful;
back slopes from
withers to rump*

*Drooping lips help
capture scent*

*Low-set tail is carried
freely when working*

*Long, pendant ears
are typical of all
coonhounds*

*Strong-boned hind legs
are straight and sturdy*

The English Coonhound is strictly an American breed, although its ancestors came from Great Britain, and probably France. In temperament it is similar to all the other coonhound breeds. It is particularly gentle with children. Recognized by the United Kennel Club since 1903, this robust dog's coat colour is usually redtick, although other colours are allowed. As with all coonhounds, females are often significantly smaller than males.

BREED HISTORY Selectively bred in the 1800s in Virginia, Tennessee, and Kentucky, the English Coonhound was developed as a smaller breed than the Black-and-tan, and is foremost a hunting dog.

KEY FACTS

COUNTRY OF ORIGIN United States
DATE OF ORIGIN 1800s
FIRST USE Raccoon hunting
USE TODAY Raccoon hunting
LIFE EXPECTANCY 11–12 years
OTHER NAME Redtick Coonhound

WEIGHT RANGE
18–30 kg (40–65 lb)
HEIGHT RANGE
53–69 cm (21–27 in)

REDBONE COONHOUND

KEY FACTS

COUNTRY OF ORIGIN United States
DATE OF ORIGIN 1800s
FIRST USE Raccoon hunting
USE TODAY Raccoon hunting, companion
LIFE EXPECTANCY 11–12 years

WEIGHT RANGE
23–32 kg (50–70 lb)
HEIGHT RANGE
53–66 cm (21–26 in)

BREED HISTORY This hound is probably named after an early breeder, Peter Redbone, of Tennessee, although much of its breeding has taken place in Georgia.

*Clean, well-modelled
head, with medium
stop between brow
and nose*

*In action,
tail is held
upright*

*Pendulous ears extend
to tip of nose when dog
follows scent*

Although some Redbones might have traces of white on the feet or chest, this affable, elegant dog is the only solid-coloured coonhound. Coonhounds are all instinctive hunters, and it is not difficult to train the breed to follow scent and tree quarry. Like other coonhounds, the Redbone is attentive, agile, and able to work in all types of weather over difficult terrain. It can be surprisingly affectionate and has a pleasant-sounding bark. If raised indoors from puppyhood, it will adapt well to family life.

*Long nose
assists scent
detection*

Skin is rich red

*Paws are compact and cat-
like, with thick, strong pads*

RED

RED/
WHITE

KERRY BEAGLE

Hindquarters are robust and powerful

Ears hang close to cheeks

Upper lip is slightly overhanging

Nose is usually black

Close-fitting, dense topcoat

Long forelegs

Strong thighs, with straight bones

An ancient breed, the Kerry Beagle is the descendant of southern Irish, stag-hunting hounds. By the 1800s, it was used almost exclusively to hunt hares, mostly in south Kerry; a century later, very few packs remained. Earlier this century, a group of Irish emigrants took their Kerry Beagles to the United States, where they contributed to the development of American strains of hound. In Ireland, breeders have stirred a resurgence of interest in this active, friendly dog. The breed is still used for hare hunting, and the rising popularity of drag trials in Ireland has created a new activity for it.

BREED HISTORY Thought to be descended from bloodhound-type dogs, the first part of this breed's name is derived from the part of Ireland where it was used as a pack hound. The second part is a misnomer – Beagle suggests a small dog, and with a height of up to 66 cm (26 in), it certainly is not that.

| TAN/ WHITE | BLUE/ TAN | BLACK/ TAN | TRI- COLOUR |

KEY FACTS

COUNTRY OF ORIGIN Ireland
DATE OF ORIGIN 1500s
FIRST USE Hare hunting
USE TODAY Pack hound, companion
LIFE EXPECTANCY 11–12 years
OTHER NAME Pocadan

WEIGHT RANGE
20–27 kg (45–60 lb)
HEIGHT RANGE
56–66 cm (22–26 in)

BEAGLE HARRIER

KEY FACTS

COUNTRY OF ORIGIN France
DATE OF ORIGIN 1800s
FIRST USE Hare hunting
USE TODAY Hare/deer/fox/wild boar hunting, companion
LIFE EXPECTANCY 12 years

WEIGHT RANGE
20–25 kg (44–55 lb)
HEIGHT RANGE
45–50 cm (18–20 in)

The Beagle Harrier was developed at the end of the 19th century as an attempt to improve on the Beagle and Harrier. The fact that it is a rare dog, seldom seen outside France, where it is kept in small packs, suggests that the attempt was less than successful. This is a pity, because this calm and gentle dog makes a good household companion, gets on well with other dogs and children, seldom snaps or bites, and is reasonably easy to train. When given the opportunity, the Beagle Harrier is an enthusiastic and tireless worker, and is used by keen sportsmen to hunt hares, deers, foxes, and even wild boars.

Tail hangs when dog is relaxed

Thick topcoat on flat undercoat

Flattish head

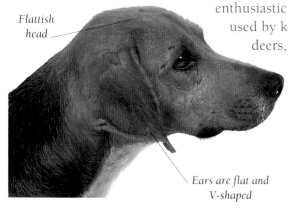

Ears are flat and V-shaped

BREED HISTORY This cross of two quintessentially British breeds – the stocky, robust Beagle and the leggy, leaner Harrier – was developed by a French sportsman, Baron Gérard who, in the late 1800s, attempted to produce a hare-hunting hound.

Nose is black and fairly large

Feet have thick, tough pads

AMERICAN WATER SPANIEL

KEY FACTS

COUNTRY OF ORIGIN United States
DATE OF ORIGIN 1800s
FIRST USE Duck hunting
USE TODAY Duck hunting
LIFE EXPECTANCY 12 years

WEIGHT RANGE
11–20 kg (25–45 lb)
HEIGHT RANGE
36–46 cm (15–18 in)

Head is moderate in length, with broad, full skull

Neck blends smoothly with shoulders

Hazel-brown, alert eyes are set well apart

Sufficiently wide nose to ensure excellent scenting ability

Long ears, with close curls

Long, broad ears are set wide, just above eyeline

Muzzle is square, with no indication of delicacy

Back is well developed and sturdily constructed

Dense coat is tightly curled and covers lively tail

Closely grouped toes on well-padded feet

LIVER

DARK CHOCOLATE

Straight, strong forelegs are feathered with water-proof hair

Upper lips hang over lower jaw

The State Dog of Wisconsin, this vibrant and active breed is similar in function to the English Springer Spaniel, Brittany, and Nova Scotia Duck Tolling Retriever. It flushes or springs game, especially waterfowl, from the water, and then retrieves for the hunter with its typically soft, retriever mouth. The dog's lean, light body allows it to accompany the hunter in his canoe or skiff, in order to work the frigid wetland waters of Michigan, Wisconsin, and Minnesota from early spring to late autumn. Pre-Civil War, tintype photographs from the 1850s show dogs similar to this breed, although it was developed to its present form during the 1920s by Dr. F.J. Pfeifer, a Wisconsin physician. Rarely, if ever, worked outside North America, the breed has a close cousin in South Carolina – the Boykin Spaniel, a water-loving, turkey-hunting dog also descended from Irish Water and Field Spaniels.

BREED HISTORY Produced in the State of Wisconsin, in the American Midwest, this breed probably descends, at least in part, from the Irish Water Spaniel. The Curly-coated Retriever and Field Spaniel may also have been involved in its development. The breed was first registered in 1940.

SEGUGIO ITALIANO

Large eyes are dark and luminous

BREED HISTORY Egyptian artefacts from the time of the pharaohs show that today's Segugio is very similar to the Egyptian coursing hounds of antiquity. Bulk was added to these hounds by introducing mastiff bloodlines.

Thin lips are neither pendulous nor prominent

The origins of this uniquely attractive breed are revealed through its conformation – it has the long legs of a sight hound and the face of a scent hound. During the Italian Renaissance, the Segugio's beauty made it a highly regarded companion. Today, it is popular as a hunting dog throughout Italy. Its sense of smell is exceptional, and once on the trail of game it is similar to the Bloodhound in its singleminded dedication to the chase. Unlike the Bloodhound, however, the Segugio is also interested in the capture and kill. As both a working dog and a companion, this breed is becoming increasingly popular outside Italy.

Dramatic, pendulous ears are set just below eye level

KEY FACTS

COUNTRY OF ORIGIN Italy
DATE OF ORIGIN Antiquity
FIRST USE Game hunting
USE TODAY Companion, gundog
LIFE EXPECTANCY 12–13 years
OTHER NAMES Italian Hound, Segugio

WEIGHT RANGE
18–28 kg (40–62 lb)
HEIGHT RANGE
52–58 cm (20½–23 in)

Coat is dense, short, and glossy

Tail is delicate and thin, even at root

Feet are oval, like those of a hare, and covered in short, dense hair

FAWN   BLACK/TAN

SABUESO ESPAÑOL

Long ears extend easily to, or beyond, tip of nose

WHITE/RED   WHITE/BLACK

KEY FACTS

COUNTRY OF ORIGIN Spain
DATE OF ORIGIN Middle Ages
FIRST USE Game tracking
USE TODAY Gundog, companion
LIFE EXPECTANCY 11–13 years
OTHER NAME Spanish Hound

WEIGHT RANGE
20–25 kg (45–55 lb)
HEIGHT RANGE
46–56 cm (18–22 in)

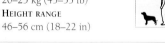

Rounded loins are rather short

Chestnut-coloured eyes are surrounded by close-fitting lids

Colour of nose blends with surrounding hair

BREED HISTORY
The Sabueso's resemblance to mastiffs indicates its antiquity. It developed from the same source as the Bloodhound, and is a probable descendant of the extinct, white Talbot Hound. Isolation on the Iberian peninsula permitted the breed to remain pure.

Forelegs are straight and strong, without being stocky

Neck is strong and muscular

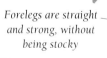

Until recently, this breed occurred in two different sizes, but the smaller Lebrero is now virtually extinct. Even in the standard variety there is a dramatic size difference, with males being 20 per cent larger than females. This breed is rarely worked in packs – it is usually a solitary hunter, working singly with its human companion. It thrives on hard work and willingly tracks from sunrise to sunset. The Sabueso can be temperamental and should be introduced to children and strangers with caution; it can also be rather troublesome with dogs that it does not know. Although the breed was not specifically developed as a watchdog, some individuals are surprisingly effective in that area.

POLISH HOUND

KEY FACTS

COUNTRY OF ORIGIN Poland
DATE OF ORIGIN 1700s
FIRST USE Large-game tracking
USE TODAY Companion, gundog
LIFE EXPECTANCY 12–14 years
OTHER NAME Ogar Polski

WEIGHT RANGE
25–32 kg (55–71 lb)
HEIGHT RANGE
56–66 cm (22–26 in)

BREED HISTORY This friendly breed's history is unknown. Its conformation and locale suggest that it is a relative of the St. Hubert Hound, and was then bred with German hounds. A smaller version, the Polski Pies Gończy, became extinct during World War II.

Large, gentle eyes are not very deep set

Body colour is black

Ears are set rather low, hang close to head, and are rounded at tips

Chest is deep, broad, and well let down

Toes are close set, with heavy, hard nails, and broad, thick pads

As happened with so many other European hunting breeds, this century's wars almost drove the Polish Hound to extinction. After World War II, Polish hunters successfully found enough survivors to perpetuate this uncomplicated, rustic dog. It is an excellent tracker, persistent and enduring, much like its distant Bloodhound relative. The breed is used to track large game, using its medium-toned voice when it latches on to a recent scent trail. It is also a companionable dog, very much at ease in the home. With the post-Communist political changes in Poland, the Polish Hound has found new admirers who will ensure its survival.

BLACK FOREST HOUND

BREED HISTORY Thoroughbred breeding began after World War II, when Czech and Slovak hunters selectively bred indigenous mountain dogs to work in rough, mountainous conditions. The breed was used to track large game, such as boars, and also small vermin.

Deep-set eyes are surrounded by black eyelids

Round, medium-long ears are set just above eyes

Neck is somewhat short and well muscled

Paws are oval, with well-arched toes

Muzzle is tipped by pointed nose

This relatively new breed's youthful temperament resembles that of the Dobermann, although that breed has played little, if any, role in its development. Young individuals are rambunctious, independent, and provocative; males, in particular, need experienced handling. With maturity comes acute orientation and scenting ability – the Black Forest Hound is an excellent tracker and uses its voice liberally when it comes upon the fresh trail of game. Slovakia's independence has stimulated a national pride in this local breed, and it is now shown in increasing numbers at local dog shows, although it is rarely seen outside the Slovak and Czech Republics. Its standard was set in 1963.

Straight, lean forearms, with well-muscled shoulders

KEY FACTS

COUNTRY OF ORIGIN Slovak Republic
DATE OF ORIGIN 1950s
FIRST USE Wild-boar/small-vermin hunting
USE TODAY Wild-boar hunting
LIFE EXPECTANCY 11–13 years
OTHER NAME Slovensky Kopov

WEIGHT RANGE
15–20 kg (33–44 lb)
HEIGHT RANGE
40–50 cm (16–20 in)

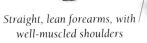

BOSNIAN ROUGH-COATED HOUND

Large, oval eyes

Muzzle narrows towards nose

Long, hard, wiry topcoat

KEY FACTS

COUNTRY OF ORIGIN Bosnia
DATE OF ORIGIN 1800s
FIRST USE Game hunting
USE TODAY Hunting, watchdog
LIFE EXPECTANCY 12 years
OTHER NAME Bosanski Ostrodlaki Gonic

WEIGHT RANGE
16–24 kg (35–53 lb)
HEIGHT RANGE
46–55 cm (18–22 in)

Fleshy ears are rounded

VARIETY OF COLOURS

Thighs are moderately long

T he harsh mountains of Bosnia are the home of a variety of game, such as hares, foxes, and even wild boars. Local hunters, wanting to produce an efficient scent hound, developed this breed in the 1800s, using the available stock of dogs. The Bosnian Rough-coated Hound is tough and perservering, and its wiry, rough coat offers insulation and protection against hostile weather. It has typical scent-hound characteristics, and also makes an excellent watchdog. It gets on well with children and with other dogs, thrives on activity, willingly sleeps outdoors, and seldom snaps or bites. Despite the Bosnian War, hunters have managed to maintain the breed.

Cat-like feet, with hard pads

Lips fit close to jaws

Compact back is muscular

BREED HISTORY A pragmatically rustic breed, this amenable hound is descended from lean, leggy sight hounds, which were brought to the Balkans centuries ago by Mediterranean merchants, and from local pariah dogs.

ISTRIAN SMOOTH-COATED HOUND

Dark, oval eyes are not too prominent

Tail reaches just below hock

Broad ears hang flat at side of head

KEY FACTS

COUNTRY OF ORIGIN Slovenia
DATE OF ORIGIN Middle Ages
FIRST USE Fox/rabbit hunting
USE TODAY Fox/rabbit hunting, tracking, companion
LIFE EXPECTANCY 12 years
OTHER NAMES Istrski Kratkodlaki Gonic, Istrian Setter

WEIGHT RANGE
14–20 kg (31–44 lb)
HEIGHT RANGE
44–56 cm (17–22 in)

Short thighs and high stifles

Glossy coat has fine texture

Long shoulders, with elbows close to body

Lean, compact feet, with solid pads and hard nails

BREED HISTORY The most ancient of the Balkan scent hounds, this handsome breed descends from crosses between Asian sight hounds, probably brought to the Balkans by the Phoenicians, and from European mastiffs and scent hounds.

Long muzzle leads to dark, well-defined nose

T his elegant hound, which comes from Istria, the region of the Balkans bordering Italy and Austria, was probably originally bred by monks. Old religious documents tell of smooth-coated hounds sent by monks, from what is now Slovenia, to monasteries in France. Such trade in working dogs between monasteries explains, in part, how scent hounds were disseminated throughout Europe. Today, this proficient hunter is an excellent cold-trail follower, and can track blood left by wounded animals which is several days old.

ISTRIAN ROUGH-COATED HOUND

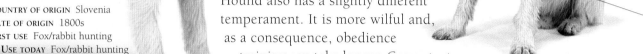

Short, thick tail tapers to tip

Ears broaden at middle and hang without folds

Eyes are dark

Broad nose, with large nostrils

Forepart of lower jaw is rounded

Hindquarters are not very prominent

KEY FACTS

COUNTRY OF ORIGIN Slovenia
DATE OF ORIGIN 1800s
FIRST USE Fox/rabbit hunting
USE TODAY Fox/rabbit hunting
LIFE EXPECTANCY 12 years
OTHER NAME Istrski
Ostrodlaki Gonic
WEIGHT RANGE
16–24 kg (25–53 lb)
HEIGHT RANGE
46–58 cm (18–23 in)

M ore rustic in appearance and better equipped to tolerate bad weather than its smooth-coated relative, the Istrian Rough-coated Hound also has a slightly different temperament. It is more wilful and, as a consequence, obedience training can take longer. Competent and versatile, this attractive, weather-resistant hound is almost always kept solely as a hunting dog, rather than as a household companion. With the disintegration of Yugoslavia, its numbers declined in the southern Balkan States while in Slovenia, its region of origin, numbers increased.

BREED HISTORY In the mid-1800s, with the aim of improving its voice, breeders crossed the Istrian Smooth-coated Hound with the French Griffon Vendéen. This resulted in the Istrian Rough-coated Hound, which was first shown in Vienna in 1866.

POITEVIN

Flat head, with slight slop onto forehead

Long, slender neck is well muscled

WHITE/ORANGE TRI-COLOUR

KEY FACTS

COUNTRY OF ORIGIN France
DATE OF ORIGIN 1600s
FIRST USE Wolf hunting
USE TODAY Fox hunting
LIFE EXPECTANCY 12 years
OTHER NAME Haut-Poitou

WEIGHT RANGE
29.5–30.5 kg (65–67 lb)
HEIGHT RANGE
58–71 cm (23–28 in)

Chest is covered by long ribs

Upper lip covers lower lip

Thin ears hang with slight fold

Large, brown, expressive eyes

Legs are long, straight, and densely boned

BREED HISTORY
Most of the original Poitevins were killed during the French Revolution. Fifty years later, a rabies epidemic destroyed the surviving packs. Using the English Foxhound, the breed was then redeveloped.

I n 1692 the Marquis de Larrye, of Haut-Poitou, received 12 foxhounds from the kennels of the French Dauphin. Cross breeding these dogs with industrious, local hounds, he produced the Poitevin. The breed proved to be a superb hunter, which used its well-developed scent-following prowess, melodious voice, courage, and speed to pursue and kill wolves, which were plentiful in the region. In the early 1800s, new packs were created in Haut-Poitou, but a rabies epidemic in 1842 killed off most of these. Rejuvenated with English Foxhound blood, today's rare breed is gentle, friendly, and alert.

POSAVAC HOUND

Long, narrow head; round ears hang flat

YELLOW   FAWN   RED

Hunting hounds evolved and thrived in all countries bordering the Mediterranean. Ancient sight hounds remained true to their origins in the African countries to the south, while in countries bordering the north of the Mediterranean, hounds adapted to a rough terrain and bad weather conditions. The sure-footed Posavac is an excellent example of adaption to environment. Lively and alert, it is a tenacious scent follower, ideal for hunting small game such as hares. It has also been used to hunt deer. The breed's gentle nature makes it a good companion, but this is a secondary role.

Tough coat is short and dense

Forearms are vertical and muscular

Narrow, compact feet

BREED HISTORY
The origins of all the Balkan hounds are lost. It is possible that traders introduced hounds from Egypt into this region via the Adriatic ports.

KEY FACTS

COUNTRY OF ORIGIN Former Yugoslavia
DATE OF ORIGIN 1700s
FIRST USE Small-game hunting
USE TODAY Small-game hunting, companion
LIFE EXPECTANCY 12 years
OTHER NAMES Posavatz Hound, Posavski Gonic

WEIGHT RANGE
16–20 kg (35–45 lb)
HEIGHT RANGE
43–59 cm (17–23 in)

Large, black (or blackish) nose

Dark eyes are alert

Lips are neither heavy nor pendulous

YUGOSLAVIAN MOUNTAIN HOUND

In times of conflict, when people suffer, so too do animals. The most recent wars in the Balkans have left many of the indigenous hounds close to local extinction. The distinctively coloured and good-natured Yugoslavian Mountain Hound is now rare in its land of origin. This breed is well adapted to hunt alone, or in packs, in mountainous regions. It has a thick, coarse, black-and-tan coat covering an abundant undercoat. Its strong voice makes it ideal for working in packs, while its stamina and agility permit it to function in difficult terrain. Usually gentle and affectionate at home, it nonetheless remains primarily a working dog.

BREED HISTORY All the hounds from the Balkans are closely related, coming from the same root stock. This breed evolved from dogs that had adapted to working in the mountainous regions of the former Yugoslavia.

KEY FACTS

COUNTRY OF ORIGIN Former Yugoslavia
DATE OF ORIGIN 1800s
FIRST USE Hunting
USE TODAY Hunting, companion
LIFE EXPECTANCY 12 years
OTHER NAME Jugoslavenski Planinksi Gonic

WEIGHT RANGE
20–25 kg (44–55 lb)
HEIGHT RANGE
46–56 cm (18–22 in)

Tail is thick at base; lower half curves

Long thighs and sloping legs

Dark-pigmented eyelids

Thick topcoat, with abundant, insulating undercoat

Broad chest has well-sprung ribs

YUGOSLAVIAN TRICOLOURED HOUND

KEY FACTS

COUNTRY OF ORIGIN Former Yugoslavia
DATE OF ORIGIN 1800s
FIRST USE Game hunting
USE TODAY Game hunting, companion
LIFE EXPECTANCY 12 years
OTHER NAME Jugoslavenski
Tribarvni Gonic

WEIGHT RANGE
20–25 kg (44–55 lb)
HEIGHT RANGE
46–56 cm (18–22 in)

The attractive Yugoslavian Tricoloured Hound shares with its close relative, the Mountain Hound, a weather-resistant coat and a love of working hour after hour on the most difficult terrain. Its long legs and superb vision assist its hunting abilities. Like most hounds, it has a typically dual personality – tranquil, relaxed, and affectionate while resting at home, but exceptionally energetic when permitted to work. It also makes a loving and obedient companion, and is always eager to please its owner. The breed is virtually unknown outside its region of origin, and sadly faces a troubled future and the risk of possible extinction.

BREED HISTORY The Yugoslavian Tricoloured evolved to track and hunt small and large game at the same time as the Mountain Hound, but was more common near the Greek border.

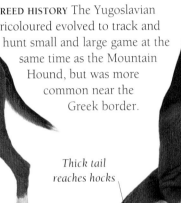

Brownish black eyes have gentle expression

Top of head is flat and wide

Short, dense, glossy coat

Thick tail reaches hocks

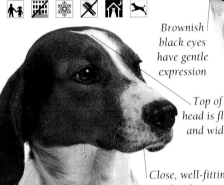

Close, well-fitting lips have black edges

White hair on solid, straight limbs

BALKAN HOUND

Until recently, the Balkan Hound frequently worked in packs, tracking and hunting large game, such as boars and deer, or small game, such as hares. In Slovenia, it is still sometimes used for these purposes. A handsome breed, with an air of calm dignity, it is a determined hunter. Its rugged build, and particularly its muscular shoulders, make it ideal for tracking through difficult terrain. Its rather high-pitched voice can be heard from a great distance – a useful feature for hunting. As with other regional hounds, local breeders have been very successful in maintaining working standards.

Bright-brown eyes

Thin, medium-length ears

Broad forehead on long head that narrows towards muzzle

Curved tail is thick and short

Wide and reasonably deep chest

Dense, black-and-tan coat, with good undercoat

Well-arched toes have exceptionally strong nails

BREED HISTORY Perhaps the first of the hounds of the Balkans to become a fixed breed, this hound was at one time the most common of all the regional hounds. It has remained relatively unchanged for at least 250 years.

KEY FACTS

COUNTRY OF ORIGIN Former Yugoslavia
DATE OF ORIGIN 1700s
FIRST USE Game hunting/tracking
USE TODAY Hunting, companion
LIFE EXPECTANCY 12 years
OTHER NAME Balkanski Gonic

WEIGHT RANGE
19.5–20.5 kg (43–45 lb)
HEIGHT RANGE
43–53 cm (17–21 in)

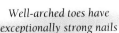

ALPINE DACHSBRACKE

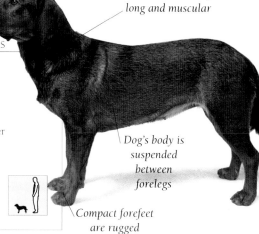

Neck is moderately long and muscular

BREED HISTORY The Alpine Dachsbracke was developed in the Austrian alps for slow ground work – following cold-scent trails of deer. To produce a robust, industrious breed, capable of working in high-altitude conditions, local hounds were crossed with the Smooth-haired Standard Dachshund.

Muzzle and nose are large for size of head

Round eyes have lively expression

KEY FACTS

COUNTRY OF ORIGIN Austria
DATE OF ORIGIN 1850s
FIRST USE Game tracking
USE TODAY Game tracking
LIFE EXPECTANCY 12 years
OTHER NAME Alpenländischer Dachsbracke

WEIGHT RANGE
15–18 kg (33–40 lb)
HEIGHT RANGE
34–42 cm (13–16½ in)

Dog's body is suspended between forelegs

Compact forefeet are rugged

Tail is carried with slight curl

Dachsbrackes are the most efficient cold-trail followers of wounded deer in Alpine Austria and Germany. The hunter's code of honour dictates that a wounded deer must not be left to die of its wounds – it must be followed and killed. In the Austrian alps, hunters independently crossed local brackes with dachshunds to create the Alpine Dachsbracke, an efficient, slow-moving, cold-trail follower. This robust breed has the endurance, stamina, energy, and dedication necessary to follow old trails through the often harsh, high-altitude conditions of the Alps. Generally used by hunters and gamekeepers, it is rarely kept as a household companion.

STYRIAN ROUGH-HAIRED MOUNTAIN HOUND

BREED HISTORY This weather-hardy, resilient hunter was bred by combining a local Austrian hound – the Hanoverian Schweisshund – with the Istrian Rough-coated Hound.

RED   WHEATEN

Long skull, with only mildly pronounced stop

Medium-length ears are set below eyeline

Rarely seen outside Austria and even there only in the possession of local hunters, this robust breed has the good voice and profound stamina necessary to work in the extreme weather conditions of the Styrian mountains. Hunters elsewhere in Austria, and on occasions in neighbouring Slovenia, use the Styrian Mountain Hound for wild-boar hunting. It has the ability to either follow trails silently or use its magnificent cry. Breeding is for sound hunting ability rather than for show, and puppies almost always go to local hunters. Its initial breeding programme began in 1870, and by 1890 Herr Peintinger had been so successful that his breed was formally recognized. Seldom kept as a companion, hunting ability remains its primary purpose.

Dense whiskers cover lips

KEY FACTS

COUNTRY OF ORIGIN Austria
DATE OF ORIGIN 1880
FIRST USE Hunting
USE TODAY Hunting
LIFE EXPECTANCY 12 years
OTHER NAME Peintinger Bracke
WEIGHT RANGE
15–18 kg (33–40 lb)
HEIGHT RANGE
44–58 cm (17–23 in)

BRUNO JURA HOUND

Head is massive, with broad skull

This hunting dog developed hundreds of years ago in the Jura mountains on the Swiss-French border. The Jura's broad head, heavy wrinkles, and rich colouring differentiate it from the other Swiss mountain hounds. An excellent hunter of foxes, hares, and even small deer, this superb scent follower is capable of following the faintest of trails over the arduous terrain of the Jura mountains and valleys. The Jura makes an equable companion, but needs resolute handling.

Large, heavy ears are set very low and hang in folds

VARIETY OF COLOURS

Strong shoulders and ribs over broad, deep chest

BREED HISTORY Similar in size to the other full-sized Swiss laufhunds, but differing in the broadness of head, this regional breed also closely resembles the neighbouring French hounds, from which it most likely descends. It is closely related to the St. Hubert Hound.

Distinctive coat is very short and glossy

Extremely powerful legs

Tail curls gently when dog is sitting

KEY FACTS

COUNTRY OF ORIGIN Switzerland
DATE OF ORIGIN Middle Ages
FIRST USE Small-game hunting
USE TODAY Companion, hunting
LIFE EXPECTANCY 12–13 years
OTHER NAME Jura Laufhund

WEIGHT RANGE
15–20 kg (34–44 lb)
HEIGHT RANGE
43–59 cm (17–23 in)

ST. HUBERT JURA HOUND

VARIETY OF COLOURS

Tail is moderately long and carried back with curl

Long, lean head has well-defined stop

This robust mountain "walking dog" accompanies Swiss hunters who trail their quarry on foot, rather than horseback. Although only slightly taller than the Bruno Jura, its flews and dewlap are distinctively different, both being dramatically pendulous. Its appearance is so similar to the Belgian St. Hubert Hound that it is highly probable they are related. Small size was a bonus in the harsh conditions of the Swiss mountains, while in Belgium the St. Hubert's larger size was retained. This is a superb scent trailer, with surprising agility and speed when necessary. It makes an attractive companion but, like the Bruno Jura, needs firm handling.

KEY FACTS

COUNTRY OF ORIGIN Switzerland
DATE OF ORIGIN Middle Ages
FIRST USE Small-game hunting
USE TODAY Companion, hunting
LIFE EXPECTANCY 12–13 years
OTHER NAME Jura Laufhund St. Hubert

WEIGHT RANGE
15–20 kg (34–44 lb)
HEIGHT RANGE
46–59 cm (18–23 in)

BREED HISTORY Similar in size to the other Swiss laufhunds, the origins of the distinctive St. Hubert Jura are unknown. However, it inhabits the French border region of Switzerland and has clearly been influenced by local French breeds.

Muzzle is long, with prolific hanging upper lips

Huge ears, with rounded tips, are set low and well back from eyes

TRANSYLVANIAN HOUND

Ears widen at their mid points, then taper to rounded tips

Brown, oval eyes look concerned

Once favoured by Hungarian kings and nobility, who used it to hunt wolves and bears, this sturdy breed has had a blighted recent history. Almost wiped out during World War II, those that survived in Romanian Transylvania were, together with the Hungarian Greyhound, exterminated in 1947 on government orders, since they were reminders of the Hungarian "occupation" of Romania. Fortunately, there were a few survivors in Slovakia and Hungary, and breeders in these countries are actively attempting to revive the breed. Slightly suspicious and introspective, this sleek hound occurs in short- and long-legged varieties.

Long head, with slightly rounded skull

BREED HISTORY This breed has changed very little in over 1,000 years. It probably arrived in the Transylvanian mountains with travellers and conquerors, moving west from Russia or north through the Balkans.

Lean lips fit well over teeth

KEY FACTS

COUNTRY OF ORIGIN Hungary/Romania
DATE OF ORIGIN Middle Ages
FIRST USE Bear/wolf hunting
USE TODAY Hunting, watchdog
LIFE EXPECTANCY 14 years

WEIGHT RANGE
Long: 30–35 kg (66–77 lb)
Short: 22–25 kg (48–55 lb)
HEIGHT RANGE
Long: 55–65 cm (22–26 in)
Short: 45–50 cm (18–20 in)

BLACK/ TAN

TRI- COLOUR

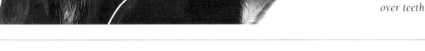

BERNER LAUFHUND

Thighs are moderately long

Rounded skull leads to distinct stop

Ancestors of the Berner Laufhund have worked with hunters in the mountain valleys around Berne for at least 900 years, hunting roe deer and smaller game. The breed's hard, tricolour topcoat, together with its softer undercoat, gives it thermal protection against the rigorous mountain climate in which it works. The Berner is a good working dog; it is also affable with children, and unlikely to fight with other dogs unless provoked. However, it is not always obedient, and needs careful training. It does not make a very good watchdog.

Moderately sized, dark eyes with gentle expression

KEY FACTS

COUNTRY OF ORIGIN Switzerland
DATE OF ORIGIN Middle Ages
FIRST USE Hunting
USE TODAY Companion, hunting
LIFE EXPECTANCY 12–13 years
OTHER NAME Bernese Hound

WEIGHT RANGE
15–20 kg (34–44 lb)
HEIGHT RANGE
46–58 cm (18–23 in)

Forelegs are long and well boned

Broad, black nose, with wide nostrils

Low-set ears are quite long and fall in folds

BREED HISTORY This breed, which is similar to the other Swiss scent hounds, was probably named after the Alps situated south of Berne, and has been used by Swiss hunters for at least 900 years. Medium in build, it closely resembles the Ariége Pointer.

LUZERNER LAUFHUND

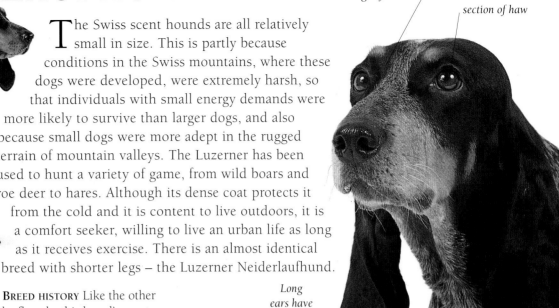

Coat has white background; when dog is wet it seems darker

Muscles of hind legs are well developed

Bridge of nose is slightly arched

Dark, oval eyes reveal small section of haw

Long ears have rounded tips

The Swiss scent hounds are all relatively small in size. This is partly because conditions in the Swiss mountains, where these dogs were developed, were extremely harsh, so that individuals with small energy demands were more likely to survive than larger dogs, and also because small dogs were more adept in the rugged terrain of mountain valleys. The Luzerner has been used to hunt a variety of game, from wild boars and roe deer to hares. Although its dense coat protects it from the cold and it is content to live outdoors, it is a comfort seeker, willing to live an urban life as long as it receives exercise. There is an almost identical breed with shorter legs – the Luzerner Neiderlaufhund.

BREED HISTORY Like the other laufhunds, this breed's exact origins are unknown. Its distinctive, tricoloured coat with mottled ticking suggests that the Petit Bleu de Gascogne may have played a role in its development.

Rounded feet, with hard, tough pads

KEY FACTS

COUNTRY OF ORIGIN Switzerland
DATE OF ORIGIN Middle Ages
FIRST USE Large-game hunting
USE TODAY Companion, hunting
LIFE EXPECTANCY 12–13 years
OTHER NAME Lucernese Hound

WEIGHT RANGE
15–20 kg (34–44 lb)
HEIGHT RANGE
46–58 cm (18–23 in)

SCHWYZER LAUFHUND

KEY FACTS

COUNTRY OF ORIGIN Switzerland
DATE OF ORIGIN Middle Ages
FIRST USE Small-game hunting
USE TODAY Companion, hunting
LIFE EXPECTANCY 12–13 years
OTHER NAME Swiss Hound

WEIGHT RANGE
15–20 kg (34–44 lb)
HEIGHT RANGE
46–58 cm (18–23 in)

BREED HISTORY Like its close relatives, this breed shares similarities with neighbouring French breeds. It may descend from the Porcelaine, or from the extinct Français Blanc et Orange. Its lean, lithe form was developed so that it could work in high mountain valleys.

Tail is distinctly pointed at tip

In profile, head is almost flat

Large, orange markings on white background

Rib cage is only moderately sprung

WHITE/
YELLOW

WHITE/
ORANGE

Ears are broad and long

Distinctive nose extends beyond lips

The bicolour appearance of this hound instantly distinguishes it from other laufhunds. Like them, this breed developed near the French border, and its evolution is closely linked with neighbouring French scent hounds. At one time the Schwyzer Laufhund occurred with wire hair, but this variety is now extinct. Although primarily a hunter's dog, this breed is also a good household companion, especially in rural parts of Switzerland. It can adapt to urban life, but it is both assertive and demanding, and does not take readily to obedience training. It does, however, get on well with children and with other dogs.

DOBERMANN

FAWN   BLUE   BROWN   BLACK

The elegant, often affectionate Dobermann is a classic example of the industriously successful dog-breeding programmes that took place in Germany just over 100 years ago. Today, this obedient, alert, and resourceful breed is a companion and service dog all over the world. Due to unscrupulous breeding, nervousness and fear biting can occur in some individuals. Good breeders, however, ensure that their dogs are neither shy nor vicious, and that they are well socialized before going to a new home. Heart disease is, unfortunately, becoming an increasingly serious problem for the breed.

Head emerges distinctly from neck, with skin fitting tightly over skull

Neck is lean but well muscled, and carries head with dignity

BREED HISTORY Beginning in the 1870s, a German tax collector, Louis Dobermann, used the Rottweiler, German Pinscher, Weimaraner, English Greyhound, and Manchester Terrier to develop this breed.

Well-proportioned chest has good width and depth

Thick hair is smooth, glossy, and hard

Feet are small, well arched, and cat-like, offering good footing for powerful stride

KEY FACTS

COUNTRY OF ORIGIN Germany
DATE OF ORIGIN 1800s
FIRST USE Guarding
USE TODAY Companion, security
LIFE EXPECTANCY 12 years
OTHER NAME Doberman Pinscher

WEIGHT RANGE
30–40 kg (66–88 lb)
HEIGHT RANGE
65–69 cm (25½–27 in)

BAVARIAN MOUNTAIN HOUND

KEY FACTS

COUNTRY OF ORIGIN Germany
DATE OF ORIGIN 1800s
FIRST USE Game tracking
USE TODAY Gundog, companion
LIFE EXPECTANCY 12 years
OTHER NAME Bayrischer
  Gebirgsschweisshund

WEIGHT RANGE
25–35 kg (55–77 lb)
HEIGHT RANGE
50.5–51.5 cm (20 in)

Rarely seen, except in the hands of professional foresters and game wardens in Germany and the Czech and Slovak Republics, this is a resourceful and ardent cold-scent follower. It usually works independently with its handler, and is frequently used when dogs with inferior blood-scenting ability have lost the trail of a wounded animal; the honour code of the middle European hunter instructs that no animal should be left to die on its own.

Masked face, with gentle expression and long, drooping ears

Thick, short, hard coat is finest on head

Body is powerful and well muscled

FAWN   RED

RED-BRINDLE   BLACK-BRINDLE

BREED HISTORY A small, agile dog with superb scenting ability was required to track wounded deer in the Bavarian mountains. The Hanoverian Hound was crossed with short-legged Bavarian hounds to produce such a breed.

Broad, strong feet, with thick pads and tough nails, enhance agility

RHODESIAN RIDGEBACK

Head is moderately long, flat, and broad between ears

Powerful neck integrates into clean, muscular shoulders

The standard for this solid dog was created at a meeting of breeders in Bulawayo, Zimbabwe in 1922, when the best attributes of five existing dogs were combined. South African big-game hunters took the breed north, to "lion country", to what was then Rhodesia. Contrary to its nickname and to myth, this muscular dog was never used to attack lions, but acted as a true hound, trailing big game, and then barking to attract the hunter's attention. Its sheer size and brute strength offered protection if it were itself attacked. Loyal and affectionate, few Ridgebacks are worked today; instead they serve as guards and companions.

BREED HISTORY References show that the Hottentots of southern Africa kept ridgebacked dogs as hunters and companions. In the 1800s, European settlers bred their Dutch and German mastiffs and scent hounds with the indigenous ridgebacks to produce today's breed.

Hair grows forwards along back

KEY FACTS

COUNTRY OF ORIGIN South Africa
DATE OF ORIGIN 1800s
FIRST USE Hunting
USE TODAY Companion, security
LIFE EXPECTANCY 12 years
OTHER NAME African Lion Hound

WEIGHT RANGE
30–39 kg (65–85 lb)
HEIGHT RANGE
61–69 cm (24–27 in)

Coat is short, dense, sleek, and glossy; in cold climates, a thick under-coat develops

Well-arched toes have tough, round, elastic pads

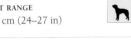

HANOVERIAN HOUND

Like its smaller descendant, the Bavarian Mountain Hound, the Hanoverian has an exceptionally fine nose and is able to follow an old, cold trail left by a wounded animal. Almost always used as a tracker, this is a professional's dog, rarely kept as a companion, but rather employed by game wardens and foresters to track wounded game, or sometimes even people. Because of its excellent nose, the breed can be used to track unwounded game, as well as for blood trailing. Generally calm, relaxed, and affable, this hound becomes dedicated and obsessive when working. At one time it was worked in packs, but today it almost always works singly.

Broad, low-set ears have round tips, and hang flat

KEY FACTS

COUNTRY OF ORIGIN Germany
DATE OF ORIGIN 1820s
FIRST USE Game tracking
USE TODAY Gundog, companion
LIFE EXPECTANCY 12 years
OTHER NAME Hannoverscher Schweisshund

WEIGHT RANGE
38–44 kg (84–99 lb)
HEIGHT RANGE
51–61 cm (20–24 in)

RED   BLACK-   BROWN
           BRINDLE

Lips are heavy and pendulous, with folds at corners

Short, dense, smooth coat has silky appearance

Forelegs are straight and moderately short

Pasterns are well boned and straight

BREED HISTORY Teutonic Common Law from the 9th century refers to a Leithund – a quiet, diligent trailing hound, used on a long line to locate quarry. Eventually the Leitbracke evolved. Breeders in the Hanover region crossed it with other, lighter local breeds, like the Haidbracke and Harzerbracke, to produce Germany's equivalent of the French St. Hubert Hound, or the English Bloodhound.

BILLY

Wide open, medium-sized eyes

Tail is long and strong

Medium-length, rounded neck is very strong

Thighs are only moderately muscled

Seldom seen outside France and rare even in Poitou, the Billy displays the grace of the Céris, the solid bone structure of the Montaimboeuf, and the superb nose of the Larrye. This is a marvellous hunter, vocal in pursuit of large game such as roe deer and wild boars. It is a relatively easygoing dog, usually safe with both adults and children, although it can be quarrelsome with other canine pack members. Typical of most scent hounds, the Billy is unlikely to snap or bite and therefore makes a poor watchdog. It responds well to obedience training and thrives on exercise. Because of the breed's exceedingly limited recent blood stock (only two survived World War II), inherited medical conditions are likely to occur.

KEY FACTS

COUNTRY OF ORIGIN France
DATE OF ORIGIN 1800s
FIRST USE Large-game tracking
USE TODAY Tracking, companion
LIFE EXPECTANCY 12–13 years

WEIGHT RANGE
25–33 kg (55–73 lb)
HEIGHT RANGE
58–70 cm (23–27½ in)

Muzzle is broad, straight, and slightly arched

Upper lip only slightly covers lower lip

Forehead is slightly domed

BREED HISTORY This breed is named after the Château de Billy, situated in Poitou and the home of its creator, Monsieur Hublot du Rivault, who combined three now-extinct breeds, the Céris, Montaimboeuf, and Larrye, to produce this refined pack hound.

Ears are set below eye level

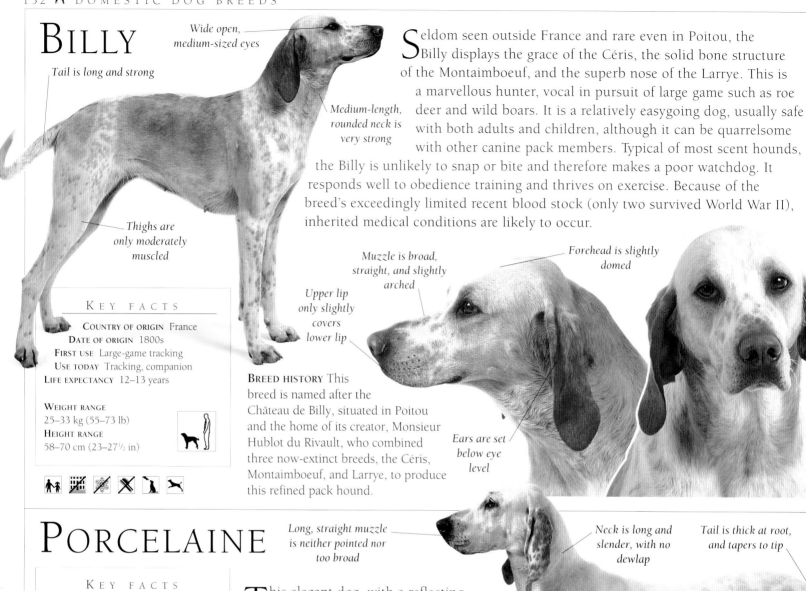

PORCELAINE

Long, straight muzzle is neither pointed nor too broad

Neck is long and slender, with no dewlap

Tail is thick at root, and tapers to tip

KEY FACTS

COUNTRY OF ORIGIN France
DATE OF ORIGIN 1600s
FIRST USE Game hunting
USE TODAY Companion, trailing
LIFE EXPECTANCY 12–13 years
OTHER NAME Chien de Franche-Comté

WEIGHT RANGE
25–28 kg (55–62 lb)
HEIGHT RANGE
53–58 cm (21–23 in)

This elegant dog, with a reflecting coat that brings to mind the lustre of porcelain, was a popular pack hunter in pre-revolutionary France. After the 1789 revolution and the subsequent turmoil and Reign of Terror few, if any, individuals survived in France. Swiss breeders, with their marvellous efficiency, took it upon themselves to restore and, some say, to recreate this breed. By 1845, it was once more prevalent in France, although today its numbers are both small and limited to France and Switzerland. With its fine, broad, musical voice, this keen-scented, active, friendly hound is an excellent example of how a breed can be "reconstructed" through selective breeding. It is a fine companion as well as an inveterate trail follower.

Powerful hind legs, with well-muscled thighs

Deep-set, gentle-looking eyes

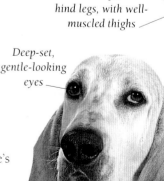

Shoulders are long and well muscled

Smooth, fine, glossy, close coat has no excess hair

BREED HISTORY After the Porcelaine's near extinction during the French Revolution, breeders developed the remaining dogs, which were situated around the French-Swiss border, incorporating some Swiss hound blood. This breed has contributed to the development of many American scent hounds.

Upper lips cover lower lips

NIEDERLAUFHUNDS

Berner Niederlaufhund

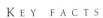

Rather large, dark eyes

BREED HISTORY Swiss walking dogs, or laufhunds, historically accompanied hunters on foot. Some hunters wanted even slower dogs, and through breeding the four indigenous laufhunds with either imported dachsbrackes or with dwarf laufhund puppies, the short-legged niederlaufhunds were created. The Schwyzer, Berner, and Luzerner Laufhunds all have recognized, short-legged, sturdier relatives, whose survival depends upon the continuing good work of Swiss breeders and the Swiss Kennel Club.

Large, pendulous ears are set below eyes

Tail falls with no noticeable curve

Body is slender; brisket does not reach below elbow

KEY FACTS

COUNTRY OF ORIGIN Switzerland
DATE OF ORIGIN 1800s
FIRST USE Small-game hunting
USE TODAY Small-game hunting, companion
LIFE EXPECTANCY 12–13 years
OTHER NAMES Small Swiss, Bernese, Lucerne Hounds
WEIGHT RANGE
9–14.5 kg (20–32 lb)
HEIGHT RANGE
30–38 cm (12–15 in)

Rough-coated variety

The Berner is the only niederlaufhund with a rough or wiry topcoat

Pendulous ears are similar to a Bloodhound's

Head is very slightly domed, with only moderate stop

Muzzle is long, clean, and robust

Large, black nose assists dog's scenting system

Long bones of forelegs are thickened and shortened

Muzzle is same length as domed skull

The direct ancestors of the niederlaufhunds, the standard-size laufhunds (*see pages 128–129*), have worked as scent trackers in the mountain valleys of Switzerland for hundreds of years. Niederlaufhunds are, however, a more recent development. All of these dogs develop thick, close topcoats and dense, fine undercoats to protect them from the harsh weather of winter. The Berner Niederlaufhund also occurs in a more unusual rough coat. Niederlaufhunds are excellent trackers. They are also highly vocal, and some individuals make moderately good watchdogs. Although Swiss breeders have been successful in perpetuating these unusual hounds, their numbers are extremely small. With the exception of the French-Swiss border region, the niederlaufunds are rarely seen outside their native country.

Schwyzer Niederlaufhund

Back is in good proportion to rest of body

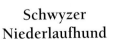

Forelimbs are sometimes only moderately shorter than a laufhund's

Luzerner Niederlaufhund

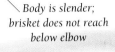

Feet are compact and cat-like

Legs are much longer than those of the other niederlaufhunds

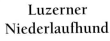

SPITZ-TYPE DOGS

NO GROUP OF DOGS has had a more influential relationship with humans than the spitz-type breeds that evolved throughout the Arctic regions of the world, in what are now the Scandinavian countries, and in Russia, Alaska, and Canada. The liaison between spitz-type dogs and many people living in these harsh regions is highly interdependent – it is likely that the tribes of people along the Arctic seas, across the tundra, and on Arctic islands would not have survived without the help of these versatile canines.

Karelian Bear Dog
Named after the province of Karelia in Finland, this striking, black-and-white dog is used to hunt large game.

COMPACT BODY, WITH DENSE TOPCOAT AND UNDERCOAT

SMALL, FOX-LIKE FACE IS SURROUNDED BY HEAVY HAIR

Pomeranian
Although it functions almost wholly as a companion, the Pomeranian is a standard spitz in miniature.

UNCERTAIN ORIGINS
The exact origin of spitz-type dogs remains uncertain. No archeological evidence has been discovered showing transition stages between the Northern Wolf and the thick-coated, muscular, short-eared, curly tailed spitz-type breeds. Skeletal remains, some of which are over 5,000 years old, indicate that it is far more likely that pariah dogs moved north and mated with the larger, more robust wolves of the Arctic. Without doubt, wolf blood has been both intentionally and unintentionally added for at least 5,000 years, producing the wolf-like, spitz-type breeds of today.

CANINE MIGRATIONS
Thousands of years ago, spitz-type dogs, descendants of dogs that had moved into the Arctic regions and interbred with wolves, spread out of the Arctic tundra, moving south into the temperate regions of North America, Europe, and Asia. With their newly acquired genetic material, they returned to the regions through which they had passed. These migrations resulted in the intermingling of material from radically different sources, thereby blurring the distinctions between breeds. This is how, for example, the African Basenji, a primitive breed closely related to the pariah dogs of Southeast Asia, could have developed anatomical attributes of the spitz-type dog. In North America, breeds such as the Alaskan Malamute and Canadian Husky remained above the Arctic Circle, but in Europe, spitz-type dogs moved south.

Prehistoric dog bones from Switzerland over 2,000 years old indicate that spitz-type breeds have inhabited central Europe for several millennia. These dogs are the likely sources of today's great variety of German spitzen, and of the Dutch Keeshond and Belgian Schipperke. They could also be ancestors of the miniaturized spitz-type dogs – the Pomeranian and the Italian Volpino. Other spitz-type dogs moved out of north-east Asia into China and Korea, evolving into today's Chow Chow and Jindo. Several centuries ago, and then again 1,500 years ago, spitz-type dogs were transported to Japan, possibly from Korea, forming the genetic foundation stock of the Hokkaido, Akita, Kai Dog, Shiba,

EARS ARE VERY LARGE, FIRM, AND ERECT, WITH ABUNDANT FRINGE

Alaskan Malamute
Bred by the Malhemut people of Alaska, this handsome dog has been a sled puller for centuries. The Timber Wolf has participated in its development.

ALMOND-SHAPED EYES ARE BROWN, BUT THEY ARE LIGHTER IN RED OR WHITE DOGS

Papillon
This breed's tail, coat, and head are typical of spitz-type dogs, but its "butterfly" ears are a cross between lopped spaniel ears and small, erect spitz ears.

BREED'S EARS ARE TYPICALLY SMALL

Standard German Spitz
The second largest of the German spitz-like dogs, this breed was developed in the 1800s. It occurs in a variety of colours and is well known throughout Europe.

DOG'S BODY IS LONGER THAN IT IS HIGH

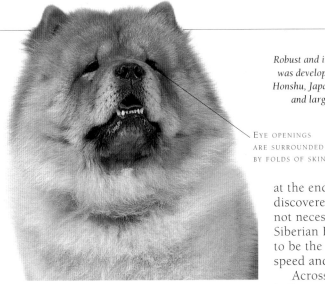

Chow Chow
The Chow Chow has pulled carts, guarded homes, and been eaten in China for thousands of years. This and the Shar Pei are the only breeds with black-pigmented tongues and gums. Self preoccupied, the Chow Chow seldom pays attention to anyone but itself.

EYE OPENINGS ARE SURROUNDED BY FOLDS OF SKIN

Akita
Robust and imperious, the Akita was developed on the island of Honshu, Japan, as a fighting dog and large-game hunter.

LUSH, DENSELY FURRED TAIL IS SET HIGH AND CURLS FORWARDS

Keeshond
This companion of Dutch bargemen is a typical spitz, with a tightly curled tail, heavy, insulating coat, and trim, small, erect ears.

at the end of the last century, racers discovered that powers of endurance did not necessarily relate to a dog's size. The Siberian Husky has subsequently proved to be the breed most suited for combining speed and endurance.

Across northern Europe and Asia, indigenous people used other breeds to herd their livestock. The Russians used their great variety of laikas, and the Sami people of Scandinavia used lapphunds. Other breeds, including the

HEAD IS IN GOOD PROPORTION TO REST OF BODY

HAIR IS LONG AND DENSE AROUND NECK

and Shikoku. The Japanese Spitz is probably of much more recent origin, developed from Samoyed stock within the last 200 years.

VALUABLE WORKERS
Through selective breeding, spitz-type breeds initially evolved to fulfil three roles. These trim and lively dogs have been adapted for hunting, herding, and the draught work of pulling sleds.

The most powerful and tenacious breeds became big-game hunters, and today's Karelian Bear Dog, Russo-European Laika, and Akita are their descendants. Others also helped hunt large game, such as elks and moose, evolving to become today's Norwegian Elkhound and Swedish Jämthund. In both Scandinavia and Japan, small, indigenous dogs were used to hunt small mammals or birds. Their descendants include the Finnish Spitz, Norbottenspets, Lundehund, the four Russian spitzen, and all the Japanese middle-sized dogs. This group of dogs also excels at pulling sleds.

The largest of these great draught dogs is the Eskimo Dog, which often weighs over 55 kg (121 lb). Other draught dogs include the Alaskan Malamute, Greenland Dog, and in Russia, the Samoyed, Siberian Husky, Kamchatka Sled Dog, and Chucotka Sled Dog. When sled-pulling races began in Canada and Alaska

EARS ARE LARGER THAN THOSE OF OTHER JAPANESE BREEDS

Kai Dog
Another of Japan's indigenous spitz-type dogs, the Kai developed in the prefecture of Yamanashi, where it was used to hunt large game.

EYES ARE INTENSE WHEN DOG IS ALERT

Norwegian Buhund
With typical spitz characteristics – a stocky body, small, erect ears, and a high-set, curled tail – the Buhund is a classic spitz-type breed.

THICK FUR PROTECTS EARS FROM FROSTBITE

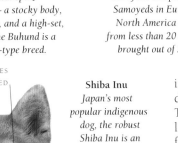

Samoyed
All of the companionable Samoyeds in Europe and North America descend from less than 20 specimens brought out of Siberia.

DARK-BROWN EYES ARE ALMOND SHAPED

Shiba Inu
Japan's most popular indigenous dog, the robust Shiba Inu is an industrious, independent breed. It has the body conformation of a typical spitz-type dog.

Lapinporokoira, Norwegian Buhund, and Iceland Dog, all with additional herding breed bloodlines, were used as farm workers. More recently, small dogs such as the Pomeranian, Japanese Spitz, and American Miniature Eskimo Dog have been selectively bred solely for companionship.

PHYSICAL CHARACTERISTICS
The anatomy of the spitz-type breeds is well suited to harsh northern climates. The insulating, water-resistant undercoat is as dense as, or even denser than, the topcoat. The small ears eliminate unnecessary heat loss and reduce the risk of frostbite. Thick fur grows between the toes, providing physical protection from razor-sharp ice.

These dogs have a distinctly rugged beauty – their conformation is closest to that of the Northern Wolf and their natural colours and wedge-shaped muzzles have a primitive attraction. Not always easy to manage, many breeds require extensive training.

ALASKAN MALAMUTE

Densely furred tail carried over back in typical spitz fashion

Small, well-furred ears lose little body heat

Almond-shaped eyes are friendly, interested, even mischievous

Panting allows body heat to escape; dense coat makes breed prone to heat stroke

Although wolf-like in appearance, the Alaskan Malamute is an affectionate dog. Not overly demonstrative, it will drop its veneer of dignity and willingly play with people or dogs it knows. This is a powerful dog with a deep chest and outstanding stamina. Although Jack London, in his novels of life in the frozen North, referred to the great strength of huskies, he was probably describing the Malamute. Popular in Canada and the United States as a family companion, the breed thrives on activity and excels in sled-racing competitions.

Heavily muscled, strong-boned legs are ideal for traction and weight pulling

BREED HISTORY Named after the Mahlemut Inuit living on the Arctic coast of western Alaska, this breed was used as a draught animal long before Europeans visited the Americas.

Bitch and dog

Females are significantly smaller than males

ESKIMO DOG

Expression of dark, well-set eyes is frank and open

The Eskimo Dog does everything – eating, working, sparring, and arguing – with an abundance of energy. It is independent and requires firm, consistent handling in order to learn to respect its human pack leaders. Eskimo Dogs have strong pack instincts, will readily fight among themselves for seniority, and scavenge food whenever they see it. They also willingly look upon other animals as food. The breed can adapt to living with people and is capable of typical canine affection, but it is most suitable for working.

Head is neat and wolf-like in appearance

Densely haired tail in classic spitz curl

BREED HISTORY For thousands of years, this dog has been the only means of transportation for the Inuit living above Hudson Bay, in what are now the Northwest Territories of Canada. It has remained a primitive, aloof breed.

Fur between toes protects pads from freezing

Dense coat protects dog from temperatures far below freezing

ANY
COLOUR

SIBERIAN HUSKY

Smaller and lighter than most other breeds of sled dog, the elegant Siberian Husky is agile, athletic, and a tireless worker. In common with other ancient northern spitz types this breed seldom barks, but engages in communal howling, much like wolves. Very popular in Canada and the United States, the Siberian Husky's coat occurs in a profusion of colours, and it is one of the few breeds that can have blue, brown, hazel, or non-solid-coloured eyes. The breed is dignified and gentle, and makes a very pleasant companion.

Tail is heavy with hair and needs grooming during moulting season

ANY COLOUR

KEY FACTS

COUNTRY OF ORIGIN Siberia
DATE OF ORIGIN Antiquity
FIRST USE Sled pulling
USE TODAY Companion, sled racing
LIFE EXPECTANCY 11–13 years
OTHER NAME Arctic Husky

WEIGHT RANGE
16–27 kg (35–60 lb)
HEIGHT RANGE
51–60 cm (20–23½ in)

Unusual patterns like this are unique to the breed

BREED HISTORY Used as a draught animal by the nomadic Inuit, the Siberian Husky was chanced upon by 19th-century fur traders and brought to North America in 1909.

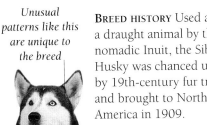

Muscular legs are straight, with substantial bone

Compact, well-furred feet, with cushioned pads

Medium-sized, triangular ears are parallel to each other when dog is alert

GREENLAND DOG

KEY FACTS

COUNTRY OF ORIGIN Greenland
DATE OF ORIGIN Antiquity
FIRST USE Sled pulling, guarding, watchdog
USE TODAY Sled racing, hunting
LIFE EXPECTANCY 13 years
OTHER NAME Grünlandshund
WEIGHT RANGE
30–32 kg (66–70 lb)
HEIGHT RANGE
56–64 cm (22–25 in)

BREED HISTORY The ancestry of this breed can possibly be traced back to dogs accompanying people from Siberia well over 12,000 years ago. As these people evolved to the Inuit of today, they may have used local wolves for further breeding.

Small, triangular-shaped ears rarely get frostbite

Typical large, bushy tail curls over back and protects face while sleeping

ANY COLOUR

Coat occurs in many colour variations

Jaws are extremely powerful

Robust head is broad and wedge shaped

Spitz-type dogs have existed throughout the Arctic regions since antiquity. With the mechanization of travel in the latter part of this century, their numbers rapidly diminished. The Greenland Dog is not as heavy as the Eskimo Dog, but is often slightly taller. Although aloof and independent, the Greenland Dog, like the Eskimo Dog, can be affectionate with its owners. It has become popular in Norway and Sweden as a hiking companion.

Legs are well feathered; toes are thickly furred with large, strong pads

POMERANIAN

CREAM,
WHITE,
SABLE

RED,
ORANGE

BLUE

GREY

BROWN

BLACK

*Feet are small and
compact in shape*

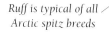

*Ruff is typical of all
Arctic spitz breeds*

*Ears are
small and
erect, like
those of
a fox*

BREED HISTORY Today's small
dog was developed in Pomerania,
Germany, by breeding from small
varieties of the large German Spitz.
Its classic spitz shape and orange
coat illustrate its Arctic origins.

Queen Victoria popularized the Pomeranian when
she added some to her kennels. In the early days, the
Pomeranian was both larger and whiter than it is now. White was
usually associated with a large-sized dog of up to 13 kg (30 lb) in
weight and breeders, selecting for a smaller size, also brought out
the now prevalent sable and orange colours. The Pomeranian,
being a naturally large breed that has been recently reduced
in size, still acts like a "big dog". It will bark unchecked,
making it a superb watchdog that will also challenge larger
dogs. The breed also makes a superb companion.

*Long, straight
topcoat covers dense
undercoat*

*Legs are fine boned
and well feathered
down to hocks*

VOLPINO

WHITE   FAWN   BLACK

*Small ears
are typical
of all spitz
breeds*

*Densely furred, small,
triangular ears are
carried neatly erect*

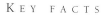

The Volpino has a more robust head
and larger eyes than the Pomeranian,
and is usually white in colour. The muzzle
is short and straight, not dissimilar to that
of a spaniel. Like the Pomeranian, the
Volpino is very fox-like in
appearance (*volpe* means fox in
Italian). In Renaissance Italy,
owners adorned these lively and
affectionate little dogs with ivory
bracelets. The Volpino is a good
watchdog, and can be trained
in obedience.

*Tail curls over body
and is carried flat
on back*

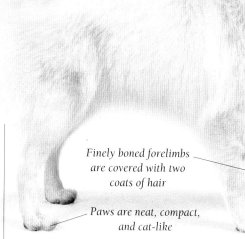

*Finely boned forelimbs
are covered with two
coats of hair*

*Paws are neat, compact,
and cat-like*

*Ruff is not
as luxurious
as a
Pomeranian's*

*Ochre-coloured
eyes have lively,
alert expression*

BREED HISTORY The
Volpino's development
probably predates the
miniaturization of the Pomeranian in
Germany. The breed was popular
with women in Renaissance Italy.

PAPILLON

Long-fringed tail arches forwards

Ears carried obliquely, like a butterfly's wings

The dainty looking Papillon is a powder puff in disguise. With dramatic ears reminiscent of a butterfly's wings (*papillon* means butterfly in French), small size, and a fine, silky, and abundant coat, this breed looks like a classic lapdog, content to spend its life watching the world go by. Not so. When trained correctly the Papillon, like the Pomeranian, excels at obedience training. It is a well-constructed, physically fit breed, suitable for town or countryside. As with most toy breeds, there is a physical tendency to suffer from slipping kneecaps and a psychological tendency to be possessive of its owner.

Abundant, silky topcoat, with no undercoat

Round-tipped ears set towards back of head

Fine, long feet like those of a hare

White, narrow, clearly defined blaze

Medium-sized, round, dark eyes

Bushy tail requires daily grooming

BREED HISTORY Stories say that the Papillon is descended from the 16th-century Spanish Dwarf Spaniel. Its shape and long coat, however, suggest northern spitz blood in its origins.

KEY FACTS

COUNTRY OF ORIGIN Continental Europe
DATE OF ORIGIN 1600s
FIRST USE Companion
USE TODAY Companion
LIFE EXPECTANCY 13–15 years
OTHER NAME Continental Toy Spaniel

WEIGHT RANGE
4–4.5 kg (9–10 lb)
HEIGHT RANGE
20–28 cm (8–11 in)

PHALENE

From the 16th to the early 19th century, this breed was a favourite of the aristocracy. The Épagneul Nain is a possible ancestor of both the Phalene and Papillon. Both breeds were painted by Goya, Rubens, and Van Dyke, and owned by Marie Antoinette and Madame de Pompadour. The two dogs are classified in the United States and Great Britain as one breed, with either erect or dropped ears. Elsewhere they are usually recognized as separate breeds. The Phalene is an effective ratter, and is cat-like in its cleanliness.

BREED HISTORY More spaniel-like in appearance because of its lopped ears, the Phalene is otherwise identical to the Papillon. It, too, combines spaniel and spitz characteristics.

CHESTNUT/ WHITE

BLACK/ WHITE

TAN/ WHITE

BLACK/ TAN/ WHITE

Ears are pendant, and covered with long hair

Tail, arched spitz-like over back, needs daily grooming

Coat is predominantly white, without undercoat

Rather low-set eyes are dark and do not bulge

Dropped ears give gentle appearance

KEY FACTS

COUNTRY OF ORIGIN Continental Europe
DATE OF ORIGIN 1600s
FIRST USE Companion
USE TODAY Companion
LIFE EXPECTANCY 13–15 years
OTHER NAMES Continental Toy Spaniel, Papillon, Squirrel Dog

WEIGHT RANGE
4–4.5 kg (9–10 lb)
HEIGHT RANGE
20–28 cm (8–11 in)

RUSSO-EUROPEAN LAIKA

BREED HISTORY Until the 1800s, all spitz-type dogs in Russia were called laikas. Intrepid elk and wolf hunters from Finland were bred with Russian Utchak Shepherds to produce this fearless breed.

Small, prominent ears

Small, brown, fiery eyes have alert expression

Straight muzzle tapers towards nose

Typical spitz curl to medium-length tail

Tail uncurls when dog relaxes

KEY FACTS

COUNTRY OF ORIGIN Russia/Finland
DATE OF ORIGIN 1800s
FIRST USE Large-game hunting
USE TODAY Hunting
LIFE EXPECTANCY 10–12 years
OTHER NAMES Karelian Bear Laika, Russko-Europiskaia Laika

WEIGHT RANGE
21–23 kg (45–50 lb)
HEIGHT RANGE
53–61 cm (21–24 in)

Full hair inside ears

Straight and stiff topcoat

Muscular shoulders slope forwards

Hind paws are lower than forepaws

In 1947, the Soviet authorities ordained that laikas existed only within the boundaries of the Soviet Union. Subsequently, they disregarded the internationally recognized Karelian Bear Dog of Finland, which was undoubtedly a laika, and replaced it with the black-and-white Russo-European Laika. Although very similar to its Finnish relative, the Russian variety is more powerful and aggressive – its fearless pursuit of big game such as elks, bears, or wolves is formidable. This large and athletic breed does not make a good companion.

EAST SIBERIAN LAIKA

Black nose at end of straight muzzle

WHITE   WHITE/BLACK   GREY

TAN, RED   BLACK

Thick paws are well insulated

Medium-short topcoat covers dense, waterproof undercoat

KEY FACTS

COUNTRY OF ORIGIN Russia
DATE OF ORIGIN 1800s
FIRST USE Large-game hunting
USE TODAY Large-game hunting, companion
LIFE EXPECTANCY 10–12 years
OTHER NAME Vostotchno-Sibirskaia Laika

WEIGHT RANGE
18–23 kg (40–50 lb)
HEIGHT RANGE
56–64 cm (22–25 in)

Dog keeps warm by holding tightly curled tail close while resting

Short, insulating fur covers small, erect ears

Muscular neck gives holding power when dog attacks animals

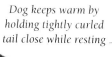

In the 1800s, Russian breeders selectively bred the indigenous spitz dogs of Siberia to work to the gun. This resulted in the East Siberian Laika, which finds game and then holds it, barking until the hunter arrives. Laikas can be trained to mark birds in trees in the same way. Although wolf-like in appearance, this breed is calm and even tempered, and makes a good companion, even in the city. It can also be trained in obedience.

BREED HISTORY This breed was developed from the working sled and hunting dogs of the indigenous people of the High Arctic. Its type was fixed in 1947.

WEST SIBERIAN LAIKA

WHITE   WHITE/   TAN,   BLACK
         BLACK   RED

KEY FACTS

COUNTRY OF ORIGIN Russia
DATE OF ORIGIN 1800s
FIRST USE Large-game hunting
USE TODAY Large-game hunting,
  companion
LIFE EXPECTANCY 10–12 years

WEIGHT RANGE
18–23 kg (40–50 lb)
HEIGHT RANGE
53–61 cm (21–24 in)

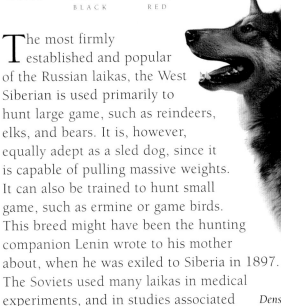

*Ears are well
covered with
insulating hair*

*Moderately close-
set eyes*

The most firmly established and popular of the Russian laikas, the West Siberian is used primarily to hunt large game, such as reindeers, elks, and bears. It is, however, equally adept as a sled dog, since it is capable of pulling massive weights. It can also be trained to hunt small game, such as ermine or game birds. This breed might have been the hunting companion Lenin wrote to his mother about, when he was exiled to Siberia in 1897. The Soviets used many laikas in medical experiments, and in studies associated with space travel. The first dog to circumnavigate the Earth in a space craft was called Laika, although it was probably a Samoyed.

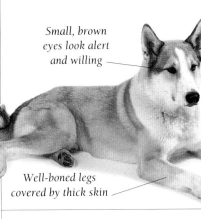

*Small, brown
eyes look alert
and willing*

*Well-boned legs
covered by thick skin*

*Dense
undercoat*

BREED HISTORY
This breed is the most numerous of the Russian laikas. Hunters from Khantu and Mansi in the Ural mountains may have bred this breed for their working purposes.

KARELIAN BEAR DOG

*Black nose at end of
wedge-shaped head*

*Dense and thick
topcoat; heavy,
protective undercoat*

*Long hair
on tail*

KEY FACTS

COUNTRY OF ORIGIN Finland/Russia
DATE OF ORIGIN 1800s
FIRST USE Large-game hunting
USE TODAY Large-game hunting,
LIFE EXPECTANCY 10–12 years
OTHER NAMES Karjalankarhukoira,
  Karelsk Bjornhund

WEIGHT RANGE
20–23 kg (44–50 lb)
HEIGHT RANGE
48–58 cm (19–23 in)

The Karelian Bear Dog, which is more numerous outside its own country than any of the Russian laikas, is used by elk hunters throughout Finland, Sweden, and Norway. Having declined in numbers in the 1960s, it has subsequently enjoyed an upsurge in popularity and is now bred in North America and many European countries. A robust, tenacious, and powerful dog, it is willing to take on virtually any game animal. Like the Russo-European Laika, the breed has a distinctive black-and-white coat, which is unusual in northern spitz-type dogs. It is not an easy dog to have as a companion, and extensive training is necessary if it is to be kept for this purpose.

*Small eyes
show intent
concentration*

*Small ears and
dense fur reduce
risk of frostbite*

*Jaws are
immensely
powerful*

*Tail curls
over back
in a typically
spitz arch*

*Thighs are
covered in thick
hair*

BREED HISTORY Closely resembling the Russo-European Laika, this breed evolved in the part of Finland claimed by the Soviet Union earlier this century. For a long time, similar dogs have been bred in Karelia for hunting large game.

FINNISH SPITZ

Small ears are sharply pointed

BREED HISTORY Descendants of the Finnish Spitz probably accompanied the ancestors of the Finns when they first arrived in Finland. For centuries, this breed inhabited the eastern part of Finland and the Karelian region of Russia. After the Russian Revolution, individuals living in Karelia became known as Karelo-Finnish Laikas.

Tail curves vigorously from root forwards and down in curve

Strong forelegs extend from relatively straight shoulders

KEY FACTS

COUNTRY OF ORIGIN Finland
DATE OF ORIGIN Antiquity
FIRST USE Small-mammal hunting
USE TODAY Hunting, companion
LIFE EXPECTANCY 12–14 years
OTHER NAMES Finsk Spets, Suomenpystykorva

WEIGHT RANGE
14–16 kg (31–35 lb)
HEIGHT RANGE
38–51 cm (15–20 in)

A hard-working, popular gundog in Finland, this independent, almost cat-like canine has a tremendous voice – an asset for its superb watchdog abilities. It listens on the forest floor for wing beats, rushes to the tree where the bird has landed, then barks continuously until the hunter arrives; it hunts squirrels and martens in a similar manner. Strong willed and independent, the Finnish Spitz thrives on exercise, and enjoys working in the coldest weather. A moderate-sized, cautious, but lively breed, it is relatively common in Great Britain and North America, and its popularity is likely to increase even more in the future.

Medium-sized eyes are dark and vivacious

Chest is deep and belly is slightly drawn up

Strong hind legs have small, rounded feet, with insulating hair between toes

LAPINPOROKOIRA

BLACK/ WHITE   BLACK/ TAN   BLACK

Pointed ears are erect

BREED HISTORY The Lapinporokoira traces its beginnings to the Finnish Lapphund, the reindeer-herding dog of the indigenous Sami people of northern Norway, Sweden, Finland, and Russia. Its present standard was written in 1966 by Olli Korhonen, then chairman of the Finnish Kennel Club.

Topcoat has moderate length of straight, rough hair

Muzzle is short and thick

Dense tail, with moderate length

Forelegs are very strong and powerfully muscled

Bridge of black nose is straight

The Lapinporokoira combines the spitz-type dog's resilience in a harsh climate with the shepherd's working ability to herd livestock. During this century, German Shepherd stock was used to improve the herding character of the breed. Until the arrival of the motorized snowmobile, the Sami people used these dogs exclusively to herd reindeer. With escalating fuel costs, their use for this purpose has recently been revived. In Finland, there is a well-organized, active breeding programme that ensures the continued working ability of this sturdy, confident breed.

KEY FACTS

COUNTRY OF ORIGIN Finland
DATE OF ORIGIN 1600s
FIRST USE Reindeer herding
USE TODAY Companion, herder
LIFE EXPECTANCY 11–12 years
OTHER NAMES Lapland Reindeer Dog, Lapponian Herder

WEIGHT RANGE
27–30 kg (60–66 lb)
HEIGHT RANGE
48–56 cm (19–22 in)

FINNISH LAPPHUND

Large, dark-brown eyes are set horizontally

Head is compact and slightly conical, with straight muzzle and jet-black nose

BREED HISTORY The historic herding dog of the Sami people, this breed is smaller than the Lapinporokoira, its descendant. It is an example of interbreeding between northern spitz-type dogs and herding dogs from further south in Europe. Originally used to herd reindeer, today it usually herds sheep and cattle.

Abundant hair is particularly profuse around hindquarters

Muzzle is short and cone shaped

Skull is broad between ears, and slightly domed; ridge above eyes is rather prominent

Tail curls well over back, a trait of spitz-type dogs

Hind parts of forelimbs have exceptionally long hair

KEY FACTS

COUNTRY OF ORIGIN Finland
DATE OF ORIGIN 1600s
FIRST USE Reindeer herding
USE TODAY Companion, herder
LIFE EXPECTANCY 11–12 years
OTHER NAMES Lapinkoira, Lapland Dog

WEIGHT RANGE
20–21 kg (44–47 lb)
HEIGHT RANGE
46–52 cm (18–20½ in)

Dense, insulating hair grows between well-arched toes

VARIETY OF COLOURS

Forelegs seem to be short in comparison with rest of body

Hind legs are very straight, with little angulation at hocks or stifles

Ears are deeply insulated on both sides to protect them from frostbite

Ears are broad at their points of insertion, short, erect, and well spaced

Throughout northern Scandinavia and the Karelian district of Russia, the Sami people used dogs to herd semi-domesticated reindeer. As interest in indigenous breeds of dog developed, both the Swedes and the Finns claimed the Sami reindeer-herding dog as their own. To avoid problems, two breeds were internationally recognized – the Swedish Lapphund, or Lapland Spitz, and the Finnish Lapphund or Lapinkoira. These are, in essence, the same breed in different countries. In Finland, selective breeding ensures that the breed's herding characteristics are not lost. Elsewhere, it is more often kept as a companion. Strongly built, it has a dense, luxurious, insulating double coat of hair. Although the breed retains a natural herding instinct, this has diminished through breeding for coat density and colour, rather than for function.

Body is longer than it is high, with straight back

Medium-length, lean, powerful neck is covered with dense double coat

NORWEGIAN ELKHOUND

Small, pointed, well-furred ears lose little heat in cold weather

Topcoat is thick, abundant, and coarse

High-set tail curls over back

Hair is longest on underside of tail

Wide, deep, and well-ribbed chest is protected by dense hair

Firm, muscular neck is of medium length

Muzzle is tapered, but not pointed

BREED HISTORY The national dog of Norway, this breed has existed in Scandinavia for at least 5,000 years. Current standards were developed in the late 1800s.

Robust, vigorous, athletic, and with a strong voice, which it willingly uses when it sees its prey, this is the most popular of the three Scandinavian elkhounds. It is the most classic of the spitz breeds, and Stone Age fossils from Norway confirm its antiquity. When working as a gundog it does not chase, but follows its prey in a hound-like manner. An extremely versatile breed, it has been used to hunt lynx and wolves, as well as elks, and is a successful retriever of small game such as rabbits and foxes. Norwegian farmers also use it to herd farmyard chickens and ducks.

BLACK NORWEGIAN ELKHOUND

Long in the leg and small in body, with a smooth and sleek coat, this handsome spitz is rarely seen outside Scandinavia. An independent and quarrelsome spirit suggests that its ancestry may be slightly different from that of its more familiar namesake. When working, however, it is equally adept. It creeps soundlessly towards its prey, and then barks and bays, dodging attacks until the hunter arrives. Its distinctive colour helps the hunter see his dog among the trees and snow. The breed is strong and dignified, and makes an excellent guard dog.

Extremely mobile ears stand firm and erect

Muzzle covers strong jaws and tight lips

BREED HISTORY With origins as ancient as its grey cousin, the smaller and more agile-looking Black Norwegian Elkhound comes from the region demarcating the boundary between Norway and Sweden. It was first acknowledged as a distinct breed in 1877.

Chest is not as deep as a Norwegian Elkhound's

High-set tail curls over on itself

Thighs are long and well boned

Coat is not as dense as its grey relative's

SWEDISH LAPPHUND

LIVER   BLACK

LIVER/   BLACK/
WHITE   WHITE

This is a very old breed, certainly as long established as the lean sight hounds of Asia, which are always portrayed as the most ancient of all dogs. The historic responsibility of the Swedish Lapphund was to herd and to guard the Sami people's herds of reindeer against predators. By the 1960s, there was sufficient concern about its guarding ability for the Swedish Kennel Club to undertake a breeding programme to enhance its working capacity. The breed is rarely seen outside its home country, although it can sometimes be found in Finland and Russia.

Ears are erect and pointed

Short, cone-shaped muzzle narrows to a point at nose

Topcoat is thick and wiry; undercoat is waterproof

Forelegs are strong and vertical

Belly is only slightly drawn up

BREED HISTORY The 7,000-year-old skeletal remains of a dog found near Varanger, Norway closely resemble today's Lapphund. It is very similar to the Finnish and Russian laikas.

KEY FACTS

COUNTRY OF ORIGIN Sweden
DATE OF ORIGIN Antiquity/1800s
FIRST USE Reindeer herding
USE TODAY Companion, sheep/ cattle herding
LIFE EXPECTANCY 12–13 years
OTHER NAMES Lapphund, Lapland Spitz, Lapplandska Spets

WEIGHT RANGE
19.5–20.5 kg (43–45 lb)
HEIGHT RANGE
44–49 cm (17½–19½ in)

SWEDISH ELKHOUND

BREED HISTORY At one time, virtually every valley in Scandinavia had its own variety of elkhound. The Jämthund, which takes its name from the Jämtland district of Sweden, eventually received official recognition, and is now Sweden's national dog.

KEY FACTS

COUNTRY OF ORIGIN Sweden
DATE OF ORIGIN Antiquity/1800s
FIRST USE Large-mammal hunting
USE TODAY Companion, gundog
LIFE EXPECTANCY 12–13 years
OTHER NAME Jämthund

WEIGHT RANGE
29.5–30.5 kg (65–67 lb)
HEIGHT RANGE
58–64 cm (23–25 in)

Rather small, well-set eyes have lively expression

Chest is broad and roomy, with flexible ribs

Hind legs are very powerful

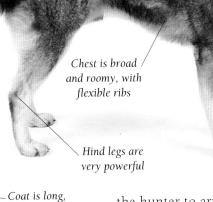

Coat is long, hard, and close fitting

Neck is long, lean, and robust

The largest of the elkhounds, this breed was probably once used for bear hunting, but as that need declined it became an ardent and successful hunter of lynx, wolves, and moose. Having successfully chased its prey across the snow, it would then corner it, while it waited for the hunter to arrive. As versatile as the other Norwegian elkhounds, this heavy-set, thick-boned, hardy breed has been used as a shepherd, watchdog, sled dog, and Swedish Army dog. It is particularly popular in Sweden, both as a working dog and as a companion. Also seen with increasing frequency in Great Britain, the Netherlands, and North America, it is likely that its popularity will soon spread worldwide.

KEESHOND

Profuse coat is densest in ruff around neck

Dense hair grows between toes, typical of spitz-type dogs

Small ears are close set

BREED HISTORY Named after Cornelius (Kees) de Gyselear, a Dutch politician, the Keeshond was once a popular guard and vermin controller in the southern Dutch provinces of Brabant and Limburg. It is the most popular large European spitz in Great Britain and North America.

Feet are very small and cat-like

Muzzle is not too long and fairly narrow

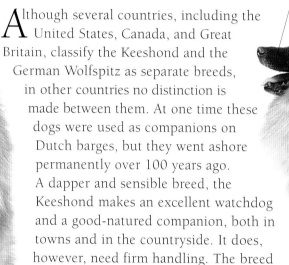

KEY FACTS

COUNTRY OF ORIGIN The Netherlands
DATE OF ORIGIN 1500s
FIRST USE Barge dog
USE TODAY Companion, watchdog
LIFE EXPECTANCY 12–14 years
OTHER NAME Wolfspitz

WEIGHT RANGE
25–30 kg (55–66 lb)
HEIGHT RANGE
43–48 cm (17–19 in)

Although several countries, including the United States, Canada, and Great Britain, classify the Keeshond and the German Wolfspitz as separate breeds, in other countries no distinction is made between them. At one time these dogs were used as companions on Dutch barges, but they went ashore permanently over 100 years ago. A dapper and sensible breed, the Keeshond makes an excellent watchdog and a good-natured companion, both in towns and in the countryside. It does, however, need firm handling. The breed remains consistently popular in North America.

Hair is tipped with black

GERMAN WOLFSPITZ

Medium-length tail bends over back

Dark, medium-sized eyes are set at slight slant

Broad skull narrows like wedge to tip of nose

Ears are densely covered with insulating hair

The Wolfspitz, and all other German spitzen, are becoming increasingly rare in their native country. In Germany, different colours of Wolfspitz became associated with different regions – the grey Wolfspitz, for example, was found along the Rhine, in the regions of Stuttgart and Mannheim. This is not an easy breed to obedience train, but because it uses its voice frequently and has an imperious presence, it makes an excellent watchdog. It is not an ideal dog with children, since it tends to nip first and ask questions later. However, it is gregarious, adaptable, relatively outgoing, and enjoys human company. Its luxurious, dense coat needs regular attention.

BREED HISTORY This vivacious breed is descended from spitz-type herding dogs, which probably arrived in Germany over 1,000 years ago. Originally used as a herder, the German Wolfspitz was an agile and proficient worker.

Abundant hair covers chest; undercoat is equally dense

KEY FACTS

COUNTRY OF ORIGIN Germany
DATE OF ORIGIN 1500s
FIRST USE Herding
USE TODAY Guarding, companion
LIFE EXPECTANCY 12–14 years
OTHER NAME Chien Loup

WEIGHT RANGE
27–32 kg (59½–70½ lb)
HEIGHT RANGE
46–50 cm (18–19 in)

GERMAN SPITZ

VARIETY OF COLOURS

Tail lies against side of body

Ears are compact, triangular, set high, and close together

Giant German Spitz

Solid-coloured, dense, long, rather harsh hair covers chest

Sturdy and solid bone gives substance to forequarters

Hair is shortest, but still very thick, on face

Standard German Spitz

Head has fairly accentuated stop

KEY FACTS

COUNTRY OF ORIGIN Germany
DATE OF ORIGIN 1600s
FIRST USE Companion (giant, toy); farm worker (standard)
USE TODAY Companion (giant, standard, toy)
LIFE EXPECTANCY 12–13 years (giant); 13–15 years (standard); 14–15 years (toy)
OTHER NAMES Deutscher Gross Spitz (giant); Deutscher Mittel Spitz (standard); Deutscher Spitz Klein (toy)
WEIGHT RANGE
17.5–18.5 kg (38½–40 lb) (giant); 10.5–11.5 kg (23–41 lb) (standard); 8–10 kg (18–22 lb) (toy)
HEIGHT RANGE
40.5–41.5 cm (16 in) (giant); 29–36 cm (11½–14 in) (standard); 23–28 cm (9–11 in) (toy)

The German Spitz occurs in three varieties of size – giant, standard, and toy. The giant and toy spitzen have always been companion dogs, while the more common standard spitz was once an efficient farm worker. In recent years, this breed has declined in popularity; even the fiesty and responsive toy variety is losing ground to the Pomeranian, an almost identical breed. This decline in popularity is not entirely surprising – spitzen demand more attention than many other breeds; in particular, their coats require routine care to prevent matt formation. Unfortunately, many individuals resent grooming, and some, particularly males, resent other dogs or strangers. Unlike many guard dogs, such as the Dobermann and German Shepherd, the German Spitz is not easy to obedience train. However, this refined and confident breed is elegant in the show ring and, when trained, makes an equable companion.

Surprisingly small feet have insulating hair between toes

Greatest length of hair is on tail

Toy German Spitz

Eyes appear proportionally large

A perfect miniature, the toy spitz's body is in exact proportion

Small ears reduce heat loss, an effective method of insulation for living in cold climates

BREED HISTORY The German Spitz is probably descended from spitz-type herding dogs, which arrived in Europe with Viking plunderers. German literature refers to the spitz as early as 1450. The three types of German Spitz are similar in conformation, only differing in size and colour. The giant spitz occurs in white, brown, or black, while its smaller relatives occur in a wider variety of coat colours. Well known, although declining in numbers in its land of origin, this breed has now reached most European countries.

JAPANESE AKITA

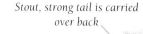

Relatively small, thick, erect, triangular ears

Rather small eyes are deep brown in colour

Stout, strong tail is carried over back

Nose is large and black

BREED HISTORY This, the largest of all Japanese breeds, was once bred for pit fighting. When this sport declined, it was used for hunting. Although by the 1930s numbers had declined to near extinction, the breed's survival was assured by the formation of the Society for the Preservation of Japanese Breeds.

ANY COLOUR

Coat is hard, with fine undercoat

Japanese breeds are all classified according to their size – large (akita), medium (shika), and small (shiba). Although there are many medium-sized breeds, there is only one large breed, the Akita. This is an impressive dog with a powerful presence. While many individuals are even tempered, some are difficult to handle. By nature the breed is undemonstrative and aloof, which means that obedience training can be irksome. Males, in particular, have a tendency to get into dog fights more frequently than many other breeds. However, well-trained individuals make excellent companions and effective watchdogs. Poised and regal, the Akita is best kept by experienced dog handlers.

Elbows fit snugly to body

KEY FACTS

COUNTRY OF ORIGIN Japan
DATE OF ORIGIN 1600s
FIRST USE Large-game hunting, dog fighting
USE TODAY Companion, security
LIFE EXPECTANCY 10–12 years
OTHER NAMES Akita Inu, Akita

WEIGHT RANGE
34–50 kg (75–110 lb)
HEIGHT RANGE
60–71 cm (24–28 in)

AINU DOG

VARIETY OF COLOURS

Small, erect ears are at right angles to brow

BREED HISTORY The Ainu tribe, whose origins are unknown, arrived in Japan over 3,000 years ago, bringing this spitz-type dog with them. As the Ainu were pushed onto the island of Hokkaido by an influx of Japanese people, their dogs gradually became restricted to that island.

Lively, dark-brown eyes, set triangularly, are somewhat small

Straight bridge leads to dark nose

KEY FACTS

COUNTRY OF ORIGIN Japan
DATE OF ORIGIN Antiquity
FIRST USE Large-game hunting
USE TODAY Companion
LIFE EXPECTANCY 11–13 years
OTHER NAMES Ainu Inu, Hokkaido Dog

WEIGHT RANGE
20–30 kg (45–65 lb)
HEIGHT RANGE
46–56 cm (18–22 in)

Tail curls in typical spitz fashion

Well-fitted lips have dark pigmentation

Topcoat is harsh and straight

This is a typical shika-inu, or medium-sized dog – headstrong, stubborn, aggressive with other dogs, but deeply submissive to its human family. At one time it was used for hunting by the Ainu, the aboriginal people of Japan. Today, it is primarily a companion, and is usually kept outdoors on a rope or chain, where it acts as a highly vocal watchdog. Many Ainu Dogs have blue-black tongues, a physical trait that suggests a distant relationship with the similarly tongued Chow Chow and Shar Pei. Through the active work of the Society for the Preservation of Japanese Breeds, the Ainu Dog was designated a Japanese Natural Monument in 1937.

Well-muscled hindquarters are covered with insulating double coat

Forelegs are straight and lean

KAI DOG

Small eyes are triangularly set and give good binocular vision

Robust tail is carried classically over back

Narrow skull and tapered muzzle

KEY FACTS

COUNTRY OF ORIGIN Japan
DATE OF ORIGIN 1700s
FIRST USE Large-game hunting
USE TODAY Companion
LIFE EXPECTANCY 11–13 years
OTHER NAMES Kai Inu, Tora Inu

WEIGHT RANGE
16–18 kg (35–40 lb)
HEIGHT RANGE
46–58 cm (18–23 in)

BREED HISTORY Nicknamed Tora Inu (Tiger Dog), this breed has existed since medieval times in the mountainous regions around the Yamanashi Prefecture in Japan. In 1934, due in part to the work of a dedicated breeder, Mr. Haruo Isogai, the Kai was designated a Natural Monument.

Ears are densely covered with hair

Hindquarters are covered with harsh topcoat

Elbows are carried close to body

 RED-BRINDLE

 BLACK-BRINDLE

After World War I, Japanese breeders began to import a variety of European dogs – this coincided with a declining interest in native breeds. In the 1930s, however, Haruo Isogai, a canine researcher, began a successful study, which resulted in the grouping and classification of all Japanese breeds. The Kai is a typical medium-sized breed, or shika-inu. It can be distinguished from other shika-inus by its narrower skull and slightly more tapered head. A one-person dog, it can be rather recalcitrant and headstrong, and is the least responsive of the Japanese breeds. The Kai has only reached North America in the last few years.

JINDO

Small, triangular, pricked ears are carried slightly forwards

Almond-shaped eyes in triangular settings

BREED HISTORY The origins of this compact, densely furred breed are unknown, but its conformation suggests that it arrived on the island of Jindo (south west of mainland Korea) centuries ago, and that it is a descendant of Nordic spitzen. In 1938, the Korean government designated it a National Treasure.

Topcoat is dense and soft

KEY FACTS

COUNTRY OF ORIGIN Korea
DATE OF ORIGIN Middle Ages
FIRST USE Hunting, watchdog
USE TODAY Hunting, watchdog, companion
LIFE EXPECTANCY 11–12 years

WEIGHT RANGE
16–18 kg (35–40 lb)
HEIGHT RANGE
41–58 cm (16–23 in)

Until recently, no Jindos existed outside Korea. In mainland Korea they interbred with other dogs, but on the island of Jindo they bred pure. Due to the recent influx of Korean immigrants to the United States, this breed has now spread to North America, where it is prized for its uniqueness and smothered with affection. By contrast, in Korea, dogs are still occasionally eaten, and this was no doubt the fate of many of the Jindo's ancestors. This is a typical spitz-type dog, protective of the family and aloof with strangers. It retains a strong hunting instinct.

Black nose and lips on straight muzzle lead to moderate stop

 WHITE

 FAWN

 BLACK/WHITE

Cat-like feet are on straight legs, with elbows close to body

JAPANESE SPITZ

KEY FACTS

COUNTRY OF ORIGIN Japan
DATE OF ORIGIN 1900s
FIRST USE Companion
USE TODAY Companion, security
LIFE EXPECTANCY 12 years

WEIGHT RANGE
5–6 kg (11–13 lb)
HEIGHT RANGE
30–36 cm (12–14 in)

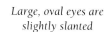

Large, oval eyes are slightly slanted

Small nose at end of wedge-shaped face

This rugged little dog is a classic example of miniaturization. It looks remarkably like the Samoyed, yet it is up to five times smaller than its presumed progenitor, and in some ways five times tougher. Lively and bold, the breed became very popular in Japan in the 1950s, and although numbers in its native land have declined, it has become increasingly popular in Europe and North America, where it acts as a house protector and guard. The Japanese Spitz can be an inveterate barker, although selective breeding has to some extent reduced this characteristic.

Pointed ears are erect

BREED HISTORY Everything about the Japanese Spitz strongly suggests that it is simply a small version of the Samoyed. The nomadic Samoyed tribe introduced that breed to Mongolia, from where it could easily have reached Japan.

Dense feathering of hair

SAMOYED

BREED HISTORY The hardy and adaptable Samoyed accompanied the nomadic tribe of that name for centuries, as it traversed the most northerly regions of Asia. The breed was not introduced into the West until 1889.

Originally a hunter and guardian of reindeer herds, today's snow-white breed retains many of its original traits. The Samoyed is an exceptionally good-natured, friendly dog. It particularly enjoys human companionship, is good with children, and is not aggressive, although it makes a reasonably good watchdog. Like most spitz breeds, the Samoyed does not take readily to obedience training, and obedience classes are advisable. Owners must be prepared to spend some time regularly grooming the breed's long and luxurious coat.

Deep-set, dark eyes contrast with white hair

Hind legs are extremely muscular

Very long and imposing tail

Small ears set wide

Chest has plenty of room for heart and lungs

Ruff of long, harsh hair grows through soft, thick undercoat

Feet are large and rather flat

KEY FACTS

COUNTRY OF ORIGIN Russia
DATE OF ORIGIN Antiquity/1600s?
FIRST USE Reindeer herding
USE TODAY Companion
LIFE EXPECTANCY 12 years
OTHER NAME Samoyedskaya

WEIGHT RANGE
23–30 kg (50–66 lb)
HEIGHT RANGE
46–56 cm (18–22 in)

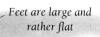

EURASIER

RED   FAWN   GREY   BLACK   MAHOGANY

Pointed, erect ears are covered with hair

Eyes are dark brown

Tongue is like that of a Wolfspitz

Densely haired tail is not as long as a Samoyed's

Neck is long and muscular

The Eurasier was developed as a "regenerated" version of the sled-pulling Russian laika, although it is now also kept as a pet. Shyness and timidity are known behaviour problems within the breed. It is not an ideal family companion, since it has a tendency to select one family member as the pack leader and then respond only to that person. Still rare outside Germany, the Eurasier seldom barks, and therefore does not make a good watchdog. Like the Chow Chow, it has a tendency to be rather snappy.

BREED HISTORY
This spitz breed originated in the 1950s in Germany. It is a cross between the Samoyed, Chow Chow, and German Wolfspitz.

Broad, slightly flat feet are good for gripping the ground

KEY FACTS

COUNTRY OF ORIGIN Germany
DATE OF ORIGIN 1950
FIRST USE Sled pulling
USE TODAY Sled pulling, companion
LIFE EXPECTANCY 11–12 years

WEIGHT RANGE
19–32 kg (40–70 lb)
HEIGHT RANGE
48–61 cm (19–24 in)

CHOW CHOW

BREED HISTORY The origins of the Chow Chow remain a mystery, although without doubt it is of spitz descent. Historians in the early 1700s described a black-tongued dog being used as food in the Orient. The Chow Chow first arrived in Great Britain in 1780.

Small, thick ears, slightly rounded at tips

Small, dark eyes; tight eyelids often cause medical problems

CREAM, WHITE   FAWN   RED

BLUE   BLACK

KEY FACTS

COUNTRY OF ORIGIN China
DATE OF ORIGIN Antiquity
FIRST USE Guarding, cart pulling, as food
USE TODAY Companion
LIFE EXPECTANCY 11–12 years

WEIGHT RANGE
20–32 kg (45–70 lb)
HEIGHT RANGE
46–56 cm (18–22 in)

The Chow Chow is probably entitled to be naturally aloof and stubborn. Throughout Mongolia and Manchuria its meat was once a delicacy, and its skin a popular fur for clothing. Its name, however, does not refer to the American cowboy's term for food. In the 1800s, English sailors named it after the term they used to describe miscellaneous ship cargo. Although it looks like an overstuffed teddy bear, the Chow Chow is not cuddly. It is a one-person dog, with a terrier-like tendency to snap or bite. The coat needs intense grooming to remove both undercoat and guard hair.

Tongue is black

Feet are small and cat-like

CHINOOK

The Chinook functions as a classic spitz – ever willing to work, especially at sled pulling in the snow. It has a strong, confident personality and needs firm handling as a puppy to ensure that it does not fight with other members of the dog team. Its numbers are small, and it is in danger of extinction, but breeders claim that it is an excellent guard dog, although some individuals are rather headstrong.

Ears hang loosely

Nose has large, wide nostrils

Ears are usually lopped or pendant

Heavily muscled hindquarters provide strength and endurance

Broad chest has excellent space for heart and lungs

BREED HISTORY By crossing Eskimo Dogs with both smooth-coated St. Bernards and Belgian shepherds, Arthur Walden, an American breeder, developed a breed with immense pulling power. The Chinook, named after Walden's favourite dog, is extremely rare.

Forelegs are thick and sturdy

Topcoat is thick and dense, with even denser undercoat that thins in summer

Thickly cushioned pads on feet

Tail is thick at root, tapering to tip

KEY FACTS

COUNTRY OF ORIGIN United States
DATE OF ORIGIN Early 1900s
FIRST USE Sled pulling
USE TODAY Sled pulling, companion, guarding
LIFE EXPECTANCY 13–14 years

WEIGHT RANGE
29.5–41 kg (65–90 lb)
HEIGHT RANGE
53–61 cm (21–26 in)

SHIKOKU

Small, erect ears face forwards

Although Japan's Buddhist Shintoist culture prohibits eating land mammals, people living in remote, rural areas once hunted game, using dogs to help them. The Shikoku is a survivor of these hunting breeds. A stubborn individual, it tends to dominate other dogs, although it is gentle with its human companions. A rare breed, it has seldom been seen outside Japan, but its future is constantly monitored by the Society for the Preservation of Japanese Breeds.

Small, dark, deep-set, oval eyes, with dark-pigmented lids

Jet-black nose is prominent on tapering muzzle

Coat is short, harsh, and very dense in winter

KEY FACTS

COUNTRY OF ORIGIN Japan
DATE OF ORIGIN Antiquity
FIRST USE Game hunting
USE TODAY Companion, hunting
LIFE EXPECTANCY 11–13 years

WEIGHT RANGE
15–20 kg (38–44 lb)
HEIGHT RANGE
46–55 cm (18–22 in)

BREED HISTORY This dog has existed in the Kochi Prefecture of Japan since ancient times, when it was used to hunt. It is one of many regional shika (medium-sized) dogs, and was declared a Natural Monument in 1937.

RED

RED-BRINDLE

BLACK-BRINDLE

Powerful hind legs support deep chest and tucked abdomen

SCHIPPERKE

Dark-brown, small, oval eyes

Small, strong, erect ears are set high

Coat is longest around neck

KEY FACTS

COUNTRY OF ORIGIN Belgium
DATE OF ORIGIN Early 1500s
FIRST USE Small-mammal hunting, barge guarding
USE TODAY Companion
LIFE EXPECTANCY 12–13 years

WEIGHT RANGE
3–8 kg (7–18 lb)
HEIGHT RANGE
22–33 cm (9–13 in)

BREED HISTORY This little barge captain's exact origins are unknown, although it has been in existence for many centuries. Anatomically, it is a classic spitz-type dog and is probably related to other continental European spitzen such as the German Spitz and Pomeranian.

Dense undercoat makes topcoat stand out, forming ruff

Deep, broad chest, covered with slightly harsh hair

Fox-like head

The Schipperke may be small, but it retains the personality of a street fighter. This compact package of energy once worked for its living on Flanders and Brabant canal barges, keeping them free from vermin and warning the bargemen of potential intruders. It was also used on land, acting as an efficient rat, rabbit, and mole hunter. Resilient and conveniently sized, it makes an ideal household companion.

Straight front legs stand directly under body

Muscular and powerful hind legs

Small, round, tight feet

SHIBA INU

VARIETY OF COLOURS

Japan's most popular indigenous dog, the Shiba is also increasing in numbers in Australia, Europe, and North America. At one time, a tendency towards poorly developed adult teeth occurred, but this was corrected through careful selective breeding. Like the Basenji, the Shiba seldom barks, preferring to shriek in an extraordinary manner. Robust and rather independent, this is a delightful breed for someone with experience and patience.

Small, triangular eyes

Pointed muzzle, with dark nose

Thick, strong tail is carried in curl

Chest is deep, with well-rounded ribs

BREED HISTORY This smallest of all the indigenous Japanese breeds has existed in the Sanin region of Japan for centuries. Bones over 2,500 years old have been found at excavation sites.

KEY FACTS

COUNTRY OF ORIGIN Japan
DATE OF ORIGIN Antiquity
FIRST USE Small-game hunting
USE TODAY Companion
LIFE EXPECTANCY 12–13 years

WEIGHT RANGE
8–10 kg (18–22 lb)
HEIGHT RANGE
35–41 cm (14–16 in)

Well-developed legs and thighs support powerful and graceful hips

Forelegs are straight, with elbows held close to body

ICELAND SHEEPDOG

OFF-
WHITE   FAWN   CHESTNUT   BLACK

*Medium-sized, alert,
dark-brown eyes*

*Forelegs are
very sturdy*

A n excellent herder, the Iceland Sheepdog has had a troubled history. Before effective tapeworm treatments were developed, the breed regularly contracted *Echinococcus* tapeworms from eating contaminated sheep carcasses, and passed on this unpleasant parasite to its owners. To control the spread of *Echinococcus* in the human population, all dogs were banned from Iceland's capital city of Rekjavik. This ban still survives today, although worming medicines can now control the parasite. The Iceland Sheepdog is a tough and vivacious dog, and looks very much like a smaller version of the Greenland Husky.

*Arched head and
rather short,
compact muzzle*

*Large nose and
black-pigmented lips*

*Double dewclaws
similar to
those of a
Lundehund*

BREED HISTORY
Descended from
dogs introduced by
Scandinavian colonists,
this breed is probably a
relative of the Buhund.

NORWEGIAN BUHUND

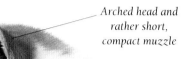

WHEATEN   RED   BLACK

*Dark-brown, bright
eyes, with dark eyelids*

*High-set tail similar
to that of an Iceland
Sheepdog*

*Snout is short
and compact*

T he word *bu* means shed or stall in Norwegian, a telling reference to this breed's original function. The Buhund has a strong herding instinct and thrives on physical activity. It has become increasingly popular in Great Britain, and has been successfully used in Australia as a sheepdog, since it does not suffer unduly from intense heat. However, inherited eye and hip problems sometimes occur in the breed. It is an excellent companion, is good with children, and is unlikely to bite or snap unless provoked. It is also a good watchdog, and is easy to obedience train.

BREED HISTORY The
Buhund was originally
used to pull sleds and as a
hunter's companion. It now
serves as both a guard dog
and a companion.

*Short, rough
topcoat, with dense
undercoat*

*Stocky, compact
body*

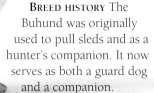

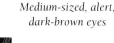

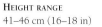

LUNDEHUND

GREY

Medium-sized, erect ears

BREED HISTORY Originating in Vaerog and Rost in northern Norway, for centuries the isolated Lundehund was used to collect puffins from nests on precipitous cliffs. It was not recognized as a distinct breed until 1943.

BLACK/WHITE **BLACK**

Brown, fairly deep-set eyes

BROWN/WHITE

KEY FACTS

COUNTRY OF ORIGIN Norway
DATE OF ORIGIN 1500s
FIRST USE Puffin hunting
USE TODAY Companion
LIFE EXPECTANCY 12 years
OTHER NAME Norwegian Puffin Dog

WEIGHT RANGE
5.5–6.5 kg (12–14 lb)
HEIGHT RANGE
31–39 cm (12–15½ in)

Small, wedge-shaped head

The small and agile Lundehund is unique in having five, rather than the usual four, supporting toes on its forepaws. The feet themselves have exceptionally large pads and double dewclaws. This combination gave the dog its superb grip as it climbed cliff pathways and traversed rocky crevasses, until it reached a nest and captured a puffin. Another unique feature is a soft fold across the cartilage of the ear. This unusual anatomical trait enabled the dog to fold down its ears to protect them, presumably from dripping water as it searched through cliff passages for its prey. A lively and responsive breed, the Lundehund is now used primarily as a companion.

Dense topcoat lies flat against body

Extra pad and double dewclaws on forepaws

Moderately muscled hindquarters suitable for agility rather than speed

NORDIC SPITZ

Very similar in size and function to the Finnish Spitz, this native of Sweden was used to hunt squirrels when squirrel pelts were valuable commodities of trade. It then graduated to hunting game birds such as black grouse. The dog listens to the sound of the bird flying, and waits for the sound to stop. It then runs to the tree in which the bird has landed, and remains there until the hunter can move forwards and shoot it. The breed has also been used as a guard dog and to pull small carts. Today, most Nordic Spitzen are kept as companions. The breed is seldom seen outside its native country.

Wedge-shaped head is flat on top and rounded at sides

WHITE/RED

WHITE/BROWN

Curled, bushy tail carried to side

Thick, rough topcoat is fairly long

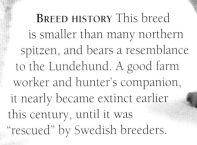

KEY FACTS

COUNTRY OF ORIGIN Sweden
DATE OF ORIGIN 1600s
FIRST USE Bird hunting
USE TODAY Companion, bird hunting
LIFE EXPECTANCY 12–14 years
OTHER NAMES Norbottenspets, Pohjanpystykorva

WEIGHT RANGE
12–15 kg (26–33 lb)
HEIGHT RANGE
41–43 cm (16–17 in)

Erect ears almost touch when dog is alert

Medium-sized, dark eyes have alert and vigilant expression

Small, compact feet, with hair between toes

BREED HISTORY This breed is smaller than many northern spitzen, and bears a resemblance to the Lundehund. A good farm worker and hunter's companion, it nearly became extinct earlier this century, until it was "rescued" by Swedish breeders.

TERRIERS

TERRIERS EVOLVED FROM HOUNDS – in appearance, German dachshunds are a classic example of a scent hound, miniaturized and dwarfed through selective breeding. Breeding also considered personality – the terrier's aggressive instinct was enhanced, so that it would work ruthlessly

and efficiently, without backing down, when confronted by a fox or badger. There is no group of dogs more expert at tunnelling than terriers; these fiesty dogs still willingly engage in head-on combat with earth-dwelling mammals on their opponents' home territories.

Border Terrier
This breed probably takes is name from the once-famous Border Hunt, which it followed on foot.

BEARD'S TEXTURE IS UNIQUE – A COMBINATION OF HARD AND SOFT HAIR

Dandie Dinmont Terrier
This breed, which dates back to the 1600s, is named after a character in Sir Walter Scott's novel Guy Mannering.

LARGE, LONG, ERECT EARS ARE COVERED IN SMOOTH, FINE HAIR

Miniature Pinscher
Germany's unique contribution to the field of terriers, the lively and demonstrative Miniature Pinscher trots with a distinctive "hackney-horse" gait, flexing its knees much more than most dogs.

ANGLO-SAXON ROOTS

Although dachshunds and many other earth dogs evolved in several European countries (for example, the Spanish Ca Rater descends from small podencos), most of the world's terriers originated in Great Britain. Their name derives from the Latin *terra*, meaning earth, although today it is not uncommon for terrier owners to blithely refer to their dogs as Yorkshire or West Highland White

"terrorists". All terriers are of relatively recent origin. Little reference is made to them until 1560, when the reknowned British writer, Dr. John Caius, described them as quarrelsome, snappy, and only to be tolerated living in stables. At that time only the short-legged terriers existed, and they were used solely to bolt down fox and badger holes. While dachshunds had smooth, close coats, the terriers described by Dr. Caius and by other British writers, such as Thomas Bewick in the 1700s, had rough coats, which were usually black and tan or mixed fawn. They had erect ears and sprightly temperaments. Anything was fair game for these robust, well-muscled dogs – badgers and foxes, but also rats, weasels, ferrets, otters, marmots, mice, and snakes.

As working dogs, no dog type was a more efficient killing machine than the tenacious, tunnel-hugging terriers. Going to ground demanded small size and also an unquestioning fearlessness, resolution, and toughness. Today, these attributes remain; this is why terriers are better at overcoming serious illness than any other dog group. Almost nothing interferes with the terrier's zest for life.

MUZZLE IS BROAD AND LONG, HOUSING A MAGNIFICENT SET OF DRAMATICALLY LARGE TEETH

"TOPKNOT" IS USUALLY LEFT UNTRIMMED

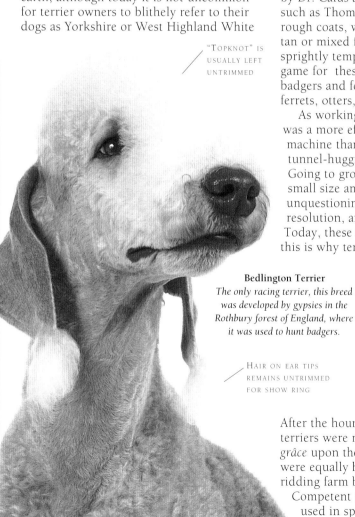

Bedlington Terrier
The only racing terrier, this breed was developed by gypsies in the Rothbury forest of England, where it was used to hunt badgers.

HAIR ON EAR TIPS REMAINS UNTRIMMED FOR SHOW RING

EFFICIENT ALL-ROUNDERS

During the 19th century, short-legged terriers, carried in saddle-bags, would accompany foxhounds on the hunt. After the hounds cornered their quarry, the terriers were released to inflict the *coup de grâce* upon the beleaguered fox. Terriers were equally happy as farmers' companions, ridding farm buildings of unwanted vermin. Competent and versatile, they were also used in sport – Patterdale and Yorkshire Terriers were developed as much for sport ratting as for any other purpose. In rat pits in Great Britain and

Lakeland Terrier
At one time each county of England had its own terrier. The Lakeland evolved to hunt vermin in England's Lake District.

Ireland, owners worked their terriers against the clock to see how many rats they could kill. Elsewhere, terriers such as the Glen of Imaal fought against each other or against other animals, in open fields or in pits. Bull-baiting breeds were originally large, mastiff-type dogs, but terrier blood was added in order to heighten their aggression, producing the English and Staffordshire Bull

NECK IS WELL
MUSCLED, GIVING
STRENGTH

Welsh Terrier
*Very similar in size to both the
Lakeland and Wire-haired Fox
Terrier, the Welsh Terrier is the
likely direct descendant of the now-
extinct Black-and-tan Terrier, once
common throughout England.*

Czesky Terrier
*This affable, attractive breed is a
good worker and an excellent
household companion. It is
becoming increasingly popular
in the United States.*

Terriers, the American
Staffordshire and, more
recently, the American Pit
Bull Terrier. Although the
Pit Bull Terrier has the worst
reputation of all dog breeds,
with reliable owners it is no
more dangerous than many
other dogs of its size. What
distinguishes the bull terriers, such as the
Pit Bull, from other large, muscular breeds,
is their tenacity. When they bite they do
not let go. In working breeds such as the
Lakeland, Welsh, and Irish Terriers, this is
called "gameness". Even show dogs must
demonstrate that they are willing to
attack a piece of animal hide.

EARS ARE ERECT,
BUT FOLD FORWARDS
TOWARDS CHEEKS

SCOTTIES HAVE
DISTINCTIVE
EYEBROWS AND
BUSHY BEARDS

they include the
Kromforländer in
Germany, and the
massive Black
Russian Terrier,
which
exemplifies
the former
Soviet Union's
desperate need to be seen to produce the
"biggest and the best". At the other end of
the spectrum, miniaturization continues –
the Miniature Pinscher, English Toy Terrier,
Miniature English Bull Terrier, Brabancon,
and Toy Fox Terrier indicate the terrier's
success as a companion.

Wire Fox Terrier
*This terrier was originally
developed to accompany
the fox hunt and to kill the
fox after it was cornered
by the hounds.*

Scottish Terrier
*Scotland is the home of a
variety of badger-, rabbit-,
and rat-hunting terriers. In
1882, this black variety was
formally given the name
of its country.*

ENTERTAINING COMPANIONS
As family pets, terriers are a joy. They love
the rough and tumble, have unlimited
energy, and provide constant entertainment.
Even the smallest individual, however,
retains its instinct to nip. Most terriers
make excellent city pets, and if excessive
yapping is controlled at an early stage, they
make superb watchdogs and loyal defenders
of their realms.

EARS WERE
ORIGINALLY CROPPED
TO REDUCE DAMAGE
IN FIGHTING RING

REGIONAL VARIATIONS
Generic, hard-working,
short-legged terriers
existed throughout Great
Britain and Ireland, but
in the 1800s breeders
began breeding to type,
producing regional
variations. In Scotland,
these became the Skye,
Scottish, Sealyham,
Dandy Dinmont, and
Cairn Terriers. White
Cairns became known as
West Highland Whites.
Breeds including the
Paisley and Clydesdale
Terriers disappeared,
although their blood
probably courses in the
veins of the Yorkshire
Terrier. Similar changes
occurred in England,
Ireland, and Wales,
producing the 29 British
breeds that exist today.

Petit Brabancon
*Belgium's delightful
Petit Brabancon comes
in a variety of colours
and makes a lively
companion.*

**American
Staffordshire Terrier**
*This breed was
developed as a heavier
variety of Britain's
Staffordshire.*

TOPCOAT IS
SHORT AND
HARD; A SOFT
UNDERCOAT
DEVELOPS IN
COLD WEATHER

occupied by British terriers, tough British
breeds were imported to create new breeds
such as the Czesky Terrier. British terriers
are the genetic base of the Japanese Terrier,
and the Australian and Australian Silky
Terriers. Terrier breeds are still evolving –

Australian Silky Terrier
*This spirited breed
developed in Australia
during the 1800s.*

Many of these terriers, including the Welsh,
Irish, Kerry Blue, Fox, and Airedale
Terriers, are descendants of hunting and
retrieving dogs. These breeds do not go
to ground but rather chase, capture,
kill, and carry. Outside Great
Britain, although dachshunds, the
Miniature Schnauzer, German,
Austrian, and Affen pinschers, and
Dutch Smoushond all fill the niche

AIREDALE TERRIER

Ears are small and V-shaped

BREED HISTORY The Airedale Terrier originated in Yorkshire, when working men in Leeds crossed the Old English Broken-haired Terrier with the Otterhound, producing this extremely versatile "King of Terriers".

Beard covers powerful jaws

KEY FACTS

COUNTRY OF ORIGIN Great Britain
DATE OF ORIGIN 1800s
FIRST USE Badger/otter hunting
USE TODAY Companion, guarding
LIFE EXPECTANCY 13 years
OTHER NAME Waterside Terrier

WEIGHT RANGE
20–23 kg (44–50 lb)
HEIGHT RANGE
56–61 cm (22–24 in)

Head, ears, and beard are always tan coloured

Forelegs are perfectly straight and thickly boned

Hard, dense, wiry coat requires expert grooming for show purposes

Small, round, compact feet, with well-cushioned pads and arched toes

Thighs are muscular and powerful; stifles are well bent

Terrier eyes are keen and alert

Although the Airedale is far too large to live up to the definition of the word "terrier", which in French means an ability to go to ground, in all other ways it is the essence of this group of dogs. A born watchdog, with a delinquent tendency to get into street brawls with other dogs, the tough, hardy, and faithful Airedale has been used as a police dog, sentry dog, and messenger. Were it not for its inherently strong, stubborn streak, it would be a popular and successful working dog.

IRISH TERRIER

Small, dark eyes are full of life

Ears have high fold and drop to cheeks

High-set tail free of feathers

BREED HISTORY Developed in the districts around Cork, southern Ireland, this sprightly breed is probably descended from old black-and-tan, and wheaten terriers.

Small, neat beard requires experienced clipping

Moderately long, widening neck usually has frills on each side

KEY FACTS

COUNTRY OF ORIGIN Ireland
DATE OF ORIGIN 1700s
FIRST USE Watchdog, vermin hunting
USE TODAY Companion, field trials, coursing, vermin hunting
LIFE EXPECTANCY 13 years
OTHER NAME Irish Red Terrier

WEIGHT RANGE
11–12 kg (25–27 lb)
HEIGHT RANGE
46–48 cm (18–19 in)

V-shaped, small ears of moderate thickness

Hard, wiry, topcoat has soft, fine undercoat

Straight legs have plenty of bone and muscle

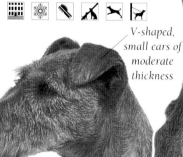

Jaws are long, strong, and powerful

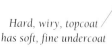

Although it is now primarily a companion dog, in Ireland the Irish Terrier's excellent hunting abilities are sometimes still put to good use. It is a superb water dog and a fiery vermin killer. In the United States, these abilities have been perpetuated through field trials and lure coursing. With its great, striding action and racy lines, this is perhaps the most elegant of all terriers. Although a good family playmate, it is a real terrorist with other dogs, is unlikely to back down from a fight, and should be kept on a lead unless fully obedience trained.

WELSH TERRIER

KEY FACTS

COUNTRY OF ORIGIN Great Britain
DATE OF ORIGIN 1700s
FIRST USE Ratting
USE TODAY Companion
LIFE EXPECTANCY 14 years

WEIGHT RANGE
9–10 kg (20–22 lb)
HEIGHT RANGE
36–39 cm (14–15½ in)

BREED HISTORY Originating in North Wales in the 1760s, this breed is probably the direct descendant of the previously common but now-extinct Old English Broken (or Coarse-haired) black-and-tan Terrier.

This lively and stubborn terrier thrives on mental and physical activity. More popular in North America than in Great Britain, the Welsh Terrier is a compact dog, suitable as a companion but still exceedingly effective as a rural vermin catcher. Coming from a working background, the Welsh Terrier is not very difficult to obedience train, but it does not back down from dog fights.

Excellent teeth not prone to tartar or decay

Slightly arched, thickish neck

Eyes are small, dark, and alert

Abundant, wiry topcoat covers fine undercoat

Good length to face and large, black nose

Strong, muscular thighs and good bone length

Small, round feet have hard, black nails and pads

Profuse beard catches food and needs routine attention

KERRY BLUE TERRIER

BREED HISTORY By government decree the national dog of Ireland, the breed has its origins in County Kerry. It was internationally recognized in 1922, when the breed standard was fixed by a British breeder, Mrs. Casey Hewitt.

Puppies of this breed are born black, and their coat colour changes to blue some time between nine and twenty-four months of age. In general, the earlier the coat changes colour, the lighter the eventual coat will be. With no undercoat and a non-shedding topcoat, the Kerry Blue is a suitable household pet. It is an all-round terrier – an excellent guard, ratter, and water retriever, and has been used as a successful herder. Rat and rabbit hunting are still a part of the life of working Kerry Blues in Ireland.

KEY FACTS

COUNTRY OF ORIGIN Ireland
DATE OF ORIGIN 1700s
FIRST USE Badger/fox/rat hunting
USE TODAY Companion, field trials, rat/rabbit hunting
LIFE EXPECTANCY 14 years
OTHER NAME Irish Blue Terrier

WEIGHT RANGE
15–17 kg (33–37 lb)
HEIGHT RANGE
46–48 cm (18–19 in)

Ears not carried as high as those of some terriers

Beard indicates how profusely coat grows

Strong neck runs to sloping shoulders

Profuse beard needs constant attention

Soft, silky, and abundant coat should be cut with scissors

Small feet covered with profuse hair

Long, lean head, with powerful neck and jaws

Bent stifle, with hocks close to ground

BORDER TERRIER

The Border, an uncomplicated and genuine terrier, little altered from its original form, is built to be small enough to follow a fox down the narrowest hole, but with enough leg to keep up with riders on horseback. It has never achieved the show-ring popularity of other terriers, and has therefore remained true to its original form and function. Its durable coat protects it from adverse weather conditions; its long legs and stamina enable it to keep up with the most demanding activity. Its amenable personality makes it a superb family dog.

Broad head and short muzzle

Dark eyes look keen and alert

Hind legs have sturdy loins

BREED HISTORY The exact origins of this breed are unknown. There is evidence that it existed in the borders between England and Scotland, in much its present form, in the late 1700s.

Harsh, dense topcoat

Small, V-shaped ears

Front legs are straight

Feet have thick pads

KEY FACTS

COUNTRY OF ORIGIN Great Britain
DATE OF ORIGIN 1700s
FIRST USE Ratting, worrying foxes from lairs
USE TODAY Companion, hunt follower
LIFE EXPECTANCY 13–14 years

WEIGHT RANGE
5–7 kg (11½–15 lb)
HEIGHT RANGE
25–28 cm (10–11 in)

WHEATEN TAN, RED

GRIZZLE BLUE/ TAN

LAKELAND TERRIER

Dark eyes look intent and fearless

Ears hang forwards

Tail is carried high

Dense, harsh topcoat

Long moustache covers very powerful jaws

COAT DETAIL

KEY FACTS

COUNTRY OF ORIGIN Great Britain
DATE OF ORIGIN 1700s
FIRST USE Small-mammal hunting/killing
USE TODAY Companion
LIFE EXPECTANCY 13–14 years

WEIGHT RANGE
7–8 kg (15–17 lb)
HEIGHT RANGE
33–38 cm (13–15 in)

BREED HISTORY The fearless and nimble Lakeland Terrier was originally bred and used by farmers in the north of England to protect their sheepfolds from predators.

The working Lakeland Terrier was an agile and ruthless hunter, adept at working the rocky ground of Great Britain's Lake District in pursuit of its quarry. It was willing to take on animals far larger than itself. The breed probably descends from extinct black-and-tan terrier stock, from which the Welsh Terrier also originates. The Lakeland has had periods of show-ring popularity, even winning Best in Show in Great Britain and the United States, but in comparison to more fashionable breeds it remains numerically small. It is a single-minded terrier, best suited to owners with patience.

WHEATEN RED BLUE/ TAN

BLACK/ TAN BLUE BLACK

SMOOTH FOX TERRIER

Tail docked in historic fashion

Round, dark, deep-set eyes

Moderately thick, V-shaped ears fold neatly over towards cheeks

Well-developed jaw

BREED HISTORY At one time, all dogs that went to earth chasing foxes were called fox terriers. It was not until 1850, however, that controlled breeding began, resulting in the breed of today.

Abundant coat is straight

WHITE

WHITE/ TAN

BLACK/ TAN

Feet are round and compact

Each English county once had its own fox terrier. The genes of the extinct white Cheshire and Shropshire Terrier are probably still present in this breed, together with those of the Beagle. The Smooth Fox Terrier was once a classic working dog, but today it is foremost an attractive, although frequently obstinate and strong-willed, companion. With persistence, this athletic dog can be obedience trained. Some individuals have even been trained to point and retrieve, others to excel in the circus ring. The breed's agility and joy in exercising off the lead make it a good dog for the countryside.

KEY FACTS

COUNTRY OF ORIGIN Great Britain
DATE OF ORIGIN 1700s
FIRST USE Fox flushing, vermin killing
USE TODAY Companion
LIFE EXPECTANCY 13–14 years

WEIGHT RANGE
7–8 kg (16–18 lb)
HEIGHT RANGE
38.5–39.5 cm (15 in)

WIRE FOX TERRIER

Dense, wiry, strong coat

More popular than its Smooth relative, the Wire Fox Terrier did not appear in show rings until the 1870s, 20 years after its cousin. It has been an intermittently popular breed, fashionable in the 1930s, then out of favour until recently, when it re-emerged as a "classic" English breed. The Wire Fox Terrier is not demonstrative with people; it is wilful, and can be a bit snappy. One of the breed's instinctive traits that has not diminished over the years is its joy in digging. Its enjoyment in challenging other dogs to fights is almost as great. Deafness can be a problem in predominantly white individuals.

Topline of ear fold is well above skull

Shoulders slope backwards

Facial whiskers are dense

KEY FACTS

COUNTRY OF ORIGIN Great Britain
DATE OF ORIGIN 1800s
FIRST USE Fox flushing, small-mammal killing, rabbit hunting
USE TODAY Companion
LIFE EXPECTANCY 13–14 years

WEIGHT RANGE
7–8 kg (16–18 lb)
HEIGHT RANGE
38.5–39.5 cm (15 in)

BREED HISTORY The now-extinct Wire-haired Terrier, from the coal mining regions of Great Britain, is a likely ancestor of the Wire Fox Terrier, which typifies the ideal terrier type.

WHITE

WHITE/ TAN

WHITE/ BLACK

Straight forelegs are lean

Weight is evenly distributed

ENGLISH TOY TERRIER

Tail is thick at root and tapers to tip that almost reaches hocks

Back curves slightly from behind shoulders to loins

Dramatic "candle-flame" ears are slightly pointed at tips

KEY FACTS

COUNTRY OF ORIGIN Great Britain
DATE OF ORIGIN 1800s
FIRST USE Ratting, rabbit hunting
USE TODAY Companion
LIFE EXPECTANCY 12–13 years
    OTHER NAMES Black-and-tan Toy Terrier, Toy Manchester Terrier

WEIGHT RANGE
3–4 kg (6–8 lb)
HEIGHT RANGE
25–30 cm (10–12 in)

A relatively rare terrier, even in its country of origin, the English Toy descends from runt Manchester Terriers. Italian Greyhound blood might have been introduced to stabilize its size, which could account for its slightly arched, or "roached", back, but its personality remains one hundred per cent terrier. Breeding has passed through various phases, emphasizing its tiny size, or arched back, or "candle-flame" ears. Breeding now appears stable, but on an international level it is unlikely that this effervescent little terrier will become as recognized or as popular as the similar Miniature Pinscher. It is, however, an enjoyable companion, and is ideally suited to the city.

Chest is narrow and deep, with straight, thin front legs

BREED HISTORY This dog, a bantam version of the Manchester Terrier, caused a sensation when it first appeared just over 100 years ago, but then for a long period it suffered from a number of health-related problems. However, since the 1950s, breeders have concentrated on improving both its constitution and its appearance.

Wedge-shaped head is long and narrow, with flat skull

Well-rounded loins lead to stifles

Thick, smooth coat, with dense, short, glossy hair

Feet are dainty and compact

MANCHESTER TERRIER

Small, V-shaped ears are folded

BREED HISTORY Vermin-hunting black-and-tan terriers existed in Great Britain for hundreds of years. John Hulme, a breeder from Manchester, is credited with crossing these terriers with the Whippet in the 1800s, producing this lithe, agile, and powerful ratter and rabbiter. Popular for a time, the Manchester is now rare.

KEY FACTS

COUNTRY OF ORIGIN Great Britain
DATE OF ORIGIN 1500s
FIRST USE Ratting, rabbit hunting
USE TODAY Companion
LIFE EXPECTANCY 13–14 years
OTHER NAME Black-and-tan Terrier

WEIGHT RANGE
5–10 kg (11–22 lb)
HEIGHT RANGE
38–41 cm (15–16 in)

Wedge-shaped muzzle does not show any cheek muscles

Small, dark, sparkling eyes are not prominent

This sleek, athletic breed reached its height of popularity about 100 years ago, when it was known as the "English Gentleman's Terrier". Exported to North America and Germany, it has been erroneously credited with lending its black-and-tan coat colour to the development of the Dobermann. Its decline began when rat baiting became unfashionable. (At one time a Manchester named Billy held the record of killing 100 rats in a wooden box in less than seven minutes.) The ban on ear cropping further reduced its popularity, and it took some time for breeders to create its V-shaped, hanging ears. Although the breed is short tempered, it makes a fine, lively, and robust companion.

Short body, with well-sprung ribs and slightly curved back

Thick, smooth, glossy, dense coat is not soft to the touch

Well-proportioned, straight, long forelimbs, with small feet

PATTERDALE TERRIER

Dark, inquisitive eyes

Short, coarse topcoat

At one time, different strains of terrier existed in each isolated village in the north of England. Breeding to Kennel Club standards reduced this great variety, but in some remote regions unrecognized breeds continued to flourish. The Patterdale, sometimes called the Black Fell Terrier, is one of these breeds. This is a robust, independent hunter, bred solely for utilitarian service as a ratter and hunting companion. Its Bull Terrier bloodlines make it too ferocious to work as a hunter with pack hounds but it is an excellent digger, tenaciously willing to encounter and attack any mammal that has gone to ground. The interest of local breeders ensures its survival.

Widely spaced ears are set high and hang in V-shaped folds

KEY FACTS

COUNTRY OF ORIGIN Great Britain
DATE OF ORIGIN 1700s
FIRST USE Rabbit hunting
USE TODAY Companion, rabbit/rat/ fox hunting
LIFE EXPECTANCY 13–14 years

WEIGHT RANGE
5–6 kg (11–13 lb)
HEIGHT RANGE
29.5–30.5 cm (12 in)

Face is stocky

Puppy

BREED HISTORY Virtually unknown outside Great Britain, this breed is generally found in Great Britain's Lake District and in Yorkshire. Used as a rat, fox, and rabbit hunter, the Patterdale Terrier is not bred for appearance.

Well-built body resembles that of a bull terrier

Legs are solid, with medium-sized feet and stable pads

RED | BLACK/ TAN | BROWN | BLACK

PLUMMER TERRIER

KEY FACTS

COUNTRY OF ORIGIN Great Britain
DATE OF ORIGIN 1980s
FIRST USE Ratting
USE TODAY Companion, ratting
LIFE EXPECTANCY 13–15 years

WEIGHT RANGE
5.5–7 kg (12–15 lb)
HEIGHT RANGE
29–34 cm (11½–13½ in)

Length from shoulders to tail is same as height

Widely spaced ears drop symmetrically in folds

Neck is strong and muscular

BREED HISTORY The neat and attractive Plummer was developed by crossing Fell-type terriers with Jack Russell-types and an American beagle. Bull Terrier and Jack Russell blood was then added. This gutsy breed has not yet received formal recognition, but its conformation is now fixed.

Coat is smooth and tight, without guard hairs

Elbows are set tight to sides of body

This compact and aggressive breed has its own breed club and a 10-year breeding plan, which will eventually lead to application for recognition by the Kennel Club of Great Britain. The Plummer is a vermin-control expert. Its proponents claim that members of the breed hold world records for swiftness of rat kill. The breed's creator, Brian Plummer, restricts all breeding to the control of three club members. By doing so, he hopes to maintain the conformation, colour, and spirit of the breed. This is a sprightly, confident, and even arrogant little dog with typical terrier energy and enthusiasm.

GERMAN HUNTING TERRIER

BREED HISTORY Early this century, four Bavarian dog breeders crossed the Welsh Terrier and the old English Black-and-tan Terrier, then bred this cross with the English Fox Terrier, producing this strong-willed, resourceful, and powerful breed. Breeding is still based upon proven ability to work.

RED   BROWN/TAN   BLACK/TAN

KEY FACTS

COUNTRY OF ORIGIN Germany
DATE OF ORIGIN 1920s
FIRST USE Vermin/small-game hunting
USE TODAY Hunting, tracking, small-game retrieving, companion
LIFE EXPECTANCY 13–15 years
OTHER NAME Deutscher Jagdterrier

WEIGHT RANGE
9–10 kg (20–22 lb)
HEIGHT RANGE
40.5–41.5 cm (16 in)

Coat is generally hard and rough, but can occasionally be smooth

Back is moderately long, strong, and straight

Long, muscular hind legs; low hocks and hind feet are smaller than forefeet

Robust lower jaw houses exceptionally large teeth

Developed as a general-purpose hunting dog, the German Hunting Terrier willingly works above or below ground, in land or water, tracking and retrieving. It is a classic, tenacious terrier, a typically good watchdog, happy to sleep outdoors, with the terrier's instinct to snap first and ask questions later. The breed thrives on both physical and mental activity – in its native land it is kept almost wholly by hunters and gamekeepers. A superb working dog, it will hunt all day, but can be a difficult companion due to its independent nature.

CZESKY TERRIER

TAWNY   BLUE-GREY

Triangular-shaped ears are of medium length and hang close to head

Hair is not clipped on head, leaving prominent beard and eyebrows

Nose is well developed and prominent

BREED HISTORY Wanting a breed that worked like a German hunting terrier, but with shorter legs for more efficient work underground, a geneticist, Dr. Frantisek Horak, from Klanovice, crossed the Sealyham and Scottish, and perhaps the Dandie Dinmont Terriers.

Robust tail is carried down when relaxed

Dark, wavy hair on legs is not usually clipped

The Czesky Terrier's unique looks have made it a favourite companion in its home countries, the Czech and Slovak Republics. In the 1980s, however, Czech and Slovak breeders felt that it had deteriorated from its original form and function, and it was again crossed with the Sealyham Terrier. The Czesky has all the ground terrier's typical attributes – it is a feisty, persistent, stubborn, and fearless dog, strong enough to subdue animals much larger than itself. Its coat requires constant attention and, like most terriers, it has a tendency to snap. Apart from this, it is an alert, inquisitive, and affable breed.

KEY FACTS

COUNTRY OF ORIGIN Czech Republic
DATE OF ORIGIN 1940s
FIRST USE Burrowing
USE TODAY Companion, hunting
LIFE EXPECTANCY 12–14 years
OTHER NAMES Czech Terrier, Bohemian Terrier

WEIGHT RANGE
5.5–8 kg (12–18 lb)
HEIGHT RANGE
28–36 cm (10–14 in)

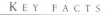

KROMFOHRLÄNDER

BREED HISTORY In 1945, American soldiers passing through Krumme Furche, Westphalia, gave Ilse Schleifenbaum a fawn-coloured dog that had been accompanying them. She bred this dog on five separate occasions with her own dog, which resembled a Griffon Fauve de Bretagne. The attractive puppies that followed formed the basis of this breed.

Close-fitting, black lips are only moderate in size, and do not hang

Coat is long, smooth, and straight

Smooth-haired variety

Wire-haired variety

Oval, medium-sized, slightly slanted eyes are dark in colour

Medium-sized, dark nose

Coat is short, rough, and somewhat wiry, with dense undercoat

No dewclaws on slightly arched hind feet

KEY FACTS

COUNTRY OF ORIGIN Germany
DATE OF ORIGIN 1940s
FIRST USE Companion, watchdog
USE TODAY Companion
LIFE EXPECTANCY 13–14 years

WEIGHT RANGE
11.5–12.5 kg (25–27 lb)
HEIGHT RANGE
38–43 cm (15–17 in)

Named after the region of Germany where it originated, this even-tempered breed, recognized in 1953, is now in danger of extinction, which is unfortunate, because it has excellent traits. It gets on well with other dogs and children, is easy to obedience train, is not snappy, and makes a good watchdog. Its only known medical problem is inherited stifle-joint disease. The Kromfohrländer is a well-proportioned dog, with a coat ranging from rough and wiry to smooth and straight. Although it was bred for companionship and to act as a watchdog, by inclination it is a true terrier.

JAPANESE TERRIER

BREED HISTORY Breeding local small dogs with the Smooth Fox Terrier, brought by the Dutch to Japan in the early 1700s, produced this breed. Systematic breeding did not begin until the 1930s, and in-breeding is a continuing problem.

Moderate-sized, dark eyes blend perfectly with dark hair on face

High-set ears of moderate size have natural folds

Fairly small head is covered in dark, short, shiny, black hair

Small nose is always black; lips are tight, with no sag

Medium-length neck is quite powerful

Predominantly white coat has random speckling

Long, lean, straight limbs have good-sized feet, with thick pads and white nails

Although this compact and athletic dog has proved itself as an efficient retriever both on land and in water, and as a resourceful and amusing companion, its numbers are declining. Fortunately, concerned veterinarians in Japan have formed a preservation society to ensure its survival (along with that of any other indigenous breed in danger of extinction). A rather refined and elegant-looking terrier, the Japanese has the racy shadow of the sight hound in its anatomy. There has been a tendency to breed down in size to create a toy variety, but most individuals remain in the robust, standard size. Due to its short coat, the breed can suffer from the cold.

KEY FACTS

COUNTRY OF ORIGIN Japan
DATE OF ORIGIN 1700s
FIRST USE Ratting, retrieving
USE TODAY Companion
LIFE EXPECTANCY 12–14 years
OTHER NAMES Nippon Terrier, Nihon Terrier

WEIGHT RANGE
4.5–6 kg (10–13 lb)
HEIGHT RANGE
32.5–33.5 cm (13 in)

CAIRN TERRIER

BREED HISTORY The Cairn may have originated on the Scottish Isle of Skye where, since at least the time of Mary Queen of Scots, it worked the cairns, searching for hiding foxes.

CREAM   WHEATEN   RED

GREY   NEARLY BLACK

No distinct indentation between eyes

KEY FACTS

COUNTRY OF ORIGIN Great Britain
DATE OF ORIGIN Middle Ages
FIRST USE Fox hunting, ratting
USE TODAY Companion
LIFE EXPECTANCY 14 years

WEIGHT RANGE
6–7 kg (13–16 lb)
HEIGHT RANGE
25–30 cm (10–12 in)

Small, pointed ears

Muzzle is powerful, but not heavy

Front feet are larger than back feet

Profuse topcoat, with furry undercoat

Forelegs are moderately long

U ntil recently, when the West Highland White and Yorkshire Terriers superseded it, this was the most popular of all Great Britain's terriers. Breeders earlier this century were careful to retain the Cairn's natural shaggy coat, sturdy body, and terrier abilities. The breed is equally at home in town or country. It makes a good watchdog, and is easier to obedience train than many other terriers. The terrier temperament is, however, always there. Males, in particular, can be bossy, and should always be monitored when meeting children for the first time. The Cairn's small size, good health, and lack of stubbornness make it a delightful companion.

NORFOLK TERRIER

W ith the exception of the ears, the appearances, origins, personalities, and function of the Norfolk and Norwich Terriers are identical. The Norfolk is a delightful little dog, although it has an instinctive terrier-like desire to attack and throttle any rodent it sees. Like virtually all terriers, it must be introduced to cats carefully, so that its natural instincts can be harnessed. Good natured and robust, the breed makes an excellent companion. It is also a good guard dog, and will bark at strangers or unusual noises. It is happy in either the town or countryside – a back garden provides all the space this short-legged breed needs for vigorous exercise.

WHEATEN   RED   BLACK/TAN

GRIZZLE

KEY FACTS

COUNTRY OF ORIGIN Great Britain
DATE OF ORIGIN 1800s
FIRST USE Ratting
USE TODAY Companion
LIFE EXPECTANCY 14 years

WEIGHT RANGE
5–5.5 kg (11–12 lb)
HEIGHT RANGE
24.5–25.5 cm (9½–10 in)

Slightly round-tipped ears drop close to cheeks

BREED HISTORY From the time it was first recognized as a breed, the Norwich produced puppies with both erect and drop ears. The arguments this created resulted in the drop-eared Norfolk being recognized as a separate breed in 1965.

Hard, straight, and wiry coat

Small, round feet have firm pads

NORWICH TERRIER

WHEATEN   RED   BLACK/   GRIZZLE
                  TAN

BREED HISTORY Packs of small, red terriers, which evolved from Irish terriers, existed in the 1800s. The Norwich may be derived from these dogs, or it may be descended from the extinct Trumpington Terrier.

Among the smallest of all terriers, the Norwich has existed in eastern England for over 100 years. In the late 1800s, students at Cambridge University used it as their mascot, but it was not exhibited as a distinct breed until 1935. The Norwich is a typically bossy terrier, which firmly believes in its own importance. It is, however, an ideal family companion, and gets on well with older children. It is not difficult to obedience train and house train, and is willing to engage in the most rigorous exercise. The Norwich is free from most serious inherited medical conditions.

Thickly muscled hindquarters give dog excellent propulsion

Ears are always erect

Head is slightly rounded

Front feet turn out slightly

Short, compact body, with wide rib cage

KEY FACTS

COUNTRY OF ORIGIN Great Britain
DATE OF ORIGIN 1800s
FIRST USE Ratting
USE TODAY Companion
LIFE EXPECTANCY 14 years

WEIGHT RANGE
5–5.5 kg (11–12 lb)
HEIGHT RANGE
25–26 cm (10–10½ in)

WEST HIGHLAND WHITE TERRIER

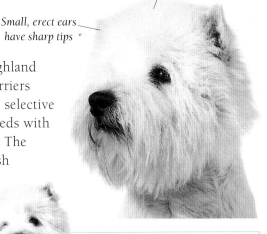

BREED HISTORY The Cairn Terrier occasionally used to produce white puppies. The Malcolm family, of Scotland, selectively bred these, producing a breed easily visible on the Scottish moors.

Head is very thickly coated with hair

Slightly sunken eyes are set wide apart

Small, erect ears have sharp tips

Although the West Highland White and Cairn Terriers share a common ancestry, selective breeding has produced breeds with quite different personalities. The Westie (along with the Scottish Terrier) is recognized worldwide because of the part it plays in advertising a Scotch whisky. White is also a fashionable colour for dogs, signifying good luck, or simply cleanliness. The consequence is that the Westie is very popular in North America, Great Britain, Europe, and Japan. The breed has a very high incidence of allergic skin conditions, and an excitable temperament. It thrives on plenty of attention and regular exercise.

Hard-haired topcoat covers fur-like undercoat

Feet have thick, black pads, and black nails

KEY FACTS

COUNTRY OF ORIGIN Great Britain
DATE OF ORIGIN 1800s
FIRST USE Ratting
USE TODAY Companion
LIFE EXPECTANCY 14 years

WEIGHT RANGE
7–10 kg (15–22 lb)
HEIGHT RANGE
25–28 cm (10–11 in)

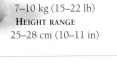

SCOTTISH TERRIER

This solid, muscular, quiet, and even dour dog has always been more popular in North America than in Great Britain. The American president Franklin Delano Roosevelt often travelled with his Scottie, Fala, and Walt Disney perpetuated the gentlemanly image of this breed in his film, *Lady and the Tramp*. Although built for penetrating underground passageways in the pursuit of small mammals, the Scottish Terrier is primarily a companion. Reserved and a little aloof, it is an excellent guardian.

Eyebrows are long and distinctive

Neat, pointed ears

Tapering tail is carried up

Hindquarters are extraordinarily powerful

WHEATEN

RED-BRINDLE

BLACK-BRINDLE

BLACK

Harsh, thick topcoat, with soft undercoat

BREED HISTORY
The Scottie of today is probably a descendant of dogs from the Scottish Western Isles, which were selectively bred in Aberdeen in the mid-1800s.

SKYE TERRIER

Abundant topcoat is long and straight

Erect ears are gracefully feathered

Long head and powerful jaws

CREAM

FAWN

GREY

BLACK

Guard hair is shorter on face than on body

BREED HISTORY
This exceptionally long-haired terrier is named after its Scottish Hebridean island of origin. At one time it was used extensively for otter, badger, and weasel tracking. Now a popular companion, it is ideal for the city.

Large feet on short legs point out slightly

Eyes are covered with hair

Nose is black, with large, wide nostrils

Popular for centuries, the Skye Terrier was at one time the favoured dog of the royal courts of Scotland and England. Scotland's most famous dog, Greyfriar's Bobby, is said to have been a Skye Terrier. For 14 years after his master's death in the mid-1800s, despite being given good homes, Bobby escaped and revisited his master's favourite cafe each day until his own death. A statue in the dog's memory stands near Greyfriar's Church in Edinburgh, Scotland. Inclined to be snappy when provoked, and perhaps not ideal for children, the Skye can be intensely loyal.

SEALYHAM TERRIER

Long, wiry coat requires expert preparation for show ring

Remarkably powerful thighs

Hair brushed forwards over eyes for show purposes

Long hair on face gives square appearance

Medium-sized ears have round tips

Dark, round, medium-sized eyes

Round, cat-like feet have thick pads

BREED HISTORY The Sealyham was selectively bred by using a variety of terriers. This produced a superb badger and otter hunter, which was willing to work in burrows, above ground, and in water.

No longer used for its original purpose, the Sealyham is an attractive, bossy, and independent companion; it also makes a distinctive show dog. Its origins as a dog willing to take on badgers or otters on their own ground are evident in its frequently aggressive attitude to other dogs. Even after almost a century of breeding for companionship, males, in particular, still need firm and experienced handling. In the 1930s, the Sealyham was an extremely popular dog, especially in North America. Today, it is almost unknown outside English-speaking countries and is uncommon even in its land of origin.

DANDIE DINMONT TERRIER

Large skull, with domed forehead

PEPPER   MUSTARD

Neck is strong and muscular

Wiry hair on top of tail, with softer hair underneath

Large, round, dark-hazel eyes are bright and expressive

BREED HISTORY Curiously named after a country gentleman in Sir Walter Scott's novel, *Guy Mannering*, paintings show that the Dandie Dinmont was owned by aristocracy for centuries before it was named. It may have its ancient origins in the gypsies' dogs of southern Scotland.

Despite the variety of hypotheses as to whether the Dandie Dinmont originates from the Skye, Bedlington, or old-type Scottish Terriers, or the Otterhound or Flanders Basset, one fact remains indisputable. It does not have the typical "take-no-prisoners-alive" terrier mentality. It is a remarkably docile breed, although its bark is deep and massive, and when aroused, it is willing to fight. Neither quarrelsome nor snappy, it is an easygoing house dog, thriving on the companionship of both adults and children. It is also extremely loyal, and makes a good guard dog. Although it enjoys vigorous exercise, this affable dog is quite content playing in the house or back garden. Unfortunately, its long back and short legs predispose it to rather painful intervertebral disc problems.

YORKSHIRE TERRIER

Ribbon holds hair away from eyes

BREED HISTORY The world's most popular terrier originated in the early 1800s in the West Riding area of Yorkshire where miners, wanting to develop a terrier for ratting small enough to carry in a pocket, probably crossed black-and-tan terriers with the Paisley and Clydesdale Terriers.

KEY FACTS

COUNTRY OF ORIGIN Great Britain
DATE OF ORIGIN 1800s
FIRST USE Ratting
USE TODAY Companion
LIFE EXPECTANCY 14 years

WEIGHT RANGE
2.5–3.5 kg (5–7 lb)
HEIGHT RANGE
22.5–23.5 cm (9 in)

Long hair needs constant attention

Hair can be either brushed to sides or clipped

Body hair is long and straight

Deep-black nose may lighten with increasing age; very thin hair on bridge

Hair has been cut from V-shaped, erect ears

Tan hair is darkest at roots, and lightest at tips

This feisty package of energy is now one of Great Britain's most numerous pure-bred dogs. In other parts of Europe and in North America it is almost equally popular, since it combines all the admirable attributes of dogs, but in miniature. Many Yorkies are spoiled from the moment they are acquired, and never have the opportunity to show their willingness to learn. Excessive breeding has also produced nervous and meek examples of the breed, but they are a minority. The typical Yorkshire Terrier is a dynamo, with little understanding of its small size. It plays hard, and has seemingly unlimited energy. Reduction in size has unfortunately brought with it many medical problems, including gum disease and collapsed windpipes. Although often regarded as a fashion accessory, the breed remains true to its origins – tenacious and stubborn.

Straight, thin legs are totally hidden by show dog's long hair

Face is very narrow, but bushy whiskers give square look

AUSTRALIAN SILKY TERRIER

KEY FACTS

COUNTRY OF ORIGIN Australia
DATE OF ORIGIN 1900s
FIRST USE Companion
USE TODAY Companion
LIFE EXPECTANCY 14 years
OTHER NAME Silky Terrier

WEIGHT RANGE
4–5 kg (8–11 lb)
HEIGHT RANGE
22.5–23.5 cm (9 in)

BREED HISTORY The Australian Silky, developed late last century, is probably the result of breeding the Australian Terrier with the Yorkshire, and perhaps the Skye, primarily as a companion.

Similar in appearance, but larger than, the Yorkshire Terrier, the blue-and-tan Australian Silky Terrier successfully colonized the United States and Canada before arriving in Europe. It is a robust breed, yappy like the Yorkie, and just as possessive of its own territory, announcing the presence of strangers in a shrill voice. Although small in size, it is quite capable of killing small rodents. It can become an independent renegade, and early obedience training is necessary if it is to live peacefully with people. A strong-willed breed, it can be intolerant of handling and of strangers, unless it experiences both while quite young. The Silky's coat mats easily and benefits from daily brushing. It does not have a dense undercoat, and can suffer in cold climates.

Hair does not cover eyes

Ears are thin, V-shaped, and erect

Tan hair grows from knees down to cat-like feet

Silver-grey hair (called blue by breeders) covers body down to pasterns

Powerful, muscular thighs

AUSTRALIAN TERRIER

Tough and willing to fight anything, the Australian Terrier was an ideal homestead dog. Capable of killing all small vermin, including snakes, it also acted as an alert watchdog, guarding isolated homes from intruders. These traits still exist today – the Aussie is unlikely to back down in confrontations with other dogs, nor is it likely to leave cats in peace, unless it has been raised with them since puppyhood. It makes an entertaining companion, however, and can be trained in obedience. Like the Silky Terrier, it accompanied armed-forces personnel and businessmen to North America after World War II. Although the breed is still most popular in Australia and New Zealand, it now exists in all major English-speaking countries.

BLUE/
TAN

SANDY

KEY FACTS

COUNTRY OF ORIGIN Australia
DATE OF ORIGIN 1800s
FIRST USE Farm ratter, watchdog
USE TODAY Companion
LIFE EXPECTANCY 14 years

WEIGHT RANGE
5–6 kg (12–14 lb)
HEIGHT RANGE
24.5–25.5 cm (10 in)

Eyes are small, dark, and vibrant

Long body in relation to height

Long, flat skull is covered by hard-textured hair

Compact, slightly pursed mouth

BREED HISTORY This sturdy native of Australia is descended from several British terriers, including the Cairn, Yorkshire, Skye, and perhaps the Norwich. Settlers brought these breeds to Australia in order to produce an efficient ratter to work the farms and ranches.

Small and compact feet have black nails

AMERICAN STAFFORDSHIRE TERRIER

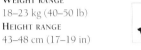

Dark-brown, oval-shaped eyes are set wide apart

Short, heavily muscled neck blends into strong forelimbs

Cheek muscles below broad skull are clearly noticeable

BREED HISTORY Originally identical to the British Staffordshire Bull Terrier, the American was selectively bred for greater height and weight, and a bulkier build. In 1936, it was recognized as a separate breed.

These ears are cropped

Like its close British relative, the American Staffordshire can be extremely gentle and affectionate with children and adults, and at the same time potentially lethal with other dogs. All members of the breed, but males in particular, need early socialization with other animals to ensure that they do not follow their instinct to attack. Most commonly seen with uncropped ears, the breed is almost always a loyal and obedient canine member of the family. It does, however, descend from bull biters and pit fighters, and still has the jaw power and tenacity to inflict horrific wounds.

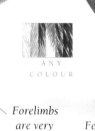

ANY COLOUR

Forelimbs are very long and thickly boned

Feet are strong, with thickly cushioned pads

AMERICAN PIT BULL TERRIER

ANY COLOUR

Tail appears quite thin in comparison to rest of body

Ears have been cropped to make dog look more dangerous

Pronounced stop between skull and muzzle

Small, oval-shaped eyes have calm look

Back is long in relation to dog's height

Massively powerful cheek muscles are clearly visible

Hysteria is now associated with this breed's name. Banned in Sweden, neutered, muzzled, and microchip-identified in Great Britain, and prohibited from entering some areas of North America, the Pit Bull is as much a victim of the press as it is of its historic breeding to fight other dogs. Some unscrupulous owners, taking advantage of its natural tenaciousness and strength, continue to use abusive training techniques to produce fighting Pit Bulls, willing to take on any animal, and even humans. When trained from an early age to obey commands, the vast majority of the breed prove to be companionable, even gregariously fawning dogs.

Coat is thick, hard, short, and silky, but not glossy

BREED HISTORY Throughout the world dogs have, at one time or another, been bred to fight. This breed descends from the Staffordshire Bull Terrier crossed with other fighting dogs, including the extinct fighting Bulldog.

AMERICAN TOY TERRIER

BREED HISTORY This breed, which was recognized in 1936, was developed by crossing "runts" from Smooth Fox Terrier litters with the English Toy Terrier and Chihuahua.

Although dome shaped, skull is not dramatically domed like a Chihuahua's

Eyes are very large, dark, and round

Tail is docked due to demands of fashion

Ears are large, V-shaped, and stand erect

Definite stop separates domed skull from small, narrow muzzle

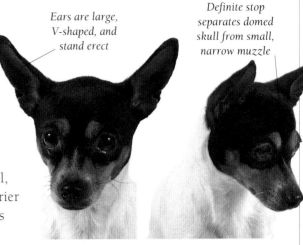

WHITE/TAN

TRICOLOUR

BLACK/WHITE

It may be physically small, but this robust little terrier retains all the passion of its fox terrier ancestors. The breed is tough and bright, but stubborn, and equally at home on a farm or the top floor of a condominium. Given the opportunity, it makes an excellent ratter, but more often it serves as a happy extension to the family, bringing smiles to the faces of nearly all who meet it, due to its energetic and forever youthful antics. It has also proved to be an excellent hearing dog for deaf people – it can be trained to take its human companion to the sources of sounds such as the telephone.

KEY FACTS

COUNTRY OF ORIGIN United States
DATE OF ORIGIN 1930s
FIRST USE Ratting
USE TODAY Companion
LIFE EXPECTANCY 13–14 years
OTHER NAMES Toy Fox Terrier, Amertoy

WEIGHT RANGE
2–3 kg (4½–7 lb)
HEIGHT RANGE
24.5–25.5 cm (10 in)

BOSTON TERRIER

KEY FACTS

COUNTRY OF ORIGIN United States
DATE OF ORIGIN 1800s
FIRST USE Ratting, companion
USE TODAY Companion
LIFE EXPECTANCY 13 years
OTHER NAME Boston Bull

WEIGHT RANGE
4.5–11.5 kg (10–25 lb)
HEIGHT RANGE
38–43 cm (15–17 in)

RED-BRINDLE

BLACK-BRINDLE

Large, round eyes, with alert but gentle expression, are set wide apart

Nose is wide and black

BREED HISTORY Developed by crossing the English Bulldog, Bull Terrier, Boxer, and extinct White Terrier, the Boston originally weighed over 20 kg (44 lb), but was bred down in size.

Well mannered, thoughtful, and considerate, this true New Englander is a perennially popular dog in North America, making a sprightly, entertaining, active, and durable companion. Terrier in name only, it has lost any ruthless desire for mayhem, preferring the company of humans, although male Bostons will still challenge other dogs if they feel their territory has been invaded. As with other proportionally large-headed breeds, Caesarean operations are sometimes needed to deliver puppies. Breeders have, however, been successful in reducing the size of the head, while retaining the dog's unique and quirky good looks.

Coat is smooth, bright, and fine textured

Thighs are strong and well muscled

Chest is only moderately deep

Thin, erect ears located at corners of skull

Slightly arched, moderately long neck carries head gracefully

MINIATURE PINSCHER

Short, glossy, dense coat is distributed evenly over body

Tail has been pointlessly amputated – an illegal mutilation in many countries

RED   BLUE

CHOCOLATE   NEARLY BLACK

When standing naturally, hind legs are well separated

Compact feet have well-arched toes

Well-set ears are large and erect

BREED HISTORY Developed from the German Pinscher hundreds of years ago, the "Min Pin" was originally a bulky, efficient stable ratter. Its refined appearance today is a result of more recent selective breeding.

Strikingly similar in appearance to the English Toy Terrier, the Miniature Pinscher evolved along completely different lines but for the same purpose, that of rodent control. Although it looks like a tiny Dobermann, it is only related to that breed by country of origin, and predates it by perhaps 200 years.

Today, this feisty little terrier (*pinscher* is German for terrier or biter) is kept strictly as a companion, but its ratting ability remains fully developed. In spite of its size, it will quite happily challenge dogs that are 10 times larger than itself, and has a tendency to snap first and ask questions later.

AUSTRIAN PINSCHER

BREED HISTORY This traditional Austrian farmer's dog was developed as a general "farm biter", used to drive livestock and to guard the home. Paintings from the late 1700s show a dog almost identical to today's breed.

Head is pear shaped, with wider part at top

Breed's ears vary greatly; these are slightly pricked

Relatively short muzzle is very powerful

Never known outside the lands of the old Austrian Empire, and today rarely seen beyond the borders of Austria itself, the Austrian Pinscher is a heavy cousin of the German Pinscher. Developed as a farm worker, and never having been selectively bred solely for companionship, it may not get on well with other dogs, and has a tendency to bite. It is, however, relaxed with people it knows. A vivacious breed, it also makes an excellent watchdog, barking at any suspicious sounds.

VARIETY OF COLOURS

Short, hard topcoat has equally short, dense undercoat

Elbows are close to body, on medium-length legs

Compact feet have well-arched toes

AFFENPINSCHER

The seriousness, intensity, and humour of this sparky breed can bring a smile to the face of the most preoccupied person. It looks like a cartoon but in fact, even with its compressed jaws, the Affenpinscher still makes a formidable ratter when given the opportunity. It is also an efficient quail and rabbit tracker. Stubborn and smug, it does not respond well to obedience training, and has a tendency to snap. It does, however, make a lively and amusing companion. Today, the breed is rare in Germany, the largest numbers surviving in North America. A larger variety of the Affenpinscher became extinct at the beginning of the century.

Large, dark, prominent eyes have bushy brows

Tail has short hair and is carried high

Face is covered in coarse hair

Moustache and beard are abundant

Well-feathered feet are short and round

Medium-length legs are straight and well boned

Broad chest is covered with dense, dry hair; there is no gloss

BREED HISTORY This ancient breed's precise history is unknown. Its anatomy suggests that it was developed from crossing small, local pinschers with pug-like dogs from Asia. It is probably the parent of the Belgian griffons, and a relative of the Miniature Schnauzer.

KEY FACTS

COUNTRY OF ORIGIN Germany
DATE OF ORIGIN 1600s
FIRST USE Vermin hunting
USE TODAY Companion
LIFE EXPECTANCY 14–15 years
OTHER NAME Monkey Dog

WEIGHT RANGE
3–3.5 kg (7–8 lb)
HEIGHT RANGE
25–30 cm (10–12 in)

GERMAN PINSCHER

FAWN

BLACK/TAN

DARK BROWN

Cropped ears are high set

Medium-sized eyes are dark and oval

Alert and expressive ears have natural half fold

Needlessly amputating a tail like this often leads to sacral arthritis

Long muzzle is bluntly tipped with medium-sized, black nose

With its sleek, handsome looks and medium-sized build, the German Pinscher should be an ideal companion dog, but inexplicably, it is now a rare breed. It is lively but docile, quite versatile, and in addition to being a good and vocal guard dog, responds reasonably well to obedience training. Like other pinschers and terriers, it does not back away from disputes with other dogs, and needs firm handling to control its pugilistic tendencies.

Body is robust and well muscled, like a schnauzer's

BREED HISTORY This tall terrier evolved as a traditional farmer's multi-purpose dog. It controlled vermin, guarded and drove livestock, and was a watchdog. It is the forebear of the Miniature Pinscher, and played a role in the development of the Dobermann.

Short coat is strong, smooth, and glossy

KEY FACTS

COUNTRY OF ORIGIN Germany
DATE OF ORIGIN 1700s
FIRST USE Vermin hunting
USE TODAY Companion
LIFE EXPECTANCY 12–14 years
OTHER NAME Standard Pinscher

WEIGHT RANGE
11–16 kg (25–35 lb)
HEIGHT RANGE
41–48 cm (16–19 in)

GRIFFON BRUXELLOIS

The Griffon Bruxellois celebrated European unity long before its human associates appreciated the value of cooperation. This is a classic "Euro-dog" – the result of blending bloodlines from diverse regions to produce a good-natured, amusing, alert, and reliable companion. There is confusion about its name – in some countries three similar dogs are classified as the Belgian Griffon. In other countries each of these dogs is recognized as unique, and is given its own name. (This method of classification is peculiar to Belgium – similar confusion exists concerning the classification of the four breeds of Belgian shepherd.) At the height of the breed's popularity between the World Wars, there were literally thousands of brood bitches in Brussels alone. Today, it has been superseded in popularity by one of its ancestors, the Yorkshire Terrier. These dogs are still most popular in Belgium.

Long, wiry hair forms fringe around face

BLACK/ TAN   **BLACK**

Belgian Griffon

BREED HISTORY The Dutch Smoushond, German Affenpinscher, French Barbet, and Yorkshire Terrier have probably been used to produce today's Brussels Griffon.

Broad, deep chest is covered by short hair

BREED HISTORY The Belgian Griffon is the direct descendant of the rat-killing, bushy-faced Stable Griffon, or Griffon d'Ecurie. This efficient terrier was crossed in the 1800s with the English Toy Spaniel, in order to reduce its size and create the compressed snout. As a result, it lost its terrier instinct to kill vermin.

Brussels Griffon

Small, black nose is set deeply back between eyes

Feet are small, round, and compact, with black pads

Red beard is profuse, and gives sagacious look to face

Wiry coat is longer than a Belgian Griffon's

Forelegs are surprisingly well muscled and boned

Chin is naturally undershot, prominent, and large

Forehead is very domed; this shape is associated with increased risk of epilepsy

Straight hind legs have typical bend at stifle

Wide-set, large eyes are prominent and surrounded by black

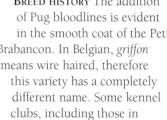

RED   **BLACK/ TAN**   **BLACK**

Small, fairly high-set ears are carried semi-erect

BREED HISTORY The addition of Pug bloodlines is evident in the smooth coat of the Petit Brabancon. In Belgian, *griffon* means wire haired, therefore this variety has a completely different name. Some kennel clubs, including those in Great Britain and the United States, continue to classify it as a Belgian Griffon.

KEY FACTS

COUNTRY OF ORIGIN Belgium
DATE OF ORIGIN 1800s
FIRST USE Vermin hunting
USE TODAY Companion
LIFE EXPECTANCY 12–14 years
OTHER NAME Griffon Belge

WEIGHT RANGE
2.5–5.5 kg (6–12 lb)
HEIGHT RANGE
18–20 cm (7–8 in)

Coat is smooth, like a Pug's

Petit Brabancon

MINIATURE SCHNAUZER

Named after its most prominent physical feature (in German, *schnauze* means nose or snout) the Miniature Schnauzer, although once a formidable ratter, is now an almost perfect canine companion. Less noisy and feisty than its British terrier equivalents, this breed has become one of North America's favourite town companions. A classically calm dog, it is easy to obedience train and is not snappy. It is good with children and other dogs, and is happy to settle into the routines of its human family. An enthusiastic barker, it also makes an excellent guard dog. It sheds very little hair, but its coat needs constant attention. Unfortunately, increased popularity has encouraged indiscriminate breeding, and inherited medical problems are now relatively common. So, too, is a rather nervous disposition.

BLACK/
SILVER

PEPPER/
SALT

BLACK

Top of head is flat and in line with muzzle

Eyes are naturally shaded with bushy, bristly eyebrows

Dense and profusely bushy beard gives aura of seriousness

High-set tail has been docked

Good angles to hind legs allow for powerful bursts of speed

Topcoat is quite hard and coarse; undercoat is soft

BREED HISTORY Almost a perfect replica of the Giant and Standard Schnauzers, the Miniature descends from this root stock, with the addition of Affenpinscher and Miniature Pinscher bloodlines. It is unlikely, as some sources suggest, that poodles played a role in the development of the breed.

KEY FACTS

COUNTRY OF ORIGIN Germany
DATE OF ORIGIN 1400s
FIRST USE Ratting
USE TODAY Companion
LIFE EXPECTANCY 14 years
OTHER NAME Zwergschnauzer

WEIGHT RANGE
6–7 kg (13–15 lb)
HEIGHT RANGE
30–36 cm (12–14 in)

Under well-trimmed fur, feet are much like those of a cat

Small ears are high set, and almost fully dropped

Dark, oval eyes are not very prominent

Nose is neat and black, at end of strong muzzle

Bushy beard gets messy after eating, and needs constant attention

Front legs are straight when seen from any angle; elbows are close to chest

GLEN OF IMAAL TERRIER

This is the rarest of Ireland's terriers, and it shares with that island's other "peasant dogs" an intense tenacity of spirit. Before selective breeding improved the Glen's social manners, it was a fierce fox and badger hunter, compact enough to go underground after its quarry and fight it to the death. The breed was used in dog fights, but in contrast to Great Britain, where the fight was staged indoors, in Ireland it took place in open fields. First exhibited in 1933, today's Glen is relatively relaxed, and makes an affectionate companion, although it certainly will not back down from a fight.

BREED HISTORY This ancient breed of unknown origins is named after a valley in County Wicklow, in eastern Ireland. It is tough, sturdy, and adaptable, and was ideal for fox and badger hunting in the rough terrains of the Glen.

KEY FACTS

COUNTRY OF ORIGIN Ireland
DATE OF ORIGIN 1700s
FIRST USE Vermin hunting
USE TODAY Companion
LIFE EXPECTANCY 13–14 years

WEIGHT RANGE
15.5–16.5 kg (34–36 lb)
HEIGHT RANGE
35.5–36.5 cm (14 in)

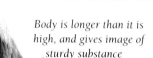

Rose-shaped, rather small ears hang naturally, but can be half-pricked

Body is longer than it is high, and gives image of sturdy substance

Powerful head has distinct stop and tapered muzzle

Rough, medium-length, tidy topcoat covers insulating, fine undercoat

Strong, slightly turned-out feet, with black nails and firm pads

WHEATEN   RED-BRINDLE   BLUE   BLACK-BRINDLE

SOFT-COATED WHEATEN TERRIER

Wavy, soft coat has loose curls, and is colour of ripening wheat

Small, thin, V-shaped ears have fringe of hair

KEY FACTS

COUNTRY OF ORIGIN Ireland
DATE OF ORIGIN 1700s
FIRST USE Herding, vermin hunting
USE TODAY Companion
LIFE EXPECTANCY 13–14 years

WEIGHT RANGE
16–20 kg (35–45 lb)
HEIGHT RANGE
46–48 cm (18–19 in)

BREED HISTORY This breed is related to both the Kerry Blue and Irish Terriers. Indigenous to the counties of Kerry and Cork in southern Ireland, for centuries it was an all-purpose worker, used for guarding, droving, herding, and hunting.

Fairly long head is covered with abundant soft hair

Moderately long, strong neck

Probably the least intense of Ireland's terriers, the Wheaten has recently become a fashionable and enjoyable companion in Canada and the United States. Its rightful popularity is based on a versatility that stems from an ancient Irish law prohibiting peasants from owning hunting dogs. The Wheaten, most definitely "peasant" in appearance, was developed to overcome this restriction. The result is, by terrier standards, a reasonably obedient and trainable companion.

Feet are quite small and compact, with black nails

BEDLINGTON TERRIER

Under profuse topknot, head is long, straight, and narrow

LIVER

SANDY

BLUE

Head is carried on long, elegant neck

Sparkling eyes have gentle, even mild look

Fringe of white, silky hair has been left unclipped at ear tips

BREED HISTORY Gypsies in the Rothbury forest near the Scottish Borders once kept functional, speedy, working terriers, known as the Rothbury Terriers. It is likely that the Bedlington Terrier, first shown in Bedlington, Northumberland, in 1870, descends from these dogs.

KEY FACTS

COUNTRY OF ORIGIN Great Britain
DATE OF ORIGIN 1800s
FIRST USE Rat/badger hunting
USE TODAY Companion
LIFE EXPECTANCY 14–15 years
OTHER NAME Rothbury Terrier

WEIGHT RANGE
8–10 kg (17–23 lb)
HEIGHT RANGE
38–43 cm (15–17 in)

L egend says that the Whippet, Otterhound, and Dandie Dinmont are the forebears of this distinctive breed. The Bedlington's hind legs and its temperament certainly suggest that the Whippet features strongly in its development. The breed's desire to "search and destroy" has been concealed under sheep's clothing – this unusual dog may look like a sheep, but it retains the terrier's need for mental stimulation, and can be destructive if it lacks sufficient physical activity.

Close-fitting lips have no flews

Coat is blend of equal parts topcoat and undercoat

Muscular hind legs are like a Whippet's

BLACK RUSSIAN TERRIER

Strong head is well covered with heavy facial hair

SALT/PEPPER

BLACK

Dark-brown, round eyes are similar to a schnauzer's

BREED HISTORY This breed, which was developed at the Soviet Union's Red Star Army Kennels by crossing the Giant Schnauzer, Airedale Terrier, Rottweiler, and perhaps other breeds, was formally recognized in the 1940s. Its standard was revised in 1993.

KEY FACTS

COUNTRY OF ORIGIN Russia
DATE OF ORIGIN 1940s
FIRST USE Watchdog
USE TODAY Companion, security
LIFE EXPECTANCY 10–11 years
OTHER NAMES Russkji Tchornji Terrier, Chornyi Terrier

WEIGHT RANGE
40–65 kg (88–143 lb)
HEIGHT RANGE
63–75 cm (25–29 in)

T his terrier, together with another "Soviet" breed, the massive Moscow Watchdog (both developed at the Red Star Army Dog Kennels), played a role in Soviet genetics. This involved Professor T.D. Lysenko's discredited idea that "acquired characteristics", from training for example, could be inherited and accumulated to a slight degree in each generation. Lysenko hoodwinked gullible Soviet authorities into believing he could break down stable hereditary constitution, make it more "plastic", and then mould heredity. Lysenko created and then used these two breeds to try and prove his theory.

Legs are covered with moderate feathering

Short-haired variety

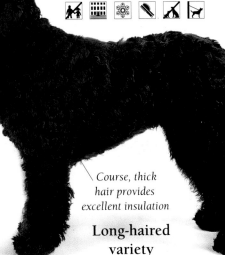

Course, thick hair provides excellent insulation

Long-haired variety

PARSON JACK RUSSELL TERRIER

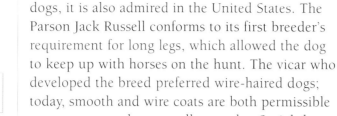

High-set ears are like dropped Vs

This is the less common version of Great Britain's most popular country terrier, the Jack Russell. One of the Netherland's most popular small dogs, it is also admired in the United States. The Parson Jack Russell conforms to its first breeder's requirement for long legs, which allowed the dog to keep up with horses on the hunt. The vicar who developed the breed preferred wire-haired dogs; today, smooth and wire coats are both permissible and are equally popular. Sprightly and robust, this breed makes a good companion, but it requires regular exercise.

Moustache and beard give mature appearance to face

Amputated tail on working dogs only

Nails are white and only moderately thick

Wiry coat may be broken or smooth, and has good undercoat

BREED HISTORY Reverend Jack Russell, a sporting parson from Devon, in the west of England, and a founding member of the Kennel Club of Great Britain, developed this strain of wire-haired fox terrier, which was long enough in the leg to accompany horses on the hunt, and small enough to burrow and bolt foxes.

Chest is not too broad, so dog can enter fox hole

Compact feet, with hair between toes

WHITE/ BROWN   WHITE/ BLACK   TRICOLOUR

JACK RUSSELL TERRIER

Long, rather pointed muzzle

The feisty, exuberant, crowd-pleasing Jack Russell is a hyperactive bundle of muscles. This popular town or country dog can be snappy and aggressive with anything that moves (including people), but is fun loving and, in most instances, overwhelmingly affectionate both with its family and with strangers. The most travelled Jack Russell is Bothy, Sir Ranulf Fiennes's companion – in the early 1980s, it accompanied him to both the North and South Poles. Because all dogs have been removed from Antarctica and none are permitted to visit, Bothy's record of playing football on the top and bottom of the world is unlikely to be broken.

Powerful, muscular hind legs

Erect ears; may also be folded

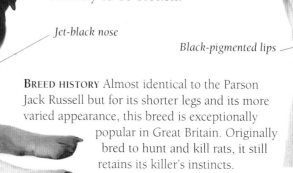

WHITE/ BROWN   WHITE/ BLACK   TRICOLOUR

Body is longer than it is tall

Jet-black nose

Black-pigmented lips

BREED HISTORY Almost identical to the Parson Jack Russell but for its shorter legs and its more varied appearance, this breed is exceptionally popular in Great Britain. Originally bred to hunt and kill rats, it still retains its killer's instincts.

STAFFORDSHIRE BULL TERRIER

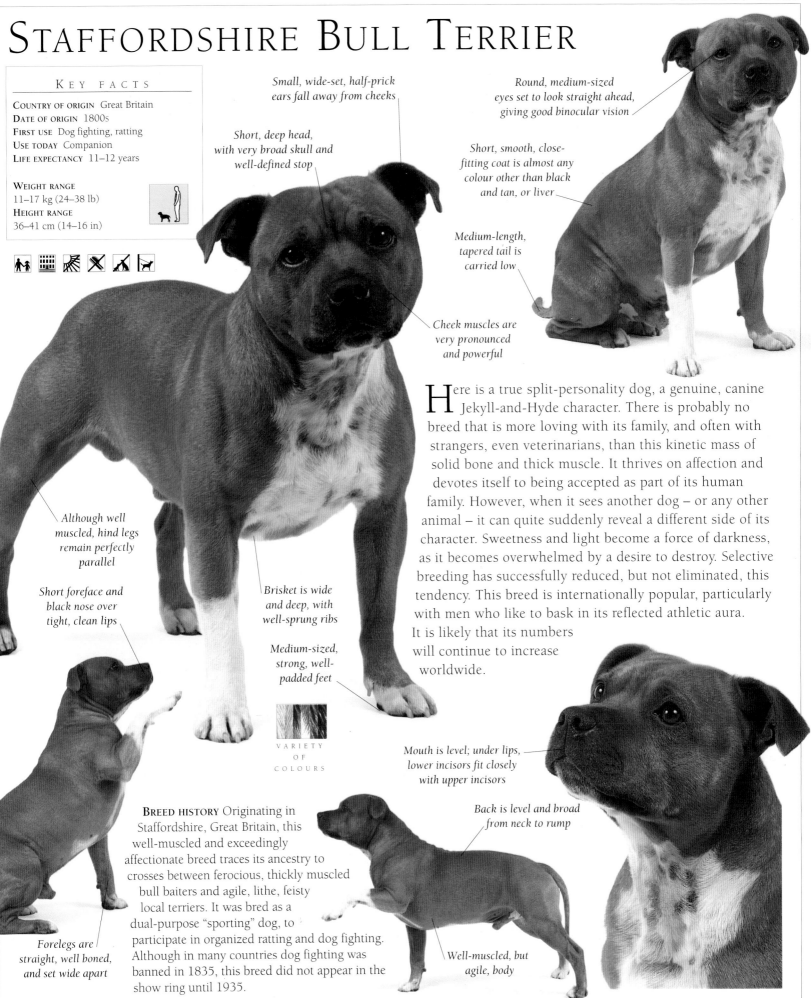

KEY FACTS

COUNTRY OF ORIGIN Great Britain
DATE OF ORIGIN 1800s
FIRST USE Dog fighting, ratting
USE TODAY Companion
LIFE EXPECTANCY 11–12 years

WEIGHT RANGE
11–17 kg (24–38 lb)
HEIGHT RANGE
36–41 cm (14–16 in)

Small, wide-set, half-prick ears fall away from cheeks

Short, deep head, with very broad skull and well-defined stop

Round, medium-sized eyes set to look straight ahead, giving good binocular vision

Short, smooth, close-fitting coat is almost any colour other than black and tan, or liver

Medium-length, tapered tail is carried low

Cheek muscles are very pronounced and powerful

Although well muscled, hind legs remain perfectly parallel

Short foreface and black nose over tight, clean lips

Brisket is wide and deep, with well-sprung ribs

Medium-sized, strong, well-padded feet

VARIETY OF COLOURS

H ere is a true split-personality dog, a genuine, canine Jekyll-and-Hyde character. There is probably no breed that is more loving with its family, and often with strangers, even veterinarians, than this kinetic mass of solid bone and thick muscle. It thrives on affection and devotes itself to being accepted as part of its human family. However, when it sees another dog – or any other animal – it can quite suddenly reveal a different side of its character. Sweetness and light become a force of darkness, as it becomes overwhelmed by a desire to destroy. Selective breeding has successfully reduced, but not eliminated, this tendency. This breed is internationally popular, particularly with men who like to bask in its reflected athletic aura. It is likely that its numbers will continue to increase worldwide.

Mouth is level; under lips, lower incisors fit closely with upper incisors

Back is level and broad from neck to rump

BREED HISTORY Originating in Staffordshire, Great Britain, this well-muscled and exceedingly affectionate breed traces its ancestry to crosses between ferocious, thickly muscled bull baiters and agile, lithe, feisty local terriers. It was bred as a dual-purpose "sporting" dog, to participate in organized ratting and dog fighting. Although in many countries dog fighting was banned in 1835, this breed did not appear in the show ring until 1935.

Forelegs are straight, well boned, and set wide apart

Well-muscled, but agile, body

BULL TERRIER

WHITE	FAWN	RED	TRI-COLOUR	BLACK-BRINDLE

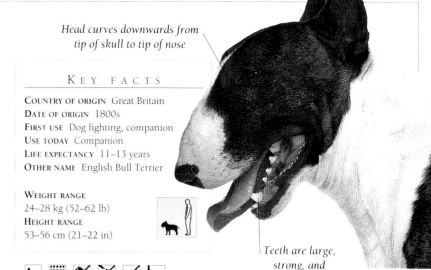

Head curves downwards from tip of skull to tip of nose

Small, thin ears are set close together

BREED HISTORY The Bull Terrier was developed by James Hinks of Birmingham, Great Britain, who bred the Bulldog with the now-extinct White English Terrier to produce a dog that dazzled observers in both the dog-fighting pit and the show ring. White was his favoured colour.

KEY FACTS

COUNTRY OF ORIGIN Great Britain
DATE OF ORIGIN 1800s
FIRST USE Dog fighting, companion
USE TODAY Companion
LIFE EXPECTANCY 11–13 years
OTHER NAME English Bull Terrier

WEIGHT RANGE
24–28 kg (52–62 lb)
HEIGHT RANGE
53–56 cm (21–22 in)

Teeth are large, strong, and perfectly regular

Short tail is carried horizontally

Shoulder blades are flat and wide

Round, compact feet have neat toes

I n the Bull Terrier, the Bulldog's strength was combined with the terrier's tenacity to create the ultimate fighting dog. James Hinks favoured white Bull Terriers, and these became, and still are, fashionable companions. Unwittingly, in selecting for this colour Hinks also selected for inherited deafness, chronic skin inflammations, and heart disease. The coloured Bull Terriers have a much lower incidence of these conditions, although inherited juvenile kidney failure can occur, with devastating effects. The breed does, however, have a lower-than-average tendency to snap and bite, and is good with people. When it does bite, the damage is considerable, because it does not let go easily.

MINIATURE BULL TERRIER

Ears point straight up when held stiffly erect

KEY FACTS

COUNTRY OF ORIGIN Great Britain
DATE OF ORIGIN 1800s
FIRST USE Dog fighting, ratting
USE TODAY Companion
LIFE EXPECTANCY 12–13 years

WEIGHT RANGE
11–15 kg (24–33 lb)
HEIGHT RANGE
25–35 cm (10–14 in)

BREED HISTORY When breeders began to consistently produce large Bull Terriers, a number of individuals decided to push in the opposite direction. This produced the Miniature Bull Terrier, which is not a true miniature in that it has not been bantomized, but is a smaller version of the Bull Terrier.

T he Miniature descends directly from small Bull Terrier puppies, which were born in the 1930s. These were bred with the survivors of a previously unsuccessful attempt to produce a genuine toy bull terrier weighing less than 4.5 kg (10 lb). With more of the terrier temperament than the Bull Terrier, the Miniature can behave like a delinquent prone to temper tantrums. It will not tolerate teasing from children and first meetings should always be supervised. The breed makes a good watchdog, and its size is ideal for urban apartment dwellers.

Eyes are narrow and deep set

Muscular thighs join stifles, which descend to hocks

Chest is extremely broad when viewed from front

Feet are neat, trim, and compact

Line from brisket to groin curves gently up

Forelegs are moderately well muscled

WHITE	FAWN	RED	TRI-COLOUR	BLACK-BRINDLE

DUTCH SMOUSHOND

Tail hangs limply when dog is not active

Skull is slightly rounded, with distinct stop

Moderately long muzzle covers strong jaws

Nose is black and eyes are dark

Long double coat of protective guard hair and down covers body

Muscular hind legs provide strength for bursts of speed

Compact, cat-like feet are densely covered with long hair

Wispy feathering on backs of forelegs

Small, bright eyes, with black-pigmented lids

Long, straight, wiry hair forms beard

Hind legs are very flexible

Forelegs are firm, straight, and well muscled

Feet are small and rounded

Strong forehead is slightly rounded

Triangular ears are set high on head

Black lips, with thick moustache

KEY FACTS

COUNTRY OF ORIGIN The Netherlands
DATE OF ORIGIN 1890s/1970s
FIRST USE Ratting in stables
USE TODAY Companion, watchdog
LIFE EXPECTANCY 12–15 years
OTHER NAME Hollandse Smoushond

WEIGHT RANGE
9–10 kg (20–22 lb)
HEIGHT RANGE
35–42 cm (14–17 in)

BREED HISTORY The Smoushond's origins are unknown, although its looks suggest that it is, in part, related to the German schnauzers. In the late 1800s, it was a popular gentleman's companion, but by the end of World War II it was almost extinct. During the last 20 years, Mrs. H.M. Barkman-v.d. Weel, from Drente, has recreated this effervescent dog through careful breeding.

Although this robust little dog was popular at the end of the 19th century, its numbers then started to decline. Attempts were made to save the breed, but World War II pushed it to near extinction. In the early 1970s, Mrs. H.M. Barkman began collecting information on the Smoushond, and by studying pictures and old pedigrees, and talking to judges who remembered the breed, she was able to recreate it through selective breeding. Today, this strong, well-muscled, ever-alert dog breeds pure for both type and temperament. A typical terrier, it is a voracious ratter, delighted to terrorize any rodent, and its yappy disposition makes it a good watchdog. The breed is now reasonably secure, with approximately 125 puppies registered each year.

DACHSHUNDS

Bushy and distinctive
eyebrows of wiry hair

Moderate-length
ears are rounded
and not too
pointed

The international name of dachshund, meaning badger dog, reflects these breeds' original purpose. For the last 100 years they have been bred as "earth dogs", the standard size being willing and able to follow badgers and foxes to earth, with the miniature version doing the same with rabbits. Show-standard dogs have deep chests and short legs, while working dogs have less robust chests and longer legs. In Germany, where these resilient dogs are still worked, they are categorized by chest circumference. The Kaninchenteckel (Rabbit-hunting Dachshund) has a maximum 30 cm (12 in) chest measurement, the Zwergteckel (Miniature) measures from 31–35 cm (12–14 in), and the Normalschlag (Standard) measures over 35 cm (14 in). All dachshunds are of hound origin, but because of their utilitarian role as Germany's most effective earth dogs, these breeds are aptly classified with the other earth dogs – the terrier group. Today, most dachshunds are kept as household companions, and they are perhaps the most recognizable of all breeds.

Wiry hair on
muzzle is longer
and more luxurious
than elsewhere
on body

Clean and sharply defined
head tapers symmetrically
to tip of nose

Short, dense, lustrous coat has
no bare patches

Wrists are slightly closer
to each other than shoulder
joints; there is a pronounced
arch to each toe

Neck is carried
with dignity and
has no dewlap

Feet rest on
pads, not just toes

Oval eyes are
set obliquely

Smooth-haired Standard Dachshund

Forehead is
not wide and is
slightly arched

BREED HISTORY Ancient Egyptian sculptures show a pharaoh seated with three short-legged dogs. The dachshund's ancestors may date back to these dwarf dogs. The Smooth-haired Standard is perhaps the oldest dachshund and was once used as a tracker.

Tightly
stretched
lips cover
jaws and
powerful
canine
teeth

Finely tapered tail
is covered with single
coat of lustrous hair

Nose is not as tapered as that of a Smooth-haired Dachshund

Eyebrows are strong and prominent above clear, friendly eyes

Hair is shorter on ears than on body, and almost smooth, but still in keeping with rest of coat

BREED HISTORY The Wire-haired was created by crossing the Smooth-haired Dachshund with rough-haired pinschers. This produced a dog with a rough coat but a small head; further crosses with the short-legged Dandie Dinmont Terrier enlarged and elongated the head, while at the same time injecting a degree of control to the dachshund's innate bloodlust.

Distinctive beard creates appearance strikingly different from other dachshunds

Wire-haired Miniature Dachshund

Buttocks are well rounded, and stifles thick and powerful

Wiry hair lies flat on tapering tail, which reaches below hocks

Chest of working- or field-trial dog is not deep

Thick and wiry, but surprisingly flat, topcoat has fine undercoat

VARIETY OF COLOURS

KEY FACTS

COUNTRY OF ORIGIN Germany
DATE OF ORIGIN 1900s
FIRST USE Badger flushing
USE TODAY Companion
LIFE EXPECTANCY 14–17 years
OTHER NAMES Zwergteckel (Miniature), Normalschlag (Standard)

WEIGHT RANGE
Miniature: 4–5 kg (9–10 lb);
Standard: 6.5–11.5 kg (15–25 lb)

HEIGHT RANGE
Miniature and Standard 13–25 cm (5–10 in)

Length of muzzle slightly exceeds that of skull

Long, smooth, silky coat is shortest on back and considerably longer on underside of body

Narrow head has distinctive, tapering appearance, narrowing smoothly towards small nose

Feet have closely set toes

Long-haired Standard Dachshund

BREED HISTORY The Long-haired Standard Dachshund was probably developed by crossing the Smooth-haired Standard Dachshund with short-legged spaniels, similar to the Sussex or Field Spaniel, and then miniaturizing the result. The Long-haired certainly has an affectionate, outgoing personality similar to that of spaniels.

Ears are set just above eyes, and are covered by luxurious, silky hair

Back is level, with slight arch above loin

GUNDOGS

FOR THOUSANDS OF YEARS, sight and scent hounds accompanied hunters in search of food or in pursuit of sport. Natural genetic variations of coat texture, length of bone, scenting ability, and levels of obedience had always occurred, but with the introduction of firearms to hunting, breeders took a far greater interest in these and other traits. Dog breeding subsequently took a dramatic leap forwards, producing highly responsive and amenable workers. Today, these trustworthy breeds are some of the world's most popular canine companions.

LEGS WILL BECOME STURDY AND THICKLY BONED

MUZZLE PROVIDES ROOM FOR NASAL MEMBRANES NECESSARY FOR SCENTING

English Springer Spaniel
This breed is a superb worker, a fine companion, and a successful show dog.

English Cocker Spaniel puppy
The English Cocker was developed in south-west England and in Wales to flush woodcock. Still used as a working dog, its responsive and affectionate nature have made it a very popular companion.

COAT IS FLAT AND STRAIGHT ON NECK

Épagneul Picard
The long-coated Picard, a gentle, active, and friendly breed, is an excellent water-fowl retriever.

BREEDING FOR ABILITY
Hunting by sight or scent, going to earth, guarding, and swimming are all natural forms of dog behaviour that require little additional training. However, finding game, then standing or crouching absolutely still, or leaping forth on command into cold water to pick up a shot bird and carry it in the mouth back to the hunter, requires the combination of instinctive ability and a willingness to be trained. In the 1700s and 1800s, from a genetic base of hounds and herders, breeders produced over 50 breeds of gundog, all willing to listen and learn. These are usually divided into five

subgroups – water dogs, pointers, setters, flushing dogs, and retrievers. Proficient water work requires a tight, waterproof coat and a strong desire to swim. The Portuguese and Spanish Water Dogs, French Barbet, Hungarian Puli, and the now exceedingly rare German Corded Poodle are among the oldest water-loving breeds. The Irish Water Spaniel, French Épagneul Pont-Audemer, Dutch Wetterhoun, American Chesapeake Bay Retriever, and English Curly-coated Retriever are all examples of regional developments of water-loving companions.

POINTERS AND SETTERS
In the 1500s, when Spain was at the height of its imperial and cultural powers, both its methods of hunting and the breeds involved were fashionable throughout Europe and the Americas. It is probable that the Spanish Pointing Hound – a dog that followed air scent,

discovered ground game, then stood stock still while hunters moved forwards with nets – was exported to France, Great Britain, and elsewhere. It is the root stock of today's pointers. The pointer searches for game silently, but on finding its prey this gundog's behaviour contradicts evolution. Rather than moving quietly forwards to capture its victim, it freezes perfectly still, often with one foreleg raised and bent, and "points". The setter behaves in an identical way, except that it crouches down, or "sets". The dog's natural inclination is to capture its prey; to stop short of that objective can produce a highly strung temperament.

At one time, there were two varieties of pointer in Spain, a light-framed one similar to today's Spanish Perdiguero de Burgos, and a heavier framed breed resembling the modern Bracco Italiano. Both were exported to Great Britain and were probably crossed with sight and scent hounds to produce today's pointer. The Spanish Pointer was also involved in the development of the British setters. In Germany, similar development of pointers and setters occurred; however, with the decline of field sports after the 1848

ROBUST LEGS ARE FEATHERED WITH SOFT, SILKY HAIR

Kooiker Dog
This lithe dog assists the Dutch hunter by waving its bushy tail and luring curious ducks forwards. At one time the ducks were netted for food, but today it is more likely that they will be leg banded and released.

CORDING SELDOM OCCURS ON POODLE'S FACE

Corded Poodle
The Corded Poodle is one of the few breeds to possess a corded coat in which an equally long topcoat, guard hair, and undercoat interweave to produce hanging cords.

CORDS COVER BODY AND PROVIDE PROTECTION FROM PREDATORS

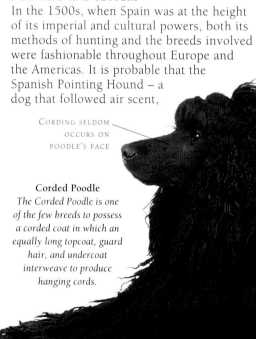

HAIR IS SHORT ON HINDQUARTERS FOR INCREASED MOBILITY IN WATER

Portuguese Water Dog
This fisherman's friend retrieved objects lost overboard and carried messages between boats.

WEDGE-SHAPED HEAD WITH FAIRLY SMALL EARS

Nova Scotia Duck Tolling Retriever
This hunter's companion lures ducks within range of the hunter's gun, then retrieves them from the water.

REGIONAL DEVELOPMENTS

While Denmark produced its own pointer, the Netherlands some fine small retrievers such as the Dutch Partridge Dog, and Hungary the elegant Vizsla, French breeders created a superb selection of gundogs. These are named according to their coat textures – the braques are short-coated pointers, the épagneuls are long-coated spaniels, and the griffons have wiry coats.

There has recently been a renewed interest in some of the oldest of the gundog breeds. The Portuguese Perdiguero and Italian Spinone have come to the attention of breeders. In Spain, hunters continue to develop their own unique selection of gundogs never seen outside Iberia. In Slovakia, the Slovensky Hruborsty Stavac is increasing in numbers, while the German Pudelpointer is being bred by several dedicated breeders.

revolutions, German pointing and setting breeds virtually disappeared. Around 1890, German hunters turned their attention back to these old breeds, and in an explosion of creative breeding activity produced pointers which occurred in three coat variations – the Weimaraner, Munsterlander and, in the German-speaking parts of Czechoslovakia, the Czesky Fousek.

Hungarian Vizsla
A superb athlete and a biddable, gentle companion, the Hungarian Vizsla was restricted to central Europe until the 1930s.

SPANIELS AND RETRIEVERS

Skilled British breeders produced another group of gundogs, the flushing spaniels, which worked their way through dense undergrowth, flushing birds towards the hunters. At one time, all British spaniels were classified as Land, Field, or Water Spaniels, according to the terrain in which they worked best. With the development of breeding for show standards, classification became more refined. English and Welsh "Springers" were separated from the "Cocker". Field, Sussex, and Clumber Spaniels were classified as distinct breeds.

HEAD IS LEAN, LONG, AND ELEGANT

Curly-coated Retriever
The oldest of the English Retrievers, the Curly-coat is affectionate, loyal, and hard working.

FACE IS COVERED WITH SHORT HAIR

At the same time, British breeders, using as a basis the water dogs of Newfoundland, produced the retrievers. This development depended upon dogs having a natural instinct to carry gently in the mouth and a great willingness to learn and obey. The Labrador and Golden Retrievers possess these qualities; not only popular as working gundogs, they are also the most successful service dogs in the world, working as guide dogs and assistance dogs for the blind or disabled.

ROUND-TIPPED EARS ARE LONG AND LOBULAR

ADMIRABLE ATTRIBUTES

This group of dogs is generally easier to train than any other. Gundogs are almost invariably relaxed with children, less inclined than any other groups to fight among themselves and, in most instances, willingly obey commands.

ELEGANT HEAD IS COVERED WITH SHORT, FINE HAIR

Épagneul Pont-Audemer
This breed developed in the Pont-Audemer region of Normandy in the 1600s, and is used to spring or flush game.

Weimaraner
This multi-purpose, German hunting dog tracks, points, and retrieves. It makes a robust household companion.

TOPKNOT OF HAIR HALOS DOG'S FACE

Ariége Pointer
The original Ariége Pointer was probably a cross between the old Spanish Pointer and a dog similar to the Bracco Italiano. Today's breed is a 20th-century re-creation.

PROMINENT NOSE, WITH LARGE NOSTRILS, IS OFTEN BROWN, EVEN TAN, IN COLOUR

Slovakian Pointer
This hard-working breed was decimated by World War II, but Czech and Slovak breeders revived it through the infusion of German Wire-haired and Short-haired Pointer blood.

COAT IS WEATHER AND WATER RESISTANT

HUNGARIAN PULI

The responsive, obedient, and virtually waterproof Puli (leader in Hungarian) is almost certainly the ancestor of the poodle. Well into this century, Hungarian shepherds continued to breed carefully for working ability. World War II virtually destroyed dog breeding in Hungary, but by then the Puli had been adopted as a companion. A group of Hungarians took their dogs abroad, and established the Puli elsewhere, particularly in North America. This adaptable dog enjoys working sheep and can easily be trained to retrieve from water.

WHITE   APRICOT   BLACK

Ears are not noticeable

Fine, round head is hidden by hair

Slightly rusty colour is not uncommon

Some cords grow to floor length

Each cord of hair has to be groomed separately

Puppy

There is no cording to puppy's coat

BREED HISTORY The Puli was probably brought to Hungary by the Magyars. Today's Pulis come mainly from a breeding programme carried out this century.

KEY FACTS

COUNTRY OF ORIGIN Hungary
DATE OF ORIGIN Middle Ages
FIRST USE Sheep herding
USE TODAY Companion, obedience, retrieving
LIFE EXPECTANCY 12–13 years
OTHER NAMES Hungarian Water Dog, Puli

WEIGHT RANGE
10–15 kg (22–33 lb)
HEIGHT RANGE
37–44 cm (14½–17½ in)

PORTUGUESE WATER DOG

Plume of hair permits tail to float

Single coat can be either long or short

Domed head is large, with long muzzle

Nose colour varies with coat colour

Eyes are set well apart

Chest is deep, with long, well-sprung ribs

Long legs from hock down

KEY FACTS

COUNTRY OF ORIGIN Portugal
DATE OF ORIGIN Middle Ages
FIRST USE Working with fishermen
USE TODAY Companion, guarding, retrieving
LIFE EXPECTANCY 12–14 years
OTHER NAME Cão de Agua
WEIGHT RANGE
16–25 kg (35–55 lb)
HEIGHT RANGE
43–57 cm
(17–22½ in)

This ancient breed of fisherman's dog has been used to pull nets in the water, as a message bearer swimming from boat to boat, and on land as a successful rabbiter. The breed is strong, loyal, and slightly suspicious by nature. Its coat was originally cut in a distinctive way in order to prevent its hind legs from dragging while swimming, and to protect its chest from thermal shock in cold water.

Long, wavy hair requires frequent grooming

Hair clipped for work and showing

BREED HISTORY This breed's ancestors arrived in Portugal either in the 400s with Visigoths from central Europe, or in the 700s with Moors from North Africa.

WHITE   BROWN   BROWN/WHITE   BLACK/WHITE   BLACK

SPANISH WATER DOG

BREED HISTORY Related to the Portuguese Water Dog and perhaps to the poodle, this breed is still almost unknown outside Spain. It has always been a multi-purpose breed, assisting in herding, hunting, and fishing.

WHITE   CHESTNUT   WHITE/   BLACK
               CHESTNUT

Non-shedding coat forms heavy cords of hair

Heavy topknot covers eyes

Hair bleaches in sunshine

Well-muscled hind legs provide endurance for swimming

This breed has not received much attention from professional breeders, one consequence being that both coat colour and body size vary considerably. Another is that inherited defects are less common in the Spanish Water Dog than in other dogs that have been more selectively bred. Although these dogs can be found on the north coast of Spain, the majority live in the south, where they are now used primarily for goat herding, but also for retrieving ducks. The breed is not difficult to obedience train, and is not snappy, but can get irritable with children.

Paws have webbed toes

IRISH WATER SPANIEL

Long, curly topknot of hair often hangs just above eyes

Large, dark, liver-coloured nose

Medium-brown eyes are bright and alert

BREED HISTORY Portuguese fishermen might have introduced their Water Dog to Ireland while visiting Galway. Ancestors could, however, include the poodle.

Powerful thigh muscles

Very long, low-set ears close to cheeks, and covered with twisted curls

Long neck carries head well above body

This breed, the most distinctive of all spaniels, is the survivor of the three varieties of water spaniel that once inhabited Ireland. Its immense stamina, excellent swimming ability, virtually waterproof coat, and muscular power make it an ideal retriever, particularly for working the cold winter waters of the tidal estuaries of Ireland. Although this is a gentle, faithful, attentive companion, as well as an excellent gundog, it has never become a popular house dog. It is, however, ideal for country walkers.

Low-set, straight, tapering tail

Well-boned forelegs straight down from shoulder

Large, roundish feet are well covered with hair

STANDARD POODLE

Well-proportioned and dignified head

BREED HISTORY Drawings by artists such as Albrecht Dürer reveal that the poodle was originally a water dog. Today's clipping is based on historic grooming to reduce water resistance while working.

Hair left on tail gives buoyancy while swimming

KEY FACTS

COUNTRY OF ORIGIN Germany
DATE OF ORIGIN Middle Ages
  FIRST USE Water retrieving
  USE TODAY Companion, security
  LIFE EXPECTANCY 11–15 years
  OTHER NAMES Caniche, Barbone

WEIGHT RANGE
20.5–32 kg (45–70 lb)
HEIGHT RANGE
37.5–38.5 cm (15 in)

The Standard Poodle is not simply a fashion accessory – it is a responsive, easy-to-train, and reliable companion, guard, and retriever. The breed has a lower-than-average incidence of skin complaints and does not moult, making it an ideal dog for people who have allergies. Dependable, calm, and not given to the hysterics that sometimes afflict its smaller relatives, the Standard remains at heart a working dog. Its French name, Caniche, meaning duck dog, is descriptive of its original purpose – a duck retriever.

Solid, long, straight muzzle is not pointed

Slightly slanted, alert-looking eyes are set at level of stop

Hair on feet increases swimming power

ALL SOLID COLOURS

BARBET

This determined hunter and retriever is certainly an ancient breed. It looks similar to the now-extinct English Water Dog and probably played a role in the development of more recent breeds, such as the Briard and French griffons. Judging from the frequency of references and illustrations, this was once Europe's most common water dog. The Barbet's waterproof coat – like that of the Irish Water Spaniel, one of its probable descendants – gives it superb protection when working in even the iciest water. Today, it is seldom seen in homes, perhaps because so much time is needed to keep its coat clean.

Ears are long and pendant

BREED HISTORY One of Europe's most ancient water dogs, and possibly the forerunner of the poodle, the Barbet was originally used to retrieve both fallen arrows and water fowl from the water.

Tail is covered with dense hair, and curls slightly

Forelegs are well boned and muscular

Large, round feet have good webbing between toes, and thick, black pads

Face is fully covered with hair

KEY FACTS

COUNTRY OF ORIGIN France
DATE OF ORIGIN Middle Ages
FIRST USE Water retrieving
USE TODAY Gundog, companion
LIFE EXPECTANCY 12–14 years
OTHER NAME Griffon d'Arrêt à Poil Laineux

WEIGHT RANGE
15–25 kg (33–55 lb)
HEIGHT RANGE
46–56 cm (18–22 in)

WHITE   CHESTNUT   FAWN   GREY   BLACK

WETTERHOUN

The square-bodied Wetterhoun (Dutch for water dog), now relatively rare, was developed in Friesland at the same time as the Stabyhoun. It specialized in killing otters, the fisherman's competitors for fish. After otters become more manageable in the northern parts of the Netherlands, the breed was used to hunt small land mammals, such as polecats, and to guard farms. It is strong willed and its guarding instinct is still sharp, so that training from an early age is imperative. The Wetterhoun is a rugged, well-built, and effective gundog, capable of flushing and retrieving on both land and water.

KEY FACTS

COUNTRY OF ORIGIN The Netherlands
DATE OF ORIGIN 1600s
FIRST USE Otter hunting
USE TODAY Companion, hunting
LIFE EXPECTANCY 12–13 years
OTHER NAMES Otterhoun, Dutch Spaniel

WEIGHT RANGE
15–20 kg (33–44 lb)
HEIGHT RANGE
53–58 cm (21–23 in)

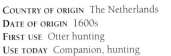

Prominent eyes are alert and penetrating

LIVER/WHITE   BLACK/WHITE

LIVER   BLACK

Coarse, thick, curly hair covers entire body, except head

BREED HISTORY Developed by the efficient breeders of the Dutch province of Friesland at least 400 years ago, this rare breed is seldom seen outside its native land.

Hocks are closer to ground than on other water dogs

Chest is very broad, keeping forelegs apart

Feet are rounded and quite large, with pronounced, thick pads

Straight forelegs are powerful

ÉPAGNEUL PONT-AUDEMER

This gentle, responsive, and effective pointer and retriever is quite rare, although an active preservation society in France ensures its survival. A breed that thrives on work, it is found mainly in the homes of serious hunters, and revels in working wetlands and marshes, where its personality instantly changes from quiet and retiring to zestful and exuberant. It is surprising that the Pont-Audemer is not more popular. It is a reliable and docile companion, and usually gets on well with other dogs. Its coat needs routine attention, but is not as oily or difficult to manage as the coats of the Barbet or poodles.

KEY FACTS

COUNTRY OF ORIGIN France
DATE OF ORIGIN 1600s
FIRST USE Game flushing, water retrieving
USE TODAY Gundog, companion
LIFE EXPECTANCY 12–14 years
OTHER NAME Pont-Audemer Spaniel

WEIGHT RANGE
18–24 kg (40–53 lb)
HEIGHT RANGE
51–58 cm (20–23 in)

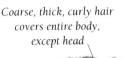

LIVER/WHITE   LIVER

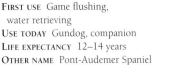

Legs are long and straight

Eyes are small and gentle

BREED HISTORY Related to old French spaniels, the Barbet, and probably the Irish Water Spaniel, this water dog became virtually extinct during World War II. It was revived after 1945, through the introduction of Irish Water Spaniel blood.

Profuse, shiny coat is not oily

Low-set ears have rather long fringes

CHESAPEAKE BAY RETRIEVER

Medium-length tail has slight feathering

Broad, round skull is covered in short hair

Thick, short hair is wavy, but not curly

BREED HISTORY Stories suggest that this breed descends from two Lesser Newfoundland puppies given to a Mr. George Law by a British army captain. These dogs were bred with local hounds to produce the Chesapeake Bay Retriever.

Wide-set eyes are enquiring

Although the Chesapeake Bay Retriever may trace its origins back to the small water dogs of Newfoundland, in form and function it is remarkably similar to the Curly-coated Retriever. This suggests that, in addition to Newfoundland blood, there is also English or Irish Water Spaniel, or English Otterhound, blood in its history. Along the duck-hunting shores of Chesapeake Bay, and throughout the United States, Canada, Scandinavia, and Great Britain, this tireless worker excels at retrieving game. It is a tougher breed than the Labrador Retriever, with a sharper personality. Like other retrievers, it is gentle with children and cordial to strangers. A loyal companion, it is happiest in a country environment.

Small ears are set well up the head and hang loosely

Toes are well rounded

Powerful hindquarters

KEY FACTS

COUNTRY OF ORIGIN
United States
DATE OF ORIGIN 1900s
FIRST USE Waterfowl retrieving
USE TODAY Companion, gundog
LIFE EXPECTANCY 12–13 years

WEIGHT RANGE
25–34 kg (55–75 lb)
HEIGHT RANGE
53–66 cm (21–26 in)

STRAW   RED-GOLD   BROWN

CURLY-COATED RETRIEVER

A classic water dog, the Curly-coat remains the least common of all the retrievers, although at one time it enjoyed great popularity, and was used extensively throughout Great Britain to retrieve from water. It has a superb water dog's coat, composed of crisp, tight, small, waterproof curls. Hip dysplasia can occur in some Curly-coats; tight lower eyelids (entropion) also occur with greater-than-average frequency. However, this is a delightfully old-fashioned breed – calm and even tempered, but powerfully alert when it is working.

Head sits comfortably on long, free neck

LIVER   BLACK

KEY FACTS

COUNTRY OF ORIGIN Great Britain
DATE OF ORIGIN 1800s
FIRST USE Waterfowl retrieving
USE TODAY Gundog, companion
LIFE EXPECTANCY 12–13 years

WEIGHT RANGE
32–36 kg (70–80 lb)
HEIGHT RANGE
64–69 cm (25–27 in)

Large eyes are not prominent

Chest is deep and broad

Small ears are set at eye level and hang close to sides of head

BREED HISTORY
This is the oldest of the British retrievers, and evidence suggests that it existed as early as 1803. It probably descends from the extinct English Water Spaniel and the Lesser Newfoundland, which was brought to Great Britain by cod fishermen.

Crisp curls cover entire body

Black nose sits at end of long, strong jaws

CORDED POODLE

Nose is pronounced and highly developed

Slightly slanted eyes are set at level of stop

Straight muzzle is almost as long as skull

Width of skull is less than half the length of head; stop is not pronounced

KEY FACTS

COUNTRY OF ORIGIN Germany
DATE OF ORIGIN 1400s
FIRST USE Retrieving from water
USE TODAY Companion
LIFE EXPECTANCY 15 years
OTHER NAMES Caniche, Pudel, Barbonne

WEIGHT RANGE
20.5–32 kg (44–70½ in)
HEIGHT RANGE
over 38 cm (15 in)

In profile, head and muzzle are long, lean, and elegant

Cords provide a protective and insulating layer

Forelegs are covered in abundant hair

Profuse hair makes head appear domed

BREED HISTORY The origins of poodles will always be unknown. They may be close relatives of the French Barbet, but historical references indicate that in the 1400s poodles travelled from Germany to France, not the reverse. Some historians claim that their ancestry lies in extinct Russian hounds.

Flat, broad ears, with round tips

Tail is set quite high, and is raised when dog is active

The Corded Poodle's coat very clearly distinguishes it from other poodles. The cords occur when the topcoat and undercoat interweave, and offer protection from both the elements and predators. Natural selection produced this type of coat in breeds that guarded herds in hostile climates. The Corded Poodle is probably closely related to the Schafpudel, but while the latter continued to be used as a sheep-guarding dog, the Corded Poodle was bred more for water work and eventually solely for companionship, producing the popular Standard Poodle of today. Unfortunately, the Corded Poodle is now extremely rare – only a few individuals remain, mostly in France. The breed's temperament is similar to that of its more popular cousin's, and its coat needs far less management once it has been properly corded.

Tufts of corded hair cover entire body

Feet are small and oval, with well-arched toes

HUNGARIAN VIZSLA

Eyes are lively and alert; no white is visible

Medium-length neck is muscular and moderately arched

Low-set tail has been docked to two-thirds its natural length

Hair is harsh, hard, loose fitting, and not glossy, with winter undercoat

Wire-haired variety

Forearm is quite long, and pastern is relatively short

Thighs and legs are long, with low hocks

KEY FACTS

COUNTRY OF ORIGIN Hungary
DATE OF ORIGIN Middle Ages/1930s
FIRST USE Hunting, falconry
USE TODAY Companion, gundog
LIFE EXPECTANCY 14–15 years
OTHER NAMES Magyar Vizsla, Drotszoru Magyar Vizsla

WEIGHT RANGE
22–30 kg (48½–66 lb)
HEIGHT RANGE
57–64 cm (22½–25 in)

Elegant and gentle, but energetic, the Hungarian Vizsla probably would not have survived World War II, had not Hungarian expatriates taken their favoured companions with them when they emigrated to other parts of Europe and North America in the 1930s. The Vizsla's original dual purpose, pointing and retrieving, has been extended to a third purpose in the last 20 years – that of a widely admired family companion, which is obedient, reliable, and healthy. It is becoming increasingly popular in Hungary, but its original purpose has not been forgotten. In Canada, the wire-haired variety is commonly seen at work as a gundog with weekend hunters. It has a good nose, follows trails diligently, and retrieves either game or thrown tennis balls with enthusiasm.

Hair forms brush on back part of forelegs

BREED HISTORY The name was first used in 1510 to describe the result of crossing the now-extinct indigenous Pannonian Hound with the Yellow Turkish Dog. By the 1850s, today's short-haired gundog was established. The wire-haired variety was developed in the 1930s.

Hair is short, smooth, dense, shiny, and lies close to body; there is no undercoat

Muzzle is slightly longer than head, tapering slightly to square end

Chest is moderately deep, reaching down to elbows

Thin, silky ears have round tips, and hang close to cheeks

Head is lean but muscular, with furrow on forehead

Thighs are well developed, with moderate angulation at stifle

Short-haired variety

Gentle and alert eyes are darker than coat colour

Cat-like, compact, round feet, with close toes and brown nails

Elbows are close on straight, strong, muscular forelimbs

Nose is quite large, with wide-open nostrils

LABRADOR RETRIEVER

Hazel-brown, medium-sized eyes express gentle temperament

Powerful jaws are of medium length, and are used deftly when working

Tail is very thick at base, and tapers gradually to tip

KEY FACTS

COUNTRY OF ORIGIN Great Britain
DATE OF ORIGIN 1800s
FIRST USE Gundog
USE TODAY Companion, gundog, field trials, assistance dog
LIFE EXPECTANCY 12–14 years

WEIGHT RANGE
25–34 kg (55–75 lb)
HEIGHT RANGE
54–57 cm (21½–22½ in)

YELLOW

MID-BROWN

BLACK

Chest has good depth and width, with well-sprung ribs

BREED HISTORY One of the world's most popular breeds, the Labrador Retriever traces its origins back to the St. John's region of Newfoundland, Canada. There it was known as the "Small Water Dog", to differentiate it from the larger Newfoundland. Trade in salted cod brought the breed to the port of Poole in Dorset, England, where local landowners acquired specimens and refined their breeding for use as gundogs.

Broad head has pronounced stop, so that skull is not in direct line with nose

Forelegs are well boned, and straight from shoulder down to ground

Medium-length tail is thickly covered in dense hair, and has no feathering

Waterproof, water loving, affable, gregarious, and family oriented – a delicious range of adjectives describes one of the world's most popular family companions. The Labrador once worked from the shores of the granite-rocked inlets of the Newfoundland coast, retrieving the cork floats of fishing nets and swimming them ashore, so that fishermen could pull in the fish-filled nets. Today, this steadfast breed is the quintessence of the agreeable canine member of the human family. Unfortunately, many individuals do not live up to the image they carry. Some suffer from hereditary cataracts, hip and elbow arthritis, and even wayward temperaments. Despite this, the Labrador Retriever is one of the most loyal and dependable breeds in the world.

Feet are round and rather compact

FLAT-COATED RETRIEVER

Dark, medium-sized eyes have alert, questioning expression

B red in Great Britain from imported Newfoundland stock, the sleek Flat-coat was the favoured dog of British gamekeepers by the turn of this century. With the advent of the Labrador and Golden Retrievers, however, it was virtually extinct by the end of World War II. Today's handsome, humorous breed, fashionable once more as a gundog, is a superb flusher, and an excellent land and water retriever. Gregarious and versatile, its popularity is bound to increase, although it does suffer from a higher-than-average incidence of bone cancer.

Dense, shiny, fine coat lies flat, and has waterproof undercoat

Short, flat tail is moderately feathered

Gentle stop delineates skull from muzzle

BREED HISTORY Crossings between the Newfoundland and the smaller working dog from the St. John's region of Newfoundland produced the Wavy-coated Retriever. Further crossings with setters resulted in the effervescent Flat-coat.

Round, strong feet, with close, well-arched toes

LIVER

BLACK

Strong, straight legs are well feathered with long hair

ENGLISH POINTER

BREED HISTORY Although its exact origins are unclear, the Pointer was developed wholly in Great Britain. At some stage in its development, Old Spanish Setter lines were probably used.

G entle, obedient, and with a tendency to take life rather seriously, the Pointer's original purpose contradicted natural dog behaviour. Upon sighting a hare it would stand and point, permitting accompanying greyhounds to chase and seize the animal. Selective breeding has created an intensely biddable, noble, and giving individual, but one that is overly sensitive. Its kindly disposition makes it an ideal family companion.

Well-defined stop separates dome of skull from muzzle

Fine, smooth, hard coat, with good sheen

Straight line goes from long, sloping shoulders to pasterns

Thighs are lean and well muscled

LEMON/ WHITE

ORANGE/ WHITE

LIVER/ WHITE

BLACK/ WHITE

Oval feet have arched toes and well-cushioned pads

High-set ears hang loose, even when dog is alert

GOLDEN RETRIEVER

Relaxed but responsive, calm but alert, sensible and serene, the Golden is, in many ways, the ideal family companion. This affection-demanding, multi-purpose, easy-to-train, and attractive breed is even more popular in North America and Scandinavia than in its native Great Britain. Bred to retrieve waterfowl, it has a gentle mouth and will rarely snap or bite – it is especially patient with children. Different breed lines have evolved for different purposes. One variety works as a gundog, another has been developed for use in field trials, while the largest line is devoted to the show ring and family life. A fourth breeding line has produced dogs that are trained exclusively as assistants for blind or disabled people. Popularity has unfortunately produced inherited defects in some lines, such as allergic skin conditions, eye problems, and even irritable snappiness.

Dark eyes, surrounded by dark rims, have kind expression

KEY FACTS

COUNTRY OF ORIGIN Great Britain
DATE OF ORIGIN 1800s
FIRST USE Game retrieving
USE TODAY Companion, gundog, field trials, assistance dog
LIFE EXPECTANCY 13–15 years

WEIGHT RANGE
27–36 kg (60–80 lb)
HEIGHT RANGE
51–61cm (20–24 in)

Hind legs are well muscled, and covered in thick skin and dense hair

Coat can be flat or wavy, with dense, waterproof undercoat

Cat-like feet have copious hair growing between pads

Forelimbs have prolific feathering

Powerful muzzle is tipped with large, black nose

CREAM   GOLD

Well-proportioned ears are of moderate size, and hang with slight fold

BREED HISTORY Records reveal that this gentle breed was developed in the late 1800s, by crossing a light-coloured Flat-coated Retriever with the now-extinct Tweed Water Spaniel. The first Goldens were exhibited in 1908.

Neck is clean and muscular, with loose-fitting skin

Coat colour varies from cream to gold, and goes lighter with age

Dark-pigmented lower lips droop naturally

NOVA SCOTIA DUCK TOLLING RETRIEVER

Head is clean cut and slightly wedge shaped

Triangular ears are set high and well back on skull

The Toller's rather unusual job is to entice ducks and geese within shotgun range, and to retrieve them from the water after they have been hit. From his concealed blind near the shore, the hunter tosses a stick parallel to the shore, and with great animation, but without barking, the Toller retrieves it. It may take dozens of throws before the ducks or geese become curious and approach the shore. When they are within shooting range, the hunter calls his dog back to the blind, stands up to put the birds to flight, and shoots. The Toller then acts as an efficient retriever.

Coat is dense, and occurs in various shades of red and orange

Deep chest is well insulated for cold-water swimming

BREED HISTORY It is likely that tolling (from the old English, *tollen*, to entice) Red Decoy Dogs accompanied their masters from Great Britain to Nova Scotia. Crossed with retrievers and working spaniels, the breed was recognized in 1945.

KEY FACTS

COUNTRY OF ORIGIN Canada
DATE OF ORIGIN 1800s
FIRST USE Waterfowl flushing/retrieving
USE TODAY Gundog, companion
LIFE EXPECTANCY 12–14 years
OTHER NAMES Little River Duck Dog, Yarmouth Toller

WEIGHT RANGE
17–23 kg (37–51 lb)
HEIGHT RANGE
43–53 cm (17–21 in)

Powerful, compact, well-muscled body on sturdy, solid legs

KOOIKERHONDJE

BREED HISTORY Dating back at least to the time of William of Orange, this breed virtually disappeared, but was recreated between the World Wars by Baroness v. Hardenbroek van Ammerstool.

Skull and muzzle are of equal length

Ears always have distinctive, black "ear-drops"

Historically, the Kooikerhondje behaved much in the same way as the now-extinct English Red Decoy Dog. With its antics and bushy white tail, it enticed ducks and geese towards nets, or within shotgun range. These dogs are still used to entice ducks, but now they do so into traps made of rush matting, for banding and identification. Only 25 of these actively curious dogs survived World War II. These are the forebears of the approximately 500 new puppies registered each year. Due to this small genetic pool, inherited diseases do occur. However, this friendly, even-tempered breed makes a very satisfying companion.

KEY FACTS

COUNTRY OF ORIGIN The Netherlands
DATE OF ORIGIN 1700s
FIRST USE Bird flushing/retrieving
USE TODAY Companion, gundog
LIFE EXPECTANCY 12–13 years
OTHER NAMES Dutch Decoy Spaniel, Kooiker Dog

WEIGHT RANGE
9–11 kg (20–24 lb)
HEIGHT RANGE
35–41 cm (14–16 in)

Heavy and luxurious topcoat conceals layer of insulating down

Body is approximately as high as it is long

Moderately deep chest is covered with protective, waterproof hair

ENGLISH SPRINGER SPANIEL

Cheeks are flat, and upper lips hang well below line of lower jaw

Lobe-shaped, close-set ears have excellent hair cover, and are set in line with eyes

BREED HISTORY Perhaps the rootstock of all working spaniels, identifiable members of this breed are portrayed in paintings from the mid-1600s. It was not until the late 1800s that springers and cockers were separated into distinct breeds.

BLACK/ WHITE

LIVER/ WHITE

A gundog with unlimited stamina, the English Springer thrives on physical activity, be it flushing game in marshes, or retrieving tennis balls in city parks. This leggy and powerful dog needs constant mental and physical stimulation; when these are denied, it can be quite destructive. Today, it is Great Britain's most popular working spaniel, although its bird-dog abilities were first appreciated in the United States. It is an excellent companion and, in spite of having diverged along separate work and show lines, even the most urban individual probably retains sound working abilities.

Straight coat is firm but not coarse, with long feathering

KEY FACTS

COUNTRY OF ORIGIN Great Britain
DATE OF ORIGIN 1600s
FIRST USE Game flushing/retrieving
USE TODAY Companion, gundog
LIFE EXPECTANCY 12–14 years

WEIGHT RANGE
22–24 kg (49–53 lb)
HEIGHT RANGE
48–51 cm (19–20 in)

WELSH SPRINGER SPANIEL

Medium-length muzzle is straight and fairly square

Ears are smaller than an English Springer's

H ard working, water loving, and with outstanding stamina, the versatile Welsh Springer is an excellent companion and superb working gundog. In Wales and elsewhere, it has also been used as a cattle drover and sheep herder. It excels at flushing (or "springing") game birds. Unlike the English Springer, it has not diverged along separate work and show lines, although it is almost equally popular for each purpose. Like all gundogs, it responds well to obedience training.

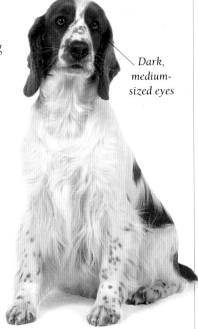

Dark, medium-sized eyes

Long, muscular neck neatly sets into long, sloping shoulders

KEY FACTS

COUNTRY OF ORIGIN Great Britain
DATE OF ORIGIN 1600s
FIRST USE Game retrieving/flushing
USE TODAY Companion, gundog
LIFE EXPECTANCY 12–14 years

WEIGHT RANGE
16–20 kg (35–45 lb)
HEIGHT RANGE
46–48 cm (18–19 in)

Thick, straight, silky topcoat is never curly

BREED HISTORY This amiable breed, which was first visually represented in the 1600s, was at one time exhibited as the Welsh Cocker. It was not recognized as a distinct breed until 1902.

FIELD SPANIEL

Low-set ears hang with graceful folds

BREED HISTORY Originally classified as a variety of cocker spaniel, the Field Spaniel received its own recognition for show purposes in 1892. Unfortunately, breeding for the show ring led to a great deterioration in the breed's working ability. By the end of World War II it was almost extinct, but by 1969 numbers had safely increased.

Tail, docked on working dogs, is carried below level of back

As in the case of the American Cocker Spaniel, the Field Spaniel's shape changed dramatically after it was recognized as a distinct breed, with separate status from its ancestor, the English Cocker Spaniel – and in this instance, the results were disastrous. Early this century, breeders selectively bred for long backs and short, heavy-boned legs. The Field Spaniel subsequently lost all ability to perform in the field. In the 1960s, English Cocker and Springer Spaniels were used to regenerate the breed, producing today's affectionate dog.

LIVER   ROAN   BLACK

Moderate-sized eyes, with grave expression

Weather-resistant, silky, glossy coat is never curled

Straight front legs, with moderately sized bones

Round feet, with short, soft hair between toes

KEY FACTS

COUNTRY OF ORIGIN Great Britain
DATE OF ORIGIN 1800s
FIRST USE Game retrieving
USE TODAY Companion
LIFE EXPECTANCY 12–13 years

WEIGHT RANGE
16–23 kg (35–50 lb)
HEIGHT RANGE
51–58 cm (20–23 in)

SUSSEX SPANIEL

BREED HISTORY Its closest relatives were developed to work to the gun in dense undergrowth, but the richly coloured Sussex was probably developed by a breeder from the county of Sussex for companionship as much as for work. With only a few individuals in North America, the breed is even rare in its home county in Great Britain.

KEY FACTS

COUNTRY OF ORIGIN Great Britain
DATE OF ORIGIN 1800s
FIRST USE Game tracking
USE TODAY Companion
LIFE EXPECTANCY 12–13 years

WEIGHT RANGE
18–23 kg (40–50 lb)
HEIGHT RANGE
38–41 cm (15–16 in)

Heavy but compact, with a thick skin and low-set ears, the Sussex may have evolved from dogs that were bred to work slowly over difficult terrain. A viable working dog, when it follows a scent trail it generally "gives tongue", and the experienced hunter can tell what animal it is trailing from variations in the tone of its voice. One of the strong visual attractions of the Sussex is its rich, liver-coloured coat, but due to the coat's dark, dense texture, this is not a suitable breed for hot, humid environments. Selective breeding has unfortunately led to drooping lower eyelids and lower lips, conditions that can cause infections.

Back is long and muscular, both in width and in depth

Large, hazel eyes, with soft expression

Coat is ample and flat, with thick, weatherproof undercoat

Feet have supportive, thick pads, and are well feathered between toes

Legs are quite short, strong, and well feathered

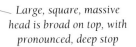

CLUMBER SPANIEL

Large, square, massive head is broad on top, with pronounced, deep stop

Very powerful hind legs, with strong loins and low hocks

KEY FACTS

COUNTRY OF ORIGIN Great Britain
DATE OF ORIGIN 1800s
FIRST USE Tracking, game retrieving
USE TODAY Companion, tracking
LIFE EXPECTANCY 12–13 years

WEIGHT RANGE
29–36 kg (65–80 lb)
HEIGHT RANGE
48–51 cm (19–20 in)

BREED HISTORY Named after the Duke of Newcastle's home at Clumber Park, Nottinghamshire, this unique breed's ancestors may include the Basset Hound, resulting in its long back, and the St. Bernard, from which it gets its massive head.

Large feet are well covered with hair

Dark amber eyes have soft expression

Square, flesh-coloured nose

Topcoat is abundant, silky and close, with dense undercoat

According to legend, the Clumber's forebears were beaters and retrievers, owned by the French Duc de Noailles. At the time of the French Revolution, he sent a number of his dogs to the Duke of Newcastle, in England, for safety. Working Clumbers perform as a team, methodically and at a leisurely pace, beating game towards the hunters. Today, a larger proportion of the breed leads its leisurely life in urban gardens, methodically tracking and retrieving insects and fallen leaves. Although this is an avuncular animal, a bored individual can be quite destructive.

GERMAN SPANIEL

Hair is long, rugged, thick, and wavy, with waterproof, insulating winter undercoat

BREED HISTORY In the 1880s, a group of German hunting enthusiasts decided to recreate the Stober, a spaniel which is mentioned as far back as 1719, and noted for its scent-following ability. Combining remnants of that breed with the English Cocker and other sporting spaniels, they produced the German Spaniel.

KEY FACTS

COUNTRY OF ORIGIN Germany
DATE OF ORIGIN 1880s
FIRST USE Quail hunting
USE TODAY Gundog, companion
LIFE EXPECTANCY 12–14 years
OTHER NAMES Deutscher Wachtelhund, German Quail Dog

WEIGHT RANGE
20–30 kg (44–66 lb)
HEIGHT RANGE
40–51 cm (16–20 in)

BROWN/
WHITE

BROWN

Moderately long, lively tail is carried straight out

Dark-brown, almond-shaped eyes

It is surprising that this multi-purpose breed is so rare. Virtually unknown outside Germany, and owned only by hunters and gamekeepers in its native country, the German Spaniel has the active, vibrant personality of the English Springer Spaniel. It is an ardent, obsessive scent follower, with a bloodhound-like persistence. Although its German name, *Wachtelhund*, means quail dog, it is an all-round bird dog, which can easily be trained to retrieve from dense undergrowth or from water. Rarely kept solely as a companion, it remains a superb working dog.

Toes are close together, and have tufts of hair between them

AMERICAN COCKER SPANIEL

Upper lip hangs down to cover lower jaw, giving square appearance

Top of head is rounded, with clearly defined stop and eyebrows

Slightly almond-shaped eyes are soft, alert, and appealing

Back is much shorter than an English Cocker's

VARIETY OF COLOURS

KEY FACTS

COUNTRY OF ORIGIN United States
DATE OF ORIGIN 1800s
FIRST USE Small-game retrieving
USE TODAY Companion
LIFE EXPECTANCY 13–14 years
OTHER NAME Cocker Spaniel
WEIGHT RANGE
11–13 kg (24–28 lb)
HEIGHT RANGE
36–38 cm (14–15 in)

Slightly wavy coat is silky in texture, with dense feathering on legs

This affectionate and most popular of all American-born breeds descends from the working English Cocker Spaniel. Although attempts have been made to work the American, and it still retains hunting instincts, its popularity lies in the gentle companionship it offers. Its beauty and charm are appreciated throughout North, Central, and South America, and also in Japan. Unfortunately, the breed suffers from a range of health problems, including epilepsy, but its generous and affable personality makes up for any physical shortcomings.

Ears are set level with eyes

Although attractive, excessively long hair on ears is almost impossible to keep tidy

Dense, fine hair must be groomed at least daily, to prevent matting

Neck is long enough to allow nose to sniff ground

BREED HISTORY Legend has it that the first spaniel arrived in the United States in 1620, with the Pilgrims on the *Mayflower*. Originally, all spaniels were classified together, but eventually the American Cocker was bred for desired traits, and in 1946 it was recognized as a separate breed.

ENGLISH COCKER SPANIEL

Bright, alert, brown eyes, with gentle expression

Head is not as distinctly domed as an American Cocker's

Well-defined, square muzzle descends from distinct stop

Pendulous, long, silky hair on ears dips in food when dog eats

KEY FACTS

COUNTRY OF ORIGIN Great Britain
DATE OF ORIGIN 1800s
FIRST USE Small-game retrieving
USE TODAY Companion
LIFE EXPECTANCY 13–14 years
OTHER NAME Cocker Spaniel

WEIGHT RANGE
13–15 kg (28–32 lb)
HEIGHT RANGE
38–41 cm (15–16 in)

An adept working dog, the English Cocker is also an extremely popular household companion throughout both Eastern and Western Europe, and in British Commonwealth countries. Unfortunately, it shares with its American relative a worrying variety of inherited disorders, including a plethora of eye conditions, numerous skin complaints, and kidney and behavioural problems, particularly rage syndrome in solid-coloured dogs. It is therefore advisable to obtain details of family history before acquiring a Cocker Spaniel. Although bred primarily for companionship, the breed performs well in field trials.

Exaggerated dome on puppy's head diminishes as it grows

Puppy

Tail is set lower than line of back

Firm, round, cat-like paws under well-feathered feet

Elegant head, with wide, well-developed nose to ensure excellent scenting ability

Back is not as short as an American Cocker's

Feathering does not hide lines of body

BREED HISTORY By 1800, the small land spaniels were divided into two groups, "starters", whose function was to spring game, and "cockers", which were used to flush and retrieve woodcock from dense undergrowth. The English Cocker descends from dogs developed in Wales and south-western England.

Slightly wavy coat is well feathered, with dense, protective undercoat

VARIETY OF COLOURS

Forelimbs are well boned, solid, and short enough for concentrated power

SMALL MUNSTERLANDER

This good-natured breed is the product of both natural and planned evolution. Its initial origins were as a bird dog, used in conjunction with the hawk and net, but until it was "rediscovered" at the beginning of this century, its survival depended upon it having a sufficiently appealing personality to exist solely as a household companion. Planned breeding then ensured the survival of traits such as trainability, a happy and carefree disposition, a natural inclination to retrieve, and an equal willingness to work in the woods or play with the family.

Light-coloured hair, with ample feathering on pointed ears

Muscular neck is slightly arched

BREED HISTORY The Small Munsterlander was developed from the remnants of ancient hawking dogs, which were crossed with other European gundogs. An attractive breed, it deserves the increasing recognition it is receiving outside its native country.

Smooth, close-fitting coat, with hint of a wave; dense undercoat

KEY FACTS

COUNTRY OF ORIGIN Germany
DATE OF ORIGIN Middle Ages/1900s
FIRST USE Tracking, pointing, retrieving
USE TODAY Companion, gundog
LIFE EXPECTANCY 13–14 years
OTHER NAMES Kleiner Münsterländer Vorstehhund, Heidewachtel, Spion

WEIGHT RANGE
14.5–15.5 kg (32–34 lb)
HEIGHT RANGE
48–56 cm (19–22 in)

Shoulders are close to each other and support well-boned, straight legs

Ample feathering on tail is longer than elsewhere on body

Well-muscled thighs support strong hind legs

LARGE MUNSTERLANDER

Broad, slightly rounded head gives impression of stability, even dignity

KEY FACTS

COUNTRY OF ORIGIN Germany
DATE OF ORIGIN 1800s
FIRST USE Tracking, pointing, retrieving
USE TODAY Companion, gundog
LIFE EXPECTANCY 12–13 years
OTHER NAME Grosser Münsterländer Vorstehhund

WEIGHT RANGE
25–29 kg (55–65 lb)
HEIGHT RANGE
59–61 cm (23–24 in)

Long, dense coat is neither coarse nor curly

BREED HISTORY Descended from the amorphous German bird dogs, this breed began as the black-and-white colour variation of the liver-and-white German Long-haired Pointer. Its breed club was formed in 1919 and, as in the case of its smaller relative, it is becoming increasingly popular outside its country of origin.

Fully feathered tail is in line with back, and tapers to tip

Plenty of feathering on long, straight forelegs

Firm, strong feet, with ample hair between black-nailed toes

Broad, round-tipped ears hang close to head

The Large Munsterlander's survival as a breed was based more upon negatives than positives. As the German Long-haired Pointer declined, a breed club was developed to save that breed, adopting as its standard only liver-and-white specimens. Black-and-white puppies continued to appear in litters, and hunters in the Münster region of Germany, interested in both form and function, continued to breed from these black-and-white dogs. They formed a breed club when it became necessary to differentiate their dogs from the Small Munsterlander. This dog thrives on close companionship.

DUTCH PARTRIDGE DOG

RED/ WHITE   BROWN/ WHITE

Look carefully at this breed and you see the root stock of later spaniels and setters. The ancestors of the last century's selectively bred gundogs must have been similar to this "half-setter, half-spaniel". It is a multi-purpose dog – a hunter, pointer, retriever, companion, and watchdog. A gentle and obedient water lover, it now has a firm base for survival, although only about 500 puppies are born each year. With sensitive training, the Partridge Dog makes an excellent companion. The only observed hereditary problem is an eye defect (progressive retinal atrophy) in some strains. The breed is rarely seen outside the Netherlands.

High-set ears hang close to cheeks

Amber-coloured eyes are wide set, with characteristic gentle expression of gundog

Dense, medium-length coat is longer on neck and chest than elsewhere

BREED HISTORY An ancient breed from the once-isolated Dutch province of Drente, this dog descends from continental spaniels used in the Middle Ages to catch partridges, cock pheasants, and black grouse under the net. Its appearance has not changed for at least 400 years.

Broad, powerful back is longer than it is high

Forelegs are straight and muscular, with elbows close to body

STABYHOUN

Although written references to the Stabyhoun date back only to the early 1800s, it probably descends from spaniels brought to the Netherlands by the Spanish during their occupation in the 1500s. Today, it is rarely seen outside its country of origin, where it is fairly uncommon (only around 200 puppies are born each year). This is unfortunate, for in many ways it is an ideal household companion. Although it is a fine hunting dog, an excellent pointer, and a soft-mouthed retriever, it is equally at home retrieving tennis balls in city parks and gardens. Calm, patient, and reliable, the breed is at ease with children and is always eager to please.

BREED HISTORY Bred for centuries in the northern Dutch province of Friesland, the Stabyhoun is a close relative of both the "Drent" and the progenitors of the Small Munsterlander. Like other multi-purpose dogs, its popularity waned considerably with the local introduction of pointers and setters in the 1800s.

Trowel-shaped, relatively low-set ears

Skull and muzzle, separated by a minimal stop, are of equal length

Muzzle narrows to nose, without coming to a point

Long, smooth topcoat, with dense winter undercoat

ORANGE   BROWN   BLACK

Long, well-feathered tail reaches down to hocks

BRITTANY

The most popular native breed in France, and the stalwart companion of hunters in Canada and the United States, the Brittany is a superb, medium-sized dog. An excellent setting and flushing gundog, the breed is often assumed to be a spaniel, much to the chagrin of its admirers, because in many countries it still carries that appellation. It may be spaniel in size, but in function it is a classic pointer, probably the world's only stumpy-tailed pointer. Rough-and-ready in appearance, the Brittany makes a trustworthy, reliable, and obedient companion.

Round head, with distinct hollow at stop

Body hair is fine and dense, with sparse feathering

Well-muscled haunches are held lower than withers

High-set, short, somewhat rounded ears

Alive, expressive, amber eyes

Lips are tighter than those of more common spaniels

BREED HISTORY

The original Brittany, as represented in old accounts and illustrations, had almost died out by the beginning of this century, when a local breeder, Arthur Enaud, rejuvenated the breed. A popular and affectionate companion, it also hunts, points, and retrieves.

LIVER/ WHITE   TRICOLOUR   BLACK/ WHITE

BLUE PICARDY SPANIEL

With looks that are strikingly similar to engravings of the early Gordon Setter, the Blue Picardy was developed in north-east France as a hunter's companion, to retrieve snipe from marshes. Although it is a hard-working gundog, this affable, fun-loving, friendly, and distinctive variation of the Picardy Spaniel makes an elegantly attractive companion. Setter-like in appearance and personality, it has a great deal of stamina and needs ample physical activity. It is not very vocal and has a low level of innate territorial aggression, so it does not make a very good watchdog. It is, however, a delight with children, and thrives on attention.

Medium-sized head is not as long as those of more common setters and somewhat broader

Oval-shaped, wide-set, dark-brown eyes are alert and expressive

Low-set ears are covered with wavy, silky hair

Deep chest, with long, flexible ribs, provides ample space for lung expansion

Lustrous, heavy coat is predominantly black (often called blue), with heavy, white ticking

BREED HISTORY
This good-natured gundog was developed by crossing the blue-lemon flecked English Setter with the reconstituted Picardy Spaniel. Completing the circle, it is likely that the English Setter was developed from Picardy crosses. Like the Brittany, the breed is more like a setter than a spaniel.

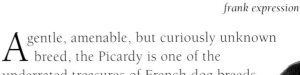

PICARDY SPANIEL

BREED HISTORY This breed may be descended from the extinct Chien d'Oysell, and from the Spanish spaniels of the 14th century. It almost died out, but was re-established in Normandy and Picardy in the first years of this century.

KEY FACTS

COUNTRY OF ORIGIN France
DATE OF ORIGIN 1700s
FIRST USE Game retrieving (waterfowl)
USE TODAY Gundog, companion
LIFE EXPECTANCY 13–14 years
OTHER NAME Épagneul Picard

WEIGHT RANGE
19.5–20.5 kg (43–45 lb)
HEIGHT RANGE
56–61 cm (22–24 in)

Deep, amber eyes have frank expression

A gentle, amenable, but curiously unknown breed, the Picardy is one of the underrated treasures of French dog breeds. Rarely, if ever, seen outside France and the Benelux countries, this docile and undemanding dog has remarkable endurance. It thrives on setting and retrieving game, from either the cold marshes or the open plains of northern France. Like its close relative, the Blue Picardy, it loves being fussed over, makes an excellent companion, and only requires a moderate amount of exercise.

Back has good proportion, with depression just behind withers

Hind legs are profusely covered in feathered hair down to hocks

Slightly wavy, heavy body hair becomes feathered on legs

FRENCH SPANIEL

Related to the German Small Munsterlander and Dutch Partridge Dog, and probably the most elegant of the French pointers, the rustic-looking French Spaniel is relatively tall and has a powerful build. In form and function more of a setter than a spaniel, this dog flushes and retrieves game birds. Easily intimidated, it needs gentle training. It is a typical working gundog – it trains well, thrives on exercise, gets on with other dogs, copes well with the cold, and rarely barks. Seldom seen outside France, the breed is becoming a popular companion.

Long skull has slight protuberance at stop

KEY FACTS

COUNTRY OF ORIGIN France
DATE OF ORIGIN 1600s
FIRST USE Game flushing/retrieving
USE TODAY Gundog, companion
LIFE EXPECTANCY 13–14 years
OTHER NAME Épagneul Français

WEIGHT RANGE
20–25 kg (44–55 lb)
HEIGHT RANGE
53–61 cm (21–24 in)

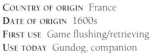

Short, flat coat has some feathering

Low-set tail is covered in long, silky hair

BREED HISTORY One theory is that this breed traces its origins back to the Barbary coast, from where it was taken to Spain, and then France. An opposing view is that it is of Scandinavian (probably Danish) descent.

Long metatarsal bones from hocks down to oval, compact feet

Rounded ears are set at eye level, and frame head

Toes, with abundant hair between them, have hard pads and dark nails

ENGLISH SETTER

Bright, gentle, dark-hazel eyes

Agraceful, elegant, quiet, and considerate breed, the English Setter is marvellous with children, easy to train, and a good, responsive worker in the field. There is an inherited tendency in a small number of setters to blindness, caused by a deterioration of the retinas. The predominantly white variety has a higher-than-average incidence of allergic skin conditions. This strong dog is capable of prolonged physical activity and needs a great deal of exercise.

LEMON/WHITE

LIVER/WHITE

BLACK/WHITE

TRICOLOUR

Topcoat is slightly wavy, long, and silky; undercoat is fleecy

Muzzle is moderately deep and square

Ears hang in neat folds, close to face

Lips are square and not too pendulous

KEY FACTS

COUNTRY OF ORIGIN Great Britain
DATE OF ORIGIN 1800s
FIRST USE Bird retrieving, bird setting
USE TODAY Companion, retrieving
LIFE EXPECTANCY 14 years

WEIGHT RANGE
25–30 kg (55–66 lb)
HEIGHT RANGE
61–69 cm (24–27 in)

Deep chest allows for great endurance

Compact feet, with hair between toes, are prone to catching grass seeds

Feathering extends along chest

Straight tail tapers to a fine point

BREED HISTORY Setters evolved from spaniels, with an ability to work as hunters. British breeder Edward Laverack developed today's English Setter.

GORDON SETTER

Head has clearly marked stop

BREED HISTORY Black-and-tan setters existed in Great Britain in the 1600s. Today's standard was started in the 1700s by the Duke of Richmond and Gordon at his home in Banffshire, Scotland.

Lean neck arches to head

Broad, black nose has large nostrils

KEY FACTS

COUNTRY OF ORIGIN Great Britain
DATE OF ORIGIN 1600s
FIRST USE Bird setting
USE TODAY Companion, gundog
LIFE EXPECTANCY 13 years

WEIGHT RANGE
25–30 kg (56–65 lb)
HEIGHT RANGE
62–66 cm (24–26 in)

Lips are clearly defined

Bright, dark-brown eyes show relaxed, but keen, expression

Fairly short tail is straight and well feathered

This breed is the strongest, heaviest, and slowest of the setters. It has never achieved the widespread popularity of other setters. Before hunting with guns became popular, this dog scented and found game, but then sat quietly, waiting for the hunter to arrive. This ability has contributed to the Gordon's friendly and relaxed disposition. The breed is loyal and obedient, and makes a fine companion. It does, however, need daily, vigorous exercise.

Deep chest gives ample space for heart and lungs

Well-arched toes are fully padded

IRISH SETTER

Once known in Gaelic simply as the "Modder rhu" or "red dog", the Irish Setter was also called a red spaniel. Today, this racy, active dog thrives on physical activity. Faster than most other companion dogs, it actively seeks out other dogs to play with, perhaps because it enjoys running rings around them. The Irish Setter is an exuberant extrovert. Its late maturing, and joy of life, give it an undeserved reputation for being flighty and overly excitable.

Oval eyes have gentle expression

Nose is black or chocolate coloured

Thin ears are set low, and hang in loose folds close to head

Upper lips are thin and close fitting

Tail set low, carried horizontal or down

Forequarters are luxuriously feathered with straight, long hair

Forelegs are straight and sinewy; feet are small, with firm, close toes

BREED HISTORY The Old Spanish Pointer (not known outside Spain), setting spaniels, and early Scottish setters have been included in the Irish Setter's evolution.

Silky coat is long; undercoat is abundant in cold weather

KEY FACTS

COUNTRY OF ORIGIN Ireland
DATE OF ORIGIN 1700s
FIRST USE Game retrieving, setting
USE TODAY Companion
LIFE EXPECTANCY 13 years
OTHER NAMES Irish Red Setter, Red Setter

WEIGHT RANGE
27–32 kg (60–70 lb)
HEIGHT RANGE
64–69 cm
(25–27 in)

IRISH RED-AND-WHITE SETTER

Alert eyes have kind expression

KEY FACTS

COUNTRY OF ORIGIN Ireland
DATE OF ORIGIN 1700s
FIRST USE Game retrieving, setting
USE TODAY Companion, gundog
LIFE EXPECTANCY 13 years
OTHER NAME Parti-coloured Setter

WEIGHT RANGE
27–32 kg (60–70 lb)
HEIGHT RANGE
58–69 cm (23–27 in)

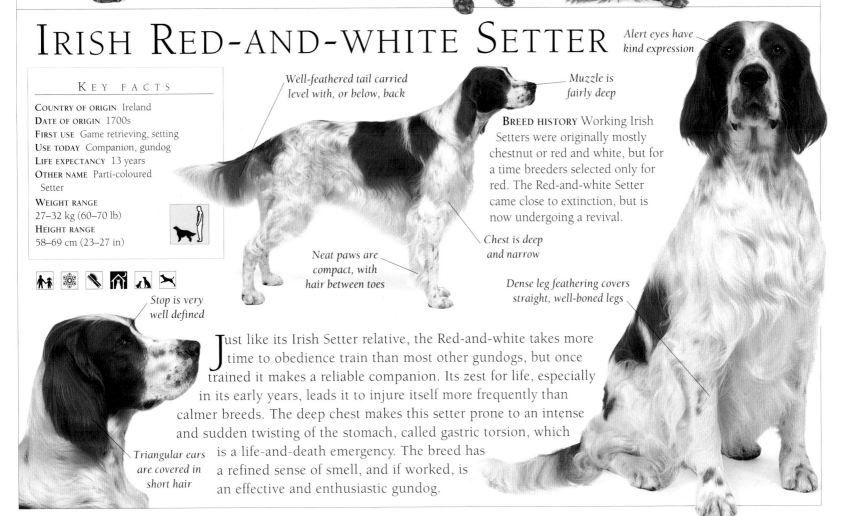

Well-feathered tail carried level with, or below, back

Muzzle is fairly deep

BREED HISTORY Working Irish Setters were originally mostly chestnut or red and white, but for a time breeders selected only for red. The Red-and-white Setter came close to extinction, but is now undergoing a revival.

Chest is deep and narrow

Neat paws are compact, with hair between toes

Dense leg feathering covers straight, well-boned legs

Stop is very well defined

Triangular ears are covered in short hair

Just like its Irish Setter relative, the Red-and-white takes more time to obedience train than most other gundogs, but once trained it makes a reliable companion. Its zest for life, especially in its early years, leads it to injure itself more frequently than calmer breeds. The deep chest makes this setter prone to an intense and sudden twisting of the stomach, called gastric torsion, which is a life-and-death emergency. The breed has a refined sense of smell, and if worked, is an effective and enthusiastic gundog.

GERMAN POINTERS

Clear, dark eyes are not deep set

High-set ears are broad, medium-sized, and not turned or folded

German Wire-haired Pointer

Broad, long, and robust muzzle leads to brown nose

Chest is prominent, with prolonged sternum

Beard is robust and coarse

Hair on head and ears is short

Tail is carried as continuation of back

LIVER/ WHITE   LIVER   BLACK/ WHITE

BREED HISTORY Developed as a reaction to specialization in gundogs, a combination of French Griffon, Pudelpointer, Short-haired Pointer, and Broken-coated Pointer produced this all-purpose, water and land-working flusher, pointer, and retriever. It was first recognized in Germany in 1870.

Although today's German pointers are a diverse group of breeds with a variety of origins, all of them are a result of the intense activity that took place in dog breeding in Germany in the latter part of the last century. Using national blood stock, but also introducing French and British breeding lines, German hunters and breeders created three distinct pointers, with different characteristics. The Wire-haired Pointer is a marvellous family dog, as well as a hardy worker. Hip and elbow arthritis are known inherited conditions in the breed, but with careful selection these problems are avoided. The Long-haired Pointer remains primarily a working dog. Some individuals may be timid, but virtually all make excellent companions and surprisingly good watchdogs. The Short-haired Pointer can also be timid, and seizures have been a problem in some lines. However, this breed has a greater life expectancy than most other breeds of its size, and makes an amenable companion in either town or country.

BREED HISTORY The German Long-haired Pointer owes its looks and temperament in part to the Épagneul Français, as well as to other long-haired continental bird dogs. Cross breeding with Irish and Gordon Setters produced red-and-black colouration, but this is generally not accepted for registration. The German Long-haired Pointer made its first public appearance in Hanover in 1879.

Tail is covered with profuse feathering

Long, straight forelegs are well fringed with soft hair

Moderately round feet have thick hair between toes

German Long-haired Pointer

Gentle-looking eyes are well spaced

Long, lean head, with sloping stop and straight muzzle

Laterally set, broad-based ears are covered with wavy hair

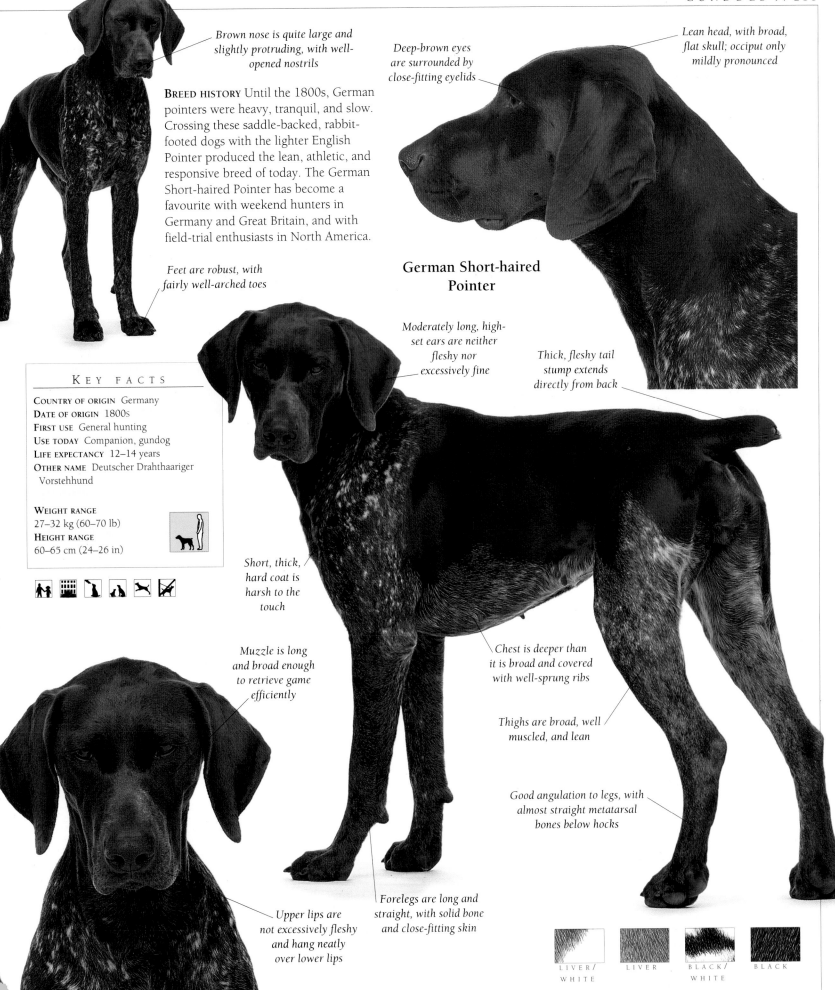

Brown nose is quite large and slightly protruding, with well-opened nostrils

Deep-brown eyes are surrounded by close-fitting eyelids

Lean head, with broad, flat skull; occiput only mildly pronounced

BREED HISTORY Until the 1800s, German pointers were heavy, tranquil, and slow. Crossing these saddle-backed, rabbit-footed dogs with the lighter English Pointer produced the lean, athletic, and responsive breed of today. The German Short-haired Pointer has become a favourite with weekend hunters in Germany and Great Britain, and with field-trial enthusiasts in North America.

Feet are robust, with fairly well-arched toes

German Short-haired Pointer

Moderately long, high-set ears are neither fleshy nor excessively fine

Thick, fleshy tail stump extends directly from back

KEY FACTS

COUNTRY OF ORIGIN Germany
DATE OF ORIGIN 1800s
FIRST USE General hunting
USE TODAY Companion, gundog
LIFE EXPECTANCY 12–14 years
OTHER NAME Deutscher Drahthaariger Vorstehhund

WEIGHT RANGE
27–32 kg (60–70 lb)
HEIGHT RANGE
60–65 cm (24–26 in)

Short, thick, hard coat is harsh to the touch

Muzzle is long and broad enough to retrieve game efficiently

Chest is deeper than it is broad and covered with well-sprung ribs

Thighs are broad, well muscled, and lean

Good angulation to legs, with almost straight metatarsal bones below hocks

Upper lips are not excessively fleshy and hang neatly over lower lips

Forelegs are long and straight, with solid bone and close-fitting skin

LIVER/ WHITE

LIVER

BLACK/ WHITE

BLACK

CZESKY FOUSEK

Muzzle is slightly longer than skull

Deep-set, dark eyes have gentle expression and close-fitting, grey-black lids

Tail is set to lengthen back

High-set ears are broad at base and pointed towards tips

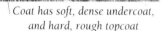

KEY FACTS

COUNTRY OF ORIGIN Czech Republic
DATE OF ORIGIN 1800s
FIRST USE Game pointing
USE TODAY Game pointing, companion
LIFE EXPECTANCY 12–13 years
OTHER NAMES Czech Pointer, Czech Coarse-haired Setter

WEIGHT RANGE
22–34 kg (48½–75 lb)
HEIGHT RANGE
58–66 cm (23–26 in)

Strong, well-muscled elbows on straight, lean legs

BROWN/WHITE

BROWN

BREED HISTORY It is possible that ancestors of the Czesky Fousek were pointing and setting wildfowl in the 1400s. This century, the breed was reconstituted with the infusion of German Wire-haired and Short-haired Pointer bloodlines.

Spoon-shaped feet, with strong, dark nails

Coat has soft, dense undercoat, and hard, rough topcoat

This responsive dog is one of Bohemia's most popular hunting dogs. A multi-purpose worker, it points, sets, and then retrieves from land or water. At ease in the home, it is almost always amenable with children. There can be a dramatic difference in size between the sexes – the largest males can be almost 50 per cent bigger than the smallest females. Some individuals can be particularly headstrong and need firm control. With regular exercise, this breed makes an attractive, amenable companion, although it is best suited to the countryside. The Czesky Fousek was first bred to written standards in the late 1800s. An excellent breed, it deserves recognition outside its native land.

WIRE-HAIRED POINTING GRIFFON

KEY FACTS

COUNTRY OF ORIGIN France
DATE OF ORIGIN 1860s
FIRST USE Hunting, retrieving
USE TODAY Hunting, retrieving, companion
LIFE EXPECTANCY 12–13 years
OTHER NAME Griffon d'Arrêt Korthals

WEIGHT RANGE
23–27 kg (50–60 lb)
HEIGHT RANGE
56–61 cm (22–24 in)

BREED HISTORY A classic "Euro-dog", this all-purpose worker was originally developed from Dutch, Belgian, German, French, and possibly English gundogs by a Dutch breeder, Eduard Korthals, who lived in both the Netherlands and Germany. This versatile gundog remains uncommon in both Europe and North America.

Beard of long, thick, harsh hair

Skull is long and narrow, with square muzzle

Bushy eyebrows cover large, yellow-brown eyes

Eduard Korthals never recorded, or certainly never revealed, the breeds he used to develop the Wire-haired Pointing Griffon, but it is a fairly safe assumption that the Munsterlander, German Short-haired Pointer, and French griffons all played roles in its development. This all-terrain, all-weather, all-game pointer-retriever was the first general-purpose European gundog to be formally recognized in the United States. It is certainly versatile, willing to hunt rodents and foxes as well as gamebirds. Its personality is that of a typical gundog – responsive and obedient, good with children, not snappy or irritable, and usually easygoing with other dogs, although males can be aggressive.

Thigh muscles are well developed

Forelimbs are straight and long, with wispy feathering of hair

WEIMARANER

High-set ears are slightly folded

Aristocratic head, with long muzzle and skull

Short-haired variety

Rather light tail is docked in working dogs, but left natural in companions

Neat lips, with delicate flews, meet brown nose

BREED HISTORY Named after the sport-loving court of Charles August, Grand Duke of Weimar, this magnificent breed's exact origins are unknown, although its root stock could come from the extinct Leithund. Selective breeding in the 1800s created today's standards.

Rippling with muscles, this uniquely coloured gundog is popular both as a worker and as a companion, although its role as a companion is taking precedence over its dual-purpose use as a tracker and retriever. The Weimaraner usually has an alert, obedient, and fearless personality, although timidity is not unknown in the breed and seems to be a trait in certain lines. In both the popular, short-haired, and less common, long-haired coat versions, this is a reliable worker – a proficient dog in field trials and obedience work, as well as in hunting. Its natural disposition and strength make it an equally reliable watchdog. The breed has grace, speed, stamina, endurance, but perhaps most important of all, "star quality". Its amber, through grey to blue, eyes, and its shimmering steel coat colour give the Weimaraner a regal presence. Its handsome carriage is almost universally admired, a fact that ensures its continuing worldwide popularity. Easy to obedience train, it is equally at home in towns or rural areas.

Hindquarters, with well-angulated stifles and straight hocks, lead to compact feet

KEY FACTS

COUNTRY OF ORIGIN Germany
DATE OF ORIGIN 1600s
FIRST USE Large-game tracking
USE TODAY Gundog, companion
LIFE EXPECTANCY 12–13 years
OTHER NAME Weimaraner Vorstehhund

WEIGHT RANGE
32–39 kg (70½–86 lb)
HEIGHT RANGE
56–69 cm (22–27 in)

Distinctive and arresting eyes have unusual colouring

Occiput is quite prominent, creating dignified-looking head

Long-haired variety

Long-haired coat is most prominent on ears

Coat is sleek, smooth, and short

Features such as nose are similar to a short-haired Weimaraner's

Deep chest, with well-sprung ribs and powerful shoulders

Forelegs are straight and strong

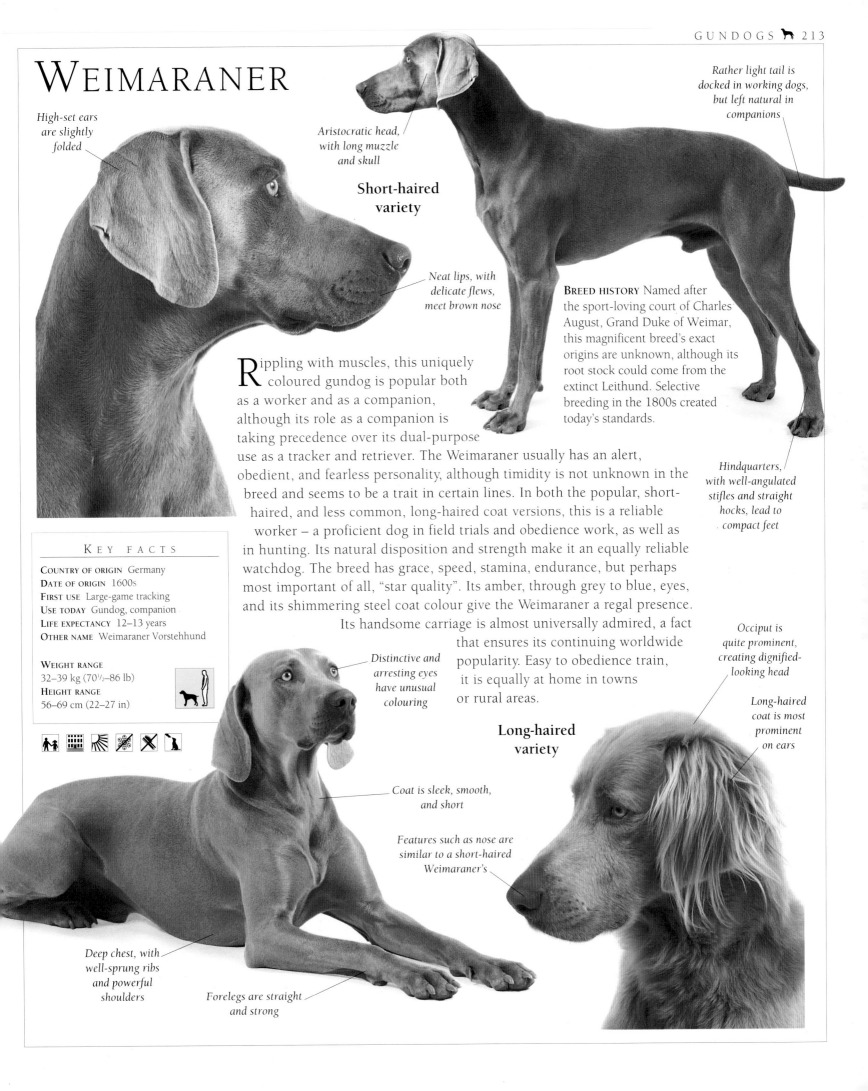

SPANISH POINTER

Prominent ridges protect dark, melancholy eyes

Stop is midway between dome of occiput of skull and tip of large nose

BREED HISTORY This breed, a relatively "new" Spanish pointing dog, probably resulted from crosses between ancient pointers, such as the Perdiguero Navarro, and light-boned pointers.

Coat may or may not have patches of colour

Long, wide, high-set, soft ears hang down in folds

Wrinkled dewlap hangs from neck

Very muscular, strong shoulders support long, straight legs

KEY FACTS

COUNTRY OF ORIGIN Spain
DATE OF ORIGIN 1500s
FIRST USE Deer hunting, pointing, retrieving
USE TODAY Companion, gundog
LIFE EXPECTANCY 13–14 years
OTHER NAMES Perdiguero de Burgos, Perdiguero Burgales

WEIGHT RANGE
25–30 kg (55–66 lb)
HEIGHT RANGE
66–76 cm (26–30 in)

The Iberian peninsula is a likely place of origin for many of Europe's pointing breeds. This fine dog was once used almost exclusively to hunt large game such as deer, but today it is employed primarily as a pointer and retriever of small, fast game such as hares and partridges. The breed is an ardent worker, equally at home in water and on land. Its appearance reveals its close relationship with scent hounds, and as a worker it retains an excellent scent-following ability. Adaptable and easygoing, it is affable with children, good with other dogs, and unlikely to snap or bite unless seriously provoked. This breed is easy to obedience train, and is consistent in its behaviour.

PORTUGUESE POINTER

Unique "dish-face", similar to that of an English Pointer

This versatile and ever-obedient pointer is the likely progenitor of the English Pointer, and probably arrived in Great Britain in the early 1700s. Stable, gentle, and intensely committed, it is rightly popular in its native land for its excellent personality and superb working ability. It is good with children and with other dogs, serious by nature, and easy to obedience train, but it does not make a very good watchdog. Its coat only needs an occasional rub down, but its body needs constant physical stimulation.

Strong fore-quarters, with long, sloped shoulders

Long, broad thighs covered in firm hair

YELLOW

CHESTNUT

Well-arched toes are evenly spaced

BREED HISTORY An ancient breed, once used as a hawking dog, the Portuguese Pointer may descend from the extinct Spanish pointing hound, the Podengo de Mastra. Its native name derives from the Portuguese word for partridge, the breed's main quarry. Breed type has been fixed for centuries.

KEY FACTS

COUNTRY OF ORIGIN Portugal
DATE OF ORIGIN Middle Ages
FIRST USE Game hunting
USE TODAY Companion, gundog
LIFE EXPECTANCY 12–14 years
OTHER NAME Perdigueiro Portugueso

WEIGHT RANGE
16–27 kg (35–60 lb)
HEIGHT RANGE
52–56 cm (20½–22 in)

BRACCO ITALIANO

Extremely fashionable in Renaissance Italy, this energetic, sensible, but slightly stubborn breed then declined in popularity. It was recently "rediscovered", first by Italian dog breeders, and then by breeders elsewhere in the European Union. Today, this powerful and well-proportioned dog is a common sight at major European dog shows. Serious, but with a gentle air, it makes a sensitive companion. It is also a vigorous hunter, capable of scenting, pointing, and retrieving both on land and in water.

Ears, set low and far back, hang with fold at front

Short, thick, glossy, fine coat covers muscular hindquarters

Light-coloured eyes

Straight, firm forelegs, with prominent back tendons

Robust, large, round feet, with strong, curved nails

Moderate bend to hocks below quite long thighs

KEY FACTS

COUNTRY OF ORIGIN Italy
DATE OF ORIGIN 1700s
FIRST USE Tracking, pointing, retrieving
USE TODAY Companion, gundog
LIFE EXPECTANCY 12–13 years
OTHER NAMES Italian Pointer, Italian Setter

WEIGHT RANGE
25–40 kg (55–88 lb)
HEIGHT RANGE
56–67 cm (22–26½ in)

BREED HISTORY This unique-looking breed evolved in Piedmont and Lombardy. Some say it is the result of crosses between the Segugio and an ancient Asiatic mastiff, while others claim that it is descended from the St. Hubert Hound.

WHITE   WHITE/ ORANGE, WHITE/ CHESTNUT

ITALIAN SPINONE

BREED HISTORY The Spinone could be descended from the Segugio, or perhaps the ancient Korthal Griffon. Its present form developed in Piedmont and Lombardy, and was apparent by the 1200s. Appealing in looks and character, this breed should increase in popularity.

Triangular ears, with short, thick hair

Coat is thick, rough, close fitting, and slightly wiry

Long, stiff hair forms distinctive eyebrows

Straight forelegs are densely boned, with distinct back tendons

Long hair on moustache and beard

KEY FACTS

COUNTRY OF ORIGIN Italy
DATE OF ORIGIN Middle Ages
FIRST USE Game retrieving
USE TODAY Companion, field trials, gundog
LIFE EXPECTANCY 12–13 years
OTHER NAMES Spinone Italiano, Spinone

WEIGHT RANGE
32–37 kg (71–82 lb)
HEIGHT RANGE
61–66 cm (24–26 in)

The Italian Spinone has recently found popularity far beyond its native land, in North America, Scandinavia, Great Britain, and elsewhere in the European Union. Rightly so. It may produce a little more tenacious saliva than some people are willing to cope with, and it may have a rather pungent canine aroma, but otherwise this is an avuncular, calm, easygoing, and obedient breed that thrives on work, be it hunting, field trials, or chasing bouncing dog toys. Although the Spinone looks dignified, reserved, and all knowing it is, in its ambling way, actively playful, even rowdy.

Large, round eyes, with relaxed expression, surrounded by well-fitting lids

Long, broad, muscular thighs have slight arch at back

 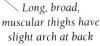

WHITE   WHITE/ ORANGE, WHITE/ CHESTNUT

FRENCH GASCONY POINTER

BREED HISTORY An ancient gundog from the Gascony region of southern France, this long-limbed dog descends from Spanish and Italian pointers, ancestors of nearly all of today's pointers and setters. It was saved from extinction at the turn of the century by two breeders, Dr. Castets and M. Senac-Langrange.

Yellow-brown eyes are well set in sockets and have gentle expression

Nose is broad, and brown in colour, with wide-open nostrils

Rather thick, smooth coat, rougher on back than on head

KEY FACTS

COUNTRY OF ORIGIN France
DATE OF ORIGIN 1600s
FIRST USE Tracking, pointing
USE TODAY Companion, gundog
LIFE EXPECTANCY 12–14 years
OTHER NAMES Braque-Français-type Gascogne, French Setter

WEIGHT RANGE
20–32 kg (45–71 lb)
HEIGHT RANGE
56–69 cm (22–27 in)

Skull is almost flat

T his long-legged gundog is an avid tracker, willingly following both ground and air scents, but favouring the latter. It also makes a fine household companion. Typical of virtually all pointers, the Gascony is a sensitive breed that trains best to modern, gentle methods. It thrives on vigorous exercise, and enjoys both canine and human companionship. Although its numbers are small, this enthusiastic breed is kept as a working dog by enough French hunters to ensure its survival.

Thighs are robust and reasonably straight

Forelegs are straight, very long, quite broad, and well muscled

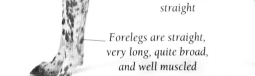

FRENCH PYRENEAN POINTER

KEY FACTS

COUNTRY OF ORIGIN France
DATE OF ORIGIN 1600s
FIRST USE Tracking, pointing
USE TODAY Companion, gundog
LIFE EXPECTANCY 12–14 years
OTHER NAMES Braque-Français-type Pyrénées, Small-sized French Setter

WEIGHT RANGE
20–32 kg (45–71 lb)
HEIGHT RANGE
47–58 cm
(18½–23 in)

BREED HISTORY This more refined-looking version of the Gascony Pointer has legs almost 12.5 cm (5 in) shorter than its relative. It was developed in the Pyrenean region of France by the Spanish border, and descends from the old Spanish Pointer and the extinct Southern Hound.

Ears are set higher than a Gascony Pointer's and are barely folded

Lips are somewhat pendant, below prominent, brown nose

T his breed is extremely agile and works exceptionally well in thick cover. Like the Gascony Pointer, it is an instinctive air scenter, turning its head to the sky and sniffing for the scent of game. Sometimes it stands on its hind legs and sniffs intently until it captures scent and begins to track. The breed makes a fine companion, and is at ease in both urban and rural homes. It learns obedience easily, and gets on well with other dogs and children. Its coat needs little attention other than the occasional rub down. Numbers are small and it is rarely seen outside France.

Neck is long, well muscled, and has no dewlap

Hair is finer and shorter than a Gascony Pointer's

Chest is deep and extends down to elbow level

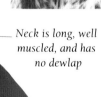

SAINT-GERMAIN POINTER

Slightly domed skull

BREED HISTORY A painting from the time of King Louis XV, hanging in the French Louvre museum, of a pointer with the colouring of this breed, indicates that the Saint-Germain Pointer is of great antiquity. After it was greatly reduced in numbers during the French Revolution, dedicated breeders revived it by crossing it with English and French Gascony Pointers.

Thin lips hang in pendant fashion over jaw

Ears are thin, supple, and longer than an English Pointer's

Set on a line with back, tail is large at root and tapers smoothly

Short, fine hair is not harsh and develops only moderate undercoat

KEY FACTS

COUNTRY OF ORIGIN France
DATE OF ORIGIN 1830s
FIRST USE Pointing/retrieving from land
USE TODAY Companion, gundog
LIFE EXPECTANCY 12–14 years
OTHER NAME Braque St. Germain

WEIGHT RANGE
18–26 kg (40–57 lb)
HEIGHT RANGE
54–62 cm (21–24 in)

Predominantly white, with orange markings, this breed looks like a rather leggy version of the English Pointer. Its docile, obedient, and loyal, but sometimes nervous disposition is another reminder of its part-English Pointer origins. Whether a working dog or a companion, the Saint-Germain Pointer requires gentle training. A superb land tracker and retriever, this breed is also easy to train and makes an amenable companion in both urban and rural households.

Shoulders are long, strong, well muscled, and slightly angled

BOURBONNAIS POINTER

Fine ears hang with slight fold

Skull is quite long and divided from muzzle by distinct stop

Heavy lips hang below level of chin

Compact and robust, the Bourbonnais Pointer is often born with no tail, or just a rudimentary stump. When worked as a general-purpose gundog, it is very versatile – tracking, pointing, and retrieving from land, marsh, or open water. Emotionally, this is perhaps the best balanced of the French pointers, with the most relaxed personality. The breed's popularity declined in the 1800s, but at the turn of this century it became a fashionable hunting companion. The World Wars brought it to the brink of extinction, but it has recently been revived as an all-round hunter.

KEY FACTS

COUNTRY OF ORIGIN France
DATE OF ORIGIN 1500s
FIRST USE Game hunting
USE TODAY Companion, gundog
LIFE EXPECTANCY 12–14 years
OTHER NAME Braque du Bourbonnais

WEIGHT RANGE
18–26 kg (40–57 lb)
HEIGHT RANGE
55.5–56.5 cm (22 in)

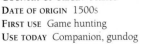

BREED HISTORY The French pointer with the longest historical record, this breed was first described in 1598 by an Italian travelling through Bourbonnais, in France. Indiscriminate breeding reduced its hunting qualities in the 1900s, but it has recently been revived.

Long, prominent ribs cover deep, broad chest

Dense coat is often rather oily, but not glossy

Hocks are broad, straight, and without deviations

OLD DANISH POINTER

BREED HISTORY It is likely that early breeding in the 1700s involved local dogs of Bloodhound descent and Spanish pointers brought from the nearby Netherlands, then under Spanish rule. A general drop in numbers this century, combined with little breeding during World War II, pushed the breed to near extinction.

Deep, comparatively short head, with broad muzzle

Neck is long, with broad chest and very distinct dewlap

Long, pendant ears are rounded at tips

Broad, powerful thigh muscles above straight hocks

Coat is short and dense, with insulating undercoat

Powerful forequarters, with straight legs

KEY FACTS

COUNTRY OF ORIGIN Denmark
DATE OF ORIGIN 1700s
FIRST USE Tracking, pointing game
USE TODAY Field trials, companion
LIFE EXPECTANCY 12–13 years
OTHER NAMES Gammel Dansk Honsehund, Old Danish Bird Dog

WEIGHT RANGE
18–24 kg (40–53 lb)
HEIGHT RANGE
51–58 cm (20–23 in)

Rarely seen outside its home country, this stocky pointer was rescued from near extinction after World War II. Today, it is one of the most popular field-trial participants and gundogs in Denmark. An excellent retriever from both land and water, its superb nose has earned it added responsibilities, such as tracking wounded game and scent detecting both ordnance and illicit drugs. The Old Danish Pointer is an agreeable companion – it is usually reliable with children and will readily adapt to urban environments.

PUDELPOINTER

BREED HISTORY From a pool of seven poodles and just under 100 various pointers, Baron von Zedlitz, a German sportsman and dog breeder, attempted to produce a breed with ideal tracking, pointing, and retrieving abilities both on land and in water. It remains rare, even in Germany.

For some inexplicable reason, the Pudelpointer, an excellent breed with no major faults, has never been popular either in Germany or elsewhere. In Germany, each individual must pass stringent field tests on land and in water before it is formally registered. This handsome, all-weather breed is only ever found in the homes of serious hunters.

Eyebrows of bushy, coarse hair cover eyes

LIVER   CHESTNUT   BLACK

Large, black nose has wide nostrils

Tail of this working dog has been docked

Strong loins on powerful, straight hind legs

Forelegs are sturdy and substantial

Coat is short, rough, waterproof, and tight fitting

Insulating hair grows between toes

KEY FACTS

COUNTRY OF ORIGIN Germany
DATE OF ORIGIN 1800s
FIRST USE Tracking, pointing, retrieving
USE TODAY Gundog, companion
LIFE EXPECTANCY 12–14 years

WEIGHT RANGE
20–30 kg (44–66 lb)
HEIGHT RANGE
53–66 cm (21–26 in)

ARIÉGE POINTER

Skull is rather narrow and slightly rounded

The Ariége Pointer is a hard and fast worker. Although it descends from plodding, steady trackers, today's working breed excels at scenting and flushing game while on a fast trot. It needs frequent mental and physical activity – when confined it can be destructive and may well howl incessantly. If this breed is kept as a companion, it should be acquired as a puppy, so that it can benefit from early exposure to the lifestyle it will lead. The Ariége does not make a particularly good watchdog, but its size gives it good presence.

Tail is historically docked

Fine, white hair is interspersed with orange markings

Straight, strong thighs above equally straight, strong feet

Shoulders are straight, slightly flat, and quite broad

Large, well-padded feet, like a hare's

KEY FACTS

COUNTRY OF ORIGIN France
DATE OF ORIGIN 1800s
FIRST USE Tracking, pointing
USE TODAY Gundog, companion
LIFE EXPECTANCY 12–14 years
OTHER NAMES Braque d'Ariége, Ariége Setter

WEIGHT RANGE
25–30 kg (55–65 lb)
HEIGHT RANGE
60–67 cm (24–26 in)

BREED HISTORY Once a heavier, slower pointer descended from the "white dogs of the King", as seen in Oudry's paintings in Versailles, today's faster, leaner dog evolved early this century through the introduction of the lighter boned Saint-Germain Pointer's bloodlines. This breed is one of the largest and strongest of all the French pointers.

SLOVENSKY POINTER

Long, soft hair over eyes grows upwards

BREED HISTORY Breeding began after World War II, by crossing the Czesky Fousek with the Wire-haired German Pointer. Their descendants were then bred with the Weimaraner. In 1975, this breed received recognition in Czechoslovakia, and in 1983 it was recognized by the International Cynological Federation.

Long, rounded ears are set above eye level

Amber, almond-shaped eyes are initially blue in colour

Long, soft hair grows around mouth, forming distinctive beard

This new and strikingly distinctive breed is an excellent example of the sophisticated gundog breeding carried out in the Czech and Slovak Republics over the last 40 years. Easy to handle, this all-weather dog is good with both novice and experienced hunters, field trialers, and pet-dog owners. In colour it resembles the Weimaraner, but it has the added protection of a tough, wiry topcoat and an insulating, woolly, downy undercoat. Very rarely seen outside the Czech and Slovak Republics, a few individuals have gone to Switzerland, where they have been trained in avalanche search and rescue. The Slovensky Pointer's conformation, appearance, and behaviour all point to a successful future.

Hard, straight, close, protective coat, with close, fine undercoat

Shoulders slant forwards over well-muscled forelegs

KEY FACTS

COUNTRY OF ORIGIN Slovakia
DATE OF ORIGIN 1950s
FIRST USE Setting, pointing
USE TODAY Gundog, companion
LIFE EXPECTANCY 12–14 years
OTHER NAME Slovensky Hruborsty Stavac

WEIGHT RANGE
25–35 kg (55–77 lb)
HEIGHT RANGE
56–68 cm (22–27 in)

LIVESTOCK DOGS

GUARDING A PERSON'S CAMPSITE or homestead is a natural way for a dog to behave. In the delta between the Tigris and Euphrates rivers, in what is now Iraq, where our hunter ancestors became cultivators and farmers, the guarding activity of dogs was extended to protecting livestock. Shepherds discovered that if dogs were raised with sheep, goats, or cattle from puppyhood, they looked after these animals as if they were members of their own pack. These guardians soon became indispensable.

COAT OCCURS IN A VARIETY OF COLOURS AND TEXTURES

Pyrenean Shepherd
Sheep have always been attended by two varieties of dog – guardians and herders. In the Pyrenees, the lithe Pyrenean Shepherd herds sheep from the lowland plains to summer highland valleys.

LEGS WILL DEVELOP THICK MUSCLES

Bernese Mountain Dog puppy
The most popular of the Swiss mountain dogs, this breed comes from the canton of Berne.

Neapolitan Mastiff
The Neapolitan probably descends from ancient Roman fighting mastiffs.

ANCIENT ROOTS

Flocks and herds of livestock were originally small, and while the herbivores rested together or grazed, dogs protected them from wolves and thieves. As flock and herd size increased, however, individual animals had to be prevented from straying. Small, agile dogs were used to move strays back to the herd – these became herders. As shepherds began to transport their animals over long distances, another group of dogs evolved, the drovers. These both protected livestock and moved them along. Bulky drovers developed to move cattle, while smaller, more agile drovers developed to move sheep and goats. These smaller drovers were the forerunners of the modern sheepdog.

The mastiff, produced through selective breeding, moved along a separate but related path. Military strategists saw its potential and turned it into a weapon of war. Protecting flocks and property that accompanied the movements of armies, it willingly imitated its master's aggressive tactics. These massive dogs spread throughout Europe and Asia, and from the fields of war they entered the arena of sport, first fighting other animals, then each other.

Many of today's mountain dogs are descended from the mastiff, including cattle, guardian, and fighting breeds. The precise origin of the mastiff remains obscure, but it is likely that primitive dogs were taken from south-west Asia into what is now Tibet, where their size increased. Armies and traders then took them further east into China and Japan, where they bred with dogs of spitz-type blood, leaving the ancestors of

today's Shar Pei, Chow Chow, Akita, and Tosa Inu. Others moved westwards – the English, French, Pyrenean, Spanish, Neapolitan, and Sicilian Mastiffs are all direct descendants of these Tibetan giants. Once more, the ever-active Phoenicians are given

Berger de Picard
About as tall as a German Shepherd, this ancient sheep-herding breed from northern France is seldom seen elsewhere.

ERECT EARS ARE WELL SPACED ON LONG HEAD

credit for spreading these Goliaths into Europe, but it was the Roman Army that actually transported them throughout their empire. Cattle-guarding mastiffs accompanied Roman legions 2,000 years ago across the Alps to Switzerland, leaving behind the ancestors of the Appenzell, Bernese, Entelbuch and Great Swiss Mountain Dogs, and the St. Bernard. In Rome, mastiffs fought either against other animals or among themselves in the gladiator's ring. Their descendants became bull and bear baiters and fighting dogs, although their main responsibility remained protecting the home. Bullmastiffs, bulldogs, the Great Dane, and Boxer descend from this source. Exported to South America, fighting dogs provided the

BROAD HEAD SITS ON THICK NECK

Australian Cattle Dog puppies
One of Australia's most numerous breeds, the robust Cattle Dog was developed from English dockyard heelers.

HEAD, LIKE THAT OF A COLLIE, IS LEAN AND ANGULAR

Shetland Sheepdog
The Sheltie was originally used to prevent sheep from grazing in gardens on the Scottish Shetland Islands.

BODY IS SLIGHTLY SMALLER THAN A COLLIE'S

Puli
Small, alert, and energetic, the Hungarian Puli is an ancient cattle herder and watchdog. It is a notable barker.

EARS ARE COVERED IN DENSE, MODERATELY HARD HAIR

MUZZLE NARROWS TOWARDS POINTED TIP

and Polish Lowland Sheepdog. In Portugal, the Estrela Mountain Dog still guards, while the Portuguese Cattle and Shepherd Dogs herd. On the plains of Europe the herding shepherd dog continued to evolve, probably from guarding breeds. In Great Britain, this produced the superb collies. Elsewhere in northern Europe, sheep herders evolved in Belgium, the Netherlands, France, and Germany. Today's Picardy Shepherd, Beauceron, Briard, Dutch Sheepdog, Schapendoes, and Belgian shepherds are all products of recent selective breeding for proficiency at herding and obedience. The versatile German Shepherd is used for a diverse range of activities that require the combination of obedience and commonsense. In the

Shar Pei
With its bristly coat and wrinkled skin, the Shar Pei has a unique appearance. Bred as a fighting dog, it still has the potential to behave aggressively.

ABUNDANT LOOSE FOLDS OF SKIN

ERECT EARS ARE BROAD AT BASE

main stock for today's powerful Argentinean and Brazilian Mastiffs, while in Iberia they evolved into the Ca de Bou and Ca de Bestiar.

GUARDIANS AND HERDERS

Livestock guarding remained a primary responsibility of mastiff-type dogs, but cattle and pig farmers and butchers required robust and agile dogs both to protect and move livestock. The Old English Sheepdog was once an excellent cattle drover. So, too, were the Corgi and Swedish Vallhund. In Germany, the Giant and Standard Schnauzers and the Rottweiler filled this role, while in France today the Bouvier des Flandres excels as a cattle mover. In Australia the Kelpie, Australian Cattle Dog, and a variety of heelers still work great herds of cattle. Other, more strictly defensive, guardian breeds spread from Asia into Europe and Africa. The fearless Greek, Albanian, Illyrian, and Istrian sheepdogs developed in the Balkans, while in Hungary the Komondor still guards and protects. Further into Europe, other massive guardians – the Kuvasz, Kuvac, Maremma, and the Pyrenean and Tatra Mountain Dogs – always white to differentiate them from marauding wolves and to bond them to their flocks, would patrol their fiefdoms, guarding but not herding. To help control their large flocks, shepherds used herders such as the Puli, Pumi, Mudi, Croatian Sheepdog, Bergamasco,

United States and Australasia, the Australian Shepherd and New Zealand Huntaway are recent additions to the list of herders.

MAIN FUNCTION

Guarding and herding breeds vary in looks and temperament. However, they all share a common background, that of guarding and protecting our forebears and their livestock, and assisting shepherds and farmers.

LONG BACK IS COVERED BY DENSE COAT

Cardigan Welsh Corgi
A traditional cattle-droving dog, the Corgi is built close to the ground to avoid the flailing hooves of cattle, whose ankles it nips.

Komondor
One of the few breeds with a naturally corded coat, the Komondor has guarded sheep in Hungary for centuries. Today, it is also used in North America to guard against Coyotes.

THIS BREED HAS AN EXCEPTIONALLY LUXURIOUS COAT

Saarloos Wolfhound
Developed by Leendert Saarloos, a Dutch breeder, attempts are periodically made to "improve" this reserved breed by reintroducing wolf blood.

COAT IS USUALLY CUT IN EARLY SPRING

Bearded Collie
There is a marked similarity in both appearance and function between the Bearded Collie of Scotland and the Polish Lowland Sheepdog.

GERMAN SHEPHERD DOG

Erect ears are feathered with sable-coloured hair

Sable, long-haired variety

Straight hair is not especially close to body

Head is rather lean and moderately wide between ears

Black, long-haired variety

BREED HISTORY The world's most numerous breed has its recent origins in the superlative breeding programme which Max von Stephanitz began at the end of the last century. Using long-haired, short-haired, and wire-haired local shepherd dogs from Wurtemberg, Thurginia, and Bavaria, von Stephanitz and other dedicated breeders produced the elegant, responsive, obedient, and handsome German Shepherd. Until 1915, both long-haired and wire-haired varieties were exhibited. Today, in most countries, only the short coat is recognized for show purposes.

Lustrous, long, black hair covers slightly shorter undercoat

While resting, tail is carried down with slight curl

In profile, muzzle is long and head is only slightly rounded

Length of back is greater than height at withers

Cream, long-haired variety

Tail reaches below hocks

Medium-sized ears are wide at base

The Roman historian, Tacitus, wrote of "the wolf-like dog of the country around the Rhine". It may well be that the German Shepherd Dog, and its close Dutch and Belgian shepherd relatives, have existed in much today's form for thousands of years. By the beginning of World War I, the German Shepherd was popular throughout Germany, and swiftly spread to other parts of the world. Indiscriminate breeding has, unfortunately, produced both physical and behavioural problems. Arthritis of the joints, eye disease, gastrointestinal disease, and other medical problems occur with significant frequency. Equally common are nervousness, fearfulness, timidity, and aggression to other dogs, the result being that the quality of individual dogs varies quite considerably. When bred carefully, however, this is an excellent breed – calm, reliable, responsive, and obedient.

Forelegs are well feathered with luxuriously long hair

Strong teeth in jaws meet in perfect bite

Slightly slanting, almond-shaped eyes do not bulge

Tail is densely feathered with long hair

Sable, long-haired variety

Coat colours and lengths

Black and tan, black and grey, and solid black are acceptable colours for exhibition. Yellow, cream, and white are not acceptable in most countries, nor are long coats, although all of these varieties are still routinely produced.

VARIETY OF COLOURS

Erect, high-set ears give impression of alertness

Upper part of head narrows gradually from eyes to nose

Large, black nose is extended to flat tip

Large litters
German Shepherds produce large litters. Their adult behaviour depends upon the genes they inherit, the way they are treated by their mother and humans, and any other experiences that they acquire.

Large, round head is typical of most young mammals

Puppy's coat consists mostly of fine down

Hair is longer and more luxurious on tail than elsewhere

KEY FACTS

COUNTRY OF ORIGIN Germany
DATE OF ORIGIN 1800s
FIRST USE Sheep herding
USE TODAY Companion, security, assistance
LIFE EXPECTANCY 12–13 years
OTHER NAMES Alsatian, Deutscher Schaferhund

WEIGHT RANGE
34–43 kg (75–95 lb)
HEIGHT RANGE
55–66 cm (22–26 in)

Chest is deep and belly only moderately drawn up

Thighs are strong and muscular, with leg bones carried slightly flexed

Arched, small, round, well-formed feet, with large pads

Black-and-tan, short-haired variety

When standing, hocks are angled, rather than perpendicular

Muzzle is half the length of head

Pointed ears are high, erect, very mobile, and capable of turning from resting, forward position to sides

While resting, dog gives impression of strength, alertness, and vigour

White, short-haired variety

Medium-length neck is robustly well muscled, with no dewlap

Lips are deeply pigmented

Legs are straight; elbows are not held too close to body

GROENENDAEL

Long muzzle tapers to narrow, black nose

Long, smooth, black hair, especially abundant around shoulders, neck, and chest

KEY FACTS

COUNTRY OF ORIGIN Belgium
DATE OF ORIGIN Middle Ages/1800s
FIRST USE Livestock herding
USE TODAY Companion, watchdog
LIFE EXPECTANCY 13–14 years
OTHER NAMES Chien de Berger Belge,
   Belgian Shepherd, Belgian Sheepdog

WEIGHT RANGE
27.5–28.5 kg (61–63 lb)
HEIGHT RANGE
56–66 cm (22–26 in)

Classifying the Belgian shepherds is not easy because national kennel clubs cannot agree on how to name them. In 1891, Professor Adolphe Reul, of the Belgian School of Veterinary Science, conducted a field study of all the existing sheepdogs in Belgium, and eventually four different breeds came to be recognized nationally. In many countries, these are classified as varieties of one breed, the Belgian Shepherd. In the United States, however, the Groenendael is the Belgian Shepherd, while the Malinois and Tervueren are recognized separately, and the Laekenois not at all. All share an extremely robust personality and need early training.

Long feathering extends from forearm to wrist

Sharply triangular, rigid, straight ears

Medium-sized, intent-looking eyes are surrounded by black rims

Long, narrow jaw provides space for well-placed teeth

BREED HISTORY At the end of the last century, breeders took an active interest in native sheepdogs, and standards were set to stabilize them into as few breeds as possible. Belgium originally recognized eight standards, including the Groenendael, which was developed by a Belgian breeder, Nicholas Rose.

Well-feathered tail is of moderate length

LAEKENOIS

Although it is as strong willed and opinionated as its three close relatives, this breed is less inclined to snap than the Groenendael, Malinois, and Tervueren. The relative rarity of the Laekenois is inexplicable – it is just as fertile, and as capable a working dog, as the other Belgian shepherds, although its rustic looks may put off potential breeders. Ever alert and highly active, it responds well to obedience training and makes an excellent watchdog. It is good with children if it is introduced to them at an early age, but it can sometimes be troublesome with other dogs.

Fawn-coloured coat is harsh, dry, and normally slightly tangled

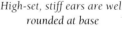

KEY FACTS

COUNTRY OF ORIGIN Belgium
DATE OF ORIGIN Middle Ages/1800s
FIRST USE Livestock herding/guarding
USE TODAY Companion, watchdog
LIFE EXPECTANCY 12–14 years
OTHER NAMES Laekense, Chien de Berger
   Belge (see also Groenendael)

WEIGHT RANGE
27.5–28.5 kg
(61–63 lb)
HEIGHT RANGE
56–66 cm (22–26 in)

Hindquarters are muscular, without looking heavy

Dense hair is bushy on tail, but there is no distinct feathering

Dark eyes and rims contrast with lighter coloured hair

High-set, stiff ears are well rounded at base

BREED HISTORY Today the rarest of the four remaining Belgian shepherds, the rough, shaggy-coated Laekenois, favoured dog of Queen Henrietta of Belgium, is named after the Château de Laeken, a residence she often visited. Similar to the neighbouring rough-haired Dutch Shepherd, the breed was first recognized in 1897.

Bristly, feathered muzzle

MALINOIS

KEY FACTS

COUNTRY OF ORIGIN Belgium
DATE OF ORIGIN Middle Ages/1800s
FIRST USE Livestock herding
USE TODAY Companion, security, assistance
LIFE EXPECTANCY 12–14 years
OTHER NAMES (see also Groenendael)

WEIGHT RANGE
27.5–28.5 kg (61–63 lb)
HEIGHT RANGE
56–66 cm (22–26 in)

Muzzle is very slightly longer than flat skull, which is of medium width

BREED HISTORY The first of the Belgian shepherds to establish type, the Malinois became the gauge by which other Belgian sheepdogs were judged. It is named after the area of Malines, where this form of sheepdog was most populous. Its conformation is closest to the German Shepherd's.

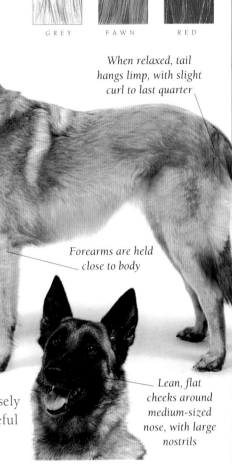

GREY   FAWN   RED

When relaxed, tail hangs limp, with slight curl to last quarter

Chest is not wide, but it is deep and roomy

Short, hard, fawn-coloured hairs are tipped with black

The Malinois has a coat similar to that of the smooth-haired Dutch Shepherd, but its temperament is closest to that of the Laekenois – active and alert, with an instinct to guard and protect. After the Laekenois, this is the least popular of the Belgian shepherds, although both of these breeds are possibly less snappy than the Groenendael and Tervueren. Its rareness could be due to the fact that it is competing with the popular German Shepherd, which it closely resembles. The Malinois is, however, a resourceful dog, and police forces are increasingly using it for security work.

Forearms are held close to body

Lean, flat cheeks around medium-sized nose, with large nostrils

TERVUEREN

BREED HISTORY In temperament and looks closest to the Groenendael (Groenendael matings occasionally produce Tervueren puppies), this breed descends from the stock that created the Groenendael. Near extinction by the end of World War II, in the last decade it has surged in popularity, especially as a drug-detecting dog.

The Tervueren's trainability and ability to concentrate have made it a favourite for agility trials, police and security service work, and assistance work with blind or disabled people. One of the success stories of the last 10 years has been the use of the breed as a scent detector – it finds drugs as they are smuggled across national borders. Its double-pigmented, long coat, in which the tip of each light-coloured hair is blackened, adds to its appeal, and is partly responsible for its increasing popularity. Like all the Belgian shepherds, this breed thrives when it is controlled by a firm and understanding hand.

GREY   FAWN   RED

Erect ears enhance alert appearance

Ruff of long hair circles neck and hides dense undercoat of fine, black hair

Dark hair on face is much shorter than elsewhere on body

KEY FACTS

COUNTRY OF ORIGIN Belgium
DATE OF ORIGIN Middle Ages/1800s
FIRST USE Livestock herding
USE TODAY Companion, security, assistance
LIFE EXPECTANCY 12–14 years
OTHER NAMES (see also Groenendael)

WEIGHT RANGE
27.5–28.5 kg (61–63 lb)
HEIGHT RANGE
56–66 cm (22–26 in)

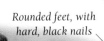

Feathering covers lean and athletic hind legs

Tapering tail is densely covered with thick guard hair

Rounded feet, with hard, black nails

BORDER COLLIE

Still the most popular working sheepdog in Great Britain and Ireland, the Border can make an affectionate but difficult pet, especially in cities. Border Collies from working lines have a strong predatory instinct, which is channelled through breeding and training into a superb herding ability. Without constant stimulation, this need to work will vent itself in destructive behaviour, such as herding other dogs or people, or snappiness.

BREED HISTORY Although shepherds in the hilly Scottish Borders used collies for many years, this breed was not given its present name until 1915.

Dense, slightly harsh, but shiny, topcoat

Mane is quite heavy

Fairly large eyes are set wide apart

Well-boned, straight forelimbs

Slightly blunt, tapering muzzle

Tail carried low, but with an up-swirl at tip

RED BLUE-MERLE

TRICOLOUR BLACK/WHITE

BROWN BLACK

KEY FACTS

COUNTRY OF ORIGIN Great Britain
DATE OF ORIGIN 1700s
FIRST USE Sheep/cattle herding
USE TODAY Companion, sheep herding, sheepdog trials
LIFE EXPECTANCY 12–14 years

WEIGHT RANGE
14–22 kg (30–49 lb)
HEIGHT RANGE
46–54 cm (18–21 in)

ROUGH COLLIE

The Rough Collie's elegant good looks first attracted the attention of breeders, and then the public. After Queen Victoria acquired the breed as a companion, its popularity increased, but it was not until Hollywood discovered it and produced the Lassie films that international recognition and popularity were assured. (Lassie, incidentally, was actually Laddie, a male.) The breed's success in the show ring has tended to override its original herding abilities. It is an excellent companion, easy to obedience train, safe with, and extremely protective of, children, and a good watchdog. Its coat mats easily, and needs daily grooming.

SABLE/WHITE BLUE-MERLE TRICOLOUR

BREED HISTORY Originating in its present form in the cold regions of northern Scotland, the working Rough Collie was shorter in leg and nose than today's elegant breed.

Almond-shaped, slightly oblique eyes

KEY FACTS

COUNTRY OF ORIGIN Great Britain
DATE OF ORIGIN 1800s
FIRST USE Sheep herding
USE TODAY Companion
LIFE EXPECTANCY 12–14 years
OTHER NAME Scottish Collie

WEIGHT RANGE
18–30 kg (40–66 lb)
HEIGHT RANGE
51–61 cm (20–24 in)

Head resembles a blunted wedge

Topcoat is dense and straight

Nose is prone to sunburn

Abundant, smooth, shiny mane

Forelegs are well feathered

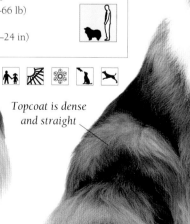

SMOOTH COLLIE

BREED HISTORY The Smooth Collie can trace its roots back to a tricoloured puppy named Trefoil, which was born in 1873. There could also be a trace of greyhound blood in its lineage.

For most of its history, the Smooth Collie has been classified with the Rough, since this breed occasionally gives birth to smooth puppies. The personalities of the two breeds have, however, diverged, perhaps because of the smaller gene pool of this rather uncommon breed. Not as popular as the Rough, the Smooth Collie is very rare outside Great Britain, and has a greater tendency to be shy and snappy. It does, however, make a good companion, and is suited to life in the city.

Ears are erect; tips hang when dog is alert

Black nose at end of long muzzle

Coat is short and dense

Forelegs are long and slender

Muscular thighs; legs long and sinewy below thighs

SABLE / WHITE

BLUE- MERLE

TRICOLOUR

SHETLAND SHEEPDOG

SABLE BLUE- MERLE TRICOLOUR BLACK/ WHITE BLACK/ TAN

Head tapers elegantly from ears to nose

Abundant hair around neck

Small, semi-erect ears are close set

Dark-brown eyes look gentle

The Sheltie is consistently one of the most popular breeds in Japan, and is popular in Great Britain and North America. Although it is rarely used as a working dog, it retains many of its guarding and herding instincts, and will efficiently protect its owner's home. Although once called the Dwarf Scotch Shepherd, the breed is a classic miniature, not a dwarf like a dachshund. It is a smaller version of the large working sheepdogs of Scotland. Miniaturization has brought with it an increased risk of fractures to long, thin leg bones, and a rather high incidence of inherited digestive problems and eye conditions.

BREED HISTORY This breed may be the result of crossing imported Rough Collies with dogs from the Scottish Shetland islands.

Frill of long hair

Long, harsh, topcoat

BEARDED COLLIE

E xuberance is the cardinal personality trait of this ancient breed. Having virtually disappeared as a working dog, the breed was revived in 1944 when Mrs. Willison, owner of Jeannie, acquired Bailie, who she saw playing on a beach at Hove, Sussex. Virtually all of today's Beardies descend from these two dogs. This high-spirited, friendly individual needs constant mental and physical stimulation, and is ideal for people who have both time and energy.

Medium-sized, drooping ears are lost under long hair

KEY FACTS

COUNTRY OF ORIGIN Great Britain
DATE OF ORIGIN 1500s
FIRST USE Sheep herding
USE TODAY Companion
LIFE EXPECTANCY 12–13 years
OTHER NAME Beardie

WEIGHT RANGE
18–27 kg (40–60 lb)
HEIGHT RANGE
51–56 cm (20–22 in)

Low-set, long tail, with abundant feathering

Long body has level back; hair naturally parts down middle

Forelegs are covered with long, shaggy hair

BREED HISTORY Mythically, the Beardie has Polish Lowland Sheepdog origins. After conquering Great Britain, it successfully colonized the United States and Canada.

GREY FAWN

BLUE BROWN BLACK

OLD ENGLISH SHEEPDOG

KEY FACTS

COUNTRY OF ORIGIN Great Britain
DATE OF ORIGIN 1800s
FIRST USE Sheep herding
USE TODAY Companion
LIFE EXPECTANCY 12–13 years
OTHER NAME Bobtail

WEIGHT RANGE
29.5–30.5 kg (65–67 lb)
HEIGHT RANGE
56–61 cm (22–24 in)

BREED HISTORY The Old English probably traces its origins back to continental sheepdogs, such as the Briard. Selective breeding began in the 1880s.

Almost square head has long, strong, square, truncated jaws

BLUE GREY

I n 1961, a British paint manufacturer launched television advertisements, using the Old English as its symbol. Sales of this breed subsequently increased as rapidly as did paint sales. Its old, aggressive instincts occasionally rise to the surface – however, early training is necessary more to control the breed's intense demands for affection. Although this burly dog is capable of behaving like the proverbial bull in a china shop, it is an excellent companion and guard.

Stands lower at shoulders than at loins

Puppy

Straight forelegs are covered with profuse, hard topcoat and waterproof undercoat

Soft puppy coat becomes harder and shaggier

CARDIGAN WELSH CORGI

BREED HISTORY Some authorities say that this breed arrived in Great Britain with the Celts over 3,000 years ago. Others say that it is a distant relative of continental bassets and reached Great Britain just over 1,000 years ago. In the 1800s, cross breeding with the Pembroke Welsh Corgi reduced the differences between the two breeds.

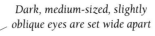

Dark, medium-sized, slightly oblique eyes are set wide apart

Smooth, protective topcoat is harsh to the touch, and covers soft, insulating undercoat

Muzzle makes up less than 40 per cent of the length of head

Head is fox-like in appearance

Powerful and slightly arched neck on sloping shoulders

ANY COLOUR

Watch your ankles when you are near a Cardigan Welsh Corgi. This robust working dog is an instinctive "heeler", which originally drove livestock by nipping at its heels; it was built low enough to the ground to avoid flailing hooves. *Cur* once meant to watch over, and in old Welsh, *gi* means dog. The Corgi lives up to its name – it is a watchful and snappy defender of property and drover of sheep and cattle. It also makes an exuberant companion.

Fox-like brush tail on body larger than a Pembroke's

PEMBROKE WELSH CORGI

SABLE   FAWN   RED   BLACK/ TAN

Erect, firm, medium-sized ears have rounded tips

BREED HISTORY Ancient records indicate that the Pembroke Welsh Corgi has existed in Great Britain since at least AD 920.

One story tells that the breed accompanied Flemish weavers brought to Great Britain by King Henry I of England.

Medium-sized, oval, brown eyes are slightly oblique

Lack of tail is an inherited trait

Muzzle is trim and compact

The Pembroke Welsh Corgi bears a striking resemblance to the Swedish Vallhund. It is possible that the Vikings took ancestors of this determined little heeler back to Scandinavia from their settlements in Great Britain. Until the 1800s, heelers were used extensively throughout Great Britain to drove cattle to markets. The stamina and efficiency of the Pembroke's ancestors made it a popular working dog. Although the breed is still worked today, most Pembrokes are kept as companions. Breeders have been moderately successful in reducing the inclination of this breed to nip.

Body is significantly shorter than that of a Cardigan

AUSTRALIAN KELPIE

FAWN   RED   BLUE   BROWN

BLACK/TAN   BLACK

Compact, robust, enthusiastic, and a tireless worker, this is Australia's most popular and successful working dog, numbering in excess of 100,000 in its country of origin. Due to its tenacious enjoyment in working any type of livestock, be it cattle, sheep, goats, or even poultry, a strong legend developed that this breed must have Dingo blood. Accurate records and the Kelpie's willingness to be trained suggest otherwise. The name kelpie comes from the water kelpie mentioned by Robert Louis Stevenson, the Scottish writer, in the novel *Kidnapped*. This responsive, restless dog is not very suitable for the confines of city life.

Small, erect ears give dog alert look

Long, narrow head

Deep, broad chest has space for lung expansion

Weather-resistant double coat

BREED HISTORY This breed is the result of a cross between a collie from the north of England, and a black-and-tan bitch from New South Wales, Australia, which was called Kelpie.

Medium-length tail is low set

Short, compact feet have well-arched toes

KEY FACTS

COUNTRY OF ORIGIN Australia
DATE OF ORIGIN 1870s
FIRST USE Livestock herding
USE TODAY Companion, livestock herding
LIFE EXPECTANCY 12 years
OTHER NAMES Kelpie, Barb

WEIGHT RANGE
11–20 kg (25–45 lb)
HEIGHT RANGE
43–51 cm (17–20 in)

AUSTRALIAN CATTLE DOG

Puppy

KEY FACTS

COUNTRY OF ORIGIN Australia
DATE OF ORIGIN 1800s
FIRST USE Cattle herding
USE TODAY Cattle herding, companion
LIFE EXPECTANCY 12 years
OTHER NAMES Blue Heeler, Hall's Heeler, Queensland Heeler

WEIGHT RANGE
16–20 kg (35–45 lb)
HEIGHT RANGE
43–51 cm (17–20 in)

In Great Britain, the now-extinct Blue Heeler, which nipped at the legs of livestock, was used at docks to herd sheep and cattle onto boats. Although its origins are dramatically different, the Australian Cattle Dog closely resembles the old dockyard breed. An Australian pioneer, Thomas Smith Hall, wanted a similar dog, but robust enough to withstand the intense hardships of droving cattle in 19th-century Australia. Exploiting the Dingo's ability to creep up silently on prey before biting, Hall created a dog very similar to the Cattle Dog of today. The breed is wary by nature, and must be introduced to other animals and people early in its development.

Dark-brown, intense, watchful eyes

Erect ears are set wide apart

TAN

BLUE

BREED HISTORY The versatile and fearless Australian Cattle Dog is the result of six decades of cross breeding. Breeds involved included the Red Bobtail, Scotland's blue-merle Collie, and the Dingo.

Deep, broad chest

Broad, round feet, with black pads

AUSTRALIAN SHEPHERD DOG

RED

LIVER

BLUE-MERLE

BLACK

Virtually unknown outside the United States, the Australian Shepherd is now increasing in popularity because of its obedient and willing nature, as well as its natural good looks. Originally bred as a working shepherd suitable for the varied climate of California, the Australian Shepherd has adapted superbly to both family life and work as a service dog, especially in search and rescue. The breed has a temperament similar to those of Golden and Labrador Retrievers. It is affectionate and playful, but maintains a basic working instinct. This is not yet a "designer" dog, although reducing its size is an objective of some breeders.

Thick ruff of fur on neck and chest

BREED HISTORY This breed originated in California in the 1800s, although its ancestors include sheepdogs from New Zealand and Australia.

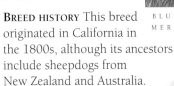

KEY FACTS

COUNTRY OF ORIGIN United States/Australia
DATE OF ORIGIN 1900s
FIRST USE Sheep herding
USE TODAY Companion, sheep herding
LIFE EXPECTANCY 12–13 years
WEIGHT RANGE 16–32 kg (35–70 lb)
HEIGHT RANGE 46–58 cm (18–23 in)

Body is moderately long

Nose is predominantly brown

Hind legs are well feathered

Moderately coarse topcoat

Solid, broad feet provide firm footing

LANCASHIRE HEELER

Wide-set, relatively large ears

With the advent of mechanized transport, the work of the old heeler breeds was no longer necessary. In Great Britain, the Yorkshire and Norfolk Heelers, the Drover's Cur, and London's Smithfield Collie all became extinct. Today's Lancashire Heeler, although in colour (black with tan markings) and size almost identical to its ancient namesake, is seldom used as a cattle dog, and has never learned to act like one. It has the alertness and rat- and rabbit-catching potential of its terrier parentage, and makes a pleasant companion.

Large, bright eyes are set wide apart

KEY FACTS

COUNTRY OF ORIGIN Great Britain
DATE OF ORIGIN 1600s/1960s
FIRST USE Cattle herding
USE TODAY Companion
LIFE EXPECTANCY 12–13 years
OTHER NAME Ormskirk Heeler

WEIGHT RANGE 3–6 kg (6–13 lb)
HEIGHT RANGE 25–31 cm (10–12 in)

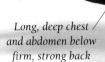

Muzzle fur is first area to change colour with age

Tail is set high and carried forwards over back

Hindquarters are very well muscled

BREED HISTORY Heelers, which drove livestock by nipping their heels, were common wherever cattle were walked to market. The Lancashire Heeler became extinct earlier this century. Today's breed, which is a 1960s' re-creation, is largely a cross between the Welsh Corgi and Manchester Terrier.

Forepaws are covered in tan-coloured fur

Legs are short in relation to body size

Long, deep chest and abdomen below firm, strong back

Short, sturdy legs; paws turn out slightly

PUMI

Elongated muzzle is most distinctive feature of face

BREED HISTORY The Pumi was created by crossing the cord-coated, herding Puli with softer coated German spitzen. It was first mentioned by name in 1815, but it was not until the 1920s that it was recognized as a distinct breed. Its function was to drove cattle rather than to guard them.

High, wide-set, erect, V-shaped ears curl down at tips

KEY FACTS

COUNTRY OF ORIGIN Hungary
DATE OF ORIGIN 1800s
FIRST USE Livestock herding
USE TODAY Security, hunting
LIFE EXPECTANCY 12–13 years
OTHER NAME Hungarian Pumi

WEIGHT RANGE
10–15 kg (22–33 lb)
HEIGHT RANGE
33–48 cm (13–19 in)

Slightly oblique, dark eyes have close-fitting lids

Chest is deep and ribs are somewhat flat

Plaited, medium-length coat does not mat easily

Feet are strong, with elastic pads and hard nails

Compact hind feet are set back from body

Hungary has produced a varied selection of livestock dogs. The Pumi is one of the lesser known breeds, perhaps because of its rustic appearance. This is a typical drover, with a fiery personality and an alert disposition. As a working dog it serves many functions, such as herding cattle, exterminating vermin, and guarding the farm. A superb watchdog, the Pumi uses its voice liberally and consistently. The breed is established in North America and across Europe, but outside Hungary its numbers remain small.

KOMONDOR

Muscular upper and lower jaws house large, regular teeth

Muscular neck, with grey-pigmented skin under hair

Heavy, coarse topcoat with dense, woolly, soft undercoat

The Komondor's corded coat historically provided protection from both the elements and from wolves, as it guarded sheep and cattle in Hungary over the centuries. Its strong guarding ability is used today to protect sheep in North America from Coyote predation. The dog is raised from puppyhood with its flock of sheep, and is shorn when the sheep are shorn. It makes an amenable companion, although its coat requires constant attention to prevent the cords from matting together.

KEY FACTS

COUNTRY OF ORIGIN Hungary
DATE OF ORIGIN Antiquity
FIRST USE Sheep guarding
USE TODAY Livestock guarding, companion
LIFE EXPECTANCY 12 years
OTHER NAME Hungarian Sheepdog

WEIGHT RANGE
36–61 kg (80–135 lb)
HEIGHT RANGE
65–90 cm (26½–35½ in)

Strong, heavy cords feel like felt when touched

BREED HISTORY It is thought that this, the largest of the Hungarian herdsmen's dogs, accompanied the Magyar tribe from the east when it settled in Hungary over 1,000 years ago. First mentioned by name in 1544, it was not until around 1910 that the Komondor was firmly established as a modern breed.

HUNGARIAN KUVASZ

BREED HISTORY Some authorities believe that this great, white guard dog arrived in Hungary in the 1100s with the Kumans – nomadic Turkish shepherds.

First mentioned as a breed in the 1600s, its name comes from the Turkish *kavas* or *kawasz*, meaning armed guard, which it certainly is.

Coat is rough, wavy, and stiff

Ears are set high and wide

Nose is pointed and black

Although Hungarian history books say that in the 15th century King Matthias I used the Kuvasz to hunt wild boars, this breed is not a natural hunter. It is an inveterate guard, content to stay with its flock rather than to participate in a hunt. Its origins probably go back to the ancient Asian shepherd dogs brought to Europe by invading armies and nomadic shepherds. The Kuvasz is a powerful dog that willingly defends its territory, and is best in the hands of capable dog handlers. However, it makes a loyal companion and is usually reliable with its human family.

Thighs and hind limbs are very muscular, with broad, long hocks

Hind feet are longer than forefeet, but just as strong

KEY FACTS

COUNTRY OF ORIGIN Hungary
DATE OF ORIGIN Middle Ages
FIRST USE Livestock guarding
USE TODAY Companion, security
LIFE EXPECTANCY 12–14 years
OTHER NAME Kuvasz

WEIGHT RANGE
30–52 kg (66–115 lb)
HEIGHT RANGE
66–75 cm (26–29½ in)

SLOVENSKY KUVAC

KEY FACTS

COUNTRY OF ORIGIN Slovakia
DATE OF ORIGIN Middle Ages
FIRST USE Livestock guarding
USE TODAY Companion, security
LIFE EXPECTANCY 12 years
OTHER NAMES Slovak Cuvac, Slovakian Chuvach, Tatransky Cuvac

WEIGHT RANGE
30–45 kg (66–99 lb)
HEIGHT RANGE
55–70 cm (22–27½ in)

Calm, powerful, and a fearless defender of its territory and pack, the Kuvac is very similar to its next-door neighbour, the Kuvasz. International recognition was secured in 1969, and today this breed is a popular companion dog. Selective breeding has produced a dog with an equable temperament and a sometimes dramatically affectionate personality with members of its family. However, the Kuvac's thick coat needs routine grooming, and it is not suited to a tidy home.

BREED HISTORY Similar in origin to the larger Hungarian Kuvasz, this mountain shepherd dog was almost extinct when Dr. Antonin Hruza, of the Brno School of Veterinary Medicine, embarked on his successful breeding programme after World War II.

Dense hair on tail

Powerful neck is of same length as head

Thick, white topcoat over dense undercoat

Very muscular hips and thighs

Broad chest, with well-sprung ribs

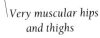
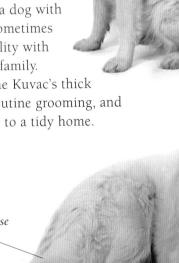

GIANT SCHNAUZER

Jet-black nose

At one time, the Giant Schnauzer was a common herding breed in southern Germany, but its extensive feeding requirements in hard times reduced its appeal. In the latter part of the last century, it regained popularity as a butcher's drover and guard. Although hardy and vigorous, the breed has a tendency towards both shoulder and hip arthritis. It does not demand unlimited exercise, making it suitable for city life. However, it is not afraid to use its considerable power to defend its territory.

Beard is long and coarse

Robust and powerful forelegs are not too close together

KEY FACTS

COUNTRY OF ORIGIN Germany
DATE OF ORIGIN Middle Ages
FIRST USE Cattle herding
USE TODAY Companion, service
LIFE EXPECTANCY 11–12 years
OTHER NAME Riesenschnauzer

WEIGHT RANGE
32–35 kg (70–77 lb)
HEIGHT RANGE
59–70 cm (23½–27½ in)

PEPPER/SALT   BLACK

BREED HISTORY The most powerful of the German schnauzers, this reliable dog was developed by increasing the size of the standard Schnauzer. When it was first exhibited in Munich in 1909, it was called the Russian Bear Schnauzer.

SCHNAUZER

High-set tail has been amputated

Ears are partly erect, dropping gracefully to sides

A vigilant guard, this is the original breed from which miniature and giant breeds later evolved. The German artist Albrecht Dürer painted dogs of this conformation, as did Rembrandt. It is possible that this ancient breed is a cross between spitz and guarding dogs. Although today it is kept primarily as a companion, the Schnauzer remains an excellent livestock dog. It learns obedience reasonably easily, and can be trained to retrieve both on land and from water.

Long muzzle and chin hair give distinct and amusing appearance

Thighs are well muscled, leading down to neat, short, round feet

Long, powerful head gradually narrows from ears to tip of nose

Strong, coarse, and dense topcoat is held up by denser undercoat

Brisket is broad and reaches below elbows

PEPPER/SALT   BLACK

KEY FACTS

COUNTRY OF ORIGIN Germany
DATE OF ORIGIN Middle Ages
FIRST USE Ratting, guarding
USE TODAY Companion
LIFE EXPECTANCY 12–14 years
OTHER NAME Mittelschnauzer

WEIGHT RANGE
14.5–15.5 kg (32–34 lb)
HEIGHT RANGE
45–50 cm (18–20 in)

BREED HISTORY Once a ratter as well as a guard, this breed is often classified as a terrier. It originated in southern Germany and adjacent regions of Switzerland and France, and was once known as the Schnauzer-Pinscher.

MUDI

Back is straight but rather short

Hind legs are surprisingly wide set

Perhaps the least known of all Hungarian dogs, both inside and outside its native country, the Mudi has served as a boar hunter, herder, farm guard, and companion. Its conformation stabilized early this century, and its standards were written down according to these original traits. Inexplicably, but perhaps in part because of its undefined origins and rustic appearance, the Mudi exists only in small numbers, and without the intervention of dedicated breeders, would be in danger of extinction. It spite of its efficiency and adaptability, the breed is rarely seen outside Hungary. It is an obedient and playful, but sometimes noisy, companion, and is happy in both urban and rural settings.

BREED HISTORY The Hungarian herdsmen's dogs were all classified together until the 1930s, when the Mudi was separated from the Puli and Pumi. This all-purpose, rural breed does not appear to be the result of planned breeding and is rare, even in Hungary.

Long, dense, wavy, and glossy hair forms tufts

VARIETY OF COLOURS

KEY FACTS

COUNTRY OF ORIGIN Hungary
DATE OF ORIGIN 1800s
FIRST USE Flock guarding/herding, boar hunting
USE TODAY Companion, security, small-mammal hunting
LIFE EXPECTANCY 13–14 years
OTHER NAME Hungarian Mudi

WEIGHT RANGE
8–13 kg (18–29 lb)
HEIGHT RANGE
36–51 cm (14–20 in)

CROATIAN SHEEPDOG

Lean muzzle on relatively long head

This "no-nonsense" canine is an uncomplicated guardian and watchdog. It evolved in northern Croatia from local shepherd dogs, themselves possible descendants of dogs brought to the region from elsewhere in the Balkans, or from Greece and Turkey. The Croatian Sheepdog is slightly larger, and more common in the Croatian countryside, than its Hungarian counterpart, the Mudi. Unlike the Mudi, which occurs in a variety of colours, this breed occurs only in black, although there may be white on its feet. An instinctive herder, it is wary of strangers; if socialized early, however, it responds well to obedience training.

Triangular, upright ears are set slightly to sides

Thick, soft, long, wavy coat is usually 8–13 cm (3–5 in) long

Muscular, broad rump slopes slightly

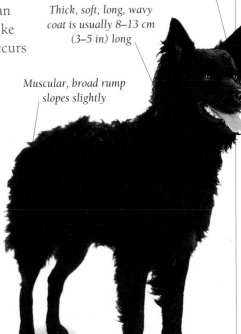

KEY FACTS

COUNTRY OF ORIGIN Croatia
DATE OF ORIGIN 1800s
FIRST USE Flock guarding
USE TODAY Companion, security
LIFE EXPECTANCY 13–14 years
OTHER NAME Hrvaski Ovcar

WEIGHT RANGE
13–16 kg (29–35 lb)
HEIGHT RANGE
40–51 cm (16–20 in)

BREED HISTORY Used as a sheepdog in the Backa and Baranja regions of northern Croatia by the Hungarian border, this breed, like the Mudi, did not develop from planned breeding to standards, but is rather the result of local matings.

Feet are rather small and elongated, with close-set toes

APPENZELL MOUNTAIN DOG

Curled tail is unique among Swiss mountain dogs

A multi-purpose breed, this impressive and sure-footed dog has been a versatile friend of Swiss farmers since the Middle Ages. Historically, this robust breed was harnessed to carts and hauled products to town on market days. It is an excellent herding dog, willing to gather cattle, sheep, or goats. An efficient guard, it uses its size, strength, and voice to warn off potential predators. In the 1800s, Appenzeller numbers diminished, and although it was saved from extinction, it is seldom seen outside Switzerland.

BREED HISTORY Although its exact origins are lost, it is likely that this breed descends from warrior mastiffs left by Roman legions as they passed through Switzerland 2,000 years ago. The curled tail suggests spitz blood in its ancestry.

Small, round eyes are particularly vivacious in young individuals

Muzzle gradually tapers to nose

Feet are rather small for a dog of such robust build

KEY FACTS

COUNTRY OF ORIGIN Switzerland
DATE OF ORIGIN Antiquity/1900s
FIRST USE Goat herding
USE TODAY Guarding, companion
LIFE EXPECTANCY 12–13 years
OTHER NAMES Appenzeller
Sennenhund, Appenzeller Cattle Dog

WEIGHT RANGE
25–32 kg (55–70 lb)
HEIGHT RANGE
48–58 cm (19–23 in)

Coat is short, thick, and glossy, with dense undercoat

BERNESE MOUNTAIN DOG

BREED HISTORY Another ancient breed, the Bernese had almost disappeared in the late 1800s when Franz Schertenleib, a breeder investigating the history of Swiss mountain dogs, found several good individuals in the Berne region. This breed was given its present name in 1908.

KEY FACTS

COUNTRY OF ORIGIN Switzerland
DATE OF ORIGIN Antiquity/1900s
FIRST USE Draughting
USE TODAY Companion
LIFE EXPECTANCY 10–12 years
OTHER NAMES Berner Sennenhund,
Bernese Cattle Dog

WEIGHT RANGE
40–44 kg (87–90 lb)
HEIGHT RANGE
58–70 cm (23–27½ in)

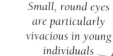

Long muzzle, with medium-sized nose

Glossy, black coat is abundant, long, and smooth

White hair on chest also occurs on bridge, feet, and tail tip

Puppy

The popularity of the Bernese is rapidly increasing in both Europe and North America. In the 1930s, a number of breeders bred for increased size and guarding ability, which left a trait of temperamental unreliability in certain lines, leading to a tendency to unprovoked aggression. Also, breeding from a small genetic stock has created certain problems, particularly shoulder lameness. A working breed, trained to herd livestock and pull carts, the Bernese readily learns obedience, and is successful in the show ring. It can be a sloppily affectionate giant, but it is best in the hands of an experienced handler.

Forelimbs are robust

Tail is fluffy and feathered, but does not curl

ENTELBUCH MOUNTAIN DOG

BREED HISTORY The smallest of the Swiss mountain dogs, the Entelbuch's origins are untraceable. Its mastiff shape strongly suggests that it is descended from the fighting and guarding mastiffs of the Roman legions. This affable breed takes its name from Entelbuch, which is situated in the canton of Lucerne.

Rather small, lively, brown eyes on massive head

Powerful, well-formed, long jaws, with ample space for teeth

Small, high-set, ears

Compact feet support muscular body

KEY FACTS

COUNTRY OF ORIGIN Switzerland
DATE OF ORIGIN Antiquity/1900s
FIRST USE Cattle droving
USE TODAY Livestock guard, companion
LIFE EXPECTANCY 11–13 years
OTHER NAMES Entelbucher Sennenhund, Entelbucher Cattle Dog

WEIGHT RANGE
25–30 kg (55–66 lb)
HEIGHT RANGE
48–51 cm (19–20 in)

Popular in Switzerland, but rarely seen outside its native land, the relatively compact and muscular Entelbuch is one of the breeds that was "rescued" through the diligent efforts of Franz Schertenleib. From the stories his father had told him, this Swiss dog breeder knew that different forms of mountain dog existed throughout the mountainous valleys of Switzerland. In the late 1800s, with the help of a Zurich show judge, Professor Albert Heim, Schertenleib scoured the Swiss countryside searching for mountain dogs before they became extinct. Always eager to please, the Entelbuch makes a good companion.

Muscular hips are covered by thick skin, and even thicker hair

Short, hard, thick, and glossy topcoat over dense, fine undercoat

Hocks are naturally well bent

GREAT SWISS MOUNTAIN DOG

When resting, stout tail is carried down and reaches hocks

Hard topcoat covers full undercoat

Robust head, with slight, median furrow down muzzle

KEY FACTS

COUNTRY OF ORIGIN Switzerland
DATE OF ORIGIN Antiquity/1900s
FIRST USE Draughting
USE TODAY Companion
LIFE EXPECTANCY 10–11 years
OTHER NAMES Grosser Schweizer Sennenhund, Great Swiss Cattle Dog

WEIGHT RANGE
59–61 kg (130–135 lb)
HEIGHT RANGE
60–72 cm (23½–28½ in)

With the exception of the Bernese, this breed is the largest of the Swiss mountain dogs, and may also be the oldest. For centuries, it was a popular draught dog in villages and on farms, pulling milk carts to market or assisting butchers by droving livestock. When Franz Schertenlieb (*see above*) showed Albert Heim the single dog he discovered on an isolated farm, Heim challenged Swiss dog lovers to search out dogs on other such farms, and enough were discovered to revitalize the breed. The Great Swiss Mountain Dog is gentle with humans, but can sometimes be troublesome with other dogs.

Strong, broad, well-muscled thighs assist endurance

Short, round feet, with arched toes

BREED HISTORY Another probable descendant of the great Roman mastiffs, this breed was "discovered" early this century by Franz Schertenlieb. He took his discovery to Albert Heim, who had thought the breed extinct. Closely resembling the Appenzeller, it achieved breed recognition under its present name in 1910.

Well-fitted, close eyelids surround medium-sized eyes

No dewlap, but fold of skin by larynx

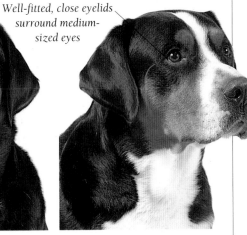

CA DE BOU

Thick, strong neck is surrounded by protective collar

Head is massive and broad, even at birth

Hips are higher than shoulders

YELLOW

LION - GOLDEN

TAN

Coat is like a Boxer's – short, hard, and smooth, with no undercoat

Exceptionally powerful jaws

KEY FACTS

COUNTRY OF ORIGIN Balearic Islands
DATE OF ORIGIN 1600s
FIRST USE Bull baiting, dog fighting
USE TODAY Companion
LIFE EXPECTANCY 10–12 years
OTHER NAMES Perro de Presa Mallorquin, Mallorquin Bulldog
WEIGHT RANGE 35.5–36.5 kg (78–80 lb)
HEIGHT RANGE 56–58 cm (22–23 in)

For centuries, this mastiff-type breed was used in contests of strength with bulls or with other dogs. Dog fighting was a popular spectator sport near the harbours of the Balearic islands, and the Ca de Bou, a bull-herding dog, was the favoured local fighter. When bull baiting and dog fighting were outlawed, it declined in numbers, but was then rescued by mainland breeders, who exhibited it at Spanish dog shows. Through breeding for the show ring, this tough-minded, medium-sized dog has become a more biddable and affectionate companion, although it remains formidably powerful and alert, and retains the tenaciousness of its bull-baiting past.

BREED HISTORY
This pugnacious bull baiter developed on the Balearic islands during the period of Catalan influence, between 1270 and 1570. By the time of the British occupation of Menorca (1708–1802), bull baiting and dog fighting were common sports, which only declined this century.

Front legs are about 2.5 cm (1 in) shorter than hind legs

CA DE BESTIAR

Thickly rooted tail tapers and extends to hocks

Long and powerful back is covered in smooth, short, hard hair

Jet-black nose at end of medium-width muzzle

BREED HISTORY This livestock-herding and guarding breed developed on the Balearic islands, off the coast of Spain, from unknown dogs that arrived from mainland Europe. It evolved according to the needs of the local, rural shepherds, who bred only for function, never for looks.

KEY FACTS

COUNTRY OF ORIGIN Balearic Islands
DATE OF ORIGIN 1700s
FIRST USE Farm guarding
USE TODAY Companion, security
LIFE EXPECTANCY 11–13 years
OTHER NAMES Perro de Pastor Mallorquin, Mallorquin Shepherd
WEIGHT RANGE 35–40 kg (77–88 lb)
HEIGHT RANGE 62–73 cm (24–29 in)

Compact feet, with thick pads and hard, dark nails

This is an enthusiastically bold and independent breed, rustic in looks because it was never bred for visual appeal. Uncomplicated, unsophisticated, and utilitarian, it is strong in both mind and body. Although it is unusual for a black-coated dog to be heat resistant, this breed can withstand high temperatures – as a consquence, some individuals have made their way to South America, where they are used as guard dogs on family estates. Its ability to work in high temperatures, guard tenaciously, and develop a thick coat in cold weather also makes it a good candidate for Coyote control on sheep ranches in North America.

Eyes naturally look timid, although breed is robust and confident

Upper lips hang just over lower lips, enclosing well-spaced, moderate-sized teeth

CANARY DOG

Powerful, square head is nearly as wide as it is long

Rump is slightly raised

FAWN

RED-BRINDLE

BLACK-BRINDLE

At one time, dog fighting was a common and popular entertainment in most European countries, and breeds were developed specifically for their tenaciousness and endurance. In some countries, such as Ireland, fights were staged in open fields, but more often – as was the case in the Canary Islands – fighting took place in rings or pits. The Canary Dog is a typical fighting dog, thick skinned, densely boned, muscular, and with a massive head, housing exceptionally large jaw muscles.

Great power emanates from deep and broad chest

Thick neck skin covers powerful muscles

BREED HISTORY This breed was developed specifically for dog fighting.Its ancestry probably includes the now-extinct local breed, the Bardino Majero, crossed with imported English mastiffs. By the 1960s the breed was nearly extinct, but it was revived by the American veterinarian Dr. Carl Semencic.

Broad muzzle

KEY FACTS

COUNTRY OF ORIGIN Canary Islands
DATE OF ORIGIN 1800s
FIRST USE Dog fighting
USE TODAY Companion
LIFE EXPECTANCY 9–11 years
OTHER NAME Perro de Presa Canario

WEIGHT RANGE
38–48 kg (84–106 lb)
HEIGHT RANGE
55–65 cm (21½–25½ in)

CATALAN SHEEPDOG

BREED HISTORY Possibly related to the Portuguese Sheepdog and a likely close relative of the long-haired Pyrenean Shepherd, the Catalan Sheepdog's standard, written in 1929, is based upon the conformation of Tac, a male, and Iris, a female.

High-set, pointed ears are covered in long hair

Dark-amber, expressive eyes are set close together

KEY FACTS

COUNTRY OF ORIGIN Spain
DATE OF ORIGIN 1700s
FIRST USE Livestock herding/guarding
USE TODAY Companion
LIFE EXPECTANCY 12–14 years
OTHER NAME Gos d'Atura Catalá
WEIGHT RANGE
17.5–18.5 kg (39–41 lb)
HEIGHT RANGE
46–51 cm (18–20 in)

With its prominent beard and moustache, its lively personality, and its willingness to learn and obey commands, the Catalan Sheepdog is rightly increasing in popularity, both inside and outside Catalonia. The short-coated version of this functioning sheepdog, the Gos d'Atura Cerda (Perro de Pastor or Catalan de Pelo Corto) is now so rare, however, that it faces extinction. Because of its size and adaptability, this breed makes a good household companion, although some individuals, especially males, are quite independent and some lines are prone to hip dysplasia.

Body is covered with long, wavy hair

Oval feet are covered with silky hair

Nose, lips, and hard palate inside mouth are black

FAWN

GRIZZLE

BLACK

RED-BRINDLE

BLACK/TAN

BLACK-BRINDLE

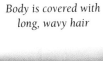

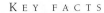

ESTRELA MOUNTAIN DOG

For centuries, this mastiff has herded and defended flocks from wolves, while accompanying shepherds in the Estrela mountains of Portugal. The dense, double coat, particularly of the long-haired variety, provides protection in cold weather. Although it still serves these functions, today this calm, but naturally dominant, dog is also kept as a companion. Outside Portugal, it has received most recognition in Great Britain, where it is often seen at dog shows. Although hip dysplasia can be a problem, this is generally a healthy breed, but one that needs firm handling.

FAWN

RED-BRINDLE

BLACK-BRINDLE

Abundant topcoat is darker than equally thick undercoat

Thick forelimbs are well boned

KEY FACTS

COUNTRY OF ORIGIN Portugal
DATE OF ORIGIN Middle Ages
FIRST USE Livestock guarding
USE TODAY Companion, livestock dog
LIFE EXPECTANCY 11–13 years
OTHER NAMES Cão da Serra da Estrela, Portuguese Sheepdog

WEIGHT RANGE
30–50 kg (66–110 lb)
HEIGHT RANGE
62–72 cm (24½–28½ in)

Oval, medium-sized eyes are set horizontally

BREED HISTORY This most popular of all Portuguese breeds is one of the oldest on the Iberian peninsula. It is descended from ancient Asiatic mastiffs brought to the West, and is related to the Spanish Mastiff. Having suffered from unorthodox cross breeding with the German Shepherd earlier this century, it is now back to a pure form.

PORTUGUESE CATTLE DOG

This breed may be rustic in appearance, but it is no rural innocent. With its unique voice (which progresses from a low growling noise and proceeds to sharp, prolonged barking), substantial size, and natural inclination to threaten first and greet later, the Portuguese Cattle Dog continues to protect sheep and cattle from wolves and other dangerous predators, including humans. Its sentinel behaviour also makes it an excellent watchdog. The breed can be difficult to control and needs experienced training and firm handling.

BREED HISTORY In the region of the town of Castro Laboreiro, between the Peneda and Suajo mountains, this muscular and fearless guardian dog developed from mastiffs and other local dogs.

FAWN   GREY

Medium-sized, almond-shaped eyes have slightly severe expression

RED-BRINDLE   BLACK   BLACK-BRINDLE

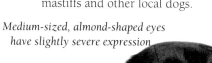

Long, thick tail reaches down to hocks

Heavy, hard, rather dull coat is smooth and abundant

Stout forelegs, with heavy shoulder muscles and dense bone

Large, well-arched toes on round feet, with thick, hard pads

KEY FACTS

COUNTRY OF ORIGIN Portugal
DATE OF ORIGIN 1500s
FIRST USE Cattle guarding/herding
USE TODAY Livestock dog, companion, guarding
LIFE EXPECTANCY 12–13 years
OTHER NAME Cão de Castro Laboreiro

WEIGHT RANGE
23–34 kg
(50–75 lb)
HEIGHT RANGE
51–61 cm (20–24 in)

Medium-sized ears

PORTUGUESE WATCHDOG

YELLOW GREY RED RED-BRINDLE BLACK BLACK-BRINDLE

With the body of a St. Bernard but with a leaner and less rugged head, the Portuguese Watchdog was a favourite of King Don Carlos, who used it as a hunting hound. Faithful to its human family, today it is a dauntless estate and farm guard in Portugal. Because of its fearlessness, attempts have been made to use the breed to control Coyote predation on sheep ranches in the United States, but the dog's naturally aggressive nature and aloof independence have made it less suitable for this purpose than other guardian breeds. A sober, utilitarian farm dog, it works exceedingly well in its assigned role.

Long, broad, and muscular hindquarters give sturdy appearance

High-set tail is well feathered, with curved tip

Strong, muscular, well-developed shoulders surround ample chest

Coat is short to medium in length, and evenly distributed over body

Dewclaws are present on hind feet; sometimes there are double dewclaws

Triangular, rather small ears fold and hang down cheeks

Stout toes are barely arched, with white nails and thick, tough pads

KEY FACTS

COUNTRY OF ORIGIN Portugal
DATE OF ORIGIN Middle Ages
FIRST USE Guarding
USE TODAY Companion, security
LIFE EXPECTANCY 11–13 years
OTHER NAME Rafeiro do Alentejo

WEIGHT RANGE
43–50 kg (95–110 lb)
HEIGHT RANGE
75.5–76.5 cm (30 in)

BREED HISTORY This is an old breed that probably developed in southern Portugal from the Estrela Mountain Dog, the Spanish Mastiff, and local dogs. The largest of all Portuguese breeds, it is still used as a guardian of homes and farms.

PORTUGUESE SHEPHERD DOG

BREED HISTORY This shaggy, all-purpose herder, drover, and guardian dog from the southern plains of Portugal may descend from Briards imported by Count de Castro Guimaraes, which then bred with local mountain dogs, or perhaps the Catalan Sheepdog.

KEY FACTS

COUNTRY OF ORIGIN Portugal
DATE OF ORIGIN 1800s
FIRST USE Livestock herding
USE TODAY Companion, herding
LIFE EXPECTANCY 12–13 years
OTHER NAME Cão da Serra de Aires

WEIGHT RANGE
12–18 kg (26–40 lb)
HEIGHT RANGE
41–56 cm (16–22 in)

Puppy

YELLOW FAWN GREY BROWN BLACK

Moderate-sized ears hang down sides of cheeks

Eyes are dark

For most of this century, the Portuguese Shepherd Dog was the companion of poor shepherds in southern Portugal, but by the 1970s it was almost extinct. Fortunately, the beauty of its coat and its pliant disposition came to the notice of breeders, and today, its appeal to middle-class Portuguese dog owners ensures its survival. An excellent breed, it is very easy to obedience train, good with children and with other dogs, and unlikely to snap or bite unless provoked. Although it is virtually unknown outside its native land, this unkempt-looking canine is a classic dog, worthy of more international acclaim.

Long fur covers firm, symmetrical forelimbs

Solid forelimbs are well covered with dense, slightly harsh hair

Beard gives look of maturity

BRIARD

BREED HISTORY The Briard's ancient origins are unknown, but it was once classified as the goat-haired variety of the Beauceron. It has been suggested that it was developed by crossing that breed with the Barbet. Named after the province of Brie, the watchful Briard has been a shepherd's guardian throughout France.

High-set, short ears covered with copious, long hair

Muzzle is square, rather than round, with black nose

Long, flexible, dry hair, like that of a goat

Long, strong head, with pronounced stop between dome of skull and tip of nose

FAWN   BLACK

Large, calm-looking, horizontally set eyes

A merican soldiers introduced this ruggedly muscular breed to the United States after World War I, but it took 50 years to gain a solid foothold. Today, this is one of France's most popular companion dogs, although it was only in the 1970s that breeders addressed the problem of shyness and nervous aggression in the breed. With careful selection, it is well mannered with its human family, yet retains superb guarding instincts. It is also an excellent herding dog, well insulated by its thick coat against harsh weather conditions.

Prominent, distinctive beard

Broad, deep chest, with ample space for efficient heart and lungs

BEAUCERON

BREED HISTORY Originally from the province of Brie, the Beauceron is closely related to the Briard – both have double dewclaws on their hind legs. In appearance a cross between the Mastiff and the Dobermann, this breed's anatomy is strikingly similar to 2,000-year-old skeletal remains found in eastern France.

Long head, with flat, but slightly domed, skull

Rough, short, dense, close-fitting coat is less than 3 cm (1½ in) long

T his strong-willed, active breed needs firm handling and a great deal of exercise – in return it gives lifelong companionship and protection. Physically uncomplicated, it has an agile, smoothly powerful body. Obedience training can sometimes be difficult, and first meetings with other adult dogs should be carried out under supervision. However, like the Briard, the Beauceron is almost invariably a safe and responsible member of its own family. A reliable working dog, it is also becoming increasingly popular in European show rings.

Horizontally set eyes vary in colour, according to coat

BLACK/ TAN

BLACK

HARLEQUIN

Long, straight forelegs, with round feet and black nails

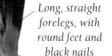

Double dewclaws on hind feet

PICARDY SHEPHERD

This solid, dependable breed has still not recovered from the ravages of World War I. With its population concentrated on the farms of north-eastern France, trench warfare in the Somme reduced it to limited numbers. Since then this lanky herding dog has been intermittently bred by isolated farmers and breeders, never gaining popularity on the French show circuit or abroad. This is unfortunate – the Picardy Shepherd's attributes include a thick, weatherproof coat, and an assertive disposition that responds quickly to obedience training, and it is a reliable and responsive member of its human family. It is also a fine sheep and cattle herder, and a good farm guard.

Erect, high-set ears are quite wide at base

Forehead is slightly vaulted on moderately broad skull

Eyebrows are thick, but do not shield eyes

Coat is harsh and crisp to the touch, and about 5–6 cm (2–2½ in) long all over body

FAWN GREY

BREED HISTORY This is possibly the oldest of all the French shepherds, arriving in Picardy and the Pas de Calais with the Celts in AD 800. This century's European wars pushed the breed to near extinction, and even today it is extremely rare.

KEY FACTS

COUNTRY OF ORIGIN France
DATE OF ORIGIN Middle Ages
FIRST USE Sheep herding/guarding
USE TODAY Herding, companion, guarding
LIFE EXPECTANCY 12–13 years
OTHER NAMES Berger Picard, Berger de Picardie

WEIGHT RANGE
23–32 kg (50–70 lb)
HEIGHT RANGE
55–66 cm
(21½–26 in)

DUTCH SHEEPDOG

Although the Dutch Sheepdog has always been an efficient herding dog, its numbers declined severely early this century due both to the war, and to the large-scale introduction into the Netherlands of the Border Collie. After World War II, Dutch breeders regenerated the breed, and were very successful in eliminating an eye problem (progressive retinal atrophy) that occurred in some lines. However, numbers remain small – only about 250 puppies are born each year. Today, this breed is kept almost solely as a companion.

Skull is hidden under profusion of moustache, beard, topknot, and ear feathering

Harsh, abundant coat has slight wave; coat is not always as wavy

BREED HISTORY Records do not exist concerning this breed's origins. It is a close relative of the now-extinct northern German Schafpudel (Sheep Poodle or Pommern). Both breeds are probably related to the Hungarian Puli, Italian Bergamasco, and Polish Lowland Sheepdog.

Tail reaches down to hocks

Topknot of hair almost completely hides eyes

KEY FACTS

COUNTRY OF ORIGIN The Netherlands
DATE OF ORIGIN Middle Ages/1940s
FIRST USE Sheep herding
USE TODAY Sheep herding, companion
LIFE EXPECTANCY 13–15 years
OTHER NAMES Schapendoes, Dutch Sheep Poodle

WEIGHT RANGE
14.5–15.5 kg (32–34 lb)
HEIGHT RANGE
40–51 cm (16–20 in)

Feet are compact, firm, and well rounded, with white nails

ANY COLOUR

Chest is deep; forelegs are carried apart to avoid squeezing on chest

CZECH WOLFDOG

Thin, short, erect, triangular ears are very mobile

Thick undercoat develops in winter under straight, close topcoat

Eskimo Dogs have benefited from periodic, unplanned introductions of Carpathian Timber Wolf blood and, with that in mind, Czech breeders produced this compact, wolf-like breed. The experiment has not been entirely successful – the Czech Wolfdog needs an extremely firm, patient hand in training. It bonds well to its handler, but not to others, and is not suitable for police work. Some individuals are afraid of strangers. However, the Wolfdog is a lively breed, with a rather pleasant howl (and a less pleasant whine).

Chest is well muscled, roomy, and pear shaped

Belly is taut and tucked up

BREED HISTORY Breeders have always been fascinated by the relationship between the dog and the wolf. In 1955, cross breeding between the German Shepherd Dog and the Carpathian Timber Wolf began, with the intention of improving the German Shepherd's working ability. This resulted in the Czech Wolfdog, which received recognition in 1982.

KEY FACTS

COUNTRY OF ORIGIN Czech and Slovak Republics
DATE OF ORIGIN 1980s
FIRST USE Improving dog stock
USE TODAY Companion
LIFE EXPECTANCY 10–12 years
OTHER NAME Ceskoslovensky Vlcak

WEIGHT RANGE
20–35 kg (44–77 lb)
HEIGHT RANGE
60–75 cm (24–29½ in)

SAARLOOS WOLFHOUND

Head is slightly arched between ears

This uncommon Dutch breed is easier to train, more amenable to urban life, and more responsive than the Czech Wolfdog. This is probably due, in part, to its longer history of selective breeding, but also because the pack-oriented Canadian Timber Wolf, rather than the lone-hunting Carpathian Wolf, has been included in its genetic background. However, this breed manifests a wolf-like wariness and, like its Czech counterpart, can be shy.

Broad, powerful neck

Long legs, with feet turning slightly outwards

BREED HISTORY In 1921, a Dutch breeder, Leendert Saarloos, began a lifelong experiment to improve trainability in the German Shepherd Dog by introducing wolf blood. Although trainability was not improved, this breed was recognized in 1975.

Densely feathered, sable-coloured tail is set low

Coat is harsh and not too long, with dense undercoat

WOLF-GREY

WOLF-BROWN

KEY FACTS

COUNTRY OF ORIGIN The Netherlands
DATE OF ORIGIN 1920s
FIRST USE Improving canine structure
USE TODAY Companion
LIFE EXPECTANCY 10–12 years
OTHER NAME Saarloos Wolf Dog

WEIGHT RANGE
36–41 kg (79–90 lb)
HEIGHT RANGE
60–75 cm (24–29½ in)

DUTCH SHEPHERD DOG

Relatively small ears are stiffly erect

No woolly undercoat on head

Curiously, while the related Belgian shepherds have become well known in the United States and northern Europe, this excellent service dog has not attracted a following outside the Netherlands. Even there its numbers are limited, with only around 400 dogs registered each year. Originally an all-purpose farm guard, drover, cart puller, and livestock dog, this breed is very similar to the Belgian shepherds, but with perhaps more German Shepherd Dog blood in its ancestry. It is a very competent working dog, excellent as a herder, guard, police and security dog, and companion. It is also very successful in field trials. The image of the German Shepherd as the supremely efficient service dog, together with difficulties experienced in defining standards as regards the look of the breed, are reasons for its scarcity.

VARIETY OF COLOURS

Hard, wiry hair, with close, dense undercoat

Wire-haired variety

Short-haired variety

Hard hair on moustache and beard

Rather hard coat, uniform over entire body

Solid, muscular, well-boned legs, with moderate angulation to stifle and hock

BREED HISTORY This breed, in its various coat textures, evolved in the early 1800s in the southern part of the Netherlands, especially the province of Brabant, and in neighbouring Belgium, which was then part of the Netherlands. Division by coat texture only occurred when dog shows began 100 years ago. The breed shares similar origins with the Belgian shepherds and German Shepherd Dog.

Long, rather stiff hair lies close

Neck is profusely covered with shiny, long hair that is neither wavy nor curly

KEY FACTS

COUNTRY OF ORIGIN The Netherlands
DATE OF ORIGIN 1800s
FIRST USE Livestock herding
USE TODAY Companion, security
LIFE EXPECTANCY 12–14 years
OTHER NAME Hollandse Herdershond

WEIGHT RANGE
29.5–30.5 kg (65–67 lb)
HEIGHT RANGE
55–63 cm (22–25 in)

Solid trunk, with deep chest and belly not too drawn up

No dewclaws on relatively small feet, which have well-arched toes, black nails, and black pads

Long-haired variety

Protective hair grows between toes

BERGAMASCO

Fine-textured facial hair covers tapering muzzle

KEY FACTS

COUNTRY OF ORIGIN Italy
DATE OF ORIGIN Antiquity
FIRST USE Livestock guarding
USE TODAY Companion, guarding
LIFE EXPECTANCY 11–13 years
OTHER NAMES Bergamese Shepherd, Cane da Pastore Bergamasco

WEIGHT RANGE
26–38 kg (57–84 lb)
HEIGHT RANGE
56–61 cm
(22–24 in)

BREED HISTORY Two-thousand years ago, Roman writers on agriculture described the ideal sheepdog – not as swift as the hound or as strong as the yard dog, but agile and fearless enough to repel the wolf and follow in pursuit. Today's Bergamasco, named after the Bergamo region of northern Italy, follows that Roman requirement.

Hare-like feet, with lean pads and black nails

Puppy

No "flocking" of hair on puppy's coat

Soft, long hair cords into strong, wavy "flocks"

In looks and temperament, this hardy and adaptable breed is remarkably similar to the Briard. However, while the Briard is popular both in France and abroad, the Bergamasco is relatively unknown, both inside and outside its native land, and has often been close to extinction. An exceptionally efficient worker, its distinctive corded coat evolved to protect it both from the weather and from the flailing hooves of livestock. Affectionate, courageous, and loyal, the Bergamasco makes a superb companion and guard dog, although it is not well suited to life in the city.

MAREMMA SHEEPDOG

This is a classic European flock-guarding dog, probably a close descendant of the great, white Eastern sheepdogs that slowly spread across Europe over 1,000 years ago. The Karabash and Akbash sheepdogs of Turkey, the Kuvac of Slovakia, the Kuvasz and Komondor of Hungary, and the Pyrenean Mountain Dog of France are all part of this migratory chain. The ancestors of the Maremma evolved to become smaller than their fellow herd guardians, while retaining the independence and aloofness of their heritage. Although it is now seen regularly in Great Britain, this breed is still rare in other countries outside Italy. It is strong willed and not easy to obedience train, but makes a superb guard.

Low-set tail is thickly feathered with dense hair

BREED HISTORY Today's Maremma Sheepdog is the descendant of the shorter coated Maremmano Sheepdog and the longer bodied Abruzzese Mountain Dog.

Deep, well-rounded ribcage extends to elbows

Black nose often becomes slightly pink-brown with age

KEY FACTS

COUNTRY OF ORIGIN Italy
DATE OF ORIGIN Antiquity
FIRST USE Flock guarding
USE TODAY Companion, security
LIFE EXPECTANCY 11–13 years
OTHER NAMES Maremma, Pastore Abruzzese, Cane da Pastore Maremmano-Abruzzese

WEIGHT RANGE
30–45 kg (66–100 lb)
HEIGHT RANGE
60–73 cm (23½–28½ in)

Pointed, rather small, V-shaped ears

Very abundant, long, harsh hair has slight wave

ISTRIAN SHEPHERD

Sabre-like tail is of medium length, reaching hocks, and is richly clad in long hair

Head is broad at ear level, narrowing gradually to nose

BREED HISTORY Now increasing in numbers in Slovenia, the Istrian Shepherd is rare elsewhere, although it is occasionally seen at European dog shows. Closely related to the Illyrian Shepherd, the breed has protected flocks and herds in the northern Karst region for centuries.

Light hair creates circles around eyes

KEY FACTS

COUNTRY OF ORIGIN Balkans/Slovenia
DATE OF ORIGIN Middle Ages
FIRST USE Flock guarding
USE TODAY Flock guarding, companion
LIFE EXPECTANCY 12–13 years
OTHER NAMES Krasky Ovcar, Karst Shepherd

WEIGHT RANGE
26–40 kg (58–88 lb)
HEIGHT RANGE
51–61cm (20–24 in)

Jaws are exceptionally strong

Slightly oblique eyes, with frank expression

The changes in the political structure of the Balkans have had a dramatic effect on the dog breeds of the former Yugoslavia. The relative physical and financial security of Slovenia, together with heightened national interest, has lead to a renewed fascination with indigenous breeds of dog. One consequence is that the Istrian Shepherd is undergoing a revival in Slovenia. This is a quietly self-confident breed, with a dense double coat which provides ideal protection in the harsh winter climate where it works.

Large, black nose at tip of black-masked face

Compact, round feet, with well-arched toes

ILLYRIAN SHEEPDOG

BREED HISTORY Thought to be older than the Istrian Shepherd (although not as old a breed as the Greek Shepherd Dog or the Turkish Akbash), this reserved guardian exists in sustainable numbers in Albania and Macedonia. First recognized as a distinct breed in 1930, the Illyrian Shepherd has recently been exported to the United States to control Coyotes.

Tail is slightly curved in repose

KEY FACTS

COUNTRY OF ORIGIN Balkans/Macedonia
DATE OF ORIGIN Middle Ages
FIRST USE Sheep herding
USE TODAY Herding, guarding
LIFE EXPECTANCY 11–13 years
OTHER NAMES Sarplanina, Sar Planina, Charplaninatz

WEIGHT RANGE
25–37 kg
(55–80 lb)
HEIGHT RANGE
56–61 cm (22–24 in)

WHITE	GREY	TAN	BLACK

Almond-shaped, dark eyes, with melancholy expression

Forearm is well boned, well muscled, and almost vertical

Tip of nose is quite large, but not protuding

Although turmoil in Bosnia has reduced this breed's population in its previous heartland, since 1975 successful exports have been carried out to the United States and Canada, and this is where its future security rests. An undemonstrative breed, the Illyrian Shepherd has an independent personality. However, it takes its work seriously – when on sheep-guarding duty it will investigate anything that catches its eye, and has no hesitation in confronting adversaries larger than itself.

Coat is 10 cm (4 in) long, dense, and evenly distributed

ARGENTINEAN MASTIFF

BREED HISTORY One of the few breeds developed in South America, the Argentinean Mastiff is the result of a breeding programme undertaken in the 1920s by an Argentinean breeder, Dr. Antonio Nores Martinez, to produce a puma and jaguar hunter.

Skull is massive; jaws are strong and tenacious

Ears are surgically amputated only to heighten aggressive look of dog

This imperious and impressive breed was initially bred to hunt in packs. Using an old type of Spanish fighting dog, the Spanish Mastiff, Great Dane, an old-style bull terrier, bulldog, and Boxer, Dr. Martinez created a bullish and fearless hunter with great stamina and a light coat capable of deflecting, rather than absorbing, heat. The breed instantly appealed to people who organize and enjoy dog fights, an activity still popular in many parts of South America and elsewhere. Argentina's first native pure-bred dog, this white mastiff needs early socialization with other animals; it also requires early obedience training and should be given ample exercise.

Chest is fairly narrow

Coat is short, glossy, thick, smooth, and always white

KEY FACTS

COUNTRY OF ORIGIN Argentina
DATE OF ORIGIN 1920s
FIRST USE Game hunting, dog fighting
USE TODAY Companion
LIFE EXPECTANCY 11–12 years
OTHER NAME Dogo Argentino

WEIGHT RANGE
36–45 kg (80–100 lb)
HEIGHT RANGE
61–69 cm (24–27 in)

BRAZILIAN MASTIFF

BREED HISTORY One of Brazil's two native breeds (the other one being the rare Brazilian Tracker), this powerful mastiff was developed from Spanish and Portuguese mastiffs and Bloodhounds in order to track and control livestock and large game.

Massive and daunting in appearance, the Brazilian Mastiff is a bold breed, amenable with its human family but often wary of strangers. Its Bloodhound ancestry is apparent in its long muzzle, pendulous skin, and superb tracking ability. When it finds its quarry it does not attack, but rather holds it at bay until the hunter arrives. This unusual ability earned it a superb reputation in the days of Brazilian slavery, when it was able to return hapless fugitives unharmed to their slave masters. The breed's presence and tracking ability has found it new homes in both North America and Europe. However, due to its size and potential for aggression, it is banned from some countries.

Strong, straight back rises gently towards hindquarters

Coat is short, dense, smooth, and soft

Extraordinarily thick neck, with dewlap

VARIETY OF COLOURS

Heavy, pendulous upper lips have typical mastiff appearance

KEY FACTS

COUNTRY OF ORIGIN Brazil
DATE OF ORIGIN 1800s
FIRST USE Tracking, large-game hunting
USE TODAY Companion, security
LIFE EXPECTANCY 10–12 years
OTHER NAMES Fila Brasileiro, Cão de Fila

WEIGHT RANGE
41–50 kg (90–110 lb)
HEIGHT RANGE
61–76 cm (24–30 in)

SPANISH MASTIFF

FAWN   RED   BLACK/WHITE   RED-BRINDLE   BLACK-BRINDLE

Coat is fine, thick, and soft to the touch

Skull is broad and slightly rounded

Eyes are surrounded by pendulous lower lids

Lower lips are particularly full

Upper part of leg is well muscled, making almost a right angle with body

Short feet are set firmly on ground, and have neatly shaped toes

KEY FACTS

COUNTRY OF ORIGIN Spain
DATE OF ORIGIN Antiquity
FIRST USE Livestock guarding
USE TODAY Companion, security
LIFE EXPECTANCY 10–11 years
OTHER NAMES Mastin Español, Mastin de la Mancha, Mastin de Extremadura

WEIGHT RANGE
55–70 kg (121–154 lb)
HEIGHT RANGE
72–82 cm (28–32 in)

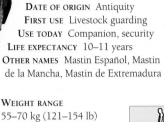

  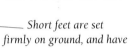

O ne of the dog world's truly great droolers, this old breed still guards sheep, as it has done for centuries. The Spanish Shepherd's Association, Mesta, records how this bulky breed has been an efficient protector from wolves since at least the 1400s. Today, some individuals are kept as companions – the Spanish Mastiff does not need a great deal of exercise and can be taken out on a lead; however, its sheer size precludes it from being a popular pet. It is a reasonably obedient guard, but it has a tendency to snap, and males can be troublesome with other dogs.

BREED HISTORY This flock guard's origins are unknown but, like the other mastiffs of the Iberian peninsula, it probably descends from dogs brought to Spain by Phoenicians and Greeks about 2,000 years ago. It is popular in Spain as a guard of both livestock and the home.

NEAPOLITAN MASTIFF

GREY   BLUE   RED-BRINDLE   BLACK-BRINDLE

BROWN   BLACK

Thick, firm, heavy upper lips

Dense, fine, short, smooth hair covers body

Withers rise slightly above back line

Very well-developed muscles cover deep chest

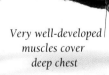 

T he Roman writer Columella's description of the perfect house guard could apply to this ponderous breed, which was saved from oblivion less than 50 years ago by Piero Scanziani, an enthusiastic breeder. A superb drooler, the Neapolitan Mastiff needs early socialization and obedience training, and males can be dominant. It does not demand frequent exercise, but its messy eating manners and sheer size make it a difficult dog to keep inside a home. This breed is best in the hands of experienced dog handlers.

BREED HISTORY Present in Campania, in central Italy, since ancient times, but not exhibited until 1947, the Neapolitan Mastiff probably descends from Roman fighting, war, and circus mastiffs. These reached Rome via Greece, transported there from Asia by Alexander the Great.

Thigh muscles are long and broad

Ears are surgically removed due only to demands of fashion

KEY FACTS

COUNTRY OF ORIGIN Italy
DATE OF ORIGIN Antiquity
FIRST USE Livestock guarding, dog fighting
USE TODAY Companion, security
LIFE EXPECTANCY 10–11 years
OTHER NAME Mastino Napoletano

WEIGHT RANGE
50–68 kg (110–150 lb)
HEIGHT RANGE
65–75 cm (26–29 in)

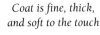 

BULLDOG

BREED HISTORY When bull baiting became illegal in Great Britain in the 1830s, this ferociously tenacious breed was in danger of extinction. However, Bill George, a breeder, transformed the Bulldog into its present form, reducing its aggressive nature.

Few breeds have altered as radically in form, function, and personality as the Bulldog. The word "bulldog" was in use in the 1600s, for the breed that was a cross between mastiff guard dogs used in bear baiting, and tenacious terriers used in game hunting. Strong and resolute, the Bulldog was an ideal pit dog, ruthlessly hanging onto the bull, regardless of the injuries it suffered. Today's gentle dog has been constructed solely for the show ring, which has caused a number of health problems. This is a great pity, since the breed has a delightful personality and makes an engaging companion.

Eyes and nose are very close together

Eyes are very wide set

Flews hang thickly over lower jaws

KEY FACTS

COUNTRY OF ORIGIN Great Britain
DATE OF ORIGIN 1800s
FIRST USE Bull baiting
USE TODAY Companion
LIFE EXPECTANCY 9–11 years
OTHER NAME English Bulldog

WEIGHT RANGE
23–25 kg (50–55 lb)
HEIGHT RANGE
31–36 cm (12–14 in)

Thick and muscular forelegs are set very wide apart

Thickly skinned feet turn out slightly

VARIETY OF COLOURS

Fine-textured, short, close coat feels reasonably soft

BULLMASTIFF

Dark, medium-sized eyes separated by distinct furrow

In theory, the Bullmastiff should be one of the world's most popular guard dogs. Its speed, strength, and endurance were developed so that it could overtake and capture intruders without mauling or killing them. Handsome and powerful, it has spread throughout all the continents of the world, but it has never attained the popularity of its German equivalent, the Rottweiler. The reason for this is that the Bullmastiff can be a stubborn breed, resistant to obedience training, and overly protective of its human family.

Small, high-set, V-shaped ears give square appearance to head

Large, but compact, cat-like feet, with rounded toes

Tail is strong at root

Wide, deep chest is covered with short, hard, flat hair

BREED HISTORY The foundation stock of the Bullmastiff is 60 per cent English Mastiff and 40 per cent Bulldog. It was produced to act as a gamekeeper's assistant, with the ability to chase and immobilize poachers on estates.

Muscular, thick neck blends into chest

Solid cheeks between eyes and nose

Powerful forelegs are thick and straight

KEY FACTS

COUNTRY OF ORIGIN Great Britain
DATE OF ORIGIN 1800s
FIRST USE Guarding
USE TODAY Companion, guarding
LIFE EXPECTANCY 10–12 years

WEIGHT RANGE
41–59 kg (90–130 lb)
HEIGHT RANGE
64–69 cm (25–27 in)

FAWN   RED-BRINDLE   RED   BLACK-BRINDLE

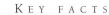

MASTIFF

BREED HISTORY The Mastiff existed in Great Britain 2,000 years ago, and was exported to Rome as a military and fighting dog. It may have arrived from Asia via Mediterranean and Phoenician traders, or with other traders across the Urals and Northern Europe.

Dark eyes are set well apart, with distinct, but not abrupt, stop

Small, thick ears are set very high on head

Large, round feet, with well-arched toes and black nails

Short, close, but not too fine topcoat covers protective winter undercoat

Tail is wide at root and tapers to tip

Throughout its long history, the Mastiff has contributed to the development of a number of dog breeds, including the Bullmastiff. The name probably evolved from the Anglo-Saxon word *masty*, meaning powerful – English court documents from 1590 record the purchase of "one masty dogge". The Mastiff is now a rare sight, both in its home country and abroad. One of the largest dogs in the world, it requires ample space to live in and large quantities of food. It is generally easygoing, but can be very protective of its owners and must be handled sensibly, since it is exceptionally powerful and can be difficult to control.

Forelegs are straight, densely boned, and set firmly apart

APRICOT-
FAWN

SILVER-
FAWN

DARK-
FAWN-
BRINDLE

FRENCH MASTIFF

Oval eyes, set wide apart, have prominent upper ridges

No feathering on deeply set, thick tail

Skull is broad and short, with abrupt stop

BREED HISTORY For centuries, the Bordeaux region of France was ruled by English kings. The large guard dogs of that region were almost certainly crossed with the English Mastiff, together with similar dogs from Spain, resulting in this powerful, and at one time ferocious, mastiff.

Small, hanging ears are slightly rounded at base

GOLDEN, MAHOGANY
FAWN

More similar to the recently developed Bullmastiff than to the ancient English Mastiff, this very old breed was originally used for boar and bear hunting in southern France, and then for cattle droving. Because of its fearlessness, it was also used in the animal-baiting arena and the dog-fight ring. It was not until the breed appeared in an American film in 1989 with Tom Hanks that it attained any recognition outside France. Unlike the sloppy star of *Turner and Hooch*, the French Mastiff possesses formidable traits, such as relentless strength, wariness of strangers, and an inclination to intimidate unknown people.

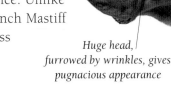

Huge head, furrowed by wrinkles, gives pugnacious appearance

BOXER

Dark mask, confined to muzzle, is in distinct relief to head colour

Tails were traditionally docked

Well-muscled, powerful loins allow for freedom of movement and an elegant stride

KEY FACTS

COUNTRY OF ORIGIN Germany
DATE OF ORIGIN 1850s
FIRST USE Guarding, bull baiting
USE TODAY Companion
LIFE EXPECTANCY 12 years

WEIGHT RANGE
25–32 kg (55–70 lb)
HEIGHT RANGE
53–63 cm (21–25 in)

Nose is black, and delightfully turned up

Top of skull is slightly arched

Long thighs are broad, curved, and very powerful

Well-ribbed, deep chest allows space for lung expansion

Legs are straight, strong, and well boned

Upper lip is thick and padded

Slight drooping of lower lip

BREED HISTORY The Boxer's primary ancestor, the old Bullenbeisser, was used in Germany and the Netherlands for hunting boars and deer. Today's Boxer was developed by crossing Danziger and Brabanter Bullenbeissers with other Bavarian and foreign breeds.

The boisterous and self-confident Boxer is one of the great successes of the high-quality "designer" dog breeding that took place in Germany 100 years ago. Today, although the size of Boxers varies from country to country, its personality remains the same – active, positive, strong, and fun loving. The Boxer is in many ways an ideal family dog, but due to its lifelong puppylike behaviour, fast reaction time, and relatively large size, it can create unintentional havoc. The breed's muscular and intimidating appearance makes it an excellent house protector; at the same time, it is as gentle as a lamb with children.

Wrinkled brow gives impression of intense concentration

Short, shiny, smooth hair covers impressive chest reaching down to elbows

FAWN   BRINDLE

Large, compact feet, with strong toes

GREAT DANE

FAWN   BLACK   BLUE   BRINDLE   HARLEQUIN

The dignified but affectionate Great Dane is the national dog of Germany. Its origins can almost certainly be traced to the dogs brought to Europe by the Alans, a Scythian tribe from what is now Asian Russia. These fighting mastiffs were probably crossed with greyhounds, producing the elegant, distinctive, and gentle breed of today. The sheer size of the Great Dane can cause medical problems, including a greater-than-average incidence of hip and elbow arthritis, and bone tumours.

No loose skin on elegant neck

Long, tapering tail is prone to injuries at tip

KEY FACTS

COUNTRY OF ORIGIN Germany
DATE OF ORIGIN Middle Ages/1800s
FIRST USE War dog, large-mammal hunting
USE TODAY Companion, guarding
LIFE EXPECTANCY 10 years
OTHER NAME German Mastiff

WEIGHT RANGE
46–54 kg (100–120 lb)
HEIGHT RANGE
71–76 cm (28–30 in)

Fairly deep-set, medium-sized eyes

Short, dense coat covers muscular thighs

BREED HISTORY
The Great Dane traces its origins back to the massive Alaunt, mentioned by Chaucer in the 1200s.

Wide, blunt, black nose, with characteristic ridge

Thick, firm lips hang symmetrically

Very deep, V-shaped chest, with well-sprung ribs

ROTTWEILER

High, wide-set ears are proportionately rather small

Black nose, with relatively large nostrils

Hind legs longer than front legs

Powerful in body and jaws, the Rottweiler can offer formidable protection. Today, this impressively handsome dog, the descendant of ancient boar hunters, is popular throughout the world, as both a family dog and a guard dog. Easy to obedience train, it can show its temper; breeders, notably in Scandinavia, have reduced this trait.

Slightly arched neck is strong, round, and very well muscled

Legs have plenty of thick bone

Strong jaws and excellent teeth

Tail amputated for fashion only

BREED HISTORY
The Rottweiler was bred in Rottweil, south Germany, in the 1800s, as a distinct droving and guard dog.

Coarse, flat topcoat

Thigh is well muscled at top and more sinewy at bottom

KEY FACTS

COUNTRY OF ORIGIN Germany
DATE OF ORIGIN 1820s
FIRST USE Cattle/guard dog
USE TODAY Companion, police dog, guarding
LIFE EXPECTANCY 11–12 years

WEIGHT RANGE
41–50 kg (90–110 lb)
HEIGHT RANGE
58–69 cm (23–27 in)

SHAR PEI

BREED HISTORY A long-time resident of China's southern province of Guangdong, the Shar Pei appears to be descended from mastiff and spitz-type dogs. It is a fairly close relative of the Chow Chow. Driven almost to extinction by China's prohibition of dogs on the mainland, the breed was rescued by Matgo Law, a Hong Kong breeder.

Muzzle is well padded, causing bulge at base of nose

Head is large in relation to body size

CREAM

FAWN

RED

BLACK

Small ears hang close to cheeks

KEY FACTS

COUNTRY OF ORIGIN China
DATE OF ORIGIN 1500s
FIRST USE Dog fighting, herding, hunting
USE TODAY Companion
LIFE EXPECTANCY 11–12 years
OTHER NAME Chinese Fighting Dog

WEIGHT RANGE
16–20 kg (35–45 lb)
HEIGHT RANGE
46–51 cm (18–20 in)

N o other breed in the dog world looks quite like a Shar Pei. Its Chinese standards eloquently describe its conformation – clam-shell ears, butterfly nose, melon-shaped head, grandmotherly face, water-buffalo neck, horse's buttocks, and dragon's legs. The first Shar Peis exported from Hong Kong and bred in the United States had severe eye problems, necessitating repeated surgery. Successive breeding has diminished these conditions, but it has not reduced the very high incidence of skin problems. The Shar Pei can occasionally be aggressive, and is suited to people who are not allergic to dogs, as well as being willing to shampoo their dogs frequently.

Prickly coat is oversized; hair stands on end

Sloping shoulders above well-boned legs

TOSA INU

D og fighting has, at one time or another, held a universal appeal in many parts of the world. Japanese dog-fighting rules in the last century demanded that dogs fight silently, without cowering, and the Tosa fought by these rules – relentlessly and silently. Although dog fighting is now illegal in Europe, North America, and Japan, clandestine pit fights continue in remote rural regions of Japan, where the Tosa, at 30–40 kg (66–88 lb) – smaller than those bred in the West – is still used for fighting. This can be a formidable breed; males in particular need excellent socialization and early training. Because of its size and background, the Tosa is banned from many countries.

Ears are small, with surprisingly thin leather

KEY FACTS

COUNTRY OF ORIGIN Japan
DATE OF ORIGIN 1800s
FIRST USE Dog fighting
USE TODAY Companion
LIFE EXPECTANCY 11–12 years
OTHER NAMES Tosa Fighting Dog, Japanese Fighting Dog

WEIGHT RANGE
89.5–90.5 kg (197–200 lb)
HEIGHT RANGE
62–65 cm (24½–25½ in)

Deep, broad chest has exceptional spring to ribs

Exceptionally strong neck generally has dewlap

Broad skull, with medium-length muzzle

Reddish-fawn, short, dense coat is uniform over whole body

FAWN

RED

DULL-BLACK

   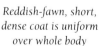

BREED HISTORY Initially bred in Japan's Kochi Prefecture, from crosses between native Shikoku fighting dogs and imported mastiffs, Great Danes, bulldogs, and bull terriers, this breed was once called the Japanese Mastiff.

Thighs are well muscled and hocks only slightly bent

TIBETAN KYI APSO

Ears are fairly long

Once used by Tibetan nomads to guard their sheep and their tents, the Kyi Apso is descended from dogs that lived in the remote, high-plateau region of Mount Kailish. Its heavy double coat provides excellent insulation against some of the harshest climatic elements that dogs face anywhere. Similar to the Tibetan Mastiff, it differs in coat quality and in the shape of its ears and tail. An attractive and engaging family dog, this alert, self-reliant breed retains its superb guarding abilities.

BREED HISTORY Arriving only recently in the United States and Canada in quite small numbers, the Tibetan Kyi Apso was developed for a functional purpose – to guard the homes and herds of the Tibetans living high on the Tibetan Plateau. Recognized as a distinct breed, the Kyi has an active breed club.

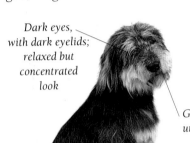

Well-feathered tail has full curl

Dark eyes, with dark eyelids; relaxed but concentrated look

Excellent growth of beard

Good topcoat and undercoat on face

Longer legs than a Tibetan Mastiff's

KEY FACTS

COUNTRY OF ORIGIN Tibet
DATE OF ORIGIN Antiquity
FIRST USE Guarding
USE TODAY Companion, guarding
LIFE EXPECTANCY 12 years
OTHER NAME Bearded Tibetan Mastiff

WEIGHT RANGE
32–41 kg (70–90 lb)
HEIGHT RANGE
63.5–71 cm (25–28 in)

TIBETAN MASTIFF

The Tibetan Mastiff once protected livestock in the Himalayas and Tibet, and is now a European-bred show dog, still uncommon but established throughout Europe. Large boned and big headed, this massive dog has provided the root stock for the mountain, livestock, and fighting dogs of Europe, the Americas, and even Japan. Easygoing and affably aloof, the Tibetan Mastiff is content to be one of life's observers, although it will not hesitate to defend what it feels to be its home and territory.

KEY FACTS

COUNTRY OF ORIGIN Tibet
DATE OF ORIGIN Antiquity
FIRST USE Livestock guarding
USE TODAY Companion, guarding
LIFE EXPECTANCY 11 years
OTHER NAME Do-Khyi

WEIGHT RANGE
64–82 kg (140–180 lb)
HEIGHT RANGE
61–71 cm (24–28 in)

Broad, massive head, with smooth face

Well-ribbed body supports heavy-boned legs

BREED HISTORY Rescued from extinction by British breeders in the last century, this is the parent breed of most European mastiffs. Orginally used to flock herds and to guard the home, the Tibetan Mastiff was prized for both its courage and its impressive size.

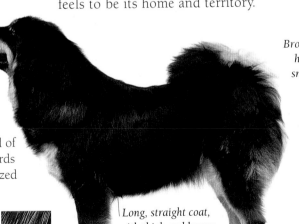

Long, straight coat, with thick and heavy undercoat

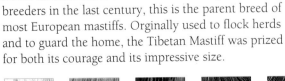

GREY   GOLD   BLACK/TAN   BROWN   BLACK

HOVAWART

Well-proportioned, triangular ears are set high and hang flat to cheeks

Strong, broad head, with convex forehead progressing to straight muzzle

The Hovawart is a classic example of the diligence of German dog breeding 100 years ago. In an attempt to recreate the great estate guarding dog of the Middle Ages, a group of dedicated breeders used selected farm dogs acquired in the Black Forest and Hartz mountain regions of Germany, and perhaps the Hungarian Kuvasz, German Shepherd, and Newfoundland, to produce this elegant worker, first recognized in 1936. The Hovawart is a reserved but pleasant family dog, although some strains are prone to fear biting, and others may be rather timid. It is, however, easy to obedience train and gets on well with other dogs and children.

Straight, strong, well-fringed forelegs, with moderate-sized feet

Long, slightly wavy, dense topcoat, with equally dense undercoat

Well-feathered tail is carried low and extends just below hock

BREED HISTORY The "Hofwarth", an estate guard dog, is first mentioned in 1220, in Eike von Repgow's *Sachsenspiegel*. Records from the 1400s illustrate and describe this breed tracking robbers. Today's Hovawart is a 20th-century re-creation of this ancient guarding dog.

KEY FACTS

COUNTRY OF ORIGIN Germany
DATE OF ORIGIN Middle Ages/1900s
FIRST USE Livestock/home guarding
USE TODAY Companion, guarding
LIFE EXPECTANCY 12–14 years

WEIGHT RANGE
25–41 kg (55–90 lb)
HEIGHT RANGE
58–70 cm (23–28 in)

LEONBERGER

Medium-sized, brown eyes, with friendly expression

YELLOW, GOLD RED-BROWN

KEY FACTS

COUNTRY OF ORIGIN Germany
DATE OF ORIGIN 1800s
FIRST USE Companion
USE TODAY Companion
LIFE EXPECTANCY 11 years

WEIGHT RANGE
34–50 kg (75–110 lb)
HEIGHT RANGE
65–80 cm (26–31½ in)

BREED HISTORY Alderman Heinrich Essig, wishing to produce a dog resembling the lion on the Imperial Coat of Arms of the Town Hall of Leonberg, Germany, used the Landseer, Newfoundland, St. Bernard, and Pyrenean Mountain Dog to create this distinguished breed.

Bushy tail is carried down, or at "half mast"

Forelegs are fairly wide set, with well-articulated joints

Smooth, dense coat has slight wave, but does not obscure body shape

Ears are as wide as they are long

This genial giant almost became extinct during World War II, but in the last 20 years has gained a good foothold, both in its home country, and in Great Britain and North America. When the Leonberger was first exhibited, it was dismissed as a mere cross of

Large, round feet, with webbed toes, facilitate swimming

several breeds, which is exactly what it is. However, the breed is a strikingly handsome dog. An inveterate swimmer, it is willing to dog paddle in the coldest weather. Its great size makes it rather unsuitable for urban living. As with many breeds that have been "recreated", hip dysplasia can be a concern to some breeders.

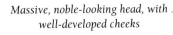

LANDSEER

Massive, noble-looking head, with well-developed cheeks

Neck is somewhat oval, muscular, and thick

BREED HISTORY Before the Newfoundland's breed standard was written, it occurred in spotted as well as solid colours. Black and brown eventually became the accepted colours, but a group of breeders continued to produce taller, lighter black and whites, which eventually resulted in the Landseer.

Long, smooth, soft coat is not as dense as a Newfoundland's

At rest, tail is carried down with slight curve

Almond-shaped rims surround moderately deep-set, brown eyes

It is not certain how dogs originally arrived in Newfoundland, but by the time Basque and Portuguese fishermen transported their water dogs and mastiffs to the world's largest fishing banks, dogs were living there with the indigenous natives. Out of this canine soup came the Greater St. John's Dog, the leaner precursor of the Newfoundland and Landseer. In North America and Great Britain, the Landseer is classified as a Newfoundland colour variation. Elsewhere, this gentle bundle of fun is classified separately. Named after the artist Sir Edwin Landseer, it is shown in his portrait, *A Distinguished Member of the Royal Humane Society*.

Large feet have toes webbed almost to tips

ST. BERNARD

Broad, powerful tail curls slightly at tip

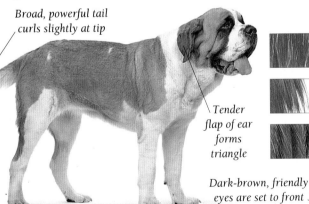

Tender flap of ear forms triangle

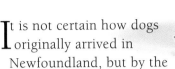

ORANGE

RED-BRINDLE

BROWN-BRINDLE

BREED HISTORY Descended from alpine mastiffs first brought to Switzerland with the passing Roman Army, the St. Bernard was once an aggressive, short-coated breed. At one time it was virtually extinct, but it was revitalized, possibly with the use of both Newfoundland and Great Dane blood. The breed's name came into general use in 1865.

Dark-brown, friendly eyes are set to front

Whether the St. Bernard ever actually rescued snowbound alpine travellers is debatable, but that image is irreversibly established. The Benardine Hospice has kept this kindly breed since the 1660s – Bernardine monks used it for draught work, and boasted to potential purchasers of its hauling abilities. It was also used to make trails through fresh snow. Today's benevolent hulk is an impressively muscular giant, whose mammoth size makes it unsuitable for most forms of indoor living.

Flews of lower jaw hang very slightly

Topcoat and undercoat are dense

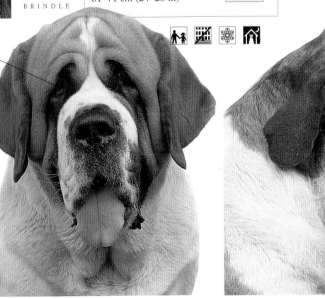

NEWFOUNDLAND

BROWN   BLACK

Broad and massive head, with short, square, clean-cut muzzle

Topcoat is flat, dense, somewhat coarse, and oily

Small, dark, rather deep-set eyes

One of the friendliest of all breeds, the Newfoundland was originally used in cod fisheries to pull nets ashore, and to pull boats. Today, teams of Newfoundlands are used in France to assist the emergency services in sea rescue. Land-based tests include draught work, hauling carts and backing them up, and manoeuvering through an obstacle course. If this benign, happy breed has a behavioural drawback, it is its inclination to rescue anyone from the water, regardless of their desire or need to be rescued. Although a little prone to drooling saliva, it is a benevolent giant and a loyal friend.

Feet are large and well shaped, with broadly webbed toes

Fairly thick tail is well covered in hair

BREED HISTORY Descended from the now-extinct Greater St. John's Dog, this large, water-loving breed has been bred to its present standard for over 100 years. Native North American, Viking, and Iberian breeds may be included in its background.

KEY FACTS

COUNTRY OF ORIGIN Canada
DATE OF ORIGIN 1700s
FIRST USE Helping fishermen
USE TODAY Companion, rescue
LIFE EXPECTANCY 11 years

WEIGHT RANGE
50–68 kg (110–150 lb)
HEIGHT RANGE
66–71 cm (26–28 in)

PYRENEAN SHEEPDOG

BREED HISTORY A slight, small relative of the Catalan Sheepdog, the Pyrenean exists in long-haired, goat-haired, and smooth-haired forms. An agile, durable breed, it evolved in the Pyrenean district between Lourdes and Gavarnie, to suit the needs of mountain shepherds.

FAWN   GREY   RED-BRINDLE   BLUE   BLACK-BRINDLE

Black-rimmed, expressive, dark-brown eyes

Long hair on head and cheeks is brushed backwards

Coat is short and fine on face

Long-haired variety

KEY FACTS

COUNTRY OF ORIGIN France
DATE OF ORIGIN 1700s
FIRST USE Sheep herding/guarding
USE TODAY Companion, herding, guarding
LIFE EXPECTANCY 12 years
OTHER NAMES Labrit, Berger des Pyrénées

WEIGHT RANGE
8–15 kg (18–33 lb)
HEIGHT RANGE
38–56 cm (15–22 in)

This is a lively breed, built for speed, endurance, and an active life. Its three different coat types are the strongest indication that it has been bred to work in specific climates, not to meet show specifications. In its mountainous home, it once worked in tandem with the Pyrenean Mountain Dog, herding and droving while the Mountain Dog guarded the flock from mountain wolves. The coat of the long-haired variety gives excellent weatherproofing, even in harsh winters. The breed's relatively small size and trainability make it a good household companion.

Smooth-haired variety

Lean, sinewy forequarters carry no needless weight

PYRENEAN MOUNTAIN DOG

BREED HISTORY One of the great, white guarding mastiffs that spread across Europe, this magnificent breed is probably related to the Italian Maremma, Hungarian Kuvasz, Slovakian Kuvac, and Turkish Karabash. It thrived principally in Andorra before it was "discovered" early in the 20th century.

The first Pyreneans to be kept as household pets had rather assertive, warrior-like personalities. In the last 20 years, breeders have been very successful in diminishing this characteristic, while at the same time retaining other, attractive qualities, such as patience, nobility, and courage. This dog will, however, still go into a defence mode if its territory is invaded. At the beginning of this century, the breed was near extinction, but today it is firmly established in Great Britain, North America, and particularly France. Its great size makes it unsuitable for urban environments, unless there is open space nearby.

Small, triangular ears are set at eye level, hanging against head

Small, obliquely set, amber eyes have serene expression

Paws are rather small and compact

Topcoat consists of abundant, flat, long, white hair

Hair on forelimbs forms "culottes" of woolly feathering

KEY FACTS

COUNTRY OF ORIGIN France
DATE OF ORIGIN Antiquity
FIRST USE Sheep guarding
USE TODAY Companion, guarding
LIFE EXPECTANCY 11–12 years
OTHER NAMES Great Pyrénées, Chien de Montagne des Pyrénées

WEIGHT RANGE
45–60 kg (99–132 lb)
HEIGHT RANGE
65–81 cm (26–32 in)

PYRENEAN MASTIFF

BREED HISTORY The trading Phoenicians acquired mastiffs in Assyria and Sumeria. They sold these in Spain, and they were bred as working dogs. The Pyrenean Mastiff is much like a cross between the Spanish Mastiff and the Pyrenean Mountain Dog. All trace their beginnings to the great Asiatic mastiffs.

Large, long, strong head, with slightly rounded skull

Supple, strong neck, with loose skin and hanging dewlaps

For centuries, every spring shepherds used to move their large flocks from the planes below the Pyrenees to graze up in the lush, high, mountain valleys. This breed assisted in moving and protecting these flocks, with four or five dogs working a flock of up to a thousand sheep. The mastiff guarded against wolf predation and, to protect its neck, each dog wore a *carlanca* – a spiked collar. This robust dog, with its powerful neck and symmetrical face colouring, was recognized as a distinct breed in the latter part of the last century. It makes a reliable, obedient, and protective companion.

WHITE/ BLACK

WHITE/ FAWN, WHITE/ ORANGE

KEY FACTS

COUNTRY OF ORIGIN Spain
DATE OF ORIGIN Antiquity
FIRST USE Sheep guarding
USE TODAY Companion, guarding
LIFE EXPECTANCY 11–12 years
OTHER NAMES Mastin del Pirineo, Mastin d'Aragon

WEIGHT RANGE
55–75 kg (121–165 lb)
HEIGHT RANGE
71–80 cm (28–31 in)

Thick, dense, rough coat is slightly longer on throat and neck

Forefeet are not very large or long; toes are closed and well arched

POLISH LOWLAND SHEEPDOG

BREED HISTORY It is likely that this medium-sized, robust sheepdog evolved from ancient, corded herding dogs from the Hungarian plains, which were bred with other small, long-coated mountain herders. The ravages of World War II very nearly led to the breed's extinction.

Breed aficionados consider the Polish Lowland Sheepdog to be an important link between ancient, corded Asian herding dogs, brought to Europe over 1,000 years ago, and more recent, shaggy herders, such as the Scottish Bearded Collie and Dutch Schapendoes. This breed was revived by diligent Polish breeders after World War II. Popular in Poland and elsewhere, it is generally kept as a household companion, although it remains an excellent herder.

Back is level and fairly broad

Loins are well muscled and broad

Copious hair on forehead, cheeks, and chin

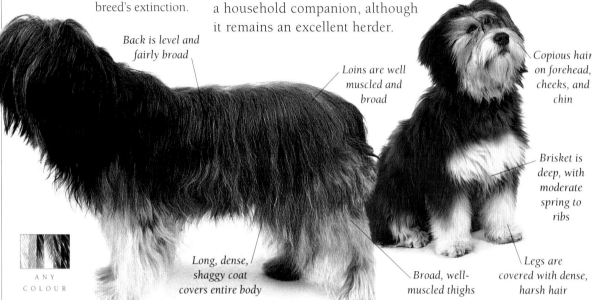

ANY COLOUR

Long, dense, shaggy coat covers entire body

Broad, well-muscled thighs

Brisket is deep, with moderate spring to ribs

Legs are covered with dense, harsh hair

TATRA MOUNTAIN SHEEPDOG

Heavily muscled, with a magnificent coat that provides protection against the harshest weather, the Tatra is a classic, herd-guarding mountain dog. Although it has been used to pull carts, and both Canadians and Americans have even tried to train it for police and military work, it remains an alert but aloof guardian whose function is to live with its flock, travel with it, and even be shorn when the flock is shorn. When danger arises from a potential predator, be it a wolf or a human, this breed offers formidable protection. Independent by nature, it makes an affable companion.

BREED HISTORY A close relative of the Hungarian Kuvasz and Slovakian Kuvac, and a probable relative of the other great mountain sheepdogs of Europe, such as the Italian Bergamasco, this guardian descends from great Asian mastiffs brought to Europe over 1,000 years ago.

Dark-black nose contrasts with almost snow-white face

Well-proportioned back is appropriately long for leg length and weight

Heavy-boned, densely muscled legs

Tail is only moderately long

Thick, dense coat is creamy white in colour

Well-muscled neck covered with thick skin

CENTRAL ASIAN SHEEPDOG

From the Ural mountains of Russia, east to Siberia, and throughout the Central Asian Republics of Turkmenistan, Uzbekistan, Kirgizia, Tadzhikistan, and Kazakstan, this independent and aloof breed has protected nomadic herdsmen and their flocks for centuries. Similar dogs may have accompanied the Mongols when they invaded eastern and central Europe, and were probably the source of Europe's herd-protecting sheepdogs. This breed is seldom seen outside the Central Asian Republics; in Russia it is in decline, losing favour to the larger Caucasian Sheepdog. The Central Asian Sheepdog does not make a suitable companion.

BREED HISTORY A likely descendant of Asian mastiffs, this fearless and bold herder has been used as a guardian of flocks in Central Asia for hundreds, perhaps thousands of years. It is a close relative of the larger, and now more common, Caucasian Sheepdog. Its coat occurs in two varieties – long and short haired.

Strong, moderately long, broad back

Long-haired variety

Dense topcoat, with dense, woolly undercoat

Muzzle is long

Skin on face is thick and may form wrinkles

Skin on neck is protective

Thighs are powerful

Lopped ears are set at eye level

Muzzle is broad and powerful, leading to defined stop and moderately flat skull

Historically, ears were amputated

Short-haired variety

Topcoat is short, moderately hard, and very dense

Well-boned forelimbs have powerful shoulder muscles

VARIETY OF COLOURS

KEY FACTS

COUNTRY OF ORIGIN Russia and Central Asian Republics

DATE OF ORIGIN Middle Ages

FIRST USE Livestock guarding

USE TODAY Livestock guarding

LIFE EXPECTANCY 11 years

OTHER NAMES Middle-Asian Ovtcharka, Mid-Asian Shepherd

WEIGHT RANGE
37–50 kg (80–110 lb)

HEIGHT RANGE
60–71 cm (23–28 in)

CAUCASIAN SHEEPDOG

Russia's most popular "ovtcharka", or sheepdog, this robust and powerful dog is commonly shown at dog shows throughout Russia and other parts of the former Soviet Union. In Poland, Hungary, and the Czech and Slovak Republics, extensive breeding programmes ensure that it remains a popular dog, even though its original use as a sheep guardian is declining. The Caucasian Sheepdog arrived in East Germany in the late 1960s to serve as a border patrol dog, especially along the Berlin Wall. In 1989, when the Wall came down, the 7,000-strong band of patrol dogs was disbanded. Many of these dogs were given new homes with families throughout Germany. Careful breeding in Germany safeguards the future of this cautious and independent dog. It is likely that as its popularity increases, breeders will selectively breed for a more amenable personality.

BREED HISTORY For centuries, flocks of sheep have existed in Caucasia, the mountainous land mass between the Black and Caspian seas, abutting on Turkey and Iran. Dogs similar to this superb guardian have protected these sheep from both human and animal predators for at least 600 years.

Dark eyes are moderate in size and deep set

Coat is thick and dense, with profuse feathering

Hips are slightly raised from line of back

Paws are large, with hair between toes providing excellent insulation and protection

Lopped ears are densely covered with hair for insulation

Deeply set eyes offer excellent binocular vision

Tail is profusely covered with long feathering of heavy hair

Forelimbs are long, straight, and densely boned

Heavy paws give firm footing in rough terrain

Nose is black and prominent, with well-opened, large nostrils

KEY FACTS

COUNTRY OF ORIGIN Russia, Caucasian Republics
DATE OF ORIGIN Middle Ages
FIRST USE Livestock guarding
USE TODAY Livestock guarding, security
LIFE EXPECTANCY 10–11 years
OTHER NAME Caucasian Ovtcharka

WEIGHT RANGE
45–70 kg (99–154 lb)
HEIGHT RANGE
64–72 cm (25–28 in)

VARIETY OF COLOURS

Puppy's legs are not yet fully calcified

Puppy's coat is finer than that of an adult

ANATOLIAN (KARABASH) DOG

Turkish shepherds never used dogs to herd sheep, only to protect them from predators. These sheepdogs were collectively classified as "coban kopegi", but in the 1970s breeders began to investigate type and found several regional differences. Karabash-type sheepdogs are found in central Turkey, and closely resemble the sheepdogs of eastern Turkey. In its native land, the Karabash remains a guardian, protecting flocks from predation by wolves, bears, and jackals. Strong willed and independent, it is not an entirely suitable companion, although with careful socialization it can adapt reasonably well to a family environment.

Triangular ears are carried high when dog is alert

Slightly pendulous, black lips

Thick, powerful, muscular neck

Long, straight forelegs are wide set

KEY FACTS

COUNTRY OF ORIGIN Turkey
DATE OF ORIGIN Middle Ages
FIRST USE Sheep guarding
USE TODAY Sheep guarding
LIFE EXPECTANCY 10–11 years
OTHER NAMES Coban Kopegi, Karabas, Kangal Dog, Anatolian Shepherd Dog

WEIGHT RANGE
41–64 kg (90–141 lb)
HEIGHT RANGE
71–81 cm (28–32 in)

Short nails on strong feet, with well-arched toes

Flat coat is short and dense, with thick undercoat

VARIETY OF COLOURS

BREED HISTORY About 1,000 years ago, the Turkic-speaking people entered Asia Minor, occupying the region that is now Turkey. They brought with them their great, herd-guarding dogs. The Karabash descends from these dogs.

AKBASH DOG

KEY FACTS

COUNTRY OF ORIGIN Turkey
DATE OF ORIGIN Middle Ages
FIRST USE Sheep guarding
USE TODAY Sheep guarding
LIFE EXPECTANCY 10–11 years
OTHER NAMES Coban Kopegi, Akbas

WEIGHT RANGE
41–55 kg (90–121 lb)
HEIGHT RANGE
71–86 cm (28–34 in)

Muzzle is straight

Broad skull is slightly rounded

Topcoat and undercoat are thick and protective

BREED HISTORY Turkish shepherds selectively bred for white-coloured guarding sheepdogs, perhaps to differentiate them from predators. The Akbash, from western Turkey, is a probable relative of the other great white herd guarders of Europe – the Komondor, Kuvasz, Tatra Mountain Sheepdog, and even the distant Pyrenean Mountain Dog.

Eyes are almond shaped

V-shaped ears are slightly rounded at tips

The Akbash's rangy shape and acute eye sight suggest that there may be sight-hound blood in its ancestry. This breed has been exported to the United States since the 1970s, and its future there is assured. It appears to function well in the western United States, where it is used to prevent Coyote predation of sheep and goats. Like the Karabash, the Akbash is a superb livestock guard. Calm and almost stately in deportment, it can be rather aloof and suspicious of strangers, be they children or adults, and requires socialization.

BOUVIER DES FLANDRES

Large size of head
is accentuated by
moustache and beard

BREED HISTORY With the exception of the nearly extinct Bouvier des Ardennes, this breed is the sole survivor of the once-wide variety of Belgian bouviers, or cattle dogs. It may have developed from griffons and the old-type Beauceron.

This robust, cattle-droving, cart-pulling farm dog existed in a number of coat and colour varieties until 1965, when present standards were written. During World War I, the French Army used the Bouvier in its medical corps, but numbers declined drastically shortly afterwards. It was only through the intervention of the Belgian Kennel Club that the breed was rescued from oblivion. This powerful and usually amiable dog can be quite aggressive, a reminder of its cattle-guarding heritage, and it makes a superb guard dog. Popular in its native land, it is also highly regarded in North America, both as a companion and as a farm worker.

High-set ears are quite small

Fluffy, fine undercoat

Back is short, broad, and powerful

Chest descends to level of elbows

Topcoat is crisp to the touch, dry, and dull

Short, round, compact feet

KEY FACTS

COUNTRY OF ORIGIN Belgium/France
DATE OF ORIGIN 1600s
FIRST USE Cattle herding
USE TODAY Companion, guarding
LIFE EXPECTANCY 11–12 years

WEIGHT RANGE
27–40 kg (60–88 lb)
HEIGHT RANGE
58–69 cm
(23–27 in)

SWEDISH VALLHUND

Rigid, pointed, pricked ears are covered in fine hair

BREED HISTORY In looks and temperament very similar to the Pembroke Welsh Corgi, it is likely that this multi-purpose drover, watchdog, and ratter arrived in Scandinavia with Vikings who had previously settled in Pembrokeshire, Wales. Its survival was ensured in the 1940s by a Swedish breeder, von Rosen.

Classified in Sweden as an indigenous breed, it is likely that this energetic, short-legged herder, like the Welsh Corgi, descends from the bassets of continental Europe. Tenacious and tough, the Vallhund is an ardent worker, and has the reckless courage typical of all heelers. An excellent multi-purpose farm dog, it efficiently guards and droves livestock, protects property, and controls rodents. It makes a rewarding companion for experienced dog handlers, but its instinct to nip never quite disappears. When kept together in large numbers, Vallhunds are likely to fight among themselves.

Hard, dense, medium-length coat, with fine, tight undercoat

Muzzle is separated from skull by distinct stop

GREY

RED-YELLOW

RED-BROWN

GREY-BROWN

Long neck has very muscular nape

Powerful legs, with short, oval feet, and round pads

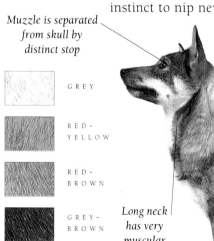

KEY FACTS

COUNTRY OF ORIGIN Sweden
DATE OF ORIGIN Middle Ages
FIRST USE Cattle herding, guarding, ratting
USE TODAY Companion, herding, guarding, ratting
LIFE EXPECTANCY 12–14 years
OTHER NAMES Vallhund, Vasgötaspets, Swedish Cattle Dog

WEIGHT RANGE
11–15 kg (25–35 lb)
HEIGHT RANGE
31–35 cm (12–14 in)

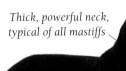

CANE CORSO

BREED HISTORY A re-creation of an old Italian herding breed, the Cane di Macellaio, this mastiff did not live on the Italian mainland, but was bred in Sicily. It was used to drove cattle to the butchers, and may well have participated in dog fighting.

Thick, powerful neck, typical of all mastiffs

The Corso is a classic mastiff, without the loose skin of geographically related mastiff breeds such as the Neapolitan Mastiff. It is a robust dog, with the typical bone and joint problems of the giant breeds. The relatively tight skin around its mouth ensures that it drools less than do the looser lipped mastiffs. This breed can be aggressive with strangers, and needs experienced handling and careful socialization. However, when fully trained, the Corso makes an amenable companion. Content to stay outside, it thrives on regular exercise.

Ears are surgically cropped only for fashion

Hindquarter muscles are less accentuated than those on forequarters

Thick, short, harsh coat over thick skin

KEY FACTS

COUNTRY OF ORIGIN Italy (Sicily)
DATE OF ORIGIN 1600s
FIRST USE Cattle droving
USE TODAY Companion, security
LIFE EXPECTANCY 10–11 years
OTHER NAMES Sicilian Branchiero, Cane di Macellaio
WEIGHT RANGE 36–63.5 kg (80–140 lb)
HEIGHT RANGE 56–71 cm (22–28 in)

VARIETY OF COLOURS

AIDI

KEY FACTS

COUNTRY OF ORIGIN Morocco
DATE OF ORIGIN Middle Ages
FIRST USE Livestock guarding, hunting
USE TODAY Livestock guarding, companion
LIFE EXPECTANCY 10–11 years
OTHER NAMES Chien de l'Atlas, Atlas Sheepdog
WEIGHT RANGE 23–25 kg (50–55 lb)
HEIGHT RANGE 53–61 cm (21–24 in)

In many ways the Aidi is similar to the Turkish livestock dogs, such as the Akbash and Karabash. For centuries, it has been employed by nomads to protect herds of sheep and goats in the Atlas mountains of Morocco, surviving the searing heat of the day and the freezing temperatures of night. Paired with the swift Sloughi, the Aidi also uses its scenting abilities to participate in hunts. The Aidi tracks game and the Sloughi brings it down. This breed's traditional guardian role makes it a superb watchdog, but it has not as yet been fully acclimatized to life as a household companion.

BREED HISTORY This moderate-sized livestock guard is a typical mountain dog, possibly related to the great, white mountain dogs that spread from the East across Europe centuries ago. The Moroccan Kennel Association has been active in ensuring this sturdy, energetic breed's survival.

Skull is broad and moderately domed

Lean, but well-muscled body, covered by coarse, insulating double coat

WHITE   TAWNY

BLACK/WHITE   RED   BLACK

Very deep chest extends below level of elbows

SOUTH RUSSIAN SHEEPDOG

Fringe of hair hangs over face

Favoured by the old Soviet Army as a guard dog, the South Russian Sheepdog is still sometimes used for this purpose by the Russian Army. Its origins probably lie in the mastiffs of Tibet, and it arrived in eastern Europe centuries, or even millennia ago, with migrating or invading Asian tribes. Recently, some individuals have been exported from Russia and are being bred in the West. Tenacious, elegant, and aloof, this independent breed is responsive to training if it is socialized as a young puppy.

Top of skull is same length as muzzle

Hair on muzzle forms distinctive moustache

Ears are long and lopped

BREED HISTORY For centuries, white guardian dogs protected flocks in the European part of Russia and in the Ukraine. About 200 years ago, smaller sheepdogs entered the region, accompanying Merino sheep from Spain. Today's South Russian Sheepdog is a cross between these two breeds.

Dense double coat provides superb waterproof insulation

Body is thickly boned

KEY FACTS

COUNTRY OF ORIGIN Russia/Ukraine
DATE OF ORIGIN Middle Ages/1800s
FIRST USE Livestock guarding
USE TODAY Livestock guarding, security, companion
LIFE EXPECTANCY 10–11 years
OTHER NAME South Russian Ovtcharka

WEIGHT RANGE
55–75 kg (121–165 lb)
HEIGHT RANGE
65–90 cm (26–35 in)

ALAPAHA BLUE BLOOD BULLDOG

Like the Plott Hound, this muscular breed is the creation of one American family, and its survival depends upon the nurturing it receives. Originating from English Bulldog stock, there is a considerable size difference between the sexes. Males can be almost twice as heavy as the smallest females. This dog's ancestors functioned as cattle and pig herders, but the Alapaha Blue Blood Bulldog is bred solely for security and companionship. With such a small genetic pool, health problems such as inversion of the eyelids (entropion) can develop.

Prominent eyes are set well apart

Muzzle is covered by loose upper lips

VARIETY OF COLOURS

Feet are cat-like; dewclaws are never amputated

Straight back is as long as dog is high at shoulders

Well-muscled hips are narrower than chest

BREED HISTORY Bred by the Lane family of Georgia, in the United States, for three generations, this rare, bulldog-type guard dog descends from Buck Lane's dog, named Otto. Buck Lane's granddaughter, Lana Lou Lane, continues the breeding programme.

Relatively short coat is fairly stiff to touch

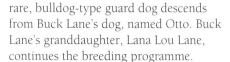

KEY FACTS

COUNTRY OF ORIGIN United States
DATE OF ORIGIN Late 1800s
FIRST USE Guarding
USE TODAY Guarding, companion
LIFE EXPECTANCY 11–13 years

WEIGHT RANGE
23–41 kg (50–90 lb)
HEIGHT RANGE
51–63.5 cm (20–25 in)

NEW ZEALAND HUNTAWAY

Velvety ears are half dropped

BREED HISTORY Most of the original British sheep-herding dogs transported to New Zealand worked silently, but shepherds saw the benefit of dogs that occasionally used voice to drive sheep. Selective breeding of barking sheep-herding dogs proved successful, resulting in the Huntaway, a breed that urges sheep forwards with its voice.

Large, black nose is a symmetrical extension of long muzzle

Muscular neck is moderately long

Deep in the throat, the voice box produces dog's effective bark

New Zealand shepherds have selectively bred sheepdogs for almost a century in order to produce a dog that uses its voice to direct sheep. The dog learns to gather the herd and follow behind it, using its voice to guide the sheep fowards. Special events were developed for these dogs at sheepdog field trials. These events were referred to as "huntaways", and eventually gave rise to the breed's name. Although it is not recognized by any kennel club, even in its land of origin, the New Zealand Huntaway breeds true for the intended purpose of sheep herding. It has been exported to Great Britain, where it works as a sheepdog and participates in field trials. It is becoming increasingly popular as a companion.

Back is long and robust

Predominantly black coat has patches of tan

Ears are set well apart

Eyes are round and alert

Thighs are powerful, providing speed necessary to cut off any break-aways from flock

Firm, straight legs provide excellent footing

Legs are leaner than a Labrador Retriever's, but better muscled than a Border Collie's

KEY FACTS

COUNTRY OF ORIGIN New Zealand
DATE OF ORIGIN 1900s
FIRST USE Sheep herding
USE TODAY Sheep herding, field trials
LIFE EXPECTANCY 12–14 years
OTHER NAME New Zealand Sheepdog

WEIGHT RANGE
18–29.5 kg (40–65 lb)
HEIGHT RANGE
51–61 cm (20–24 in)

Tail is thick and well plumed

COMPANION DOGS

ALL DOGS OFFER COMPANIONSHIP – they seem to understand our emotions. Most look upon the people they live with as members of their own family – even the fiercest guardian dog usually acts like a teddy bear with the people it knows. Almost all cultures in the world

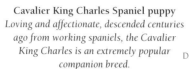

keep pets, usually dogs, for no obvious purpose other than companionship. Some breeds evolved for no functional reason other than to offer warmth, company, and entertainment. These were generally small breeds, originally created for the amusement of women.

Cavalier King Charles Spaniel puppy
Loving and affectionate, descended centuries ago from working spaniels, the Cavalier King Charles is an extremely popular companion breed.

DARK HAIR SURROUNDS EQUALLY DARK NOSE

Tibetan Spaniel
Bred by Tibetan monks for no purpose other than companionship, the Tibetan Spaniel is closely related to the Pekingese.

Labradoodle
The Labradoodle is the result of an attempt to combine the obedience of the Labrador Retriever with the non-shedding coat of the Standard Poodle.

HAIR DOES NOT SHED AND NEEDS CONSTANT TRIMMING

friends, and are increasing in popularity faster than most other companion breeds. In their quest for new and useful varieties of dog the ancient Chinese perpetuated the hairless dog, originally no doubt as a curiosity, but then latterly as a comforting hot-water bottle.

IN HIGH ESTEEM
In Japan, the Japanese Chin assumed the role of élite companion of aristocracy, as did the Pekingese in the Chinese royal court. On the other side of the world a similar dog, a miniature spaniel, filled the same role in the English royal court. This breed was so synonymous with the king that it was given his name, the King Charles Spaniel. Like its close relative, the Cavalier King Charles

Spaniel, this breed never worked the field, but rather provided affection and constancy to the king and his favoured friends.

The English king was not alone in keeping small dogs for companionship. Throughout other parts of Europe, small bichons were the favoured friends of royal courtiers. Close ancestors of the Bichon Frise, Lowchen, Maltese, and Bolognese are seen in similar forms in portraits of the ruling classes of Portugal, Spain, France, Italy, and Germany. The Coton de Tulear accompanied the wives of French administrators to Madagascar, while the Havanese became the house pet of wealthy Italians in Argentina, and latterly, Cuba. Chihuahuas are unique companions and vibrant sentinel dogs. They have never been used as ratting terriers, although the larger ones have the sizes and feisty personalities to excel at the job. Larger in size are the Pug, French Bulldog, and American Bulldog, all miniaturized versions of working dogs. So, too, are the

MINIATURE FORERUNNERS
Archeological evidence from China and from central Europe shows that dwarfism, where the skull becomes domed and relatively large, and the long bones shorten and the joints thicken, occurred naturally in primitive dogs. These dwarf dogs were probably kept for their oddity value and are the forebears of today's short-legged breeds – the dachshunds and bassets. Another form of size reduction – miniaturization – occurred, in which all parts of the skeleton are equally reduced in size. These forms of size reduction sometimes took place together, producing breeds such as the Pekingese, the oldest recognizable companion dog and sleeve-dog of Chinese empresses over 2,000 years ago.

The Pekingese is probably related to the Shih Tzu and to the small working Tibetan dogs – the Lhasa Apso, Tibetan Terrier, and Tibetan Spaniel. All of these were herders or sentinel dogs, although the Tibetan Spaniel also acted as a talisman of luck for travellers. Today, these breeds are sturdy

Miniature Poodle
Once the world's most popular breed, the Miniature Poodle is a bantam version of the Standard Poodle, a one-time guarding breed. It makes an excellent watchdog.

LOPPED EARS ARE COVERED IN DENSE HAIR

POODLE IS TRIMMED FOR SHOW

Dalmatian
At one time a carriage dog accompanying travellers and offering protection, today the Dalmatian makes an affable and alert companion.

LONG LEGS ARE CAPABLE OF ACCOMPANYING A HORSE-DRAWN CARRIAGE

French Bulldog
This dwarfed mastiff's forebears were used as bull baiters, but reduction in size eliminated this vocation.

LEGS HAVE DENSE BONE AND ARE WELL MUSCLED

Miniature, Toy and Medium Poodles, kept entirely for companionship, while retaining the trainability of the Standard Poodle. Unique among companion dogs is the Dalmatian. Its conformation indicates that it comes from a hound background, but breeding for its striking black-spotted coat has obliterated all instinctive, scent-hunting activity. Its exuberant personality makes it a resourceful, exhilarating companion.

NEW BREEDS
Companionship is central to our relationship with dogs today, and breeds continue to evolve. The Moscow Long-haired Toy Terrier,

Short-haired Chihuahua
The name Chihuahua comes from the Mexican state of that name, but whether this breed originated there is unknown.

MUZZLE IS SHORT AND POINTED

recognized by the former Soviet Kennel Club in 1966, is a cross between toy terriers and small mongrels. In North America, small poodles are frequently crossed with other breeds, producing companion dogs known as the Cockerpoo and Pekepoo. These have become so popular that it is possible that they will eventually be recognized as new breeds. Elsewhere, particularly in the state of Victoria, in Australia, the Standard Poodle has been crossed with the Labrador Retriever, producing the Labradoodle. Some of these cross

breeds have non-shedding coats, and have been trained to act as guide dogs for blind people who are allergic to shedding dog hair. It is possible to combine almost any two breeds. The combination of a Staffordshire Bull Terrier and a Boxer produces a handsome and rugged individual, while crossing a Bichon with a Yorkshire Terrier results in a sparkling companion. The Markiesje, a toy Dutch breed soon to be recognized by the Dutch Kennel Club, is the result of crossing toy continental spaniels with the Toy Poodle. While miniaturization creates new breeds like the North American Shepherd and

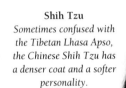

THIS BREED IS ONLY 20 CM (8 IN) HIGH WHEN FULLY GROWN

NECK IS THICK AND EXTREMELY POWERFUL

FORELEGS ARE STRAIGHT AND WELL BONED

Olde English Bulldogge
Developed by American breeder David Leavitt, this re-creation of the 18th-century Bulldog is a feisty and courageous dog, without being overly aggressive.

Japanese Chin
Perfected by Japanese breeders centuries ago, the Japanese Chin makes a fine friend and an excellent watchdog.

COAT IS SHORT AND SMOOTH, WITH IRREGULAR SPOTTING

Miniature Shar Pei, enhancement produces others, such as the Shiloh Shepherd, a giant, straight-backed German Shepherd, which is bred for soundness of hips and increased body weight. Its role is one of companionship. Some "new" breeds are, in fact, very ancient breeds that have never been recognized by kennel clubs. The Thai Ridgeback has lived in rural regions of Thailand for hundreds of years, but was not seen in the West until very recently. For centuries, the ancient Danish Chicken Dog was regarded as a random-bred dog (mongrel), until breeders eventually realized that many of these so-called "mongrels" were, in fact, almost identical. As they increase in numbers, breeds such as these will probably be kept primarily as household companion dogs.

Prazsky Krysavik
Not yet officially recognized, this breed is still very rare and only exists in the Czech and Slovak Republics.

Shih Tzu
Sometimes confused with the Tibetan Lhasa Apso, the Chinese Shih Tzu has a denser coat and a softer personality.

TOPCOAT IS LONG AND DENSE

RANDOM-BRED DOGS
Random-bred dogs (mongrels) make up the majority of dogs in the world. Only in a few countries do pure-bred dogs outnumber random breds. Because they are not inbred, harmful, inherited conditions such as hip dysplasia or blindness occur much less frequently in them than in pedigree dogs. Random breds are, however, far more expendable in the eyes of callous people, because they have no social or commercial value. They remain, nonetheless, the world's most popular companions and house dogs, offering amusement and affection worldwide.

BICHON FRISE

Round, dark eyes also have dark rims

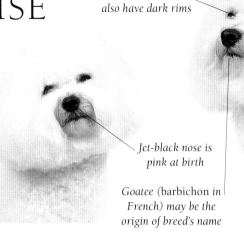

Hair from tail falls against, but does not press on, back

Jet-black nose is pink at birth

Goatee (barbichon in French) may be the origin of breed's name

Drooping ears are smaller than a poodle's

When dog is relaxed, tail hangs limp

Nails are usually white, although breeders prefer black

Attractive, adaptable, happy, bold, and lively, the Bichon has found a large following since its emergence from obscurity in the late 1970s. As well as being the ultimate companion dog, this breed is game and hardy – in Norway, farmers recently discovered that it could be trained to round up sheep. Regular grooming is essential. The teeth and gums require attention, since there is a tendency for tartar formation and gum infection. Although many white-haired breeds suffer from chronic skin complaints, the Bichon is free of allergic skin problems.

BREED HISTORY The exact origins of this vivacious and affectionate breed are unknown. By the 14th century, sailors had introduced it to the island of Tenerife, and by the 15th century it was a royal favourite.

MALTESE

BREED HISTORY Phoenician traders probably brought the ancient "Melita" (archaic name for Malta) breed to Malta more than 2,000 years ago. Today's Maltese is possibly the result of crossing miniature spaniels with the Miniature Poodle.

Ears are heavily feathered with long hair

Glossy coat is heavy and long

Large, round, dark eyes protrude very slightly

Weight of long, abundant hair causes tail to curve to side

Ribbon in hair permits Maltese to see clearly

Once called the Maltese Terrier, this good-tempered, sweet-natured, sometimes sensitive breed does not shed its hair and develops a long, luxurious coat. This creates a matting problem, especially at around eight months of age, when the puppy coat is replaced by adult hair. Daily grooming is absolutely essential. The breed is almost invariably good with children. It relishes exercise, but when the opportunity for it does not exist, it will adapt to a more sedentary life.

Hair is pure white, with hint of ivory or lemon

HAVANESE

CREAM GOLD SILVER BLUE BLACK

Tail is covered with long, silky hair

BREED HISTORY The Havanese could be descended from either Bolognese dogs crossed with small poodles, or Spanish-owned Maltese.

Rather pointed ears, covered with dense hair, fall in slight fold

Large, dark eyes covered by hair

Body has profuse feathering of hair

Straight legs, with lean toes

KEY FACTS

COUNTRY OF ORIGIN Mediterranean region/Cuba
DATE OF ORIGIN 1700–1800s
FIRST USE Companion
USE TODAY Companion
LIFE EXPECTANCY 14–15 years
OTHER NAMES Bichon Havanais, Havana Silk Dog

WEIGHT RANGE
3–6 kg (7–13 lb)
HEIGHT RANGE
20–28 cm (8–11 in)

Revolutions are seldom kind to dogs. New regimes often look upon pure-bred dogs as totems of the *ancien régime*. Following the French, Russian, and Cuban revolutions, the cherished breeds of the overthrown classes were actively or passively eliminated. Now rare in Cuba, the Havanese is experiencing a resurgence in popularity in the United States. Sometimes shy, and always gentle and responsive, the Havanese is a natural companion dog, which attaches itself firmly to its human family and is very good with children. The profuse, soft coat varies from wavy to curly.

BOLOGNESE

The Bolognese closely resembles the Maltese, and served a similar role among the ruling families and aristocracy of Renaissance Italy, particularly the courts of the Medicis, Gonzagas, and d'Estes. Rare today even in Italy, the affectionate Bolognese is slightly more reserved and shy than its more popular cousin, the Bichon Frise. Its white, cottony coat makes it suitable for hot climates. The Bolognese enjoys the companionship of people, and forms a close relationship with its owner.

BREED HISTORY Although it takes its name from the northern Italian city of Bologna, it is possible that the Bolognese is descended from the Bichons of southern Italy. Descriptions of this breed have been recorded since the 1200s.

Ears set wide, giving square appearance

Hair on lips is shorter than on other parts of body

Button nose is pink until three months of age, then turns black

Hair falls in tufts

Small, compact feet, with pink or black nails

Legs covered in tufts of long hair; no undercoat anywhere

Tail hangs limp when relaxed, and curls over back when dog is alert

KEY FACTS

COUNTRY OF ORIGIN Italy
DATE OF ORIGIN Middle Ages
FIRST USE Companion
USE TODAY Companion
LIFE EXPECTANCY 14–15 years
OTHER NAME Bichon Bolognese

WEIGHT RANGE
3–4 kg (5–9 lb)
HEIGHT RANGE
25–31 cm (10–12 in)

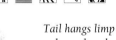

CHIHUAHUA

Large, erect ears slope outwards

BREED HISTORY The origins of the Chihuahua are shrouded in mystery. Experts speculate that small dogs arrived in the Americas with the Spanish armies of Hernando Cortes in 1519. Another theory is that the Chinese voyaged to America, bringing with them miniaturized dogs before the arrival of Europeans. The breed was first exported to the United States in the 1850s.

Distinctive, round head is related to increased risk of epilepsy

Small, neat mouth; prone to tooth loss

Prominent, relatively large eyes

Short-haired variety

Robust, well-muscled neck, with fragile, thin windpipe

Compact body is long

Very thin bones in front legs can break easily

Glossy coat forms slight collar around neck

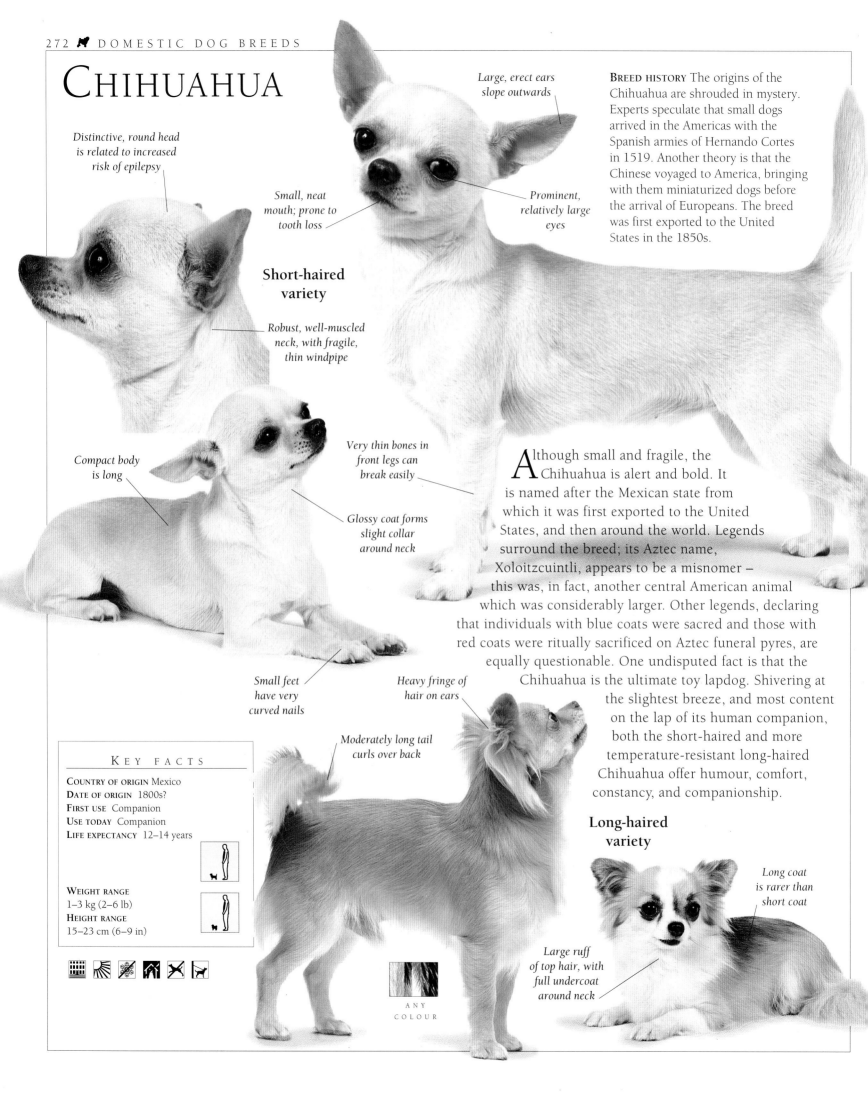

Although small and fragile, the Chihuahua is alert and bold. It is named after the Mexican state from which it was first exported to the United States, and then around the world. Legends surround the breed; its Aztec name, Xoloitzcuintli, appears to be a misnomer – this was, in fact, another central American animal which was considerably larger. Other legends, declaring that individuals with blue coats were sacred and those with red coats were ritually sacrificed on Aztec funeral pyres, are equally questionable. One undisputed fact is that the Chihuahua is the ultimate toy lapdog. Shivering at the slightest breeze, and most content on the lap of its human companion, both the short-haired and more temperature-resistant long-haired Chihuahua offer humour, comfort, constancy, and companionship.

Small feet have very curved nails

Heavy fringe of hair on ears

Moderately long tail curls over back

Long-haired variety

KEY FACTS

COUNTRY OF ORIGIN Mexico
DATE OF ORIGIN 1800s?
FIRST USE Companion
USE TODAY Companion
LIFE EXPECTANCY 12–14 years

WEIGHT RANGE
1–3 kg (2–6 lb)
HEIGHT RANGE
15–23 cm (6–9 in)

ANY COLOUR

Long coat is rarer than short coat

Large ruff of top hair, with full undercoat around neck

COTON DE TULEAR

WHITE

BLACK/
WHITE

*Light-textured
hair requires
daily grooming*

KEY FACTS

COUNTRY OF ORIGIN Madagascar/France
DATE OF ORIGIN 1600s
FIRST USE Companion
USE TODAY Companion
LIFE EXPECTANCY 12–14 years

WEIGHT RANGE
5.5–7 kg (12–15 lb)
HEIGHT RANGE
25–30 cm (10–12 in)

BREED HISTORY Related to French bichons
and the Italian Bolognese, the Coton
possibly arrived in Madagascar
with French troops, or with
the administrators who
followed. The breed was
virtually unknown
until it was
reintroduced to
Europe and America
in the last 20 years.

*Long topcoat; there is
no undercoat*

For centuries, the Coton de Tulear was a favoured
companion of the wealthy residents of Tulear, in southern
Madagascar, where it continued to breed to type. A dog with
similar origins was popular on the French island of Reunion, off
the east coast of Madagascar, but became extinct. This is a typical
bichon-type dog. Its dominant characteristics are its cotton-candy,
fluffy coat of long hair (which needs careful grooming), and the
tendency, unlike European bichons, to have yellow or black patches
of hair. A gentle, affectionate, and alert breed, the Coton de Tulear
is becoming increasingly popular in the United States.

*Fluffy hair covers thin,
lightly muscled forelegs*

LOWCHEN

BREED HISTORY The Lowchen's origins
are probably similar to those of the
other bichons of Mediterranean
Europe. Although uncommon,
it is no longer rare.

French in origin, this sparky breed is a true
European, with progenitors throughout the countries
of southern Europe. Goya is one of many artists to have
featured this lively little dog on canvas. Its lion-cut coat
makes it look fragile and rather undignified, although
this is definitely not the case. The Lowchen is a
robust, even tough dog, which can be strong willed
and arrogant. Males, in particular, are quite willing
to challenge other, larger household dogs for
leadership. As in the case of poodles, the breed's
hair needs to be clipped only for show purposes.

*Plume of hair on
medium-length,
curled tail*

ALL
COLOURS

*Coat is long and
wavy, especially
around ears*

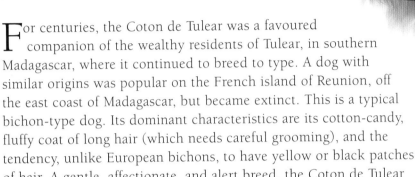

*Earth-brown nose;
colour varies according
to coat colour*

*Delicate coat provides
little insulation in
freezing climates*

KEY FACTS

COUNTRY OF ORIGIN France
DATE OF ORIGIN 1600s
FIRST USE Companion
USE TODAY Companion
LIFE EXPECTANCY 12–14 years
OTHER NAME Little Lion Dog

WEIGHT RANGE
4–8 kg (9–18 lb)
HEIGHT RANGE
25–33 cm (10–13 in)

*Hair has been carefully
clipped on forelegs*

*Feet are small
and cat-like*

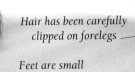

LHASA APSO

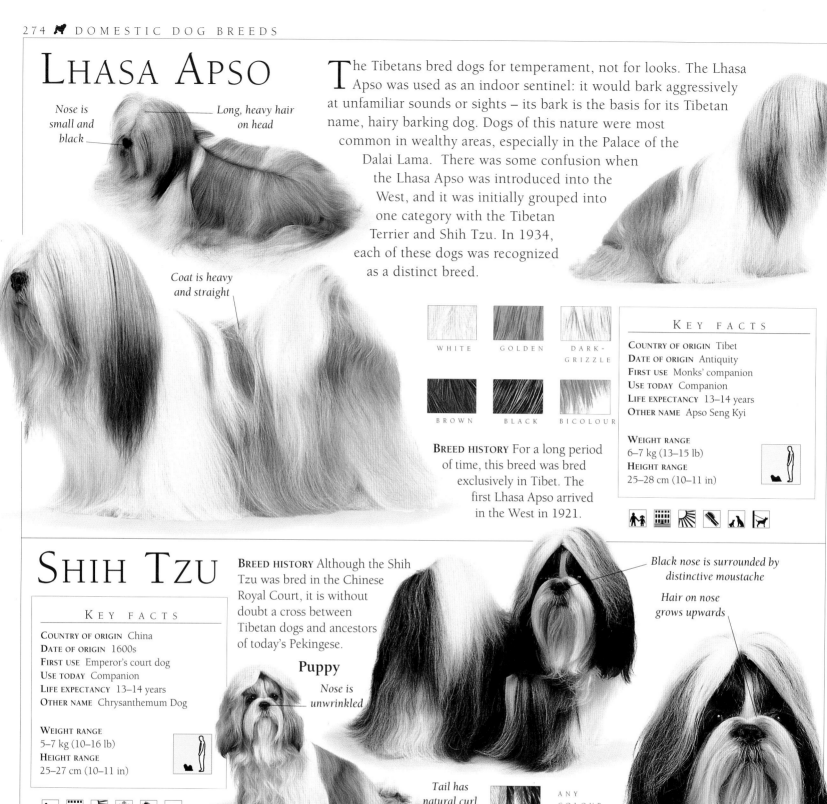

Nose is small and black

Long, heavy hair on head

Coat is heavy and straight

The Tibetans bred dogs for temperament, not for looks. The Lhasa Apso was used as an indoor sentinel: it would bark aggressively at unfamiliar sounds or sights – its bark is the basis for its Tibetan name, hairy barking dog. Dogs of this nature were most common in wealthy areas, especially in the Palace of the Dalai Lama. There was some confusion when the Lhasa Apso was introduced into the West, and it was initially grouped into one category with the Tibetan Terrier and Shih Tzu. In 1934, each of these dogs was recognized as a distinct breed.

WHITE GOLDEN DARK-GRIZZLE

BROWN BLACK BICOLOUR

BREED HISTORY For a long period of time, this breed was bred exclusively in Tibet. The first Lhasa Apso arrived in the West in 1921.

KEY FACTS

COUNTRY OF ORIGIN Tibet
DATE OF ORIGIN Antiquity
FIRST USE Monks' companion
USE TODAY Companion
LIFE EXPECTANCY 13–14 years
OTHER NAME Apso Seng Kyi

WEIGHT RANGE
6–7 kg (13–15 lb)
HEIGHT RANGE
25–28 cm (10–11 in)

SHIH TZU

BREED HISTORY Although the Shih Tzu was bred in the Chinese Royal Court, it is without doubt a cross between Tibetan dogs and ancestors of today's Pekingese.

KEY FACTS

COUNTRY OF ORIGIN China
DATE OF ORIGIN 1600s
FIRST USE Emperor's court dog
USE TODAY Companion
LIFE EXPECTANCY 13–14 years
OTHER NAME Chrysanthemum Dog

WEIGHT RANGE
5–7 kg (10–16 lb)
HEIGHT RANGE
25–27 cm (10–11 in)

Black nose is surrounded by distinctive moustache

Hair on nose grows upwards

Puppy

Nose is unwrinkled

Tail has natural curl

ANY COLOUR

Long, dense topcoat

Although it is very similar in looks to the Lhasa Apso, the Shih Tzu is different in origin and temperament. A translation of the pre-revolutionary Peking Kennel Club's breed standard for the Shih Tzu says it should have, "a lion head, bear torso, camel hoof, feather-duster tail, palm-leaf ears, rice teeth, pearly petal tongue, and movement like a goldfish". The Shih Tzu is less aloof and more playful than its Tibetan lookalike, and this probably accounts for its greater worldwide popularity. The hair on the bridge of its nose tends to grow upwards, and is often tied up on the top of its head.

KYI LEO

BREED HISTORY This breed's history began in the 1950s, with the accidental mating of a Lhasa Apso and Maltese in San Francisco. Line breeding continued in San José, California, where Harriet Linn was responsible for choosing the name and setting the standard.

KEY FACTS.
COUNTRY OF ORIGIN United States
DATE OF ORIGIN 1972
FIRST USE Companion
USE TODAY Companion
LIFE EXPECTANCY 12–14 years

WEIGHT RANGE
6–7 kg (13–15 lb)
HEIGHT RANGE
23–28 cm (9–11 in)

Head is completely covered with long hair

Profuse beard and whiskers

Muzzle is moderately long

Tail curls over back when dog is alert

Forelegs are long and straight

This delightful dog is the result of a happy accident followed by planned selective breeding. Crossing the Lhasa Apso with the Maltese has produced an effervescent companion, full of voice and energy. The breed is extremely affectionate, and is always eager to please. Although sociable, it is slightly wary of strangers, as are most Lhasas, and stubborn, as are so many small dogs. Generally black and white in colour, with time the breed's silky hair often changes to silvery grey, an elegant sign of maturity.

PEKINGESE

BREED HISTORY At one time the exclusive property of the Chinese Royal Courts, and strongly associated with Buddhism, the first four Pekes arrived in the West in 1860.

Large, clear, lustrous eyes

Profuse double coat conceals bowed legs

Nose is compressed flat between eyes

Heavy mane, and ruff of long, coarse hair

Breathing through mouth helps dissipate excess heat

KEY FACTS
COUNTRY OF ORIGIN China
DATE OF ORIGIN Antiquity
FIRST USE Companion
USE TODAY Companion
LIFE EXPECTANCY 12–13 years
OTHER NAME Peking Palasthund

WEIGHT RANGE
3–6 kg (7–12 lb)
HEIGHT RANGE
15–23 cm (6–9 in)

According to the rules set by the Chinese Dowager Empress Tzi Hsi, the Pekingese should have short, bowed legs so that it cannot wander far, a ruff of fur around its neck to give it an aura of dignity, and selective taste buds so that it should appear dainty. She omitted to mention other striking qualities, including the stubbornness of a mule, the condescension of the haughty, and the speed of a snail. The Pekingese is a pleasure for those who enjoy the companionship of an amusing, calm, independent dog. Chinese legend says that it is the result of a union between a lion and a monkey, combining the nobleness of the former with the grace of the latter – this is an apt description.

JAPANESE CHIN

BREED HISTORY Although in some ways this breed is similar to the Pekingese, it probably evolved from the Tibetan Spaniel. It first reached Europe in the 1600s, when Portuguese sailors presented some Chins to Princess Catherine of Braganza. Queen Victoria acquired a pair from the American Commodore Perry, after his warships visited Japan.

Large, dark eyes are set wide apart, with a little white showing

Small, V-shaped ears are carried slightly forwards

BLACK/
WHITE

RED/
WHITE

Well-plumed tail is carried over back

Large head, with very short, wide, well-cushioned muzzle

Long, profuse, straight coat is free from curl

B ritish breeders probably crossed this breed with their own toy spaniels, accounting for the similarity between the Chin and King Charles Spaniel of today. Like all other breeds with flat faces, some individuals unfortunately suffer from breathing and heart problems. The feisty little Chin is robust and independent. As in Japan, where these dogs were owned by noble ladies, so too in Europe and America they were companions of the wealthy.

KEY FACTS

COUNTRY OF ORIGIN Japan
DATE OF ORIGIN Middle Ages
FIRST USE Companion
USE TODAY Companion
LIFE EXPECTANCY 12 years
OTHER NAMES Japanese Spaniel, Chin

WEIGHT RANGE
2–5 kg (4–11 lb)
HEIGHT RANGE
23–25 cm (9–10 in)

KING CHARLES SPANIEL

BREED HISTORY Early in the Middle Ages, spaniels of various sizes occurred in single litters. By the 1600s, selective breeding of the smallest individuals had produced a "toy" spaniel, later named the King Charles Spaniel, after one of its most obsessive admirers.

BLENHEIM   RED/
TAN

BLACK/   TRICOLOUR
TAN

Puppy

Long, well-feathered, low-set ears hang flat to cheeks

Nose is turned up

Large, wide-set, dark eyes, with pleasing expression

KEY FACTS

COUNTRY OF ORIGIN Great Britain
DATE OF ORIGIN 1600s
FIRST USE Companion
USE TODAY Companion
LIFE EXPECTANCY 12 years
OTHER NAME English Toy Spaniel

WEIGHT RANGE
4–6 kg (8–14 lb)
HEIGHT RANGE
25–27 cm (10–11 in)

R eports by Samuel Pepys and other British diarists tell that King Charles II seemingly spent more time with his spaniels than with affairs of state. His dogs were larger and had longer noses than today's breed, but with the demands of fashion, both the dog and its nose shrank to the proportions that exist in present standards. It is possible that crosses with the Japanese Chin helped to bring about these changes. Delightfully affectionate, the breed makes a superb urban companion.

Long, silky coat can be straight or wavy

Straight legs, with compact, well-fringed feet

CAVALIER KING CHARLES SPANIEL

Puppy

Head is almost flat between ears, and without dome

BREED HISTORY In the 1920s, an American, Roswell Eldridge, offered prize money at Cruft's Dog Show in London, to anyone exhibiting King Charles Spaniels with long noses, as they appeared in Van Dyck's painting of King Charles II and his spaniels. By the 1940s, these dogs were classified as a unique breed and were given the prefix Cavalier, to differentiate them from their forebears.

Moderate length to slightly arched, solid neck

Puppy

Moderately muscled thighs, with solid bone

Shallow stop, with well-developed nose and wide nostrils

Long ears, set high, with plenty of feathering

A success story of the last decade, the friendly, affable, and energetic Cavalier has become extremely popular. In many ways it is an ideal urban canine companion, willing to curl up on a sofa in bad weather, but equally willing to walk and run for miles when the occasion arises. The breed's increasing popularity has led to intensive in-breeding, and this has unfortunately contributed to an overwhelming increase in lethal heart conditions. The devastating consequence is that the life expectancy of affected dogs is reduced from fourteen to only nine or ten years. This is a heartbreakingly high incidence of inherited disease, perhaps the highest of any serious disease in any breed. When selecting one of these dogs, it is extremely important to check the medical history of several previous generations.

Silky feathering along straight, well-boned forelegs

Long, silky coat has slight wave, but no curl

Large, round, dark eyes are not too prominent

Face is substantial, and well filled out beneath eyes

Upper lips hang just slightly over lower lips

BLENHEIM

RUBY

BLACK/ TAN

TRI-COLOUR

KEY FACTS

COUNTRY OF ORIGIN Great Britain
DATE OF ORIGIN 1925
FIRST USE Companion
USE TODAY Companion
LIFE EXPECTANCY 9–14 years

WEIGHT RANGE
5–8 kg (10–18 lb)
HEIGHT RANGE
31–33 cm (12–13 in)

TIBETAN TERRIER

Body is compact and powerful

The Tibetan Terrier is not a true terrier – it was never bred to go to ground. Historically, it was kept by Tibetan monks for companionship, acting as a very vocal watchdog. Transported to the West by a British medical doctor, Dr. Greig, this alert and inquisitive breed has not attained the popularity of its close relative, the Lhasa Apso. However, it makes a loving companion, requires little exercise, and is reasonably easy to obedience train. Wary of strangers, it has retained its guarding attributes, using its loud voice at the slightest provocation.

Large feet are hidden beneath profuse, fine hair

Profuse hair on head

VARIETY OF COLOURS

Medium-sized, fairly narrow head

BREED HISTORY The Tibetan Terrier was historically treasured as a gift of tribute. Stories tell that Buddhist monks gave these dogs to nomadic tribes for good luck. The breed was introduced to Great Britain in the 1930s.

KEY FACTS

COUNTRY OF ORIGIN Tibet
DATE OF ORIGIN Middle Ages
FIRST USE Guarding
USE TODAY Companion
LIFE EXPECTANCY 13–14 years
OTHER NAME Dhoki Apso

WEIGHT RANGE
8–14 kg (18–30 lb)
HEIGHT RANGE
36–41 cm (14–16 in)

TIBETAN SPANIEL

Well-feathered, pendant ears are set quite high

Richly plumed tail carried in curl over back

A spaniel in name only, this breed never participated in the hunt. Legend says that in Tibet it was used as a "prayer dog", trained to turn the monk's parchment-covered prayer wheel. It has certainly been a monastery companion for centuries, and probably served as a watchdog. Anatomically similar to the Pekingese, the leggier, longer faced Tibetan Spaniel has far fewer breathing or back problems. Independent and self confident, this breed makes a satisfying companion.

Silky, double coat forms slight ruff

Mouth is tipped by black nose

Bones in front legs are slightly bowed

ALL COLOURS

BREED HISTORY Dogs resembling this breed existed in the 8th century, in what is now Korea, but whether they arrived there from China or Tibet is uncertain. The Tibetan Spaniel may be a founder breed of the Japanese Chin.

KEY FACTS

COUNTRY OF ORIGIN Tibet
DATE OF ORIGIN Antiquity
FIRST USE Companion in monasteries
USE TODAY Companion
LIFE EXPECTANCY 13–14 years

WEIGHT RANGE
4–7 kg (9–15 lb)
HEIGHT RANGE
24.5–25.5 cm (10 in)

CHINESE CRESTED

Ears are quite large in proportion to size of head

Head shape is very similar to that of a Yorkshire Terrier

Erect ears are covered with long, sparse hair

BREED HISTORY Although historically, the Chinese are considered to be the world's most successful "domesticators" of animals, creating distinct and unusual varieties, there is no documented proof that the Chinese Crested originated in China. Some evidence actually suggests that hairless dogs developed in Africa, and were then taken by traders to Asia and the Americas.

The similarities in conformation between the Chinese Crested and hairless African dogs suggest that these breeds might be distantly related. Genetically, hairless dogs do not breed very successfully – they usually have teeth and toe-nail abnormalities. However, matings between hairless individuals often produce coated puppies, called "powder-puffs". Breeding hairless dogs with powder-puffs, which are genetically more sound, ensures the continuity of this striking breed. The Chinese Crested is lively and affectionate, and makes an affable companion, but it needs to be protected from both hot and cold weather.

Body is lean, with straight back and fairly narrow ribcage

Plain or spotted skin lightens in summer

Hairless variety

Chest is not particularly deep

Although most of the body is hairless, the tail carries a fine display of long hair

Triangular head, with muzzle narrowing to a point

Hair on ears is almost 12 cm (5 in) long

KEY FACTS

COUNTRY OF ORIGIN China/Africa
DATE OF ORIGIN Antiquity
FIRST USE Companion/comforter
USE TODAY Companion
LIFE EXPECTANCY 12–13 years
OTHER NAMES Hairless, Powderpuff

WEIGHT RANGE
2–5.5 kg (5–12 lb)
HEIGHT RANGE
23–33 cm (9–13 in)

Fine, cat-like feet are covered with hair of moderate length

Erect ears are not weighed down by hair

Powder-puff variety

Ears droop under weight of fine, luxurious hair

Deep chest is well insulated against the elements

Lean, elegant body is covered in long hair

Long tail is well feathered with fine hair

VARIETY OF COLOURS

FRENCH BULLDOG

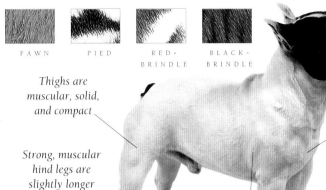

FAWN   PIED   RED-BRINDLE   BLACK-BRINDLE

Thighs are muscular, solid, and compact

Strong, muscular hind legs are slightly longer than forelegs

Cylindrical, barrel-like rib cage

Very short, thick, glossy, soft coat

BREED HISTORY In the 1860s, French dog breeders imported some very small Bulldogs from Great Britain and bred them with French terriers. By the turn of the century, the French Bulldog was a popular butcher's and coachman's companion in Paris.

Broad, short, snub nose has slanting nostrils

Ears amputated for fashion purposes only

Although stories persist that the French Bulldog descends from a Spanish bull baiter (the Dogue de Burgos), there is convincing evidence that this often opinionated little dog descends from "miniature" Bulldogs produced in Great Britain. Curiously, it was first recognized as a distinct breed not in France or Great Britain, but in the United States. Originally bred for the utilitarian purpose of tenacious ratting, this muscular companion then became the fashion accessory of working-class Paris. No longer as numerous as it once was, the French Bulldog has moved up the social ladder and now resides in more affluent households.

KEY FACTS

COUNTRY OF ORIGIN France
DATE OF ORIGIN 1800s
FIRST USE Bull baiting
USE TODAY Companion
LIFE EXPECTANCY 11–12 years
OTHER NAME Bouledogue Français

WEIGHT RANGE
10–13 kg (22–28 lb)
HEIGHT RANGE
30.5–31.5 cm (12 in)

PUG

Short, deeply wrinkled muzzle

Short, cobby body, with wide back

Strong, straight legs

Pugs are an acquired habit, but once someone is habituated to them they become addictive. Pugnacious and individualistic, this vibrant breed is extremely tough and opinionated. It is independent and resolute – it knows what it wants and stands its ground until it is satisfied. Its muscular, compact body, flat face, and unblinking stare give it a strong presence and personality. Although it is strong willed and forceful, it is rarely aggressive. Affectionate with its human family, it makes an amusing and rewarding companion.

Large, dark, prominent eyes

Thin, soft, small, velvety, high-set ears

Tightly curled, twisted tail

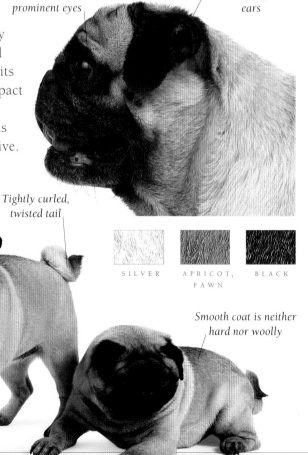

SILVER   APRICOT, FAWN   BLACK

Smooth coat is neither hard nor woolly

BREED HISTORY Miniaturized from mastiffs in the Far East at least 2,400 years ago, the Pug's ancestors were once companions of Buddhist priests. Introduced into Holland in the 1500s via the Dutch East India Company, this dog then became the companion of aristocrats and kings.

KEY FACTS

COUNTRY OF ORIGIN China
DATE OF ORIGIN Antiquity
FIRST USE Companion
USE TODAY Companion
LIFE EXPECTANCY 13–15 years
OTHER NAMES Carlin, Mops

WEIGHT RANGE
6–8 kg (14–18 lb)
HEIGHT RANGE
25–28 cm (10–11 in)

AMERICAN BULLDOG

Although it breeds true to type, the American Bulldog is not recognized by any of the large-breed-registering organizations in the United States, and has not been accepted into the show circuit. This bold and lively breed varies considerably in size and colour, and is similar to the original English working bulldog used for bull baiting in the 1700s. Robust and well muscled, it appeals to those who want a powerful companion. To ensure good manners, it needs experienced handling and broad socialization while it is young.

BREED HISTORY In the 1800s, a number of European immigrants were accompanied by their dogs when they emigrated to the United States. The American Bulldog is descended from these dogs, many of which were livestock workers.

Broad, square skull, with wide-set eyes

Small, high-set ears

Typically large, muscular male body

Short, tapering tail is normally thick

Thick, muscular, broad shoulders

Short, dense, glossy coat

Robust, hard, powerful muscle covers heavy-boned hind legs

KEY FACTS

COUNTRY OF ORIGIN United States
DATE OF ORIGIN 1700s
FIRST USE Guarding, dog fighting
USE TODAY Companion
LIFE EXPECTANCY 11–12 years
OTHER NAME Old Country Bulldog

WEIGHT RANGE
30–58 kg (65–130 lb)
HEIGHT RANGE
48–71 cm (19–28 in)

VARIETY OF COLOURS

OLDE ENGLISH BULLDOGGE

High-set, small ears are set well back on head

Short, broad muzzle, with moderately pendulous lips, has distinct stop

BREED HISTORY Attempting to recreate the old-type Bulldog, David Leavitt, a breeder in Pennsylvania, United States, developed this breed by crossing the English Bulldog, American Bulldog, Bullmastiff, and American Pit Bull Terrier.

VARIETY OF COLOURS

Short, close coat

Heavy-boned, straight forelegs

Head is large in proportion to body

Neck is as wide as head

This dog resulted from a breeder's attempt to recreate the ancient English Bulldog, but without its tendency towards aggression. By combining the affable modern English Bulldog with the more resolute American Pit Bull Terrier, Bullmastiff, and American Bulldog, he was successful in eliminating the English Bulldog's breathing problems and tail abnormalities, while at the same time diminishing the tenacity of some of the other breeds. However, this breed still has a profoundly aggressive personality and should be handled with extreme care.

Dramatically broad chest

KEY FACTS

COUNTRY OF ORIGIN United States
DATE OF ORIGIN 1900s
FIRST USE Companion
USE TODAY Companion
LIFE EXPECTANCY 11–12 years

WEIGHT RANGE
29.5–48 kg (65–105 lb)
HEIGHT RANGE
51–64 cm (20–25 in)

POODLES

KEY FACTS

COUNTRY OF ORIGIN France
DATE OF ORIGIN 1500s
FIRST USE Companion
USE TODAY Companion
LIFE EXPECTANCY 14–17 years
OTHER NAME Caniche

WEIGHT RANGE
Toy: 6.5–7.5 kg (14–16½ lb)
Miniature: 12–14 kg
 (26–30 lb)
Medium: 15–19 kg (33–42 lb)
HEIGHT RANGE
Toy: 25–28 cm (10–11 in)
Miniature: 28–38 cm
 (11–15 in)
Medium: 34–38 cm
 (13–15 in)

ALL
SOLID
COLOURS

*Woolly,
springy hair*

*Lively eyes are
slightly slanted*

*Ears are
covered with
wavy hair*

Toy Poodle

BREED HISTORY Herd-guarding and
water-retrieving Standard Poodles
were probably taken from
Germany to France at least
500 years ago. Certainly by
that time, the poodle had been
"bantomized" to the reduced
size of today's
Toy Poodle.

*Curly, resilient, non-
shedding hair grows
abundantly and needs
frequent trimming*

*Regardless of
style, hair is
never shaved*

*Pom-poms on
hind legs give
clown effect*

Miniature
Poodle

*Muzzle is
straight*

*Feet are small and
oval, with nails that
vary with coat colour*

BREED HISTORY A miniaturized
version of the Standard Poodle,
this breed became extremely
popular during the 1950s and
1960s. Slightly larger than the
Toy Poodle, the agile Miniature
was once a regular performer
in the circus ring.

F ifty years ago, the poodle was the world's
most popular dog – a fashion accessory in
cities worldwide. With popularity, however, came
indiscriminate breeding for quantity, not quality.
Both physical and behavioural
problems crept into this
alert and highly trainable
breed and it fell from favour,
replaced by the German
Shepherd and Yorkshire Terrier as
the world's most popular large and
small breeds. Today, safe in the hands of knowledgeable
breeders, small poodles are once more reliable
companions. Miniaturization sometimes brings with
it a heightened puppy-like dependence upon people,
but in the case of poodles, sound individuals
retain powerfully independent personalities.
At their best these dogs are exceptionally
responsive, trainable, and thoughtful.

*Forearms are
straight*

*Hair is
left uncut
on tail
tip*

Medium Poodle

*Forelegs are straight
and parallel*

BREED HISTORY Although the
Medium Poodle has not received
formal recognition everywhere, it
is accepted in some countries as a
separate breed. In size midway
between the Miniature and
Standard, it has the same
characteristics as its cousins.

DALMATIAN

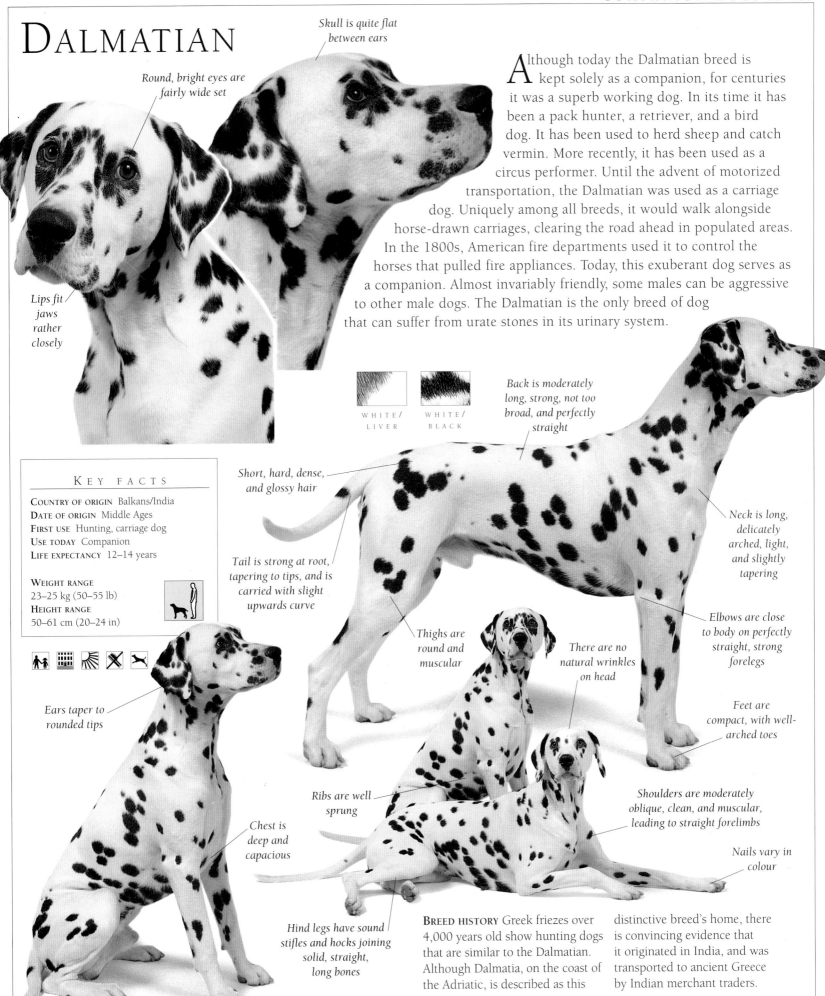

Skull is quite flat between ears

Round, bright eyes are fairly wide set

Lips fit jaws rather closely

Although today the Dalmatian breed is kept solely as a companion, for centuries it was a superb working dog. In its time it has been a pack hunter, a retriever, and a bird dog. It has been used to herd sheep and catch vermin. More recently, it has been used as a circus performer. Until the advent of motorized transportation, the Dalmatian was used as a carriage dog. Uniquely among all breeds, it would walk alongside horse-drawn carriages, clearing the road ahead in populated areas. In the 1800s, American fire departments used it to control the horses that pulled fire appliances. Today, this exuberant dog serves as a companion. Almost invariably friendly, some males can be aggressive to other male dogs. The Dalmatian is the only breed of dog that can suffer from urate stones in its urinary system.

WHITE/LIVER   WHITE/BLACK

Back is moderately long, strong, not too broad, and perfectly straight

Short, hard, dense, and glossy hair

Neck is long, delicately arched, light, and slightly tapering

KEY FACTS

COUNTRY OF ORIGIN Balkans/India
DATE OF ORIGIN Middle Ages
FIRST USE Hunting, carriage dog
USE TODAY Companion
LIFE EXPECTANCY 12–14 years

WEIGHT RANGE
23–25 kg (50–55 lb)
HEIGHT RANGE
50–61 cm (20–24 in)

Tail is strong at root, tapering to tips, and is carried with slight upwards curve

Elbows are close to body on perfectly straight, strong forelegs

Thighs are round and muscular

There are no natural wrinkles on head

Feet are compact, with well-arched toes

Ears taper to rounded tips

Ribs are well sprung

Shoulders are moderately oblique, clean, and muscular, leading to straight forelimbs

Chest is deep and capacious

Nails vary in colour

Hind legs have sound stifles and hocks joining solid, straight, long bones

BREED HISTORY Greek friezes over 4,000 years old show hunting dogs that are similar to the Dalmatian. Although Dalmatia, on the coast of the Adriatic, is described as this distinctive breed's home, there is convincing evidence that it originated in India, and was transported to ancient Greece by Indian merchant traders.

LABRADOODLE

VARIETY
OF
COLOURS

Body is slightly heavier than that of a poodle

Topknot has been cut, exaggerating poodle-like look of face

Muzzle is slightly narrower than a Labrador Retriever's

Tightly curled hair grows without shedding

Ears are set just above eye level

Forelimbs are robustly muscled

KEY FACTS

COUNTRY OF ORIGIN Australia
DATE OF ORIGIN 1980s
FIRST USE Guide dog
USE TODAY Guide dog, companion
LIFE EXPECTANCY 13–15 years

WEIGHT RANGE
25–35 kg (55–77 lb)
HEIGHT RANGE
54–65 cm (21–26 in)

BREED HISTORY
In 1989 Wally Conron of Kew, Australia, began crossing the Labrador Retriever and Standard Poodle, wanting to create a guide dog suitable for blind people allergic to dog hair.

This is a classic example of logical and planned cross breeding – the aim being to create a new "breed" with the best attributes of the original breeds. It is still too early to say whether this particular cross – between the Labrador Retriever and poodle – will be successful. Wally Conron's objective is to produce assistant dogs that do not shed hair. Labradoodle guide dogs have been successfully trained and placed in Australia and Hawaii, but as yet the non-shedding characteristic of the Standard Poodle has not become a fixed attribute. As regards temperament, however, this appears to be a very successful combination.

BICHON/YORKIE

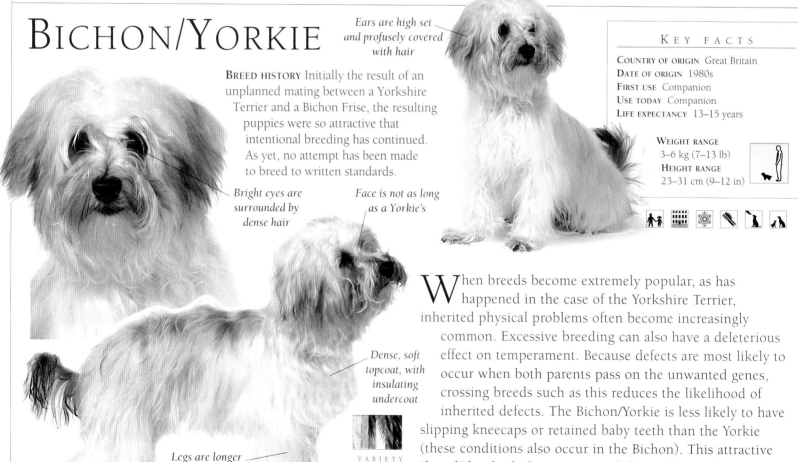

Ears are high set and profusely covered with hair

BREED HISTORY Initially the result of an unplanned mating between a Yorkshire Terrier and a Bichon Frise, the resulting puppies were so attractive that intentional breeding has continued. As yet, no attempt has been made to breed to written standards.

Bright eyes are surrounded by dense hair

Face is not as long as a Yorkie's

KEY FACTS

COUNTRY OF ORIGIN Great Britain
DATE OF ORIGIN 1980s
FIRST USE Companion
USE TODAY Companion
LIFE EXPECTANCY 13–15 years

WEIGHT RANGE
3–6 kg (7–13 lb)
HEIGHT RANGE
23–31 cm (9–12 in)

Dense, soft topcoat, with insulating undercoat

Legs are longer than a Bichon's

VARIETY
OF
COLOURS

When breeds become extremely popular, as has happened in the case of the Yorkshire Terrier, inherited physical problems often become increasingly common. Excessive breeding can also have a deleterious effect on temperament. Because defects are most likely to occur when both parents pass on the unwanted genes, crossing breeds such as this reduces the likelihood of inherited defects. The Bichon/Yorkie is less likely to have slipping kneecaps or retained baby teeth than the Yorkie (these conditions also occur in the Bichon). This attractive "breed" has both the tenacity and the resilience of the Yorkshire Terrier, as well as the insulating coat of the Bichon.

COCKERPOO

Jaws provide ample space for well-spaced teeth

Sturdy back is as long as dog is high

Hip joints do not suffer from inherited problems

VARIETY OF COLOURS

KEY FACTS

COUNTRY OF ORIGIN United States
DATE OF ORIGIN 1960s
FIRST USE Companion
USE TODAY Companion
LIFE EXPECTANCY 13–15 years

WEIGHT RANGE
9–11 kg (20–24 lb)
HEIGHT RANGE
35–38 cm (14–15 in)

Face resembles that of both poodle and cocker spaniel

Hereditary slack kneecaps seldom occur

Dense coat protects skin

BREED HISTORY Crosses between the Miniature Poodle and American Cocker Spaniel have existed for over 30 years. The Cockerpoo is now so common in North America that it may well soon obtain breed standards and formal recognition.

Tail is long and close

The Cockerpoo – a cross between the American Cocker Spaniel and Miniature Poodle – is much sought after in North America. Like other crosses, the first dogs were the result of unplanned matings, but more recently, as numbers have increased, matings between Cockerpoos have become planned. The poodle is evident, both in the face and coat texture, and in the personality of this new "breed". Like the poodle, the Cockerpoo is an intent observer, not given to the hyperactive excesses of many American Cocker Spaniels. An added bonus is that the Cockerpoo has a much lower incidence of skin problems than the American Cocker.

BULL BOXER

Lopped ears are set above eye level

Eyes are wide set

KEY FACTS

COUNTRY OF ORIGIN Great Britain
DATE OF ORIGIN 1990s
FIRST USE Companion
USE TODAY Companion
LIFE EXPECTANCY 12–13 years

WEIGHT RANGE
17–24 kg (37–53 lb)
HEIGHT RANGE
41–53 cm (16–21 in)

The resulting dogs of this cross between the Boxer and Staffordshire Bull Terrier have characteristics that make them in some ways superior to their parents. While Boxers seldom outgrow puppy behaviour until they are over three years old, Bull Boxer puppies mature earlier. And while many Staffordshires are unreliable with small animals, this cross is less inclined to chase; it has also inherited the Staffie's gregarious nature. It is possible that this crossing reduces the Boxer's predisposition to skin cancer and the Staffordshire's predisposition to heart disease.

Back slopes slightly

Powerful hind legs are indicative of this dog's mastiff heritage

Coat is close, smooth, hard, shiny, and dense

BREED HISTORY Another consequence of unplanned breeding, in this instance between a Boxer and a Staffordshire Bull Terrier, the resulting puppies were so attractive that breeding has continued.

Forelimbs are leaner than a Staffordshire's

Feet are small and compact

VARIETY OF COLOURS

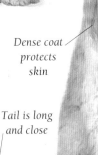

NORTH AMERICAN SHEPHERD

KEY FACTS

COUNTRY OF ORIGIN United States
DATE OF ORIGIN 1968
FIRST USE Companion
USE TODAY Companion
LIFE EXPECTANCY 12–13 years
OTHER NAME Miniature Australian Shepherd

WEIGHT RANGE
7–13.5 kg (15–30 lb)
HEIGHT RANGE
33–46 cm (13–18 in)

The North American Shepherd is the result of a specific breeding programme to produce small companion dogs for people living in towns. Breeders have attempted to maintain the attractive temperament characteristics of the Australian Shepherd, the breed's progenitor, such as calmness and sensitivity, while reducing its size. A fine companion, it also enjoys working small stock.

BREED HISTORY A breeding programme was initiated in 1968, involving two small Australian Shepherds. By 1980 conformation was fixed, and the breed's name was established in 1993.

Top of skull is quite flat and clean cut

Slightly wavy coat is of moderate length

Lips do not hang over lower jaw

Feet are oval and compact

Hindquarters are same length as forequarters

VARIETY OF COLOURS

HIMALAYAN SHEEPDOG

BREED HISTORY This is an ancient breed, and may be closely related to the root stock of the great mountain sheepdogs that spread from northern India across central Asia into Turkey and then on into Europe.

Deep-set eyes are quite close together

Rounded ears are set high, and are of medium length

Stop separates muzzle from broad head

Medium-sized head is rather flat at top

Bushy, medium-length, high-set tail curls loosely

KEY FACTS

COUNTRY OF ORIGIN India
DATE OF ORIGIN Antiquity
FIRST USE Livestock guarding/herding
USE TODAY Livestock guarding/herding
LIFE EXPECTANCY 10–11 years
OTHER NAMES Bhotia, Bangara Mastiff

WEIGHT RANGE
23–41 kg (50–90 lb)
HEIGHT RANGE
51–66 cm (20–26 in)

Thick, harsh topcoat

VARIETY OF COLOURS

Strong back is moderate in length

Deep, strong, well-ribbed chest

Cat-like, medium-sized, compact feet

Well-boned, straight front legs

Professor Panwar of Lucknow University, writing for the Indian Kennel Club, tells of growing up among these powerful, muscular guardian dogs. He believes that India's Bangara Mastiff and Bhotia are, in fact, the same breed, collectively known as the Himalayan Sheepdog. This dog is a robust, efficient guard and herder, although it is likely that in the future it will be kept primarily as a companion.

THAI RIDGEBACK

KEY FACTS

COUNTRY OF ORIGIN Thailand
DATE OF ORIGIN Middle Ages
FIRST USE Guarding, hunting
USE TODAY Companion, guarding
LIFE EXPECTANCY 12–13 years
OTHER NAME Mah Thai

WEIGHT RANGE
23–34 kg (51–75 lb)
HEIGHT RANGE
58–66 cm (23–26 in)

SILVER

BLUE

CHESTNUT

BLACK

Top of skull is flat and slopes gently to stop

Rather large, high-set, triangular, pricked ears incline forwards

Almond-shaped, dark-brown eyes have alert expression

Large, black nose

Muzzle is wedge shaped and powerful looking

Strong, muscular shoulders

Head is carried high on strong, firm, clean-cut neck

Streamlined, muscular body

Jet-black nails on fine feet

Back is strong and firm, and covered with dense hair

Tail tapers towards tip

Ribs are well sprung, with no hint of barrel appearance

Hind legs are long and moderately lean, with slight bend to stifles

Pliant rolls on neck when dog is alert

Thighs are solid and muscular

Straight, long forelegs lead to well-muscled shoulders

BREED HISTORY Only recently "discovered" by Western dog owners, the Thai Ridgeback has bred pure in eastern Thailand for centuries. Physical isolation ensured that it seldom, if ever, had the opportunity to cross breed with dog breeds of European origin.

In Thailand, isolated populations of dogs have bred true for hundreds of years. This unique breed is relatively unknown outside eastern Thailand, but was chanced upon recently in Bangkok by an American dog enthusiast, Jack Sterling, who has exported a number of individuals to California. Known locally simply as the Mah Thai (Thai Dog), this ridge-backed breed served as a house guard and hunting companion for centuries. Its body is a classic example of a cross between a spitz-type dog and a primitive hound. A Thai kennel club (The Dog Association of Thailand) is now ensuring that this unusual breed continues to thrive in its native land.

DANISH CHICKEN DOG

All-purpose farm dogs exist wherever farmers need canine helpers to control vermin and drive livestock. This is a remnant breed from Denmark and southern Sweden, almost completely forgotten until recently, when Scandinavian breeders revived it. Although it is not yet recognized by any national or international breed clubs, the Danish Chicken Dog is occasionally seen at regional dog shows.

Lips fit neatly over strong jaws, with rather large teeth

Close, shiny, soft, smooth coat

No dewlap on tight skin over neck

VARIETY OF COLOURS

Chest is moderately deep, just reaching elbows

Lopped ears are set to sides of head

Muzzle is moderately long

Compact, round feet, with soft pads, and firm white nails

Hindquarters are robust and powerful

KEY FACTS

COUNTRY OF ORIGIN Denmark/Sweden
DATE OF ORIGIN 1700s
FIRST USE Livestock control
USE TODAY Companion
LIFE EXPECTANCY 12–13 years
OTHER NAME Danish Farm Dog
WEIGHT RANGE
12–14 kg (24–30 lb)
HEIGHT RANGE
26–30 cm (14–18 in)

BREED HISTORY Medium-sized dogs, with origins in Germany, France, and Great Britain, arrived in Denmark centuries ago and functioned as ratters and livestock dogs. The Chicken Dog accompanied the Danes when they occupied southern Sweden.

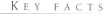

LUCAS TERRIER

Ears are set above eye level and hang away from head

Not unlike the internationally recognized Czesky Terrier, this rare British breed's type is somewhat variable. However, the Lucas Terrier is an adaptable and friendly dog; it is unlikely to bite aggressively and is good with children, but like many terriers, has a hard mouth and snaps unwittingly. Its future remains rather uncertain.

Thick, hard pads

Neck is moderate in length

Large feet are covered with protective hair

KEY FACTS

COUNTRY OF ORIGIN Great Britain
DATE OF ORIGIN 1950s
FIRST USE Pack hunting
USE TODAY Companion, pack hunting
LIFE EXPECTANCY 14–15 years

WEIGHT RANGE
4.5–6 kg (10–14 lb)
HEIGHT RANGE
25–30 cm (10–12 in)

Large, gentle-looking eyes

Moustache and beard give aura of dignity

VARIETY OF COLOURS

Chest is not excessively deep

BREED HISTORY Sir Jocelyn Lucas, feeling that the Sealyham Terrier was too big to work efficiently, bred Sealyham bitches with Norfolk Terrier dogs, creating the breed that carries his name. It has not yet received formal recognition.

SHILOH SHEPHERD

Overall appearance is rather heavy

Back is broad, strong, and solid

BREED HISTORY An American breeder, Tina Barber, unhappy with the degree of nervousness that she saw displayed in the German Shepherd Dog, began breeding for size, sound hips, and steady temperament. This resulted in the Shiloh Shepherd, which received formal recognition in 1990.

Ears are moderately pointed and erect

KEY FACTS	
COUNTRY OF ORIGIN United States	
DATE OF ORIGIN 1980s	
FIRST USE Companion	
USE TODAY Companion	
LIFE EXPECTANCY 11–12 years	
WEIGHT RANGE 36–73 kg (80–160 lb)	
HEIGHT RANGE 66–76 cm (26–30 in)	

Muzzle is very long, almost like that of a collie

I n the United States, the Shiloh is now recognized as a distinct breed. Breeders are very particular about size, temperament, and the condition of its hips. The breed club promotes temperament testing and issues certificates for individuals which it considers to be neither fearfully shy nor dominantly aggressive. Although the Shiloh is still relatively unknown, it makes an agreeable companion.

Both upper and lower thighs are well muscled

Tail, hanging like a plume, is quite long and thickly covered in dense guard hair

PRAZSKY KRYSAVIK

S eldom seen outside the Czech and Slovak Republics, the Prazsky Krysavik (meaning beautiful Prague dog) has been selectively bred as an urban companion. Although there are fewer than 600 individuals, most of them in Prague, breeders have successfully fixed this personable little dog's type, and it is now being exhibited at European dog shows.

KEY FACTS	
COUNTRY OF ORIGIN Czech Republic	
DATE OF ORIGIN 1980s	
FIRST USE Companion	
USE TODAY Companion	
LIFE EXPECTANCY 12–14 years	
WEIGHT RANGE 1–3 kg (2–6 lb)	
HEIGHT RANGE 19.5–20.5 cm (7–8 in)	

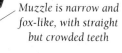

Muzzle is narrow and fox-like, with straight but crowded teeth

Chest is broad but not at all deep, descending only partly to elbows

Neck is moderately long and narrow, supporting delicate head

BREED HISTORY The Prazsky Krysavik was developed by Czechs and Slovaks who wanted to create a distinctly non-utilitarian breed. This slight and delicate breed is probably the most recent, strictly companion dog to develop in central Europe.

Lean, delicate body is covered with thin skin

Very short, thin, glossy hair

Thin-boned legs are susceptible to injuries

RANDOM-BRED DOGS

REFERRED TO BY DIFFERENT NAMES at different times – for example, as mongrels or curs – random-bred dogs all share a characteristic trait. They have never been bred for an exclusive purpose and are therefore far less likely to suffer from the wide range of inherited medical problems, such as blindness, heart disease, and hip dysplasia, that occur with distressing frequency in certain pure-bred dogs. However, random-bred dogs are inexpensive to buy and plentiful. As a result, they are valued less by society than pure-bred dogs, even though the companionship they provide is just as rewarding.

GENETIC AND ENVIRONMENTAL INFLUENCES

A dog's personality is determined by many factors, the most important being genetics and early environment. Genetics are profoundly influential – breeding dogs of similar temperament is more likely to produce dogs of like temperament than breeding dogs of random temperaments. This, of course, is the basis of selective breeding – if you choose a specific breed it is more likely that you will acquire a dog with known behaviour than if you choose a random-bred dog.

Genetics, however, do not determine the whole personality. Early environment is very critical. Random-bred puppies raised properly in a family environment grow to become reliable adults. Unfortunately, random-bred dogs are often the results of unplanned pregnancies, and owners sometimes disregard or even discard them. These individuals consistently show a high level of anxiety-related behaviour problems.

FERALS AND STRAYS

Feral dogs are random bred; they eat, breed, give birth, and survive outside homes, but depend upon the detritus of human habitation for survival. Few feral dogs exist in North America and northern Europe, but they are common in Central and South America, in parts of the Balkans and the former Soviet Empire, in Turkey and the Middle East, and in Africa and Asia. Although they breed randomly, they often breed true to type – if their breeding were brought under human control, regional random-bred dogs would be redesignated into categories of pure-bred dogs. Stray dogs are different. Unlike feral dogs, they are raised in homes and often return to them after a day's wandering. However, the random-bred dog's desire to wander is no stronger than that of pure-bred dogs. It is lack of human responsibility that produces this kind of behaviour.

Alert guardians
Regardless of background, all dogs willingly protect their home territories. This short-legged dog alerts its family when it hears any unexpected noise.

RESCUED DOGS ARE MORE LIKELY TO BARK THAN THOSE RAISED AT HOME FROM PUPPYHOOD

ACQUIRING A RANDOM-BRED DOG

The best place to acquire a random-bred dog is from a neighbour or from a friend's litter of puppies. The mother's temperament, and possibly also the father's, can be observed. By selecting a puppy, you eliminate the unknown variables of early learning that can so dramatically affect later temperament.

Random-bred dogs are not common in Scandinavia, but account for the majority of dogs in virtually all other countries. They certainly form the vast majority of dogs in dog shelters, which always have a surplus needing good homes. Some organizations, such as the charity Hearing Dogs for the Deaf in Great Britain, which trains dogs to act as ears for profoundly deaf people,

Acquiring puppies
It is unlikely that you will inherit known behaviour problems if you acquire a random-bred dog while it is still a puppy.

GENTLE EYES SUGGEST THAT THIS DOG WILL BE A GOOD COMPANION

LONG MUZZLE INDICATES NO LIKELY BREATHING PROBLEMS

LOPPED EARS SUCH AS THESE ARE COMMON IN MOST EUROPEAN RANDOM-BRED DOGS

BODY IS COVERED WITH A DOUBLE COAT OF LUSH, DENSE HAIR

FACE IS LEAN, WITH COLLIE SHAPE, SUGGESTING THIS DOG'S POSSIBLE HERITAGE

Needing good homes
Dog shelters are more likely to be filled with random-bred dogs than with pure-bred ones. Behavioural problems are more likely to occur in these dogs, not because they are prone to them, but because they have been lost or abandoned.

LUSH AND DENSE COAT NEEDS DAILY BRUSHING TO KEEP IT FREE FROM ODOUR AND TANGLES

Relaxed companions
When rescued, these dogs initially preferred each other's company to that of humans. Now they are content household canine companions.

POWERFUL THIGH
MUSCLES HELP DOG
JUMP OVER OBSTACLES

COAT IS SHORT,
DENSE, GLOSSY,
AND HARD

HEAD IS MASSIVE
AND BROAD,
SUGGESTING THAT
THIS DOG HAS A
MASTIFF
BACKGROUND

LOOK OF
INTENSITY
IN EYES

Grooming needs
*The coats of random-bred dogs
vary considerably from short and
smooth, to heavy, dense, and wiry.
This rough coat needs routine
brushing to prevent
matting. Matts can be a
particular problem in
the beard.*

CHEST IS DEEP AND
ROBUST, WITH AMPLE
ROOM FOR HEART
AND LUNGS

Requirements for exercise
*This dog is an ideal companion for
someone who enjoys exercise. Some
random-bred dogs are content with
minimal exercise; others need
frequent exercise.*

WIRY BEARD
GIVES LOOK
OF DIGNITY

rescue random-bred dogs brought to dog-
welfare organizations and find that they
readily respond to both standard obedience
training and complicated sound-response
training. Eventual adult size can be difficult
to estimate with some random-bred
puppies, and can vary dramatically among
members of the same litter. So, too, can coat
length and texture. Random-
bred dogs are less expensive
to purchase than pure-
bred dogs, but this can be
curiously detrimental to
their well being. When a substantial
investment is made in the purchase of a
dog, typical owners wish to protect that
investment. One result is that the dog is
likely to receive good routine veterinary
attention. Random-bred dogs are just as
susceptible to infectious disease, but
because they are inexpensive to buy they
may not always receive the same degree of
care. Bearing this in mind,
good dog shelters now charge
reasonable fees for "recycled"
random-bred dogs and "vet"
potential buyers for
responsible attitudes.

Trainability
*This cross breed looks
predominantly
Rottweiler, and thrives
on both obedience and
agility work.*

THIS ATHLETIC
DOG NEEDS
FREQUENT
EXERCISE

THIS TYPE OF RANDOM-
BRED DOG WAS MADE
POPULAR BY THE
BENJIE FILMS

observe the dog's
reaction to them. By
carrying out a range of
simple tests, you can
roughly determine the
personality of any random-
bred dog. In its ability to offer
companionship and affection, or
to bark a warning about potential
intruders, the random-bred dog is generally
as efficient as any pure-bred dog. In its
doggedness, nothing outshines it.

TEMPERAMENT TESTING
There is no doubt that dogs which have
been housed in dog shelters and rescue
centres have a higher level of temperament
and behaviour problems than dogs that
remain in stable households. Pragmatically,
this means that random-bred dogs have a
high incidence of potential problems like
destructiveness, fear biting, excessive
barking, or a lack of "manners".
When considering offering your
home to a rescued dog, ask the
rescue centre whether it has
carried out temperament testing.
Make sure that the dog's size,
exercise requirements, and feeding
demands are compatible with your
own living environment.
If temperament testing has not
been carried out, do it yourself,
concentrating on areas that apply
to your circumstances. For
example, if you have children,
take them with you and

Behaviour problems
*Recoiling when it is approached, this
dog shows fearful behaviour – a typical
problem in dogs that have been mistreated.*

Chapter Six

CARING FOR YOUR DOG

When we actively chose to breed dogs for our own needs, we undertook an obligation to care for them. Today, the dog is an integral part of human society, dependent upon us for its well being. Choosing the right dogs for our lifestyles is our first responsibility. Keeping them mentally and physically alert, well nourished, properly groomed, and free from disease are further demands. For most dog owners these are rewarding responsibilities, the basis for the great satisfaction canine companionship can offer.

CHOOSING A DOG

THE VARIETY OF DOGS to choose from is enormous, and it is important to select carefully, according to your interests, your lifestyle, and your current and future circumstances. Consider the differences between raising a dog from puppyhood or acquiring it as an adult. Consider the benefits or drawbacks of each sex, as well as the pros and cons of neutered dogs. Then think about size – large dogs do not necessarily need more exercise than small ones, but almost always require more space. Then you must decide whether a random-bred, cross-bred, or pure-bred dog is right for you. Finally, you should make sure you choose your new dog from the best source.

Cute today, unwanted tomorrow
A puppy looks cuddly while young, but when it grows as large as this French Mastiff eventually will, it may lose some of its charm. Consider the attributes of the adult-sized dog, not just its size at eight weeks of age.

PENDULOUS LIPS CREATE TENDENCY TO DROOL STRINGY SALIVA

LOOSE SKIN FOLDS AROUND EYES MAY CAUSE EYE PROBLEMS

Fashionably unique
Breeds vary in fashion and status. A recently revived breed like the Shar Pei becomes a talking point because it is distinctive and rare. It also has a higher-than-average incidence of medical problems that can be costly to treat.

PUPPY OR ADULT?

The primary advantage of acquiring an adult dog is that it usually arrives house trained. There are few other advantages. Although it may have a delightful temperament with you, there is the possibility that it has hidden behavioural problems such as a dislike of children. If you plan to get an adult dog, carry out simple tests to try and determine its

personality. Watch its behaviour as you approach it; put it on a lead and take it for a walk among people. Walk it past a dog and a child it has not met. Open an umbrella in its presence to see if it takes fright easily. Command it to sit. Leave it alone with a toy for 10 minutes. By carrying out these or other suitable tests, you can make a rough evaluation of its temperament and anticipate any potential problems that might arise. Puppies are still at the impressionable, early-learning stage of life, but even eight-week-old members of the same litter each have their own distinct personalities. The shyest individuals cling to their mother or cringe in corners, while the boldest march confidently forwards to inspect you. These are the extremes of temperament within the litter. Choose according to what you want from a dog.

destructive, and likely to be snappy with children. Females are easier to obedience train and house train. They also demand more affection. There is no difference between the sexes in excitability, nervous barking, or defensive barking. Male dogs are more likely to urine mark territory and to wander. Females have two heat cycles each year that involve blood-tinged vaginal discharges lasting about a week.

LARGE OR SMALL?

Small dogs have small appetites, but some individuals can be exceptionally selective about what they eat. A consequence is that they may demand high-quality, expensive food. Pet-food manufacturers are familiar with this small-dog ploy and produce ranges of particularly tasty food for them. Small dogs almost invariably need as much exercise as large breeds, but can get their exercise in more confined locations. Some small dogs, such as terriers, need more exercise on a more regular basis than do some large breeds, such as the St. Bernard and Irish Wolfhound. Although many breeds of small dog were created solely for companionship, not all of them are equally companionable. Aggression in small dogs becomes almost comical because of size; however, some small breeds, particularly small terriers and the Chihuahua, can be as aggressive as any other dogs, or more so.

Companion or worker?
A pure-bred dog is not always an ideal companion. The English Foxhound is bred primarily to work with its pack. It has not as yet been selectively bred solely for companionship. When choosing a pure-bred dog, consider the individual dog's background, and whether it comes from working or companion stock.

BODY IS ROBUST AND NEEDS FREQUENT, VIGOROUS EXERCISE AND ACTIVITY

MALE OR FEMALE?

Even in pre-pubertal puppies, there are sex differences in behaviour. Male puppies have "masculinized" brains, affected by a surge of testosterone just before birth. Females remain behaviourally "neutral" until puberty. There are distinct differences in behaviour between the sexes. Males are more likely to try to be dominant over their owners, act aggressively with other dogs, defend their territories, and be generally more active. To a lesser extent, they are more playful,

Background unknown
Random- and cross-bred dogs are less likely to suffer from inherited medical disorders than are pure-bred dogs. Conversely, adult temperament is generally less predictable. Because random- and cross-bred dogs frequently find themselves in dog shelters, they can have a high incidence of separation-anxiety problems.

Small dogs are ideal for apartments or compact homes with limited space, but still need daily physical and mental exercise and stimulation. While the yapping and barking of the small dog acts as a good deterrent to criminals, larger dogs are more impressive. This is one of the main reasons why large dogs are so popular. However, a large breed takes up more physical space in the home. A giant breed can be overwhelming, especially in small homes. Large dogs eat more, but are often less fickle about their diet.

Size is not an indicator of temperament. Large breeds like the Dobermann and German Shepherd can be more puppy-like and dependent than smaller breeds such as the Fox Terrier. Large breeds, especially those with dense coats, are not very suitable for house-proud individuals. The choice of coat texture depends upon where you live and on your willingness to groom your dog. Dogs with dark, thick, dense coats are not suitable for hot, sunny climates. Similarly, sparse, short, smooth coats offer little insulation in cold, wet climates. Smooth coats like the Boxer's need only intermittent maintenance. Lush, dense coats such as the Afghan's need daily brushing and combing. Dogs with non-shedding coats, like poodles, are the most suitable for people with allergies.

PEDIGREE OR MONGREL?

Deciding whether to acquire a pure-bred or random-bred dog is as much an ethical decision as it is a practical one. The advantages of acquiring a pure-bred dog are numerous. There

HAIRY MOUSTACHE MAKES THIS DOG ENDEARINGLY ATTRACTIVE

are hundreds of different breeds, with differing mental and physical characteristics. The choice is daunting, but with careful selection you can choose a breed that is most suitable for your needs and lifestyle. Most important, you are bringing into your home a known quantity. There is a range of behaviours within each breed, and statistically you know that a member of a breed is more likely to develop according to the norm than otherwise. You know its attributes and deficits, and even its potential life expectancy.

The main disadvantage of pure-bred dogs is that by creating breeds – groups of dogs with similar conformation and behaviour – we accidentally concentrate deleterious genes as well. This results in a relatively high potential for inherited disease. This can be manifested in skin allergies; in other circumstances, it means serious heart disease, as in the Dobermann or Cavalier King Charles Spaniel.

A random-bred dog, by the very randomness of its breeding, is less likely to suffer from inherited disease than a pure-bred dog. Its potential, size, feeding, grooming requirements, and temperament are, however, unknown. Although society places more value on pure-bred dogs (*see pages 290–291*), it is random-bred dogs that are most often in need of good homes.

Physically demanding
Certain breeds need more exercise and grooming than others. This long-haired, white German Shepherd Dog needs good quantities of both. Some breeders believe that the white coat is associated with a nervous disposition.

ROBUST BODY NEEDS LARGE, OPEN SPACES FOR EXERCISE

HEAVY COAT NEEDS FREQUENT GROOMING TO REMOVE DEAD HAIR

Easy to exercise
Although dachshunds are very active, because of their short legs they need less physical space for exercise than many breeds. They have a higher-than-average incidence of slipped discs.

SHORT LEGS REDUCE SPEED AND NEED FOR OPEN SPACES

ACQUIRING A DOG

Dogs can be acquired from breeders, pet shops, animal-rescue centres, breed-rescue groups, friends, through veterinarians, or straight off the street. Some sources are better than others. Knowledgeable breeders often know more than almost anyone else about the behaviour of their breed. They are generally frank about the breed's advantages and disadvantages, although some breeders may gloss over the potential problems inherent in their breed. Commercial breeding establishments that sell dogs primarily as a business venture are rather less reliable than breeders affiliated with breed clubs.

Good breeders employ vets to carry out preventative medical examinations – to vaccinate and eliminate any parasites contracted from the parents. Dog shelters and rescue centres often carry out medical examinations, neutering programmes, and behavioural evaluations of their dogs (explaining each dog's assets and potential problems), as well as keeping track of dogs they have homed. Breed-rescue centres are usually excellent, and often very protective of their charges. Friends are an excellent source of dogs, especially if you know the dog or its parents. So too are local vets, who usually know behavioural as well as medical backgrounds.

ESSENTIAL EQUIPMENT

THE DOG'S BASIC FURNISHING requirements are simple. It needs to be properly identified, safely controlled, securely housed, nutritiously fed, and kept mentally and physically active and alert. Choose a collar, and walking and training leads, according to your dog's weight, strength, and level of activity. In some circumstances, a head halter or body harness is advisable. Provide your dog with its own bed – this is its own personal space. Dogs are generally content to use crates as beds, provided they have been trained to do so from early puppyhood. Use strong, hygienic food and water bowls, and provide a limited number of well-made toys for your dog's amusement, for playing either on its own or with you.

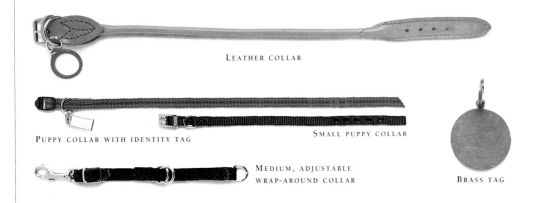

LEATHER COLLAR

PUPPY COLLAR WITH IDENTITY TAG

SMALL PUPPY COLLAR

MEDIUM, ADJUSTABLE
WRAP-AROUND COLLAR

BRASS TAG

Collars and tags (left)
Inexpensive, easy-to-clean, soft, nylon collars are excellent for growing puppies, and can be replaced with larger models as a dog grows. Rolled leather collars cause less damage to the hair on the neck than flat ones. Attach an identity tag, with a relevant contact telephone number, to the collar. Augment this with temporary information when you take your dog on holiday.

Leads (below)
Use a reliable, strong, short lead for walking your dog. During training, use a long training lead to ensure that your dog is committed to respond to command. If your dog is unreliable off its lead, use the long training lead for exercise and keep alert to its activities.

LEATHER LEAD

NYLON LEAD

2-M (20-FT) COTTON-
WEBBING LEAD

IMMEDIATE NEEDS
Quality equipment is usually an excellent investment. It is unlikely to be damaged and it is long lasting. The most immediate needs for a newly acquired dog are food and water bowls, a bed, a collar and lead, and an identity tag with a contact telephone number. For hygienic as well as practical reasons, avoid using your own tableware for feeding your dog. Provide sturdy, shatterproof, non-slipping food and water bowls. It is useful to place these on a mat that absorbs any water which might splash while the dog is drinking. Consider buying a special can-opener and knife and fork for preparing your dog's food.

Bedding should be comfortable and easy to clean. Wicker baskets are attractive but easily chewed, especially by puppies, and extremely difficult to clean when soiled. Beds made of moulded plastic are easy to clean. They appeal to dogs because they provide secure "walls" to lie against. "Bean-bag" beds are very attractive to dogs, since they provide both comfort and insulation. This form of bedding usually has a removable cover and is machine washable. Finally, a useful piece of puppy equipment is a crate, which provides the dog with a safe space.

Halters, harnesses, and muzzles
A head halter is excellent for controlling a powerful dog. It should not be used on a dog with very short legs – its nose would be pulled too close to the ground when it surged ahead. Body harnesses eliminate tension on the neck, especially in the area of the windpipe. Well-designed muzzles prevent scavenging and reduce the risk of bites.

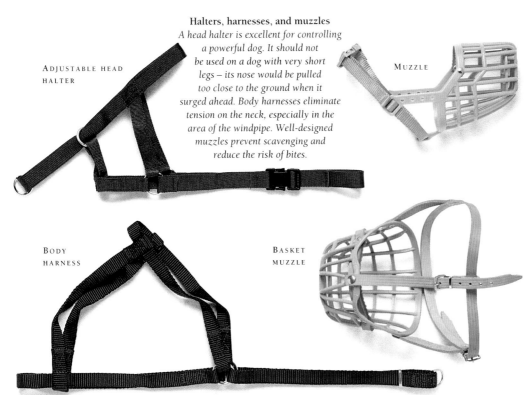

ADJUSTABLE HEAD
HALTER

MUZZLE

BODY
HARNESS

BASKET
MUZZLE

EQUIPMENT FOR CONTROL
When selecting appropriate collars and leads, your dog's temperament and size are important considerations. Your local veterinary clinic or dog-training club will provide experienced advice on what is best for your dog. In virtually all outdoor

FIRM, HYGIENIC BASKET IS EASY TO CLEAN

FORM-FITTING BEDDING RETAINS BODY HEAT

Beds and bedding
A bed is a dog's personal place. The basket (top) *is firm, with strong sides to sleep against. Washable bedding fits inside and provides a comfortable and hygienic resting place. A beanbag* (above) *also makes an extremely luxurious dog bed.*

FOOD AND WATER BOWLS

Food and water utensils
These food and water bowls are safe, hygienic, and robust. The ceramic bowl is heavy, while the lighter steel bowl is mounted on rubber to prevent it from slipping. Clean the food bowl after each meal. Wash the water bowl daily, replenishing water when necessary.

TYPES OF TOY

ROPE

THROW BALL

TUG TOY

CHEW TOY

CHEW TOY

CHEWY BONE

FRISBEE

PLASTIC BONE

SQUEAKY TOYS

Well-made toys satisfy the dog's natural inclination to chase, chew, and tug. Avoid cheap and shoddy toys that are easily damaged or can be swallowed. Rubber and rope tug-of-war toys are excellent for playing indoors with most dogs. Frisbees and throw toys on ropes are wonderful for outdoor exercise, and for training a dog to retrieve. Dogs learn to anticipate the flight patterns of frisbees and the symmetry of a ball's bounce. The oddly shaped rubber "Kong" bounces eccentrically, and provides agility exercise for dogs. A small selection of chewable rubber, nylon, and rawhide toys is excellent for dogs that are left alone for short periods. Leave your scent on a toy by handling it – this will make it more attractive. A hollow "Kong" filled with cheese makes a good toy for a dog to amuse itself with in your absence.

situations, you will need a soft, light training lead – these are often made of cotton or meshed nylon. Available in various lengths, they can be geared to the size of your dog and the level of training you have reached. Start with a 2 m- (6 ft-) length lead and use this both indoors and outdoors to ensure that your dog responds to commands. For exercise, a body harness may well be appropriate for breeds with potentially delicate windpipes, such as the Yorkshire Terrier, or for breeds with robust necks, like the Pug. Head halters act much like horse halters and are extremely useful for controlling large, enthusiastic young dogs. When the dog surges ahead, its momentum pulls on the halter and draws its head downwards. The dog stops pulling on its own. Dogs should be trained to wear muzzles to prevent potential conflict with other dogs, and to obey local laws.

CRATES AND PLAYPENS

PUPPY CRATE

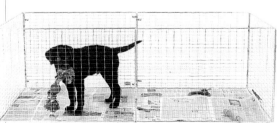

PUPPY PLAYPEN

Safe space
A crate is an ideal "home" for a dog. Puppies willingly learn that it is a comfortable and secure bed and personal territory. By training a puppy to eat, play, and sleep in a crate, you train it to accept and enjoy staying in its "den" during transport or on other occasions. Crate training provides the solution to a variety of behaviour problems before they happen.

Practical play area
A playpen is an expanded version of a crate, useful for puppies that are not yet house trained. Soiling accidents in the home are avoided when a puppy is left temporarily unattended, if it is restricted to a newspaper-lined playpen. Never use a playpen or crate as punishment – both are meant to be enjoyed.

HEALTH AND SAFETY

DOGS DEPEND UPON US for their physical and emotional well being. It is not enough to simply provide food and shelter. During daily activities with your dog, carry out routine physical checks to ensure that your companion is healthy. Worm your dog regularly, and arrange for a yearly veterinary examination and preventative vaccination against infectious diseases. Make your home safe by removing anything dangerous, such as household chemicals or toxic plants, from your dog's reach. Never let your dog run free if it is a hazard to people or other animals. Train it in basic obedience – walk it on a lead, and keep public places tidy by cleaning up after it.

Examining your dog
Routine checks of your dog's health are advisable. Observe its behaviour when you play with it. Check its physical activity, but also carry out a simple physical examination. Feel its body, look in the ears for discharge, odour, or inflammation, at the eyes for redness or discharge, and in the mouth for gum or tooth damage or offensive odour. Check the body and between the toes for bits of vegetation, mats of hair, or lumps. Finish these activities with a reward.

FOOD REWARD IS POWERFUL INCENTIVE FOR HEALTHY DOG TO SIT STILL

HEALTHY LOOKING DOG SHOWS TOTAL CONCENTRATION ON FOOD REWARD

Veterinary care
A yearly veterinary examination of your dog is a prudent investment. Future problems can be caught at an early stage when they are much easier and less expensive to treat, cure, or prevent from developing further. Later in life, when age-related problems are likely to occur, the frequency of visits should increase according to the vet's advice. Health insurance is often available to cover the sometimes significant costs of technically sophisticated diagnostics and treatments.

WELL-TRAINED CAVALIER KING CHARLES SPANIEL STANDS QUIETLY

VET CARRIES OUT COMPLETE PHYSICAL EXAMINATION, INCLUDING LISTENING TO HEART SOUNDS FOR ANY ABNORMALITIES

HEALTH PRECAUTIONS
Routinely observe your dog for signs of illness, but still arrange for a thorough veterinary examination once a year. During a routine physical examination, a vet will examine all parts of your dog's anatomy, listen with a stethoscope to its heart and lung sounds, and feel for any possible abnormalities in the abdomen and over the body. The vet will ask questions regarding what you feed your dog and its stool consistency, and might ask you to bring in a stool specimen for analysis for worm eggs. You may be asked about your dog's day-to-day activities.

Preventative vaccination protects against canine diseases that may be endemic in the region in which you live. These include distemper, parvovirus, leptospirosis, kennel cough, rabies, and hepatitis. The vet will recommend suitable worming according to the risks in your area. Worming dogs to

VISUAL COMMANDS ARE USEFUL FOR CONTROLLING DOG

DOG CONCENTRATES OBEDIENTLY ON SPOKEN AND VISUAL COMMANDS

Obedience training
Teaching your dog to obey simple commands is as important for its health as are physical health checks. This well-trained dog responds to both verbal and visual commands to "sit". The obedience-trained dog is under your control. Even when it is running free, it responds to your commands when you see a potentially dangerous situation.

prevent roundworms is as much a human health precaution as it is beneficial for your dog. Roundworms are often inherited by dogs from their mothers while they are still in the womb. Children, especially those with allergies, can contract canine roundworms. Occasionally, this will lead to vision impairment. Because of the roundworm's sophisticated lifestyle, dogs should be wormed frequently, about four times a year, to prevent both the home and public places from being contaminated.

SAFETY IN THE HOME

Ensure that your home is safe by securing doors and windows and making your fencing "dog-proof". Dogs enjoy outdoor activity and should be allowed to go out of the house whenever possible; however, they should not be left alone to bark and disturb the neighbours.

Bored dogs often attempt to jump fences or dig their way to freedom. Ensure that the fence goes down far enough into the ground to prevent escape by digging. Garden sheds and swimming pools should be off limits to dogs. Sheds contain delicious but often toxic substances. Swimming pools are very easy to get in to, but often impossible to get out of. Never cut the grass with your dog present, and keep all wonderfully smelly fishing tackle well out of its reach.

All puppies and many adult dogs derive great satisfaction from chewing. Give your dog a maximum of three toys to chew, and make sure they are different from any other chewable articles, such as shoes, socks, and pillows. Never leave a dog that enjoys chewing alone in a room with live electric wires. Turn electric items off at the plug, or preferably unplug them. Check your plants and flowers to see if any of them are toxic. Some, such as Dumbcane, have dangerous sap and are especially hazardous to dogs. If your dog is able to open cupboards, either use latches on their doors, or keep all kitchen and bathroom chemicals and cleaners out of your dog's reach.

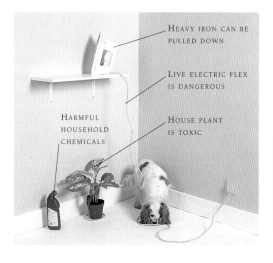

HEAVY IRON CAN BE PULLED DOWN

LIVE ELECTRIC FLEX IS DANGEROUS

HARMFUL HOUSEHOLD CHEMICALS

HOUSE PLANT IS TOXIC

The unsafe home
Our seemingly secure homes can be extremely hazardous to inquisitive or bored dogs. Puppies, in particular, enjoy chewing on rubbery items like electric flex. Dogs are omnivores, willing to eat all types of vegetation, and in the absence of succulent grass will chew on house plants. They willingly taste almost anything, especially if it is on the floor and comes in an easy-to-chew, plastic container.

DANGEROUS SUBSTANCE, TOXIC PLANT, AND LIVE FLEX ARE OUT OF HARM'S WAY

The safe home
Here, all sources of danger have been removed. The Dumbcane plant contains toxic sap – avoid all toxic house plants. The electric flex has been unplugged to prevent shock, and removed so that the dog does not pull the iron off the shelf. Harmful toilet-bowl cleaner has been placed out of reach. Secure all dangerous or toxic substances, but always give your dog appropriate items to chew.

PUBLIC RESPONSIBILITIES

When we domesticated the dog, it became dependent upon us for survival. From the dog's point of view, this has been an overwhelmingly successful operation. Dogs are more numerous than any other members of the canine family. We have taken upon ourselves a number of responsibilities, both for their welfare and for the welfare of the communities in which they live.

All dogs should be trained in basic obedience – to come, sit, stay, and lie down. Most dogs are able to learn these commands. The best time to teach obedience is when a puppy is still in its formative, early-learning stage. Puppy classes for dogs under 16 weeks old are ideal to give dogs a head start in life, although obedience training can be taught at any age. Dog clubs and vets have names of trainers and times of local classes. Barking can be a serious social nuisance. This, too, can be prevented by effective

training. A dog should be trained to walk on a lead in public places, and owners should remove its droppings from parks and pavements. Even the gentlest dog carries the potential to nip or bite in anger, fear, or pain. Never leave unattended infants with dogs. Prevent potential bites by teaching your dog to wear a muzzle, and use a muzzle when it first meets children. Only remove the muzzle when you are sure there is no risk.

Risk prevention
This dog has been trained to wear a muzzle when it is outdoors, to prevent it from scavenging and developing gastrointestinal problems. All dogs, even those with the most affable temperaments and generosity of spirit, such as this Cavalier King Charles Spaniel, have the potential to bite. Dogs should never be left alone with infants. Dogs meeting unknown children should be muzzled until the relationship is secure. Any potentially aggressive dog should be muzzled when it is taken to a public area. A comfortable muzzle that fits well is no hardship for a dog.

CORRECTLY FITTED MUZZLE IS LIGHTWEIGHT AND COMFORTABLE

Canine hygiene
The responsible dog owner understands the aesthetic problems, as well as the health hazards, created by dog droppings. Disease transmission is a minor health hazard. More important is the simple unpleasantness of dog mess, especially in public areas in urban environments. Clean up after your dog. Use a purpose-made scoop such as the one shown here, or simply a biodegradable bag. Deposit the mess in an appropriate receptacle, or flush it down the toilet.

PLASTIC SCOOP IS LINED WITH BIODEGRADABLE PLASTIC BAG

FEEDING AND NUTRITION

GIVEN THE FREEDOM OF CHOICE, dogs behave carnivorously, preferring to eat fresh meat. However, unlike the truly carnivorous cat which cannot survive without eating meat, the dog is really more like a human – an omnivore – willing to eat and able to digest most types of food, including fruit and vegetables. Pet-food manufacturers produce a variety of nutritious foods with different textures, tastes, and energy levels. Fed in correct quantities these foods, together with fresh water, provide the protein, fat, carbohydrate, minerals, and vitamins necessary for a dog's well being. If you follow sensible feeding guidelines, you will help to prevent nutritional and behaviour problems.

Canned foods
A variety of nutritious and tasty canned foods is prepared worldwide by reputable dog-food manufacturers to appeal to both dogs and their owners. Canned foods vary in content and texture. The highest energy foods are prepared for growing puppies and working dogs, while lower calorie foods are available for under-active canines.

Complete semi-moist food
Complete dog foods have less moisture than canned foods, and three times the number of calories on a weight basis. These foods often have high carbohydrate or sugar contents. They are suitable for dogs that eat intermittently rather than finishing quickly, and are unsuitable for diabetic dogs.

A BALANCED DIET

Protein, which consists of amino acids, is the building material for animal tissue. Meat is an excellent source of easily digested protein, but dogs can also digest plant protein, such as soya. In addition, cheese and eggs provide good digestible protein. Carbohydrates in the form of cereals, bread, pasta, rice, and potatoes provide dogs with energy. Carbohydrates are converted to glucose – essential "fuel".

Fat consists of fatty acids. Some of these are converted to glucose for energy; others are beneficial for different body functions. Certain fatty acids are also necessary to maintain the skin and coat in prime condition. Vitamins and minerals are needed for a variety of body functions, such as building teeth, bones, or new blood cells, assisting absorbtion of food from the intestines, and aiding tissue

repair. The dog needs a balance of these nutrients to remain healthy. Excesses can be just as harmful as deficiencies. Make sure that you provide a good balance of all the daily requirements, not just the right number of calories. Alternatively, provide a prepared dog food manufactured by a reputable company.

Never leave old or stale food for your dog and always provide a bowl of fresh, clean water. Serve food at room temperature, not refrigerated, and dispose of any canned food that is not immediately eaten. Soft, moist food can be left in the bowl for several hours, and dry foods all day. Never feed brittle bones. Dogs wolf their food and easily swallow sharp pieces of chicken or lamb bone.

CALORIES AND QUANTITIES

Meats vary considerably in protein, fat, and calorie content. For example, tripe is low in all categories (9 per cent protein, 3 per cent fat, and 63 calories per 100

Mixed food from our table
Food for human consumption is excellent for dogs, but it requires planning and knowledge of a dog's nutritional requirements. An equal mix of meat and vegetables is likely to provide all the ingredients needed for a nutritious diet.

Nourishing chicken
Chicken is easily digested and has slightly fewer calories than other meats. Dogs enjoy meat, but meat on its own does not provide a balanced diet. Always mix meat with dog biscuits, pasta, rice, or vegetables to ensure a constant supply of vitamins and minerals.

Digestible rice
Rice is easily digested by dogs, and is an excellent source of nourishment, especially for convalescing dogs with gastrointestinal problems. White and brown rice are both suitable for dogs, but brown rice provides more beneficial roughage than white rice.

Clean water
Fresh drinking water should always be available. Dogs that are fed dry food drink more than dogs that are fed canned or table food. Dogs drink more in hot weather and after heavy exercise. Any other increase in thirst warrants a visit to the vet.

DRY PUPPY FOOD

DRY, LOW-CALORIE FOOD

Complete dry foods

Dramatic advances have been made in the technology of producing complete, tasty, and nutritious dry dog foods. These are available for all breeds of dog. Specialty dry foods are manufactured for dogs with medical conditions.

grams), while lamb is considerably higher (20 per cent protein, 8.8 per cent fat, and 162 calories per 100 grams). Chicken and beef are very similar in nutritional content (20 per cent protein, 4.3–4.6 per cent fat, and 122 calories per 100 grams), but dogs appear to be able to digest chicken more readily than beef. There is also the possibility that diets high in red meat are related to skin itchiness in some dogs. Choose the best meat source for your dog's particular needs.

Carefully calculate your dog's calorie needs. A Yorkshire Terrier weighing 5 kg (11 lb) needs about 210 calories each day, while a Golden Retriever weighing 35 kg (77 lb) requires about 1,500

calories. Giant breeds like the Bernese Mountain Dog, which weighs 80 kg (176 lb), need about 2,800 calories per day. These suggestions should only act as guidelines – needs vary among individual dogs. If feeding your dog on canned foods, refer to the manufacturer's instructions on the food label, but alter these if your dog is either gaining or losing weight.

THE RIGHT DIET

Humans have complete control over a dog's food consumption. However, dogs are excellent at manipulating owners, convincing them to feed them more, or to feed them specific diets. Most canine nutritional problems are a result of owner behaviour. Dogs may become obese because of under-active thyroid function, but this is rare. Thirty per cent of companion dogs are fat because their owners feed them too many calories. A dog may refuse to eat food, having learnt that if it refuses long enough it will be fed something tastier. Pet-food manufacturers are aware of this dog ploy and produce very tasty premium brands of food. A perverse result is that some dogs continue to eat after hunger has been satisfied, because the food is so delicious.

Manufacturers produce a range of specialty diets, such as low calorie for weight control and low protein for dogs with kidney problems. Good pet-food producers buy up surplus food from the human market, and convert it into reliable products for dogs. The best manufacturers not only carry out nutritional analyses on their foods, but also monitor the amount of waste dogs produce, an important factor in a hygiene-conscious world.

TREATS AND CHEWS

CHEWS

BEEF CHEWS

BONE-SHAPED TREATS

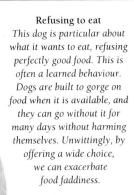

RAW-HIDE CHEWS

Eating is an enormous pleasure for dogs. Pet-food manufacturers produce a range of snack foods in the form of biscuits and chews. These can be used as rewards during training, or to provide interest and amusement when a dog is left alone. Biscuits are high in fat and carbohydrates. They contain as many calories as dry food. Remember to include these calories when calculating your dog's daily needs.

PUPPY EATS FOOD PREPARED TO PROVIDE IDEAL NOURISHMENT

Separate bowls, separate meals

Food is very important to dogs. Some can be very possessive of it. Each dog should have its own food bowl and should be fed so that it cannot watch the other one eat. However, to encourage an ill dog to eat, allow it to see another dog being fed. Select a diet most appropriate for your dog. A puppy has more calorie requirements than a mature, non-working dog.

THIS DOG EATS LOW-CALORIE FOOD, PREPARED FOR NEEDS OF INACTIVE DOG

Refusing to eat

This dog is particular about what it wants to eat, refusing perfectly good food. This is often a learned behaviour. Dogs are built to gorge on food when it is available, and they can go without it for many days without harming themselves. Unwittingly, by offering a wide choice, we can exacerbate food faddiness.

NUTRITIOUS FOOD IS LEFT UNEATEN, DUE TO POOR TRAINING

GROOMING

ALL ANIMALS GROOM THEMSELVES, but social species like the dog also groom each other as a way of maintaining bonds within the group. Dogs are reasonably good at grooming themselves, but changes that have occurred as a result of selective breeding have increased the dog's dependence upon us for assistance. Fortunately, the typical dog accepts and even enjoys simple grooming, as long as it is not associated with discomfort. Routine grooming involves cleaning the face, checking the nails, and tending to the coat according to its length and thickness. This may involve rubbing down, brushing, combing, cutting, or bathing, and should always be associated with rewards for good behaviour.

GROOMING EQUIPMENT

TOOTHBRUSH

CANINE TOOTHPASTE

SYNTHETIC BRISTLE BRUSH

NARROW-TOOTHED COMB

CHAMOIS CLOTH

SOFT PIN BRUSH

RUBBER BRUSH

EAR FORCEPS

COTTON WOOL

NAIL CUTTERS

Grooming items are designed for different coat densities, skin textures, and sensitivities. A rubber brush and chamois leather are all that is needed for short, close coats like the Boxer's, while a soft pin brush and wide-toothed comb are used on long, fine coats like the Yorkshire Terrier's. Breeds with dense coats need rigorous grooming with a soft pin brush and comb, and also with a good, firm bristle brush. Damp cotton wool is ideal for cleaning the eyes. Use scissors to clip away excess hair from the anal region and between the toes, or to thin down feathering on the legs and tail. Clip nails as necessary, and provide the dog with its own toothbrush.

DUAL-PURPOSE BRUSH, WITH SOFT PINS ON ONE SIDE, AND FIRM BRISTLES ON OTHER SIDE

DOG SITS QUIETLY; IT HAS BEEN TRAINED TO ENJOY GROOMING AND IS THEN GIVEN A REWARD

Massaging the skin
A firm but pliable rubber brush penetrates through the coat and gently stimulates the skin. It loosens and lifts flakes of dead skin and other debris that are subsequently brushed out of the hair. Most dogs like this stage of grooming because it is enjoyable.

GREAT CARE IS TAKEN WHILE COMBING EARS

Gentle brushing
A flexible, non-irritating brush is used to remove dead hair from the coat. It has no sharp tips that might potentially scratch, damage, or irritate this dog's relatively thin and sensitive skin. Most dogs like to be brushed along their heads and backs. They are sensitive about their feet, and particularly sensitive about their tails and anal regions.

Removing tangles
This Chihuahua is combed to complete its grooming. Combing removes the finest tangles and is carried out only after brushing has broken down any large mats of hair. This is the most delicate part of grooming. Take care that while combing you do not scratch, pull, or otherwise cause skin discomfort. Grooming should always be associated with pleasure, not pain, and should finish with a suitable reward.

Clipping the nails
The trained dog willingly permits its nails to be cut. Inspect the feet each time you groom your dog. Spread the toes and check between them, looking for accumulated debris or matted hair. If the nails are too long, trim them carefully, avoiding cutting the living tissue, or "quick". A vet will show you exactly how to do this. Always reward good behaviour.

NAIL-CLIPPER SHEARS NAIL, RATHER THAN CRUSHING IT, AVOIDING DELICATE LIVING TISSUE

LIP IS RAISED TO BRUSH FOOD FROM BETWEEN TEETH

Teeth and gum care
Look inside your dog's mouth each day, checking for odour, inflammation, and debris. At an early age, train your dog to allow you to brush its teeth and gums with a soft toothbrush, and either dilute salt water or special canine toothpaste, available from a vet. Avoid using toothpaste made for humans, since most dogs dislike both its taste and its foaming sensation.

MUCUS IS REMOVED, BUT EYE ITSELF IS NOT DIRECTLY TOUCHED WITH TISSUE

Facial hygiene
Check your dog's eyes daily, cleaning away any mucus that builds up in the corners with damp cotton wool or tissue. Lift the ears and check for wax, odour, or inflammation. Never push a cotton-wool bud into the ear, since it may push unseen wax or debris down towards the ear drum. If your dog has facial wrinkles or excessive lip folds, check these for odour or accumulated debris.

TRAINED DOG ALLOWS ITS ANAL REGION TO BE INSPECTED, AND IS REWARDED AFTERWARDS FOR GOOD BEHAVIOUR

SELECTIVE GROOMING AND BATHING

Selective breeding has produced a great variety of coat textures and densities. Smooth, short-haired coats such as the Boxer's are easiest to maintain. Once or twice weekly, with a rubber brush, work against the lie of the coat to loosen surface dirt and dead hair, then remove this debris with a bristle brush. Coat conditioner may be used to add sheen, although a chamois cloth is usually just as effective.

Regularly groom short-haired breeds with dense undercoats, such as the Labrador Retriever, removing mats and tangles with both brush and comb. Long topcoats with dense undercoats, such as those of the St. Bernard, need gentle but vigorous and frequent brushing.

There are occasions when it is necessary to bath a dog, especially if its coat has been contaminated with oily or malodorous substances. Medicated shampoos are a treatment of choice for a variety of skin conditions. Bath the dog in a sink or bathtub, preferably outdoors if the weather permits. Place cotton wool in the ears to prevent water from getting in, and provide a rubber mat for the dog to stand on. Use warm rather than hot or cold water. Make the experience as pleasant as possible, by offering regular food rewards for staying still. Lather the dog well, but avoid getting shampoo in any body opening.

Thorough rinsing is crucial, especially under the forelegs and between the hind legs – where shampoo might accumulate and possibly cause skin irritation. You will be pleased with the results, but your dog's inclination will be to roll about and cover itself with natural environmental smells.

Tail-end inspection
The anal region should be inspected for accumulated debris or inflammation. If your dog drags its bottom along grass or carpet, it is likely that its anal sacs are causing irritation and need emptying. A vet will show you how to do this. Routinely clip away excess hair from around the anus to prevent unnecessary soiling.

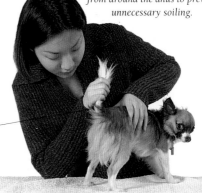

TRAVELLING AND BOARDING

As HONORARY MEMBERS of human families, dogs often travel with us in our vehicles. Urban dogs, in particular, are regularly driven to parks for exercise. Some dogs accompany their owners on holidays, or travel by car to kennels for boarding. Travelling problems, such as motion sickness or agitation, are diminished through early and frequent exposure to car travel. Potential hazards are reduced by using travel containers. You should avoid exposing your dog to excess heat, and stop frequently if journeys are over two hours long. Obey local regulations for dog owners. If your dog is to be kennelled, seek veterinary advice on disease prevention and choice of kennel.

Crate training
This puppy has been introduced to its crate at an early age and now thinks of it as her own personal space. She feels relaxed and content when she is inside it. Crate training is the simplest way to ensure safe, secure, and contented travelling for dogs. Later in life, wherever the dog goes, her portable home can accompany her.

PUPPY WILLINGLY USES HER CRATE, WHICH SHE REGARDS AS HER OWN PRIVATE "DEN"

SUN BLIND REDUCES HEAT BUT DOES NOT PREVENT CAR BECOMING OVEN FOR DOG

CRATE HAS BEEN CHOSEN FOR ADULT-SIZED DOG, BUT ALSO TO FIT IN CAR

Travelling safely
Hatchbacks and estates are ideal vehicles for dogs to travel in. Ensure that the travelling crate fits securely. Alternatively, install a dog guard to prevent your dog from jumping into the passenger section of the vehicle. Provide washable bedding for comfort.

Preventing heat stroke
Sun shades have been attached to these windows to reduce the risk of heat stroke. In sunny or hot weather, body temperature may rise rapidly. Heat stroke can be lethal within minutes.

Respecting local laws
This obedient dog normally walks to heel without a lead, but for its own safety and to abide by local laws, it is walked on a lead when it is away from familiar territory. Obey local regulations for parks and beaches when you travel with your dog.

DOG IS SAFE AND SECURE ON HOLIDAY

TRAVELLING BY CAR
Some dogs are extremely relaxed during car journeys. Others suffer from motion sickness, pace constantly, or bark excitedly. Car travel is an abnormal activity for the dog. It needs to learn to behave in the way you want it to. For protection and security, the safest way for a dog to travel is in an appropriate container.

Dogs that are crate trained as puppies *(see pages 306–307)* will happily travel on extended journeys, secure in their own crates. For shorter journeys, a dog can be protected behind a dog grill in the back of an estate car or hatchback. If it must sit on a passenger seat, consider securing it with a purpose-built seat belt. If it is a small dog, train it to enjoy sleeping in a purpose-built, moulded plastic travel container and place this in your car where it will not shift if you brake suddenly.

Exercise your dog before you start any extended journey, and stop every two hours to allow it a sniff of fresh air and a drink of water. Never leave your dog in a car in hot weather, even with the windows slightly open in partial shade. Compared to humans, the dog has very poor control of its body temperature. It cannot sweat. Each year, thousands of dogs quite literally cook to death in cars from heat stroke.

When you reach your destination, behave conscientiously. If dogs are prohibited from a beach or park, avoid those areas. For safety, walk your dog on its lead and only let it off where it is safe and permissible to do so. Amend its identification tag to include a local telephone number. Just as you would do in your local park or street, clean up after your dog and deposit waste properly.

COMMERCIAL TRANSPORT
Plane, train, and bus journeys can be frightening for dogs, because they are often separated from their owners. Crate training ensures that your dog can feel secure in its own "den" during travel. Walk your dog before the journey begins, and withhold food for six hours before. Provide a safe and familiar chewable toy for the journey. A vet will suggest whether your dog will benefit from sedation or anti-nausea medicine for the journey.

If you are travelling abroad, make sure that you have all the necessary travel documents. Usually these include an up-to-date rabies vaccination certificate, and a document signed by a vet verifying that your dog is fit to travel and free from infectious or contagious disease. Many countries require these documents to be in

Preventing illness
This Cavalier King Charles Spaniel is being vaccinated against kennel cough with a nasal-spray vaccine. Follow the advice of your vet or kennel staff to prevent your dog from introducing or picking up infection while it is boarding.

VACCINE IS GIVEN IN NOSE

OWNER ASKS ABOUT FACILITIES, SAFETY, AND COST OF BOARDING DOG

VET OFFERS ADVICE ON A VARIETY OF KENNELS

Choosing a kennel
Seek professional advice on what type of kennel is best for your dog. Then inspect several and decide for yourself whether the facilities and the staff are to your satisfaction. Good kennels demand preventative vaccination and willingly permit extensive inspections.

their own language. In some countries, such as Japan, Australia, and Great Britain, where rabies does not exist, dogs are quarantined for a period of time upon entry. Whenever possible, try to obtain advice from someone in the country of destination about the range of quarantine kennels available.

Some rabies-free countries, such as Ireland, permit private quarantine on your own premises. Others, such as Norway and Sweden, allow dogs to enter, provided they are individually identified by tattoo or injected microchip transponder, vaccinated against rabies, and have a laboratory-verified level of immunity. Check the regulations with the embassy or consulate of your destination country before planning to travel with your dog.

CHOOSING A KENNEL

Boarding is unsettling for many dogs, especially those with deep attachments to their owners, and it is advisable to begin boarding a dog at an early age. Once a dog has had an experience of boarding, it should know that this is only a temporary episode and that it will rejoin its owners.

Boarding kennels vary considerably. Generally, the more you pay, the more extensive the facilities. Inexpensive kennels usually provide secure accommodation and basic food. The most expensive kennels are canine hotels, with heated indoor accommodation,

comfortable beds, planned daily activity, and a variety of meals. All good kennels permit personal inspection. Good kennels also demand up-to-date vaccination records to prevent the introduction of contagious disease. If possible, visit kennels before making a choice. If not, select a local boarding kennel by recommendation from friends or a vet.

Ultimately, the quality of a kennel depends upon the staff who work there. Look for staff who genuinely enjoy their work. Inspect the dogs that are there. Ask if they are exercised and groomed. Find out whether your dog will be kennelled with a compatible dog. An alternative is to employ a dog sitter in your home. A vet will be able to put you in touch with an approved house- and dog-sitting agency.

THE HEALTHY TRAVELLER

The incidence of many canine diseases varies from one locality to another. Keep your dog's preventative immunization up to date. If your dog is to be boarded, consider having it vaccinated additionally against airborne infectious disease.

The presence of skin parasites varies locally even more than virus infection. Wildlife and livestock parasites such as ticks seem to find urban dogs particularly attractive. If you plan to walk your dog in forests, woods, pastures, or on a natural beach, examine it thoroughly afterwards for any fellow travellers it has acquired during its walk. A vet can supply you with effective flea and tick control. As soon as you arrive at your destination, find the location of the nearest veterinary facility, in case of an emergency.

Having a break
Keep routines as regular as possible when you travel. On long journeys stop every two hours to allow your dog to have a walk on its lead and relieve itself. When there is safe, open space and it is legally permissible, play with your dog in order to provide mental and physical stimulation. A dog is stimulated by new sights and scents.

ACTIVE DOG ENJOYS RETRIEVING GAME DURING BREAK IN JOURNEY

BEHAVIOURAL PROBLEMS

LEFT TO THEMSELVES, dogs act like dogs. Within a pack, a leader emerges that dominates other pack members. The pack survives by hunting, killing, and eating prey, or by scavenging. Members of the pack mark their territory with urine and faeces; they communicate vocally with each other by howling. In the circumstances of living with humans rather than other canines, some dogs develop problems. Lack of early experience can lead to nervousness when confronted with new situations. Being left alone can create anxiety that the dog may release by howling or chewing. Many behaviour problems can be prevented, and most problems that occur can be solved with training.

LEAD IS HELD SLACK, BUT DOG IS STILL UNDER CONTROL

Nervousness
Lack of early learning or unpleasant early experience may lead to fear of adult humans. Often this is directed at only one sex. Direct eye contact as here, between a towering stranger and a dog, could be intimidating. However, the handler controls the dog and rewards it with soothing words for not showing fear.

WITH NO SIGN OF AGGRESSION, ONE DOG SNIFFS THE OTHER

Aggression with dogs
Both of these dogs are under their owners' control, and if either dog shows aggression, training is necessary. It should be rewarded for showing no aggression, first at some distance from the other dog. Over a period of several weeks, the distance should be reduced, with a reward being given each time the dog remains quiet.

Anxiety with children
This dog comes from a rescue centre, and is being carefully introduced to a child in order to monitor its response. The child has been instructed to avoid staring at the dog. If the dog shows fear or aggression, it undergoes training, with rewards for behaving affably in the child's presence, and admonishment for misbehaviour.

Fear of loud noises
This dog is being tested for its response to a loud noise. It has dropped its head and tail and is cowering – these are signs of nervousness. It can be trained to accept loud noises through controlled exposure to them, starting with mild noise and gradually increasing the intensity of the noise. Each time the dog shows no tension, it should be rewarded.

DOG REACTS NERVOUSLY TO SUDDEN LOUD NOISE BY ADOPTING SUBMISSIVE POSTURE

PREVENTING PROBLEMS

Prevention is always easier than cure. Early obedience training gives you control over your dog's activities. Each dog has its own unique personality, but there are often personality similarities between members of a breed. The amount of training that is necessary varies with the individual, but also with the breed. Some breeds train faster than others. Although weekly classes are an excellent way for you to learn how to train your dog, most training takes place at home. A dog is lucidly aware of your attitude, and good obedience training is as much in your attitude as it is in the exercises themselves. Prevent behaviour problems from developing by training your dog from as early an age as possible to come to you, stay, sit, and lie down. When you start training, liberally use potent rewards such as food, touch, and praise, and accompany these rewards with appropriate command words, which your dog will eventually learn. Within a short time, verbal rewards will be sufficient. After training your dog in simple obedience, train it to walk by your side and on a lead. Train your dog to retrieve objects and, just as important, to drop them on command. Finally, gently expose your dog to as wide a variety of activities as possible when it is still under 12 weeks old. By doing so, you will reduce the likelihood that it will be frightened by new experiences later in life.

AGGRESSION

Different types of aggression demand different approaches. If your male dog is aggressive with other male dogs, neutering is likely to reduce the behaviour. If your dog aggressively protects its food, toys, or resting place, growls at you when you give a command, or shows sibling rivalry when you talk to or touch any other dogs (or children), neutering will only marginally diminish the problem. Your dog's luxuries should be withdrawn, and it should be trained to earn rewards through acceptable behaviour. Obedience training is very important for this type of problem.

Dogs that are aggressive through fear need a gentler approach. You should reduce your dog's fear of a particular situation through gentle and controlled

Separation anxiety
Test for separation anxiety by leaving a dog alone in a room with only a bed and a toy. If it howls or becomes destructive, its feeding and exercise routines can be altered and it can be trained to play with stimulating toys.

DOG REMAINS ALERT BUT RELAXED

feed your dog, even to exercise it. Reduce physical contact with it. When boredom is the cause of destruction, increase the amount of time devoted to your dog's activity. When you leave the dog alone, leave an interesting object, like a rubber chew toy filled with cheese, to interest your dog in your absence. However, bear in mind that dogs should never be left alone for long periods at a time.

NERVOUSNESS

Fear of strangers, children, uniforms, loud noises, unexpected objects like umbrellas or prams, other dogs, or any other living or inanimate object is more common in some breeds than in others, but may occur in any individual. Often it is a consequence of restricted early learning. The first 12 weeks of a puppy's life are extremely influential on its future development. Discuss with a vet how to overcome the conflict of interests in protecting your puppy from disease, with the need for it to have as much experience as possible during these formative weeks before it has been fully vaccinated. Reduce nervousness in specific circumstances by initially avoiding the causes, if at all possible. Train your dog to sit and stay with food rewards. Over a period of a few weeks, gradually expose your dog to the situations that make it nervous, such as loud noises or a particular place, always rewarding calm behaviour. Also identify circumstances where your dog does not show nervousness, and reward it for showing no signs of nervousness.

GETTING HELP

Even the most affectionate and obedient dog has the potential to develop behaviours that you,

exposure to it, always rewarding calm behaviour. Chasing livestock or other animals is the most difficult behaviour to overcome; seek professional assistance.

ANXIETY

Virtually all anxiety problems have their origins either in boredom or in over dependency upon people. Dogs show their anxiety at being left alone by barking, and by emptying either or both the bladder and the bowels indoors, sometimes in unexpected places like a bed or sofa. Some become exceedingly destructive, and chew carpets, doors, and walls. Some dogs dig in a fixated, obsessive fashion – on carpets or walls indoors, or in the ground or under fences outdoors.

To eliminate anxiety-related activities, determine whether your dog is behaving in these ways because it is bored or because it is anxious in your absence. If part of the problem is emotional dependence upon you, reduce this by giving fewer rewards less often. Cool the relationship. Arrange for someone else to

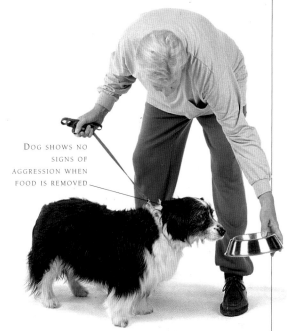

DOG SHOWS NO SIGNS OF AGGRESSION WHEN FOOD IS REMOVED

Possessiveness
Some dogs are very possessive of their toys, food, or resting places. Test possessiveness in an unknown dog by taking food away while the dog is eating. Possessiveness is often a form of dominance aggression, and diminishes when the owner reasserts leadership of the dog.

NEITHER ANIMAL SHOWS WORRY OR CONCERN

Meeting other animals
These animals grew up with other dogs and cats, and show neither fear nor predatory behaviour. Early experience is most important in relations with other animals. Introduce dogs to cats and vice versa under controlled conditions, allowing the resident animal to inspect the new arrival.

DOG SHOWS NO FEAR WHEN CONFRONTED WITH VARIETY OF NEW SIGHTS

Unexpected sights
Some dogs react unexpectedly to unusual everyday situations such as the sight of umbrellas, beards, or hats. A new dog's responses can be tested through controlled meetings. If it shows anxiety or nervousness, it can be trained under controlled circumstances to be less fearful.

your family, or others find unpleasant. Sending your dog to a trainer may be easy for you, but it does not necessarily solve a behaviour problem. Early participation in weekly puppy classes is the best way to minimize future problems. Use a good, practical dog-training book, and involve all the family. Older dogs and their owners benefit from attending weekly obedience-training classes. Dogs respond best to reward-based training, and physical discipline is rarely necessary. Local dog-training clubs and veterinary clinics are excellent sources of training information. Training does not limit a dog's freedom; through training we teach our dogs how to get the best out of life.

GLOSSARY

ACTION The way the dog moves

ANGULATION The angle at which the bones meet at the joints

BAT EAR An erect ear, broad at the base, and rounded at the top

BLENHEIM Chestnut and white

BLUE MERLE Marbled blue and grey mixed with black

BRACHYCEPHALIC HEAD A short, flattened, and rather broad head

BREED STANDARDS Description of breeds against which dogs are judged at shows

BRINDLE A mixture of black hairs with lighter gold, brown, red, or grey hairs

BRISKET The part of the body below the chest and between the forelegs

BROKEN COAT Wire-haired coat

BUTTON EAR An ear in which the flap folds forwards, with the tip close to the skull

CANINE TEETH The two upper and lower long teeth lateral to the incisors

CARNASSIAL TEETH The first lower-molar and the last upper-premolar teeth, enlarged and modified for tearing flesh

CARPALS The wrist bones

CAT FEET Short, round, compact feet resembling those of a cat

COBBY Short, compact body

CORDED COAT Coat consisting of separate, rope-like twists of hair formed from intertwined topcoat and undercoat

CORKSCREW TAIL A twisted tail

CROPPING The amputation of the ears to enable the remaining part to stand erect

CROSS BREED The progeny of parents of two different breeds

CROUP The part of the back above the hips extending to the root of the tail

CRYPTORCHID DOG A dog whose testicles have not descended to the scrotum

CULOTTE Long hair on thighs

DEWCLAW The fifth digit (thumb) on the inside of the leg

DEWLAP The loose, pendulous skin under the throat

DISH-FACE A type of face with an upwards-slanting, or concave, nasal bone

DOCKING Amputating the tail

DOLICHOCEPHALIC HEAD A long head

DOMED SKULL Evenly rounded skull

DOUBLE COAT Warm, waterproof undercoat and weather-resistant topcoat

DRAWN-UP CHEST Small, rather than naturally deep chest

DROP EAR A folded, drooping ear

ECTROPION Condition in which the lower eyelid hangs loosely, exposing the inner lining, or haw

ENTROPION The eyelids turn in, causing the lashes to contact the eye

EYE TEETH The upper canines

FEATHERING The long fringe of hair on the ears, legs, tail, or body

FEMUR The thigh bone that lies between the hip and the knee

FLANK The sides of the body between the last rib and the hip

FLEWS Pendulous upper lips

FRONTAL BONE The skull bone over the eye

GAIT The pattern of stride

GAZEHOUND A sight hound

GENETIC Concerned with hereditary factors or genes

GUARD HAIRS The long, thick, heavy hair that creates the topcoat

HACKLES The hair on the back and the neck that can be raised involuntarily

HARE FOOT A long, narrow foot, with toes that are not too arched

HARLEQUIN Patched colours of black or blue on white

HAUNCH The region that is directly above the hips

HAW The inner lining of the lower eyelid

HEAT The female dog's oestrus period

HEIGHT The distance from top of the withers to the ground

HOCK The tarsal bones forming the joint between the knee and the toes

HORMONES The chemical substances produced by endocrine glands that circulate in the blood

HUMERUS The bone of the upper arm

ILIUM The part of the pelvis into the cavity of which the head of the femur fits

IN-BREEDING Mating of closely related dogs

ISCHIUM The hind portion of the floor of the pelvis

LINE BREEDING Mating of related dogs within a family or to a common ancestor

LIVER Coat colour – also called chocolate or brown

LOINS The anterior thigh muscles

MANDIBLE The lower-jaw bone

MAXILLA The upper-jaw bone

MERLE Blue-grey with flecks of black

MERLE EYE Flecked brown or blue eye, with black iris

METATARSALS The bones between the hock and the foot

MONORCHID DOG A dog with only one testicle descended into the scrotum

MOULT The shedding of the coat

MUZZLE The foreface – the head in front of the eyes

OCCIPUT The highest, upper-back point of the skull

OESTRUS The period during which a female ovulates and mates willingly

OVERSHOT JAW Jaw in which the front upper teeth overlap and do not touch the teeth of the lower jaw

PADS The thickened cushion beneath the toes and on the sole of the foot

PARTI-COLOUR Two colours that are in variegated patches

PASTERN The region between the wrist and the toes

PATELLA The kneecap

PEDIGREE A record of a dog's ancestry

POINTING Freezing on sight of game and pointing in direction of game

PRE-MOLAR TEETH The teeth situated between the canines and the molars

PRICK EAR An erect, pointed ear

PURE-BRED DOG A dog whose parents both belong to the same breed

RADIUS The second bone of the foreleg lying parallel to the ulna

RANDOM-BRED DOG A dog whose parents do not both belong to recognized breeds

ROSE EAR A small, drop ear folding over and back

SABLE Black-tipped hairs on a background of gold, silver, grey, or tan

SABRE TAIL Tail carried in a curve

SACRUM A mass of fused vertebrae situated between the lumbar vertebrae and the bones of the tail

SCAPULA The shoulder blade

SCENT HOUND A hound that hunts by ground scent

SCISSOR BITE Bite in which the upper teeth closely overlap the lower teeth

SEASON A bitch's heat or oestrus period

SECOND THIGH The region of the hindquarters from the stifle to the hock

SEMI-PRICK EARS Erect ears, with tips breaking fowards

SEPTUM The division between the nostrils

SETTING Freezing on sight of game and flushing game upon command

SICKLE TAIL Tail carried out and up in a semicircle

SIGHT HOUND A dog that hunts more by sight than by scent

SOUND Term used generally to describe ease of movement

STIFLE The joint between the thigh and second thigh

STOP The depression before the eyes between the skull and the muzzle

STRIPPING A COAT The removal by hand of old hair from a wire-haired coat

TAIL SET The position of the tail

THICK SET Broad and solid

THIGH The region from the hip to the stifle

TIBIA The bone between the stifle and the hock

TOLL To lure (for example, a duck tolling retriever entices ducks to come ashore, capering in a fox-like manner)

TOPCOAT Heavy, primary, or guard hair

TOPKNOT The long, fluffy hair on the crown of the head

TRICOLOUR Three coloured – black, white, and tan

TUCKED-UP The line of the abdomen is drawn up at the loins

ULNA The larger of the lower-foreleg bones, the point of which is the elbow

UNDERCOAT The dense, usually short, soft coat closest to the skin

UNDERSHOT JAW Jaw in which the lower-front teeth stick out beyond the upper-front teeth

WELL-DROPPED THIGHS Back thigh muscles in good proportion to front thigh muscles

WELL LET-DOWN CHEST Deep chest

WELL-SPRUNG RIBS Rounded, rather than flattened, ribs

WHEATEN Pale yellow or fawn colour

WITHERS The highest point on the body just behind the neck

WRINKLES The loose folds of skin around the skull

INDEX

PLAYER'S CIGARETTES.

BULLDOG.

ACKNOWLEDGMENTS

Author's Acknowledgments

During my 25 years of practising clinical veterinary medicine I have met quite a few dogs. I have also had the good fortune to be invited by veterinary associations and universities in over 20 countries to speak to both undergraduate and practising veterinarians. I have visited dog shows and dog shelters on four continents, yet still many of the breeds illustrated in this encyclopedia were new to me. My lack of knowledge was overcome through help from veterinarians, dog breeders, and dog-show judges around the world. These experts on breeds that originate in their own countries researched and translated information for me about the origins, uses, numbers, and behaviour of many rare breeds. They sent me anecdotes and stories, illustrations, and personal comments. My grateful thanks go to: Dr. Walter Poduschka (Austria); Elizabeth Dunn (Canada); Roger Abrantes (Denmark); Dr. Tina Toomet (Estonia); Dr. Isabelle Park (France); Binke Durr, Dr. Ulrich Durr, and Dr. Hellmuth Wachtel (Germany); Professors Imre Bodo and Pal Rafai (Hungary); Ashley McManus (Ireland); Dr. Keitaro Kurabayashi and Keiko Yamazaki (Japan); Dr. Simon Roos and Joop Lamers (The Netherlands); Torhild Aabergsbotten and Professor Jorunn Grondalen (Norway); Isabel Reinhards (Portugal); Miss Elena Mychko and Professor Eugene Yerusalimsky (Russia); Peter Heidinger and Pavol Galo (Slovakia); Marjan Kocbek (Slovenia); Dr. Antonio Prats and Dr. Jaume Camps (Spain); Professor Ake Hedhammer (Sweden); Pamela Harrow (Great Britain), and Dr. I. Lehr Bribin (United States).

As always, the staff at the Royal College of Veterinary Surgeons Library either immediately found information I requested in their own documents or obtained it through The British Library Document Supply Centre within days. Tim Scott – an experienced and discriminating Senior Art Editor – created the production line of images, while Cangy Venables, the Project Editor, fluently honed my copy into shape. Managing Editor Krystyna Mayer and Managing Art Editor Derek Coombes as always kept the project gliding forwards. Thanks to them all. And finally, thanks to my wife and family, for letting me work on this encyclopedia during "their" time, and to my veterinary nurses for willingly taking on added responsibilities.

Publisher's Acknowledgments

Dorling Kindersley would like to thank photographer Tracy Morgan for her invaluable contribution to the book. Thanks also to the following for their hard work: Stella Smyth-Carpenter and Sally Roose (Tracy Morgan's photographic assistants), Juliette Cunliffe, Gerald D'Aoust, Janet Edmonds, Sarah Goodwin, Peter Heidinger, Carol Ann Johnson, Daniel McCarthy, Gerard McLaughlin, M. Noblet, Luise Roberts, Maryann Rogers, and Karin Woodruff (who compiled the index).

Dorling Kindersley are very grateful to the following dog owners for allowing their dogs to be specially photographed for the encyclopedia: Alapaha Blue Blood Bulldog: J. Otterbein; Alpine Dachsbracke: W. Lehmann; American Staghound: R. Mullens; American Water Spaniel: A. Raas; Ariége Pointer: A. Bostyn; Ariégeois: R. Caujolle; Austrian

Pinscher: P. Hansen, I. and B. Strate; Azawakh: A. Hellblom, Heaney; Beagle Harrier: G. Thomas; Bergamasco puppy: M. Andreoli; Berner Laufhund: R. Luchtmeijer; Berner Niederlaufhund: M. Deucher, W. Rueedi; Bernese Hound: A. Klepper; Bichon Yorkie: C. Ravden; Black Norwegian Elkhound: K. Bonaunet; Black Russian Terrier: J. Kielan, Szczepanscy; A. Bostyn; Bull Boxer: Rebecci; Cairn Terrier: S. Dolan; Cavalier King Charles Spaniel: S. Webb, A. Schofield; Cockerpoo: C. Ravden; Corded Poodle: S. Maurette; Czech Wolfdog: J. Jedlicka, L. Krivanek; Danish Chicken Dog: M. Merling; Dutch Shepherd Dog (wire-haired): J. Meenderng; Dutch Smoushond: Zuydeweg-Roxs; English Foxhound: M. de Rothschild; English Springer Spaniel: P. Grimshaw, B. Lancaster; Français Blanc et Noir: Rallye Saintongeais; Français Tricolore: P. Gervreau; French Mastiff: C. Steiner; German Long-haired Pointer: H. Schmid, R. Aeberhard; German Shepherd Dog: S. Moore, G. Elliott, S. Bergh-Roose, S. Mann; Grand Anglo-Français Blanc et Noir: M. Aviat, M. Conquard; Grand Anglo-Français A. Dauchez; Harrier: D. Christopher, G. Hughes; Ibizan Hound: F. Benecke; Istrian Smooth/Wire-haired Hounds: J. Ryzek; Jack Russell: G. Elliot; Jindo: J. and T. Rabinowitz; Labradoodle (Guide Dog Training Centre): J. Taylor; Giant Spitz (black): M. Vongehr; Luzerner Laufhund: M. Mervaille; Luzerner Niederlaufhund: W. Schirmer; Medium Poodle: B. and L. Warming; Miniature/Toy Mexican Hairless: S. Corrone, L. Woods; Miniature Pinscher: A. Coull; Miniature Schnauzer: M. Roloff; New Zealand Huntaway: F. and R. Banfield; North American Shepherd: J. Aldrow; Petit Griffon Bleu de Gascogne: R. Gaychet; Plummer Terrier: G. Welby; Podengo Canario: Jesus F. Melian Lorenzo; Poitevin: Jean François Lescop de Moÿ; Polish Lowland Sheepdog puppy: J. Cole; Prazsky Krysavik: H. Janková; Pudelpointer: D. Lengronne; Schwyzer Laufhund: Bonslet; Schwyzer Niederlaufhund: A. Egli; Shar Pei: Sommeryns Demoor; Shiloh Shepherd: P. and J. Dawson; Sloughi: Karen Schirmer; Slovensky Pointer:

M. Kern, L. Geffroy; Smålandsstövare: K. Skolmi; South Russian Sheepdog: M. Valle; Spanish Water Dog: Marisol Alvarez; Styrian Rough-haired Mountain Hound: J. Vester; Thai Ridgeback: J. Sterling; Tibetan Kyi Apso: Jesse Taylor Ide; Transylvanian Hound: D. Solymosi.

A particular debt is due to the hundreds of dog fanciers from around the world who gave up their valuable time and allowed their special dogs to be photographed for the encyclopedia.

Photographic credits

KEY: l = left, r = right, t = top, b = bottom, c = centre

All photography by Tracy Morgan except:
BFI Stills, Posters, and Design: 29cl; The Bridgeman Art Library: 21bl; Christies, London: 21c; Bonhams, London: 21br; Grosvenor Estate: 22c; The British Library: 22bl; Galleria Palatina, Florence: 22br; Courtesy of Board of V and A: 23tl; Roy Miles Gallery: 23tc (detail); Louvre, Paris: 23bl; The British Museum, London: 22t; © The Brontë Society: 26t; Burton, J: 35tl, 53c, 56, 57–58t,c, 60b, 62t,b, 290bl,cl, 291tl; Jean-Loup Charmet: 27c; Christie's Images: 25c; Bruce Coleman Ltd.: Stephen J. Krasemann: 12t; Rod Williams: 13c; Gerald Cubitt: 13bc; Bob and Clara Calhoun: 14c; Hans Reinhard: 31r; Uwe Walz: 61tr; J. Cunliffe/C. A. Johnson: 68b, 69tl; G. D'Aoust: 93t, 286bc; C. M. Dixon: 20cr, 21tl, 23br, 24t; E.T. Archive: 24br, 25tl, 26bc, 30c; Mary Evans Picture Library: 27bl,br, 30t,b, 32tl,cl,b, 68tr; © Elizabeth Banks: 26cl; N. Fletcher: 113tl,b; L. Gardiner: 114tl, 266bl, 287; N. Goodall: 5 (postage stamps), 25tr,bl, 308b, 309t, 288b; Ronald Grant Archive: 28bl,br, 29br; Hearing Dogs for the Deaf: 33cl; P. Heidinger: 121b; M. Henrie: 100b, 101t, 104t; © Hush Puppies/British Shoe Corporation: 29bl; The Image Bank/Grafton Marshall Smith: 24bc; Images Colour Library: 20tc,cl,bc, 27tl; K. Jamazaki: 152bl; D. King: 40l, 76bl,tr, 84cl, 86tr, 95bl, 159br, 175br, 182t, 257b, 290r, 291bl,tr; M. Kocbek: 123t, 235br; The Mansell Collection: 27tc; NHPA: Stephen J. Krasemann: 12cl, 14tr; Orion Press: 12bl; John Shaw: 14b; OSF: Richard Packwood: 14t; Eyal Bartov: 15b; Popperfoto: 33tl; Rex Features Ltd./ Tatiner/Sipa-Press: 33c; T. Ridley: 7br, 29lbr, 31br, 34, 53t, 61b, 65cr, 290t, 296–303, 304b,tl, 305–306; S. Russell: 110, 111t, 112b, 144b, 235; Sporting Pictures (UK): 31tl,bl; © 1988 Universal Studios Inc: 29t; D. Ward: 4, 40r, 60t,c, 61tl, 62c, 63t,br, 64, 65t,b, 291cr, 304tr; © D. Watkins: 25tr,bl, 309t; J. Young: 10–11, 12br, 13 tl,b, 15 tr,c, 74t; Zefa Pictures: E. and P. Bauer: 14br; Minden: 15tl

Every effort has been made to trace the copyright holders and we apologise in advance for any omissions. We would be pleased to insert the appropriate acknowledgment in any subsequent edition of this publication.

Illustrations

Rowan Clifford: 15; Samantha Elmhurst: 41, 45, 49t,r, 51t,r; Janos Marffy: 10 (silhouettes), 18, 38, 40, 43, 44, 46, 48, 49bl, 52, 53, 71; Yak El Droubie (Cartography): 11, 14–15; Amanda Williams: 10 (Canids), 39, 42, 47, 51bl, 53t